The Ethics of Oneness

The Ethics of Oneness

Emerson, Whitman, and the Bhagavad Gita

JEREMY DAVID ENGELS

The University of Chicago Press
Chicago and London

The University of Chicago Press, Chicago 60637
The University of Chicago Press, Ltd., London

Published 2021
Printed in the United States of America

30 29 28 27 26 25 24 23 22 21   1 2 3 4 5

ISBN-13: 978-0-226-74597-8 (cloth)
ISBN-13: 978-0-226-74602-9 (paper)
ISBN-13: 978-0-226-74616-6 (e-book)
DOI: https://doi.org/10.7208/chicago/9780226746166.001.0001

Library of Congress Cataloging-in-Publication Data

Names: Engels, Jeremy, author.
Title: The ethics of oneness : Emerson, Whitman, and the Bhagavad gita / Jeremy David Engels.
Description: Chicago ; London : The University of Chicago Press, 2021. | Includes bibliographical references and index.
Identifiers: LCCN 2020038660 | ISBN 9780226745978 (cloth) | ISBN 9780226746029 (paperback) | ISBN 9780226746166 (ebook)
Subjects: LCSH: Monism. | Philosophy, American—19th century. | Emerson, Ralph Waldo, 1803–1882. | Whitman, Walt, 1819–1892. | Bhagavadgītā—Influence. | Monism—Moral and ethical aspects. | Democracy—United States. | United States—Civilization—Indic influences.
Classification: LCC B906.M66 E64 2021 | DDC 147/.3—dc23
LC record available at https://lccn.loc.gov/2020038660

♾ This paper meets the requirements of ANSI/NISO Z39.48-1992 (Permanence of Paper).

To Sunny,
for it all.

Contents

An Invitation to All

One is a mighty orbic word.
Too bold for jagged edges, it's
a prime parabola of sound,
an English synonym for *aum*.

And yet it's more: the answer to
a question I asked you as
we lay on our backs cloud-watching,
falling into perfect stillness

Nothing reckoned, reasoned, ribboned—
no thing is done without the one.
Whoever finds it is not lost.
Can you hear it whistle us home?

Perhaps one is not an answer,
then, but a generous
invitation to a place
where the arcane and the mundane meet.

Can you hear it beckoning us?

To word the unwordable

Shanti

To emplace the individual

Shanti . . .

To reunite the *dvi*-ded world

Shanti.

Introduction

Yo yat shraddhah sa eva sah.
As a person's faith is, so are they.
BHAGAVAD GITA, 17.3

During my first trip to study yoga in India, I asked one of my teachers for the name and location of her favorite bookstore in Chennai. After a white-knuckle rickshaw ride through town, my driver dropped me off in front of a nondescript apartment building down a long alleyway across the street from the local Sanskrit college. Three floors up, dodging chickens and giggling, pointing children, shoes off, I opened the door and entered Hogwarts—at least, that's how it felt. It was a giant room with books piled floor to ceiling, in all the world's languages, ugly, yellowing paperbacks right next to the most beautiful leather-bound books that surely cost a fortune. I grew alarmed as I calculated the shipping costs in my head. The owner greeted me kindly, and I asked her for her favorite book about yoga. She smiled, asked me if I read Sanskrit; I replied that I was learning; she said no matter, and disappeared into some backroom labyrinth only to emerge, several minutes later, with a small volume: Ralph Waldo Emerson's *Essays: First Series*, printed in Boston in the 1850s. "This is the best book about yoga for you," she said, handing me the tiny tome.

Even years later, thinking about this moment gives me chills. To travel halfway around the world to the birthplace of yoga to have a Chennai bookseller hand me a copy of Emerson and then recommend that book to me as a resource about yoga was just so unexpected, so wonderful, so strange! Of course I bought the book, no questions asked. With the biggest grin and a grateful "namaste," I turned to leave—no other books were going home with me that day—but the kind bibliopole was not finished with her surprises. She tapped me on the shoulder and presented me with another book, a tattered paperback Bhagavad Gita from the 1960s. "You should take this book, too," she said—"it has many answers, and many questions." She then sent me on my way without charging me for the Gita.

Emerson (1803–1882) was a literary and oratorical giant.[1] He invented a rich vocabulary that even today continues to shape how Americans talk about themselves, their place in the world, and their democracy.[2] Emerson adored Plato and Plotinus, Shakespeare and the Quakers. He also treasured the Bhagavad Gita. Indeed, Emerson stands at the beginning of a long American tradition of fascination with Indian thought. Most historians recognize the influence of Indian philosophy on Emerson's writing, and position him as one of the earliest and most important interpreters of Indian philosophy for nineteenth-century Americans.[3] As I left the bookstore, I wondered, Did the Chennai bookseller know that the Bhagavad Gita was one of Emerson's favorite works? To Emerson, the Gita was "the first of books."[4] Opening its pages, he wrote, "it was as if an empire spake to us, nothing small or unworthy but large, serene, consistent, the voice of an old intelligence which in another age & climate had pondered & thus disposed of the same questions which exercise us."[5] "Let us . . . cherish this venerable oracle," he advised, for it speaks "more to our daily purpose than this year's almanac or this day's newspaper."[6]

I spent much of the long plane ride home from India asking myself whether it was random chance or cosmic fate that led me to that bookshop. Employing one of his favorite metaphors for the human experience, water, Emerson observed that "man is a stream whose source is hidden. Our being is descending into us from we know not whence."[7] According to Emerson, all our insights and good ideas come from being receptive to the wisdom of the world. The world is constantly talking to us; the question is whether or not we will listen. What was the world trying to tell me? Why these two books? I still ponder these questions today, though I've turned them over and over enough to recognize that there is no definitive answer. The distinction between chance and fate is one of temperament. More important than attributions of divine providence is whether or not we are open to serendipity when it strikes.

The Bhagavad Gita and Emerson's *Essays* are joined across centuries and continents and climates, for both center on the ancient theme of oneness. In the Gita, "out of kindness" Krishna teaches the warrior Arjuna the "greatest secret" (*paramam guhyam*)—namely, that the individual soul is an incarnation of the universal soul.[8] This means that individuals are not separate from divinity and, in truth, everything is one (in Sanskrit, *ekatva*).[9] For Emerson, oneness was also the highest secret, a truth hidden in plain sight that could liberate Americans from their suffering and fix the world's most vexing political and social problems. As I read Emerson's *Essays* on the airplane, it quickly became clear to me that the Emerson on the page is unlike his public perception as a stubborn prophet of American individualism, with its hands-off, leave-me-alone, I-can-do-it-myself spirit.[10] That Emerson does make an appearance from time to time. Yet in his most famous essay, "Self-Reliance," he writes, "This is the ultimate fact which we so quickly reach on this, as on every topic, the resolution of all into the ever-blessed ONE."[11] Emerson is emphatic: people are not monads bouncing through space; it is impossible to go it alone. All of us exist in a "condition of universal dependence"; we are ever-reliant on our connection to "the One."[12] Emerson reassures his American readers that they are right to pursue happiness, but at the same time he reminds them that they should know that true happiness can only be found by acknowledging, and nurturing, our deep interconnectedness to other people and to the world in all its mysterious, omnipresent, baffling wonder.

Emerson was born in 1803, and he died in 1882. His life bookended a turbulent century as a new nation grew and expanded and nearly destroyed itself, all the while grasping for a national identity and a shared sense of democratic purpose. Americans are not known as philosophers, but nineteenth-century Americans carried on a wide-ranging, freewheeling debate about a number of philosophical questions. They discoursed about the meaning of life and the true nature of reality: Is the world one thing, or is it many parts? Is the universe a force for good or evil or is it simply neutral? Is death real or an illusion? Is there life after death? Do ghosts and spirits walk among us? If so, can we talk with them? And what of God? Is there a place for God in a demystified, Newtonian universe in which science claims victory over religion? Is there more to the story of God than what Sunday sermons disclose? If there is a God, what does this divinity look and feel like? Does this divinity lord over us or live through us? How should we address it? Americans pursued these questions with a cold, steely determination that might seem foreign to us today—as though something real was at stake, because it was. Indeed, my ancestors recognized that philosophy is not an armchair activity but a thing of the world. To study philosophy is to change one's life. Real philosophy breathes.

As their young nation became more urbanized and capitalist, many Americans wondered whether there was more to life than material acquisition. The philosophies of oneness that Emerson and others developed emerged out of this disquietude, serving to counterbalance the dominant national philosophy of individual liberty, or liberalism, which is for Americans "like water for a fish, an encompassing political ecosystem in which we have swum, unaware of its existence."[13] Liberalism is the foundation for many of our culture's most cherished rights (including privacy, free speech, and freedom of religion), but in their obsessive focus on individual autonomy, liberals often become blind to the interdependence of people as well as to the importance of human relationships in supporting life. During the nineteenth century, liberalism emphasized individualism; oneness emphasized solidarity. Liberalism praised competition; oneness praised cooperation. Liberalism lauded material acquisition; oneness championed appreciating things that on the surface have little monetary value. Liberalism instructed Americans that they must find success on their own, with hard work and good old-fashioned pluck and grit; oneness taught Americans to lean into support. Liberalism said, hands off, leave me alone, for the economy is guided by an "invisible hand"; oneness extended a hand of assistance and said, let's work together to build a better world. At their best, the nineteenth-century philosophies of oneness emphasized human interconnectedness and recognized that life is a shared project. At their best, these philosophies of oneness sanctified life while challenging doctrines of individuality run amok.

It was during the 1820s and '30s that Indian philosophical and religious texts—including the Laws of Manu, the Upanishads, the Bhagavad Gita, and the devotional Puranas—first began to arrive in the United States in English, French, German, and Latin translations of varying quality. Unlike many Europeans, when curious and broad-minded Americans including Emerson, Henry David Thoreau, and Walt Whitman first encountered these texts, they did so free from the inherited dogma of centuries of oppressive theological traditions, and this created space for a profound emotional reaction of wonder and admiration. Not content to understand these texts as abstract inquiries into abstruse philosophical topics, these writers and others were determined to put them into use in daily life. These texts inspired Emerson and Whitman as they developed philosophies of oneness that challenged the hegemony of liberalism.[14] (Thoreau was less interested in the Gita's teachings on oneness than he was in Krishna's words concerning dharma, or duty, which is why I do not focus on his philosophy at great length in this book—though fret not, Thoreau fans, he will indeed make a guest appearance from time to time.) The Bhagavad Gita in particular helped Emerson and Whitman imagine a different way of life than most Americans had adopted, a life based on something deeper and richer and more vast than the market and the pleasures of the senses. "Life is comic or pitiful, as soon as the high ends of being fade out of sight, and man becomes near-sighted, and can only attend to what addresses the senses," Emerson concluded.[15] The philosophies of oneness he and Whitman invented returned Americans' focus to the "high ends" of life, and ultimately proved a source of comfort and inspiration for generations of Americans to come.

Over the course of the eighteen chapters of the Bhagavad Gita, Krishna and Arjuna discuss many of the questions that most interested Americans.

Over the course of the nineteenth century, Emerson and Whitman also contemplated these questions. At the core of their philosophies is the central key question: *What does it mean to live a life committed to oneness?* The answers they offer often diverge—Emerson and Whitman differ from the Gita at key points, and Whitman breaks from Emerson at key points, too. Emerson and Whitman were more than conduits or cultural way stations; they were active participants in a cultural conversation that struggled to understand what a life of oneness might look like in such an individualistic nation. Approaching the Bhagavad Gita with their own cultural preoccupations and personal biases, these authors did not simply adopt the Gita's doctrine of oneness, they transformed it. The philosophies that grow out of their dialogue with the Bhagavad Gita are the product of controversy and contestation. At many moments, Emerson and Whitman modified or even rejected ideas they found in the Gita when these ideas were not so easily incorporated into the American scene, or when Krishna's teachings ran afoul of native temperament. The philosophies they developed are often surprising and unexpected. My goal in this book is to describe and critique these philosophies of oneness, telling a long-neglected story of the history of American ideas that I firmly believe has something to teach us, even today.

In the early twenty-first century, individualism has been taken to extremes, and it has actually become hard to notice human interconnectedness. Though humankind has perhaps never been so connected—economically, biologically, environmentally—the urge to retreat into our mediated shells is real. Our world is fractured in its hyperconnectedness. The language of a common good has gone out of fashion. It is difficult to see ourselves sharing a common destiny. The impulse is to quantify and put a monetary value on everything, and I am regularly shocked at how little we seem to value life, especially the lives of people who are in one way or another different from us.[16] Life itself has been commodified—given a market value, and weighed against the demands of the market—with predictably damning consequences for the most vulnerable.

I argued in my book *The Art of Gratitude* (2018) that one of the most alarming things about our society is a widespread attitude of "casual whateverness" toward the fragile miracle that is life.[17] Many of my academic friends and colleagues chuckle and roll their eyes when I speak about life as a miracle, as though I am but a naive boy from somewhere out on the plains, unwise to the dark and brutish ways of the world (which is perhaps true!). Academics are not supposed to speak such tenderhearted, sentimental refrains, but what else can we call life but a miracle?[18] We undersell life if we do not recognize it for the marvel that it is, a fragile, beautiful, shared wonder that transcends all others. I disavow any philosophy that does not sanctify life—not just my life and the lives of those I love, but the lives of strangers, too. One of the daunting ethical challenges of our time is how to build healthy forms of solidarity that enrich and sustain life and that are not premised on the enemyships of racism, sexism, xenophobia, and homophobia—healthier, more cooperative forms of solidarity that emphasize what we share without downplaying what we do not; communities of belonging rather than of exclusion. This is the high standard I hold all philosophies to, including philosophies of oneness.

Philosophies of oneness speak to an ancient longing, to a deep and primal need for connection with others and with the world we inhabit. Oneness has been called the perennial philosophy.[19] Though Americans are constantly striving to be different, to stand out from the crowd, in the end we all desperately crave "at-one-ment," to use a neologism coined by an American writer in the 1890s.[20] We want to feel rapport, that the universe has our back. We want to feel at home in the world, that we belong. We want to feel as though we are being held up by loving, caring, tender hands, that in the end it will all work out, because the universe is not a cold and dark place devoid of feeling. Oneness can bring comfort, and inspire us to be better than we currently are. But the longing for oneness can take a very dark turn into the dangerous territory of exclusivity, restriction, and violence. Indeed, it is amazing how rapidly rhetorics of oneness become rhetorics of twoness, how quickly an "us" invites a "them."

How easily, how naturally, how quickly humans adopt what I call the rhetoric of enemyship![21] Unlike friendship, whose bonds are forged by mutual affection, enemyship fabricates bonds of a false oneness based on mutual antagonism toward an enemy. At its most effective, enemyship actualizes a state of us-against-them: *you're either with us or against us*. Enemyship demands unity in the face of danger, and though this unity is never quite achieved, the demand for togetherness offers a powerful justification for the repression of dissent. "Acquiescence in the establishment," Emerson concludes, "indicate[s] infirm faith" and "heads which are not clear."[22] The oneness of enemyship, of *e pluribus unum*—out of many, one—is not how Emerson or Whitman imagined oneness. Their oneness does not mean sameness. It is not the oneness envisioned by philosophers like Thomas Hobbes, one of the philosophical founders of liberalism, who fantasized about all people becoming one in their shared obedience to an absolute authority figure.[23]

Emerson and Whitman hoped to inspire Americans to think more deeply about oneness so that they might direct the human urge for connection toward democratic, rather than authoritarian, outcomes. This was especially true for Whitman, America's greatest democratic poet and my favorite writer.

He observed, "We have frequently printed the word Democracy. Yet I cannot too often repeat that it is a word the real gist of which still sleeps, quite unawaken'd."[24] For Whitman, awakening democracy meant awakening people to the reality of oneness, for oneness gave democracy its modus operandi and offered divine sanction to the foundational democratic virtue of equality. Democracy's challenge, he astutely recognized, is to indulge, rather than deny, the urge toward oneness while creating a oneness that is not predicated on division and that, at the same time, is not personally, socially, and politically repressive—a oneness that results in friendship, not enemyship; in inclusion, not exclusion; in peace, not war.[25]

Talk of oneness tends toward platitudes that make for great memes and gifs but offer very little guidance for how we should actually live our lives. In this book I move past commonplaces and inanities and hackneyed phrases to consider how Emerson, Whitman, and a gaggle of other figures imagined what it might mean to live a life of oneness. My goal is to better understand oneness not as an abstract, timeless, philosophical concept but as a concrete, practical, ethical challenge.

My central question is, What are *the ethics of oneness*? A number of additional questions immediately follow. Some questions are *metaphysical*: If the world is one, in what way is it one? And toward what end? Some are *psychological*: If the world is one, then why do people feel separate and alone? Some are *rhetorical*: If the world is one, how should we represent this oneness with words? Some are *ethical*: If the world is one, what does this entail, in concrete terms, for how we should live our lives? What are what I call our *everyday democratic obligations* to others? Toward the earth? How should we act? How should we speak? What are our responsibilities toward those who disagree and dissent, toward those who deny oneness, toward those who are hateful, intolerant, and perhaps even violent? And, finally, some are *spiritual* and *political*. If the world is one, should we try to make it a better place? And what is "better," anyway? How do we fix the problems we see around us?

The Ethics of Oneness

My goal in this book is to recover two long-forgotten philosophies of oneness, Emersonianism and Whitmanism, both born from cross-cultural dialogue and a genuine desire to offer Americans a richer and more rewarding life than that offered by conventional individualism. In this book I will describe these philosophies in all their rich perplexity. But that is not my only aim. I will also critique these philosophies. No philosophy is perfect; every worldview has its blind spots. I tend to think of philosophies as maps.[26] There is no such thing as an "objective" map. No map is a perfect mirror of reality. Maps are human inventions that tell a story about the world that highlights some features while ignoring others. All maps have cardinal directions—north, south, east, and west—but north matters only in reference to where I am now, and where I want to go. (Moreover, where I find myself on the map changes the felt experience of direction. It always feels like I am going north when climbing up a mountain, even if the summit is to the east.) Though all maps are inventions, some are better than others—and their value depends on our purposes. Multiple goals, multiple goods, sometimes in competition, form the backdrop to our biographies. Both Emerson and Whitman offer maps to life, and both seek to persuade us, in their own unique ways, to let oneness be our guide through life's adventures.

How should we evaluate a philosophy of oneness? When it comes to questions of ontology, I believe we must tread lightly and with great care, for we are talking about people's most deeply held beliefs. For many people, ontology is beyond argument; it simply is. Mystical traditions tend toward adamance on this point. Many mystics argue that there is no case for oneness, because oneness is beyond case-building; oneness is an experience that cannot arise from argument or practical knowledge (*phronesis*). It doesn't matter how early we rise or turn in. Hard work and the American can-do spirit is not enough to achieve it. And we cannot talk our way into this state. "We do not get it," Emerson muses, with "verbs and nouns."[27]

Neither Emerson nor Whitman makes a case for oneness. Oneness is. The one, the oversoul, the all: this is an a priori for Emerson, and the mystical root center of Whitman's poetry. But surely, given his repeated, emphatic attacks on convention and his spirited defense of self-reliance and independent thought, Emerson would not have believed his rhetoric of oneness to be beyond critique and judgment. I cannot imagine that Whitman wouldn't have welcomed a spirited debate about oneness, either.

To evaluate a philosophy of oneness, it is necessary to keep in mind three different claims that such a philosophy tends to make: the ontological claim, the goodness claim, and the ethical claim. Ontology is an argument about the nature of being. Within every ontology, if we seek it out, there is also an argument about the good (or perhaps goods, plural). In turn, what is good by definition entails certain ethical commitments. Ethics is not the domain of abstract talk; ethics is concerned with concrete practices that are designed to bring the self in line with the good. To think ethically means asking, What changes must we put into place, what habits and practices must we develop, in order to better align ourselves with the highest good, the summum bonum?

It is difficult to judge ontology. What are we going to say in response to an argument about the nature of being—that you're wrong, that the nature of reality is not that way? Good luck with that argument. It is not impossible to argue ontology, but there is little that pluralists can say to move monists to their side, and vice versa. Again, while not impossible, it is difficult to judge claims about "the good." We are on much firmer ground, I believe, when it comes to practices. To assess an ontology of oneness, I propose that we focus on its practical consequences; namely, how it encourages people to speak and act in the world.

Here, I follow the spirit of the pragmatic method as William James describes it in *Pragmatism* (1907). Whenever we engage in a philosophical dispute—such as, *Is the world one thing or many parts?*—we must ask, What difference would it practically make to anyone if this notion rather than that notion were true? "If no practical difference whatever can be traced," James concludes, "then the alternatives mean practically the same thing, and all dispute is idle. Wherever a dispute is serious, we ought to be able to show some practical difference that must follow from one side or the other's being right."[28] With these phrases, James pulls philosophy out of the clouds and brings it home to the world. "How much water does it draw?" Emerson asks about every philosophy he encounters.[29] Krishna would have approved of this question, at least concerning the value of a philosophical system. The Bhagavad Gita discusses many Indian philosophical traditions, and, as Richard Davis notes, "the philosophical criterion Krishna employs in his discussion of theses schools of knowledge is not their metaphysical accuracy but rather the psychological consequences for one who adopts that perspective."[30] Critiquing ontology means observing its practical consequences on the real, embodied, concrete ethical lives of those who believe it. Does the philosophy embolden our most beneficent, loving tendencies? Does it prepare us to act so that we are capable of doing what must be done? Does it draw out our worst instincts, leaving us wracked with guilt, writhing in resentment, wallowing in woe, incapable of action that is not reactionary?

During the nineteenth century, Americans debated a number of topics of deepest concern, including salvation and damnation, heaven and hell, *the one and the many*—the last being the issue, again if James is to be believed, on which all philosophy, and all religion, ultimately turns. "I myself have come, by long brooding over it, to consider it the most central of all philosophical problems, central because so pregnant. I mean by this that if you know whether a man is a decided monist or a decided pluralist, you perhaps know more about the rest of his opinions than if you give him any other name ending in *ist*. . . . To believe in the one or in the many," James concludes, "is the classification with the maximum number of consequences."[31] You can learn a lot about people by listening to the words they use to describe their beliefs, their *isms* and *ists* and *ities*, just as we can learn a lot about ourselves by listening to our own words on the matter. To define oneself as a monist—as a believer in oneness—as Emerson and Whitman do, is to stake out a position that entails a number of ethical commitments. To study the ethics of oneness involves asking after its consequences.

The pragmatic method treats all truth claims as fallible and therefore subject to revision. Truth is made—and unmade—in experience, James insists. However, Emerson and Whitman were not pragmatists, though they are often described as precursors to American pragmatism. For both Emerson and Whitman, oneness is a truth that precedes and shapes experience. Oneness is an a priori, a given, an article of absolute personal faith. Oneness is not the product of cogitation (as faith was for Descartes with his cogito, ergo sum) or a gambler's rationalizations (as faith was for Pascal with his wager). Oneness is not a theory to be tested against reality. Oneness underlines, and buttresses, both Emerson and Whitman's philosophies and their lives. Even as we ask after the ethical consequences of their faith in oneness—and I believe we must ask after these consequences—we also must be very careful not to instrumentalize oneness, to transform it into just another variable in the calculus of everyday life. Oneness is the bedrock—the sine qua non—of democracy. To treat this bedrock as a working hypothesis that can be discarded when a better theory comes along is to misunderstand the nature of bedrock.

I do not question the truth of oneness in this book. Emerson, Whitman, and most of the other figures I consider follow the Bhagavad Gita in assuming the truth of oneness—and also assuming that this is a timeless truth. And yet even the wisdom that claims to be without time or place, clime or creed, still requires a voice to pronounce it. The universal can manifest itself only in the particular. The timeless can only be known in time. The question, then, is not if oneness is true.[32] The question is, How are we asked to think and feel and act because all things are one? To get a handle on the ethics of oneness, I investigate how we talk about oneness—I focus, in short, on its rhetoric. I ask, How do Emerson and Whitman make oneness matter?[33] How do they make this deeply personal experience available to others? How do they bring oneness before the eyes?[34] What types of relationships, communities, and worlds do they build on the ontological foundation of oneness? What difference do they say it makes to us, in practical terms, that all things are one? By asking these questions, the ethical consequences of oneness come into sharper focus.

James marked the choice between monism and pluralism as the most consequential choice a person can make. But say, for a moment, that one is committed to monism. What does this entail practically? Does it demand retreating from the world—to a monastery, perhaps, or a lovely mountain cabin—and passing one's days in quiet contemplation of the universe's mysteries? Or does it demand committing oneself to "justice" by vanquishing one's enemies on the battlefield of life? These choices might seem extreme, running the gamut as they do from peace to war; but in the Mahabharata—the epic Indian poem that contains the Bhagavad Gita—they are two possible ways to live a life committed to oneness. Not all monisms are created equal.

Recognizing that not all readers will be familiar with the Bhagavad Gita, let me take a moment to describe its context, and its argument. The Bhagavad Gita ("the Lord's song") is a pivotal book in the ancient Indian oral epic poem the Mahabharata.[35] Most contemporary Sanskrit scholars believe that the Mahabharata was composed by many bards, likely over the period of hundreds of years, and that the Gita originated at some point during the larger compositional process, incorporating the arguments and perspectives of rival philosophical schools. It is likely that the Gita was composed in northern India, sometime between the reign of the Mauryan king Ashoka (r. ca. 269–232 BCE) and the Gupta dynasty (320–547 CE).[36] It is a product of the interregnum, as people dealt with the collapse of the first great Indian empires and the resulting change in material and political realities, and as a widespread cultural debate played out about what makes a good king and who should have his ear.[37]

The Mahabharata tells the story of a terrible war over succession to the throne of Hastinapur between two rival camps of cousins, the five Pandava brothers and the hundred Kaurava brothers, that engulfs and nearly destroys an entire civilization. This made-for-television conflict—at times Homer, at times Shakespeare, at times a really scandalous telenovela—climaxes in a catastrophic war at Kurukshetra that lasts for eighteen days, a war that draws in all the surrounding kingdoms and their armies, a war that also involves the gods and their celestial weapons. Nearly everyone dies. The story resists easy moralizing—the "good guys," the Pandavas, at times do horrible things in the service of their noble ends, and even the "bad guys," the Kauravas (and they are certainly bad guys), have their own ethics, the heroic ethics of a warrior culture drunk on machismo. Though both sides display ethical virtues and iniquities in general the Mahabharata portrays a world out of whack, in which dharma, what is right and what is wrong, is not so clear.

The Bhagavad Gita occurs at a key moment in the story, right before the climactic battle is set to begin. The greatest warrior in the land, the third

Pandava brother, Arjuna, looks across the battlefield and sees his cousins, his teachers, his mentors, and his friends. Knowing that he will have to destroy them to win the war, he breaks down and refuses to fight. On the surface and taken quite literally, the Bhagavad Gita is war rhetoric—it is a sustained discussion between two characters in the Mahabharata: one, Arjuna, who refuses to fight a battle against his kith and kin; the other, his adviser and a god-in-disguise, Krishna, who implores Arjuna to abandon his pacifist delusions, fulfill his duty as a member of the warrior class, and fight. Arjuna argues that it is unethical to fight a war against one's family, even when they are clearly in the wrong. To persuade Arjuna to fight, Krishna teaches him a number of lessons, including the truth of oneness. The individual soul (*atman*) is in fact the universal soul, the divine substratum of all existence (*brahman*); everything is God. The world is "woven" on the divine background like "pearls on a string" or "beads on a thread."[38] Because the individual *atman* is immortal and imperishable, this means that death is an illusion, for the divine can be neither harmed nor killed. The body is killed, but the soul lives on. Krishna therefore implores Arjuna not to fret about slaughtering his cousins; Arjuna will destroy their bodies, but their souls are immortal and beyond harm. Stand up and fight! Krishna instructs Arjuna. In the end, Krishna's arguments—which culminate in the revelation of his cosmic form—are convincing. Krishna wins the argument; Arjuna wins the war.

The Bhagavad Gita is a master class in war rhetoric. Indeed, the Gita is a product of its time, which celebrated violence as central to manhood and framed battle as an instrument of divine justice.[39] Consequently, the Gita's critics see it as a celebration of slaughter. According to Bhimrao Ambedkar, the anticaste reformer who served as the chief architect of the contemporary Indian constitution, "To say that killing is no killing because what is killed is the body and not the soul is an unheard of defense of murder. . . . If Krishna were to appear as a lawyer acting for a client who is being tried for murder and pleaded the defense set out by him in the Bhagvat Gita there is not the slightest doubt that he would be sent to the lunatic asylum."[40] Read as a defense of war, as a persuasive case for killing, the Gita is a massive moral letdown. However, Emerson and Whitman did not read the poem primarily as a call to physical warfare. Following the German Romantics, instead they read the Gita as a book of timeless wisdom more concerned with issues of religious salvation than war.[41] They interpreted the Gita's "war" as an allegory for the conflict between good and bad, light and dark, in the human soul. This is a psychological war, a human battle that has been raging in each of us since the dawn of consciousness.

Most pandits and yogis read the Gita similarly. About the Gita Mahatma

Gandhi observes, "Under the guise of physical warfare, it described the duel that perpetually went on in the hearts of mankind, and that physical warfare was brought in merely to make the description of the internal duel more alluring."[42] The Gita invites such a reading with its opening scene-setting verse: "Dharmakshetre kurukshetre," "in the field [*shetre*] of dharma, in the field of the Kurus."[43] The dialogue of the Gita is situated on the battlefield of Kurukshetra—but this is no normal battlefield. It is also a moral battlefield, a battlefield where the central question is dharma, what is right and what is wrong.[44]

As an allegory that takes place on the *dharmakshetra*, the Gita dramatizes many of the psychological conflicts that characterize human life. Two mental battles are especially relevant to *The Ethics of Oneness*: first, the battle between greed and the countervailing capacity to act in the interests of a common good; and second, the battle between the human tendency to run away from our problems and the courage it takes to face these problems and do what needs to be done. Interpreted allegorically, the Bhagavad Gita models a central ethical conflict at the heart of monism, between withdrawal and engagement.

It is certainly valid to read the Bhagavad Gita as a parable. However, as I will argue later, to understand the Gita, as well as Emerson and Whitman's interpretation of it, we must never forget that it is a chapter in the story of a horrific war and that it serves as one of the most persuasive cases for war ever written. Of course, the Gita did not become one of the world's bibles because of its case for war. Instead, it is the poem's affirmative teachings about oneness, yoga, duty, devotion, and love that have consistently drawn Americans in, beginning with Emerson and his contemporaries. According to Krishna, a chief cause of human suffering and interpersonal cruelty is "duality delusion"—the misperception of reality as a realm of division.[45] Reality is not two, or many; it is one. Division is not real; it is a mistaken belief that must be overcome by practicing yoga.

In the Rig Veda, the word *yoga* tended to mean "action" (as opposed to *kshema*, "rest") and was in particular applied to martial actions like warfare and cattle rustling.[46] Clearly, then, the Gita preserves yoga's bellicose roots in Krishna's commandment that Arjuna fight. Later, in the Upanishads and the Gita, the word *yoga* came to mean something more peaceful and spiritual—namely, "binding together," "joining," or, as it was often translated during the nineteenth century, "marriage," of the individual soul and the oversoul. Things appear separate, but in reality everything is unified and united. Yoga is about overcoming the beguiling appearance of difference. Krishna teaches Arjuna a yoga of oneness, *ekatva*. Yoga in the Bhagavad Gita is a practice of focusing the mind and reigning in the senses so that when we look at the world with one-pointed focus (*ekagrata*), we see oneness and not division. Though the world is a playground of variation, underlining the many differences we espy is a common divine substance. Krishna affirms that the yogi knows that everyone, and everything, is born from *brahman*. Once the yogi becomes skilled in seeing oneness, then they can recognize that the *atman*, the immanent, individual self, or soul, is and always has been yoked to *brahman*, the universal, divine substratum of life and the absolute principle of all existence. In reality, all things are one and the individual is divine.

Krishna's yoga aims at an enlarged, universal perspective of the world that perceives all beings as interconnected in their shared divinity. According to Krishna, the yogi is *ekabhakti*, devoted to oneness.[47] The yogi practices this devotion (bhakti) by seeing the divine in all beings:

> Arming himself with discipline [*yoga*],
> Seeing everything with an equal eye,
> He sees the self [*atman*] in all creatures,
> And all creatures in the self [*atman*].[48]

This yoga strives toward a resolute vision of oneness rooted in common divinity—Krishna instructs Arjuna to practice seeing every person, friend or foe, as an incarnation of divine oneness. This yogic vision of innate divinity must not be shaken by the ups and downs of everyday life; oneness must be *samadarsana*, "seen equally," and *sarvatra*, "at all times, everywhere, in all cases."[49] "The yogi who abides in oneness," Krishna proclaims, gains "transcendent bliss"—"happiness beyond end."[50] "Resting in the one" (*ekastha*), the yogi finds peace and the power to do what is necessary.[51] That such beautiful lessons are part of a case for war is a profound paradox of the human experience.

The Bhagavad Gita is one of the world's bibles. For many it is sunlight in darkness. For others—contemporary Dalits ("untouchables") in India, or anyone else condemned by Krishna's words and marked by Brahmins as *mleccha*, "barbarian" or "sinner"—the Gita is the darkness itself. The Gita is a paradoxical, vexing, contradictory, frustrating, and, to say the least, morally troubling book. The meaning of the Bhagavad Gita is not settled. It changes depending on who is reading it, what language and time period they read it in, what philosophical map they are using, and where they are hoping to go. Historically, there is no Gita; there are only Gitas. Like the Mahabharata itself, which was intended to be an encyclopedia of India's cultural wisdom, the Gita is a polyphonic text. Krishna speaks in diverse accents and voices a number of often-inconsistent philosophical positions. Generally, the Gita reads like a straightforward defense of the nondualism typical of the Advaita Vedanta school of Indian philosophy.[52] However, Krishna also invokes Buddhist and Jain concepts and ideas.[53] Sometimes he couches his arguments in the dualistic language of Samkhya metaphysics, with its absolute distinction between soul (*purusha*) and matter (*prakriti*).[54] At his most elliptical, Krishna employs the head-scratching language of Bhedabheda (*bheda-abheda*, distinction-nondistinction) Vedanta, which teaches that the *atman* is both different (*bheda*) from and not different (*abheda*) from *brahman*. However, it was unquestionably Advaita Vedanta and its philosophy of oneness, *ekatva*, that most resonated with Americans during the 1800s.

Advaita dominated in large part because of the texts that were available to Americans and the choices made by translators to present the Gita as a statement of oneness. The Advaitic interpretation of the Gita offered Americans an inspiring language for critiquing the liberal, individualistic, materialistic, Protestant strains of their culture that they found so problematic. Indeed, numerous Americans during this period turned to oneness to counter the greedy capitalism that dominated their lives. In oneness, they found an anecdote to the spiritual nihilism hastened by Newtonian physics, which popularized a picture of a cold, mechanistic universe in which humans are little more than cogs in a disenchanted machine. In oneness many Americans discovered the meaning of life.

In *The Ethics of Oneness*, I describe and critique Emerson and Whitman's philosophies of oneness, including the ontological, goodness, and ethical claims they make. In the first two chapters, I consider Emerson's (chapter 1) and Whitman's (chapter 2) metaphysics. These chapters are primarily about ontology—and make no mistake: American democracy requires, for both authors, a firm ontological foundation of oneness that is beyond debate if democracy is to survive and thrive. Emerson calls oneness "the Over-soul," his Americanization of the Bhagavad Gita's *paramatman*. Whitman calls it "All," "rondure," "ensemble," "mélange," and "kosmos." I tell the story of how they arrive at these terms, and the functions they serve, in these opening chapters. I also recount the various techniques these writers describe for overcoming the illusion of separation and realizing the truth of oneness, including the practice of what I will call *communication as yoga*.

When I speak about "yoga" here, I do not mean the elaborate physical postures (asana) that have become so closely associated with contemporary practice.[55] Yoga is more than moving bodies, though it is that, too. The Bhagavad Gita presents many definitions of yoga. When I speak about yoga in this book, I have one particular definition in mind. Yoga is the practice of focusing the mind (which is constantly wandering off, pulled this way and that by the senses) on one object and then sustaining that focus without distraction.[56] Krishna compares the yogi's mind to "a lamp in a windless place that does not flicker."[57] Yoga in the Bhagavad Gita means focusing so deeply, so fully, so completely on oneness that subject and object merge and we become conscious embodiments of the divine all. And so Krishna implores Arjuna to practice seeing everything with an equal eye that illuminates the divine soul in all creatures.

The soul is unkillable; the practice of seeing the divine in everything becomes a combat technique in the Gita. But this practice, of becoming attuned to the divine oneness of all creation, need not lead to war. Inspired by the Bhagavad Gita, in different ways both Emerson and Whitman imagine every interaction with another person as an opportunity to ask, Would I treat the divine this way? Because whenever we engage with another person, that is what we are doing—we are talking with a divine being who might well be mistaken about their true nature, but who is divine nonetheless. Speaking to others as divine is a way of becoming oriented toward an experience of oneness in our lives. Of course, one can relate to divinity in many ways. Some shield their eyes in fear and refuse to utter the holy name. Some raise their voices in loving worship. Some jeer and dismiss. How to see the divine equally, and everywhere, is an open question, and its answer might influence how we live a life committed to oneness.

In the next two chapters I consider the ethical consequences of Emerson and Whitman's philosophies of oneness. In chapter 3, I focus on the question of the body. In the Advaita Vedanta of the Bhagavad Gita—and also, as we will see, in Emerson's Advaita, especially his poem "Brahma"—the practice of communication as yoga becomes a powerful argument for war, for if the soul is immortal and the body is an illusion, a trick of divine maya, then there is no harm in killing, for in reality there is no killing, since the divine cannot be killed. The body, for Emerson, is disposable.

Initially, I held an oversimplified portrait of Whitman as the inheritor and expositor of Emerson's Advaita and his philosophy of the oversoul; this is how he is often described in histories of American yoga and mysticism.[58] It is true that Whitman redoubles Emerson's cosmic optimism, his healthy-minded and tenderhearted belief that the universe is not cold and dark but alive and quick for the good. And yet Whitman's ontology and his ethics diverge from Emerson's, as does his vision of everyday democracy. Whitman's Vedanta is closer in spirit to the Bhedabheda interpretation of the Bhagavad Gita than the Advaita interpretation that Emerson preferred.[59] Whitman never denies the reality of the body, as Emerson did, and Whitman did not warm to the theory of maya, or illusion, like Emerson did.

Whitman pronounces an ethics of oneness that is grounded in the reality of lived, bodily experience. His oneness makes space for diversity and recognizes the reality of division. Difference and division are not simply delusions; they have a degree of reality, as both are contained within the divine oneness. Whitman also practices communication as yoga—but rather than addressing the divine soul and ignoring the body, he imagines the body, too, as divine, celebrating it as worthy of dignity and as a vital site of spiritual practice. We experience oneness through our bodies. Contra Emerson, Whitman was emphatic that people do not have to transcend the human to have a mystical, meditative experience. It is by delving deeply into the human that we realize oneness. Whitman holds the individual and the cosmic, the many and the one, in a delicate balance. This is one of the many balancing acts that an ethics of oneness must undertake. The ethical implications of chapter 3 are clear: to ignore the body is to court catastrophe.

As is to downplay the power of language. The mystics testify that oneness is beyond words. Whitman muses, "I do not know it—it is without name—it is a word unsaid, / It is not in any dictionary, utterance, symbol."[60]

> When the subtle air, the impalpable, the sense that words and reason hold not,
> surround us and pervade us,
> Then I am charged with untold and untellable wisdom, I am silent, I require
> nothing further.[61]

Both Emerson and Whitman join countless mystics across history in equating an experience of oneness with an eloquent silence. When it comes to mystical experiences, perhaps it would be best not to speak; but this is harder than one might think. Extraordinary experiences exercise an extraordinary pull on the human need to communicate ourselves to others, because it is by vocalizing such experiences that we process them and ascribe them meaning. "If utterance is denied, the thought lies like a burden on the man. Always the seer is a sayer," Emerson mused at his most Delphic.[62] Oneness is an experience that is beyond language, but the map to this experience is written in words. Though oneness, and the words we use to represent it, are not equivalent—the word that points at the moon is not the moon—nevertheless, our words matter, for they gesture, guide, and goad.

Perhaps the Rig Veda is correct when it argues, "Ekam sad, vipra bahudha vadanti"—"the truth is one, sages call it variously."[63] One truth, many names. If I learned anything from writing this book, however, it is that the words and phrases and names we use to describe *ekatva*, oneness, *do* matter, for they orient us toward infinity while priming us to experience the world and its transcendence in particular ways. Talk of oneness is inherently moral, for such talk builds a template in our expectations for, and perceptions of, reality. To understand the ethical consequences of a philosophy of oneness, we must ask how oneness is portrayed in poetry, dialogues, stories, analogies, fables, fairy tales, parables, and philosophical disquisitions. Accordingly, in chapter 4, I compare and contrast Whitman's attempt to represent oneness in his cosmic poem "Salut au Monde!" with Arjuna's divine vision in chapter 11 of the Bhagavad Gita. Here we will see that oneness can be the inspiration for peace or for war, depending on how it is represented. Even infinity is shaped by human motivations.

In the concluding chapters of *The Ethics of Oneness*, I offer an evaluation of the two philosophies of oneness I have described in this book, focusing on Emerson in chapter 5 and Whitman in chapter 6. To evaluate their philosophies, I ask three questions:

> First, *What type of relationship does this philosophy encourage us to form with ourselves, with others, and with the world where we make our home?*
> Second, *How does this philosophy treat diversity and difference?*
> And third, *How does this philosophy teach us to view life itself?*

Why these questions? Because to me they address the most important consequences any philosophy can have, on how we build our lives in common with others, on whether we treat differences with dismissal or respect, and on how we perceive life itself.

If William James is to be believed, Emerson's interpretation of the Bhagavad Gita gave birth to the first truly American religion, which he dubbed Emersonianism.[64] Whether or not this eponymous faith constitutes a religion, I cannot say. There are no Emersonian churches or ashrams, no annual pilgrimages to Emerson's birthplace. Emerson never taught anyone how to pray. But Emersonianism is in America's bones, as the kind Chennai bookseller surely knew when she presented me with his book. Emerson's essays—which as a general rule were first delivered as public talks on the lyceum circuit to large and enthusiastic audiences—continue to shape how many Americans think and speak about our spiritual and religious lives. When we talk about the wisdom of the "soul" and "the inward eye" and "divine energy" that flows like "water," we speak the language of Emersonianism.

In the end, I conclude that the kind Chennai bookseller was correct: we have much to learn from Emerson, and about yoga, too. Emersonianism represents the faith that human beings are worthy of life's challenges, ad astra per aspera. "Our philosophy is affirmative."[65] From podium and pen, Emerson gave voice to the upbeat optimistic American attitude that no matter how difficult life might be, no matter how bad things get, no matter how badly humans have messed up their world, nothing is beyond redemption, for deep within each of us there is a reservoir of strong, courageous, compassionate power that can be drawn on to meet the demands of the moment. He observed that "great men, great nations, have not been boasters and buffoons, but perceivers of the terror of life, and have manned themselves to face it."[66] People prove their worth at the crossroads.

I cheer the spirit of Emersonianism—in particular, I applaud his intuition that Americans have something valuable to learn from Indian philosophy, and I celebrate his attempt to expand our philosophical vision to become more global. Oneness is a theme that borders could never contain. I also raise serious ethical questions about Emerson's philosophy of oneness. In chapters 2 and 3, I follow Emerson's brilliant contemporary Margaret Fuller and question its sexism; in chapter 3, I question its idealism and its neglect of the body; and in chapter 5, I question its tendency to take oneness too far, to the point that it almost entirely erases the individual and its agency. Emerson's greatest contribution to the history of American yoga is, I believe, also his greatest contribution to everyday democracy: he democratizes the divine avatar of the Bhagavad Gita by encouraging people to address everyone they meet as an incarnation of the divine. Emerson had much less faith in democracy than his transcendentalist friends, however, and his vision of social reform tended to be antidemocratic: as a cosmic optimist, he advised people to stop worrying so much about making the world better and to put their faith in a benevolent universe that is constantly working for the good; and, as a believer in heroism, he celebrated those rare individuals, those few enlightened geniuses who rose above convention to receive a revelation of divine oneness as the true agents of social change. Both visions of social reform had precursors in the Bhagavad Gita, and while Emerson's reading of this text has much to offer, I conclude that his interpretation also demonstrates the challenges of articulating a philosophy of oneness that withstands the rigors of everyday democracy. Oneness should balance and ground individuality, not erase it.

Whitman had none of Emerson's ambivalence about democracy. Whitman has been called the "seer" of democracy, and, indeed, Whitman approached democracy more like a seer or a mystic than a political scientist.[67] Whitman roots democracy in an ontology of oneness. For Whitman, the purpose of democracy is to use words to transcend words, to empower the "soul-sight," and to facilitate a direct meditative "intuition"[68] of oneness—"to enter the pure ether of veneration, reach the divine levels, and commune with the unutterable."[69] For Whitman, it is ethically good for people to develop their soul-sighted capacity for meditation, and democracy is the superior form of government because it respects *spiritual equality*. Oneness, in turn, gives democracy divine sanction, for it provides an ontological argument for the chief democratic virtue of equality. Whitman's poetry positions the shared human capacity for mystical insight at the core of democracy. Intuition, or soul sight, is an indispensable ingredient for democracy.[70] Democracy creates a gymnasium in which people can develop their capacity to experience oneness, and it is the responsibility of the poets, the prophets, the bards, the storytellers, and the orators to awaken.

I've long been interested in questions of the one and the many, identification and division, both as a scholar of rhetoric and as a teacher of yoga and meditation. I've spent a number of years examining and critiquing the most common rhetorical techniques used to divide and conquer. My research is driven by the hope that if we truly understand what causes division, then it might be possible to see beyond it toward something deeper, and more real, that unites us, so that we might be able to talk to each other, to learn from each other, to understand each other and live together more peacefully, in justice. As I look forward to democracy's future, I take inspiration from Whitman's philosophy of oneness. Indeed, I make no attempt in this book to hide my love for Whitman's poetry and his unparalleled ability to give voice to a dream of democratic oneness. The impressive vocabulary that Whitman develops to represent oneness remains conscious of difference, as does his vision of communication as yoga. He is steadfast: the goal is not to obliterate differences, but to attune people to the oneness that underlines all individualism and all conflict.

Though democracy aims at helping people achieve a transcendent experience beyond language, democracy is enriched by those who pursue this experience, *even if it never comes*. Democracy is a life of interaction, engagement, and relationship-building. As we work to develop our capacity for intuition, Whitman suggests that we will be more compassionate, loving, mindful, and grateful citizens. We will become accustomed to speaking to other people as though they are divine and worthy of dignity. We will also become more attuned to our fundamental interconnectedness, both with other human beings and with the rest of the natural world. We will develop skills and capacities that are vital to building healthy relationships and hence a healthy democracy. We will also learn how to call out hatred and intolerance for the abuses that they are. In the end, I agree with Whitman that oneness can be democratic, and that it can deeply enrich our broken-down democratic culture.[71] Properly conceptualized, I believe—and hope to demonstrate—that oneness can meet the ethical challenges of everyday democracy and heal "the decays of things."[72]

While I might sound harsh in my evaluation of Emerson, in relationship to America's often materialistic and greedy individualism—and in contrast to a very different nineteenth-century philosophy of oneness, Theosophy, which was deliberately recherché and antidemocratic as it lorded its secretive furtive teachings over the unenlightened masses—I would evaluate both Emerson and Whitman's work as ethical statements of oneness.[73] It's just that Whitman's philosophy is more democratic, more inclusive, more worldly, more sensitive to difference, more human and humane. But there would be no Whitmanism without Emersonianism, for while Whitman is not a direct philosophical heir, nevertheless he builds on important themes in Emerson's work. And there would be no Emersonianism (and by extension no Whitmanism)—at least, not in the way that it came to be—without the Bhagavad Gita. Americans frequently trace their conception of democracy to Periclean Athens and republican Rome. In fact, our democratic ideas and practices are influenced by many traditions and cultures. Consequently, in the coming years, I hope to see the study of democracy move in a more global, transnational direction—because American democracy has always been global and multicultural, and we are stronger politically, and smarter philosophically, when we recognize this. And I hope that my book can be a humble contribution to this project.

People often speak about "new beginnings," but I'm just as interested in *old* beginnings, in the creativity and inventiveness that can be found by looking over old terrain, old maps, and old books with new eyes. Life is full of beginnings, but they are rarely "new." We are constantly in dialogue with the past. The past is the ground on which we stand. The past informs the words we speak, the thoughts we think, the air we breathe. We bear the past in muscle and sinew and bone and gait. The past limits who we are and who we can be, but these limits are not total, for the past can also empower and inspire us to be something different, something more, than we are now.

I do not see the turn to Emerson, Whitman, and the Bhagavad Gita as a form of spiritual bypassing or an attempt to retreat from the world's troubles.[74] I see it as a chance to reassess many of the assumptions that have become commonplace about democracy, assumptions that like anything else seem more true the less we question them. Perhaps by looking at an old American philosophy from the nineteenth century—neglected, sure, but one that has profoundly shaped the spiritual practices of Americans for generations—and putting it in dialogue with its Indian, yogic influences, including the Bhagavad Gita, we can invent something new: an ethics of oneness worthy of everyday democracy.

1

Oversoul

Yoga = the effort to unite with the Deity.
Concentration.
EMERSON, *Notebook Orientalist*

Two recent histories—Philip Goldberg's *American Veda: How Indian Spirituality Changed the West* (2010), and Stefanie Syman's *The Subtle Body: The Story of Yoga in America* (2010)—make the provocative claim that the founder of American yoga was not some extravagantly dressed master clad in brightly colored robes hailing from foreign shores. The gurus came later. The founder of American yoga did not travel to the United States on a boat or a plane. He was born here. He was none other than the sage of Concord, Ralph Waldo Emerson (1803–1882).[1] Emerson never self-identified as a yogi. And Emerson did not practice asana, the physical practices of yoga. In fact, many of the elaborate physical practices associated with contemporary yoga were not developed until after Emerson's death.[2] When scholars argue that Emerson introduced Americans to yoga, they are speaking about *the philosophy of yoga*, specifically the Advaita (nondualistic) Vedanta of the Bhagavad Gita.

"Emerson" is not a name you hear in contemporary yoga circles. There are no invocations to Emerson chanted at the beginning of yoga classes or statues of Emerson placed reverently on meditation altars. Personally I do not know anyone who walks the earth with a transparent eyeball tattooed on their arm or back. Emerson was aware of yoga from his reading of Indian philosophy, but he never claimed to be a yogi or to practice yoga.[3] Emerson was never as bold as Thoreau, who observed, "To some extent, and at rare intervals, even I am a yogin."[4] Nevertheless, Emerson's essays have long influenced the vocabulary by which Americans understand the Bhagavad Gita and its articulation of a philosophy of oneness (*ekatva*). In his essays, Emerson engaged in a double hermeneutics, interpreting Indian philosophy from the perspective of America as he understood it and America from the perspective of Indian philosophy. In the process, Emerson helped create something new: a rhetoric of transcendentalist yoga that speaks with an American accent.

There are many genealogies of American yoga. The story I tell in this book is unique—not because it starts with Emerson, for, as we have seen, others start with Emerson, too, though most histories start much later, at the place where my tale will end, when the yogis come from India in the 1890s and early 1900s. The story I tell is unique because it focuses on communication as foundational to living an ethical life dedicated to oneness. In the sixth chapter of the Bhagavad Gita, Krishna instructs Arjuna to see the divine in all beings at all times.[5] Ordained as a preacher, famed as a lecturer, and trained as a student of rhetoric, Emerson interprets this passage as a clarion call to change how Americans communicate. In his essay "The Over-Soul" (1841), which I read as an early attempt to grapple with the implications of the Bhagavad Gita, Emerson imagines communication as a type of yoga. When talking with others, he advises his readers to picture their interlocutors as incarnations, or avatars of the divine—and to speak to the divinity in them, as though their individual souls are no different than the universal cosmic divine soul that is the foundation of all creation, the oversoul. For Emerson, living a life committed to oneness means practicing communication as yoga, the active devotion to the shared divinity of all beings in speech. Emerson opines that speaking to the divine in others will open Americans to the divine in themselves. It will also pave the way for a better world.

Yoga as Retreat: The View from Europe

Emerson never traveled to India. He did not read or speak Sanskrit or any of the other Indian languages. Like most Americans of his time, he knew Indian philosophy secondhand, via Europe. The British colonization of India in the 1700s introduced the foundational works of yoga philosophy to Europe.[6] The British tended to engage with Indian philosophy in one of two antithetical ways (and these two patterns of interpretation were symbolic of how Europeans and Americans engaged with India more generally during the nineteenth century).[7] On one side were the first generation of Orientalists, including Sir Charles Wilkins and Sir William Jones, who believed in British superiority but who were also deeply sympathetic to both Hinduism and Buddhism. These scholar-bureaucrats attempted to understand Indian philosophy so that the British could better govern India with the cooperation of Indians. On the opposite side were the Anglicists like James Mill, whose three-volume *History of British India* (1818) also forwarded a vision of British superiority but who far surpassed the Orientalists in his racist, patriarchal condemnation of Indian inferiority.

Rooted in the demands of the colonial project but at the same time driven by a genuine interest in and sympathy for Indian culture, the early Orientalists translated the sacred texts of Hinduism that Brahmin pandits were willing to share with them into English, French, German, and Latin during the late eighteenth and early nineteenth centuries. Hinduism makes a distinction between wisdom that is *shruti* ("that which has been heard"), the canonical, unquestionable, eternal wisdom of the Vedas, and *smriti* ("that which has been remembered"), the commentaries on the Vedas found in texts including the Laws of Manu, the Upanishads, the Bhagavad Gita, and the Puranas. *Smriti* texts address eternal themes, but the messages of these texts are time- and context-bound and are acknowledged to evolve as the perspective of interpreters change. Brahmins generally did not reveal the *shruti* Vedas to the British.[8] These Brahmins did share and help translate *smriti* texts like the Bhagavad Gita. The translation of these texts staked a surge of interest in Indian philosophy and religion in Europe and the United States. The Bhagavad Gita proved especially popular for a number of reasons, including its dramatic setting, its familiar dialogic form, its timeless subject matter (duty and war), and the figure of Krishna, who many Europeans envisioned as an Indian Jesus Christ.[9] When the Gita was first translated into English in 1785, the linguist Sir William Jones (1746–1794), a hero in America for supporting the cause of independence, advised his European readers that "if they wish to form a correct idea of Indian religion and literature, let them begin with forgetting all that has been written on the subject by ancients or moderns, before the publication of the Gītā."[10]

Though aspects of the Bhagavad Gita seemed familiar to Europeans, much of it was completely foreign—including the importance it placed on the mysterious, esoteric practice of "yoga." The word *yoga* is capacious. In Sanskrit, it has over eighty meanings, ranging from "yoking" and "joining" to "meditation," "magic," "astrological calculation," and "the equipping of an army for battle." Yogis can be "pandits," "secret agents," "liars," "great warriors," "sorcerers," "mercenaries," "circus performers," "philosophers," and "business people."[11] Given its wealth of possible meanings, the word *yoga* caused considerable trouble for the original translators of major Indian philosophical works. In the first English translation of the Gita, published in 1785 as *Bhăgvăt-Gēētā, or Dialogues of Krěěshnă and Ărjŏŏn*, Sir Charles Wilkins (1749–1836) said this about it: "There is no word in the Sănskrěět language that will bear so many interpretations as this." Because there was no one English word that could capture the expansiveness of yoga, Wilkins chose to leave *yoga* untranslated—a choice many translators continue to make today. He explained that yoga is an active discipline of the "yōgēē," "a devout man," who hoped to live his life in line with universal divinity—*yoga* means "junction," "union," "devotion," and "the application of the mind in spiritual things."[12]

In 1823, the German Romantic A. W. Schlegel (1767–1845) translated the Bhagavad Gita into Latin, believing that the flexibility of this language captured the beauty and textual nuance of the poem better than German or French. Schlegel also was likely inspired by the common belief that as a sacred, religious, liturgical language, Latin was the European parallel to Sanskrit. Unlike Wilkins, Schlegel chose to translate the term *yoga* with several Latin words. Yoga is *destinatio* (acting with determination, purpose, great resolve); *exercitatio* (exercise, training, discipline); *applicatio* (accommodation, inclination); *devotio* (devotion, consecration, a vow); *disciplina activa* (a way of life, a doctrine); *mysterium* (a secret); *facultas mystica* (a mystical branch of knowledge); *maiestas* (excellence, distinction); and *contemplatio* (consideration of eternal secrets with the mind).[13] "The word yoga is a true Proteus," Schlegel concluded, and "its intellectual metamorphoses compel us to use cunning and force to tie it down and make it present itself to us and reveal its secrets."[14] He explained that he considered translating yoga simply as *conjugium*—"connection" or "marriage," as between an individual (*atman*) and the divine (*brahman*)—but opted instead for a range of expressions that spoke to the diverse definitions of yoga.

Schlegel's edition of the Bhagavad Gita prompted a heated, intensely personal, and at times downright vicious scholarly debate in Europe concerning translation.[15] Some philosophers, including G. W. F. Hegel (1770–1831), argued that it was perhaps impossible, but almost certainly unnecessary, to translate Sanskrit works like the Bhagavad Gita into European languages. As he composed and revised his lectures on the philosophy of history during the 1820s, Hegel portrayed Indian philosophy as childish and fatalistic. In his reading of the Bhagavad Gita, Hegel denied that yoga was an active practice because, he surmised, Indian culture precluded the development of free individuality. For Hegel it was not the case that Europeans could never understand yoga, though it was unclear why they should want to. Instead, Hegel believed that Indians could never understand European philosophy because they had not yet advanced to being properly free. India was a land of blind obedience. Yoga was a kind of nihilism, "the intuition of nothing" (*das Anschauen des Nichts*), a flight from the world into mystical nothingness.[16] Hegel doubted that yoga had anything to offer the West, and he attacked those like Schlegel who said otherwise as being hopelessly naive and philosophically unsophisticated. Schlegel and others disagreed, believing that Westerners had much to learn from the study of yoga in the Bhagavad Gita.

The popular French philosopher Victor Cousin (1792–1867) was an admirer of Hegel, and the two carried on a long and engaged correspondence. In his Paris lectures of 1828 and 1829, Cousin divided the anatomy of the history of philosophy into four archetypical forms—sensationalism, idealism, skepticism, and mysticism—that recur throughout history, and always in that order. India was the starting point of it all, "the cradle of civilization and philosophy."[17] The philosophy of India represented "the first epoch of the history of philosophy" and "the beginning of the human mind."[18] "We come from the Romans, the Romans from the Greeks, and the Greeks took from the East their language, their arts, their religion."[19] For Cousin, the Bhagavad Gita was the textbook of yoga, and yoga the beating heart of Indian mysticism.[20]

In his 1828 lectures, Cousin accurately glossed Krishna's teaching in the Bhagavad Gita concerning the illusion of separation: "Why do you speak of friends and of family? Why of men? Family, friends, men, beasts or stones, all are one. A perpetual and eternal force has created all which you see and renews it without cessation. . . . The principle of every thing is eternal; what value does anything else have? . . . Nothing exists but the eternal principle; being, in itself."[21] The world was animated by "a perpetual and eternal force" (*une force perpétuelle et éternelle*), and the goal of yoga was to meditate with "eyes focused unceasingly upon the absolute principle" so that the yogi might devote himself fully to realizing the divine life.[22] Following Hegel, however, Cousin concluded that yogic devotion (bhakti) demanded a slavish obsession with quiet contemplation. The true yogi must shun action and "let things pass" (*de tout laisser-faire*).[23] For Cousin, all yoga was bhakti yoga, and by definition bhakti yoga required abandoning the world. Cousin translated *yoga* as a synonym for *retreat*. The "true yogi," he concluded, must turn his back on the world, becoming "Mouni and Sannyassi, that is, a recluse."[24] Ultimately, the Bhagavad Gita encouraged people to recuse themselves from the world and its affairs, paving the way for "a formidable theocracy" to "oppress humanity, seizing all liberty, all movement, all practical interest, and consequently all true morality."[25]

Cousin's interpretation of the Bhagavad Gita was mistaken, his errors born from a determination at all costs to see Indian thought as quietism and from bad translations of the Sanskrit. In verse 2.58, Krishna describes the yogic practice of withdrawing the senses:

> When he draws [*samharate*] the senses
> In from what they're sensing,
> All together, just like tortoise limbs,
> His mysticism stands fast.[26]

This is Krishna's call for Arjuna to take control over his thoughts and emotions and not let his mind, or his heart, be overwhelmed by the demands of the situation he finds himself in. Schlegel translated *samharate* into Latin with the verb *abstraho*, to drag oneself away from the world and retreat into the self.[27] In his 1829 lectures, Cousin—who, unlike Schlegel, did not read Sanskrit, and thus only read the poem in translation—translated *samharate* with the reflexive French verb *se recueillir*: "He retires into himself, 'like a turtle who retracts into itself.' "[28] Cousin interpreted the Gita through the lens of Romanticism, which stressed the importance of inward, subjective experience.[29] However, while the Romantic looked inward in order to become more sensitive to a spontaneous, aesthetic experience that illuminated a person's place within the cosmic order, Cousin claimed yoga demanded that practitioners divorce themselves from the world completely. In this way, it was both quietistic and nihilistic.

To defend his damning interpretation of the Bhagavad Gita, Cousin repeatedly mistranslated Schlegel's Latin and ignored passages that contradicted his conclusions, in effect making the text say what he wanted it to say. Quoting Schlegel's translation of verse 2.50, Cousin wrote: " 'In this world, the true devotee disdains all action.' What, all action, good as well as bad, true virtue as well as false? Yes, in this world the true devotee disdains all actions, good as well as bad."[30] Krishna speaks here not of disdaining all action, but of avoiding action undertaken for selfish reasons and personal gain. And, indeed, Krishna later counsels Arjuna to act in a way that that holds the world together (*loka-samgraha*)—that is, for the common good of society.[31] Krishna denounces selfish action, not action in general. This is clear in the Sanskrit, for Krishna certifies that "yogah karmasu kausalam," "yoga is skill in action," which Schlegel appropriately translated as "devotio dexteritatem in operibus praebet," "yoga grants skill in all things."[32] Cousin simply ignored the conclusion to this verse, making his Bhagavad Gita a testament to passivity, acquiescence, and retreat.

Yogis had a terrible reputation during Emerson's day. Widely circulated newspaper accounts reported that yogis wandered around India in dangerous gangs, practicing their black magic and selling the use of their *siddhi* powers to the highest bidders. At the time yogis were seen as the equivalent of modern-day terrorists.[33] The yogis who were not armed bandits were said to be the worst sort of dropouts, the kind who abandoned their families and worldly duties in order to punish themselves with body-breaking austerities. In *A Dictionary of All Religions* (1817), the American writer Hannah Adams (1755–1831) offered the following definition: "Yogeys, (Sanaisys, or Sunasees,) Hindoo Devotees, who practice a variety of self-tortures, and mortifying the body in order to merit heavenly felicity, and obtain the immaterial nature of Brahma, the supreme."[34] With this definition, she went one step further than Cousin in his critique of yoga: yogis were, as Cousin argued, sannyasis who withdrew from the world, but they did so, Adams wagered, to punish themselves because of their mistaken belief that mortification is a path to God. She continued to list the many brutal ways that yogis tortured their bodies to achieve enlightenment, including piercing their tongues with pins, lying down on spikes, and stabbing themselves with hooks tied to strings festooned from trees and spinning around for hours on end. Hindu reformers including Rammohan Roy (1772–1833) also attacked such awful practices—including human sacrifice, a ritual that continued in Hindu communities into the middle 1800s.[35] An article in the *North American Review* in March 1818 quoted Roy, who decried the "barbarous sacrifices and idol worship" of Indian yogis.[36]

In the popular press, white Protestant American missionaries portrayed India as a backward land of heathen idolatry, and "Hindooism" as a barbarous, evil religion of "violence, blood, sex, and noise."[37] Their condemnation, and their racism, knew no bounds. Breathing in the animus of these Protestant missionaries, Emerson initially interpreted Indian philosophy like most Western chauvinists of his day. Aping accounts of India in the popular press, Emerson wrote in his journal in 1821 that "the poor inhabitants of Indostan are distressed & degraded by the horrors of a flimsy & cruel Superstition. The iron hath entered into their souls, & their situation is in all respects abominable. Why is it their misery is thus darkened & deepened far different from the lot of the rejoicing nations of Europe & America?"[38] Emerson also composed an awful poem at Harvard called "Indian Superstition" that denounced India as a backward land where people worshiped idols and yogis physically abused themselves to get to heaven.[39] Fortunately, these immature, embarrassing sentiments soon passed. In the 1820s, Emerson's aunt Mary Moody Emerson repeatedly urged him to reconsider his position on Indian thought in poignant letters that testified to the contemporary importance of Hinduism. Emerson looked up to his aunt, and she exercised a profound influence on his intellectual development. Heeding her advice, he eventually did give Indian philosophy a second chance.

Over the course of the nineteenth century, the Orientalism of Wilkins and Jones—which affirmed British superiority, but which also expressed a genuine interest in and respect for Indian culture—grew into something more patronizing, racist, and ugly. The second and third generations of British Orientalists held that "everything from Egypt to Japan is essentially the same, and is the polar opposite of the West."[40] These Orientalists affirmed Hegel and

Cousin's stereotype that Oriental thought is childish, naive, and ultimately nihilistic in its world-denying quietism. Following Edward Said, when contemporary scholars invoke "Orientalism," they tend to refer to the belief that "the Orient" is totally inferior to European (and American) thought—"the West" is a land of action, reason, and freedom, "the East" of inaction, irrationality, and slavery. Because "the Orient" is all the same, its philosophy arrives in Europe and the United States "preinterpreted"—Orientalists assume there is little need for Westerners to engage Indian or Chinese or Persian philosophy, because we already know what it says, and what it says is not nearly as sophisticated or significant as what our own philosophers teach.[41] For hundreds of years, Orientalist rhetoric justified colonial oppression in India. This propaganda asserted that Indians were incapable of governing themselves and needed the "help" of the British to raise them into freedom, or, at the very least, to keep them from destroying themselves.

Emerson unquestionably was guilty of the Orientalist tendency to oversimplify "the East" as an exotic, mysterious land where people sit in silence all day long meditating and contemplating the eternal mysteries of the universe. He was never a typical Orientalist, however. Unlike many European Orientalists, and also unlike the American Christian missionaries who filled the pages of the popular press with their theological opprobrium and racist censure, Emerson was not interested in intellectually dominating India or slighting it as inferior. He turned to Indian philosophy out of curiosity and a broad-minded, humanistic interest. He found that Indian philosophy confirmed many of his philosophical predilections while providing him with a vocabulary for critiquing his own culture. He was attracted to Indian philosophy out of "a sense of the insufficiency of his home culture and the desire to confound its provincial stuffiness."[42] As he matured, Emerson was not guilty of the wrongheaded, shortsighted assumption that Westerners have nothing to learn from India: "Europe has always owed to oriental genius, its divine impulses," he concluded.[43] Indeed, in essays including "The Over-Soul," he frequently subverted both Orientalist and Christian stereotypes about India and Indian philosophy.

Emerson's efforts to bring Vedanta to the United States became known the world over. While researching this book, I had a lovely conversation with Swami Tattwamayananda, the director of the Vedanta Society of Northern California, about Emerson, and he suggested that Indian intellectuals warmly embraced Emerson not necessarily because he got Vedanta right, but because he articulated a Vedanta that was right for Americans at that time. And, indeed, after Emerson's death, many Indian intellectuals claimed him as a lost son. Surely they wouldn't have done this if they believed that his project was inherently colonialist or completely off base.[44]

In his 1885 retrospective essay "Emerson as Seen from India," Protap Chunder Mozoomdar (1840–1905)—a prominent member of the Hindu reform movement Brahmo Samaj, and the popular author of *The Oriental Christ* (1869), a book that described a number of similarities between Christianity and Hinduism—called Emerson "the best of Brahmins," and suggested that his philosophy so perfectly expressed the insights of the Upanishads and the Bhagavad Gita that a fundamental, cosmic mistake had been made: Emerson should have born in India, not the United States.[45] Though he hailed from Concord, Emerson was in fact a child of the Himalayas and the Ganges: "Amidst this ceaseless, sleepless din and clash of Western materialism, this heat of restless energy, the character of Emerson shines upon India serene as the evening star. He seems to some of us to have been a geographical mistake."[46] Paramahansa Yogananda (1893–1952) cited Emerson at least fifteen times in his bestselling *Autobiography of a Yogi* (1946), employing Emerson's work as a cultural reference point for relating complex Indian philosophical ideas to his American audience. And thus things came full circle: in the 1840s and '50s, Americans were exposed to Indian philosophy by reading Emerson; in the late nineteenth century, Indians were exposed to American philosophy by reading Emerson; in the 1940s and '50s, Americans were again exposed to Emerson by reading bestselling Indian philosophers including Yogananda.

Swami Vivekananda (1863–1902)—the young Hindu reformer who exploded onto the American scene with his electrifying public oratory at the World's Parliament of Religions in Chicago in 1893, and the founder of the Vedanta Society of Northern California in San Francisco (as well as the Vedanta Society of New York)—arrived in the United States familiar with Emerson's philosophy.[47] This was due to Unitarian missionaries like Charles Dall, who trucked thousands of copies of Emerson and the other transcendentalists' essays to India to be read by Brahmo Samaj reformers, including Vivekananda.[48] (I assume that Dall, or some kindred missionary, was the original source of the copy of Emerson's *Essays: First Series* I purchased in Chennai.) On his second trip to the United States, in the winter of 1900, the swami talked warmly of Emerson to his audience in Pasadena, California, and attributed Emerson's theories of self-reliance and the oversoul to his reading of the Bhagavad Gita: "I would advise those of you who have not read that book to read it. If you only knew how much it influenced your own country even! If you want to know the sources of Emerson's inspiration, it is this book, the Gita."[49] If Mozoomdar and Vivekananda had their way, Emerson would be seen as the founder of an American Vedanta, a nondualistic philosophy of oneness inspired by Bhagavad Gita and other *smriti* texts. Also, if these

Indian pedants had their way, Americans would trace their democracy not just to Athens but also via Emerson back to the battlefield at Kurukshetra.

There is little question that the Bhagavad Gita, the dialogue between Krishna and Arjuna that took place in the no-man's-land between the two armies poised on the precipice of battle, inspired Emerson's rhetoric. "Let us . . . cherish this venerable oracle," he wrote in his journal.[50] Cherish, but not sanctify. As he worked to develop an interpretation of the Bhagavad Gita that might inspire Americans to loftier heights, far above the conformity, conflict, and naked materialism of their culture, Emerson entered into the European controversy over the value of the Gita. The result was his 1841 essay "The Over-Soul," included in *Essays: First Series*. Emerson wrote this essay in dialogue with, and ultimately in rejection of, Cousin's interpretation of the Gita, as well as many other dismissive European readings of the treatise.

Emerson revered Cousin, whose lectures on the history of philosophy he first read in May 1831.[51] Emerson studied and annotated Cousin's works in both French and English. He owned a copy of Cousin's French lectures of 1828 and 1829 and the English translation of the 1828 lectures, published in Boston under the title *Introduction to the History of Philosophy*.[52] Until Emerson borrowed James Elliot Cabot's copy of Wilkins's *Bhăgvăt-Gēētā* in 1844 (he finally tracked down a copy he could purchase for his personal library in 1845), he primarily knew the Gita through Cousin's lectures. Even after he read Wilkins's translation, he continued to testify to the power of his initial encounter with Cousin.[53] In August 1873, Emerson wrote to his friend and admirer the English Indologist Max Müller expressing his great admiration for Cousin's gloss of the Bhagavad Gita: "I remember I owed my first taste for this fruit to Cousin's sketch, in his first Lectures, of the Dialogue between Krishna & Arjoon, & I still prize the first chapters of that Bhagavat as wonderful, & would gladly learn any accurate date of their age."[54] On many points, Emerson concurred with Cousin concerning the Bhagavad Gita. Emerson also believed that philosophy began in India and then migrated to ancient Greece.[55] Though Emerson adored Cousin, his interpretation of the Bhagavad Gita rejected Cousin's harsh conclusion concerning devotion. The Gita, it turned out, did have something important to say to Americans, and it was not that they should retreat from the world.

I read "The Over-Soul" as Emerson's earliest attempt to grapple with the Bhagavad Gita and its ontology of oneness. Emerson agrees with Cousin that the yogi "searches only for God, and he finds him equally in every thing," but this does not lead, as Cousin argues (and, it should be noted, as many contemporary gurus *continue* to argue), to "l'indifférence."[56] In "The Over-Soul,"

Emerson demonstrates how the recognition of God in everything and then the devotion to this universal divine principle, which Cousin calls "une force perpétuelle et éternelle" and Emerson calls "Over-soul," could fundamentally reorient how Americans lived their lives and related to each other. Indeed, Emerson finds in the Bhagavad Gita a new language for God and a guide for how a person might live an active life devoted to oneness, by practicing what I call communication as yoga.

Transcendentalism

Emerson was a transcendentalist, which, according to the rhetorical scholar Nathan Crick, means he practiced a particular kind of rhetoric—*the rhetoric of transcendence*, which "is a way of crossing a divide or reconciling a contradiction through a radical act of imagination whereby people are able to see and judge themselves from the perspective of some distant and different 'beyond.'"[57] "The accomplishment of Emerson and the Transcendentalists," Crick rightly concludes, is to make transcendence "a self-conscious rhetorical strategy whereby an audience would 'find itself' by interpreting its present from a future time and distant place, by looking at the part from the perspective of the whole, by seeing the particular in light of the universal, or by seeing existence from the distance of a star."[58] The transcendentalist is a mapmaker and science fiction writer who charts new and brighter futures far beyond the everyday, far beyond anything we have imagined. The imagination is pen and canvas. The transcendentalist is a poet and magician who uses rhetoric to inspire the audience to see the world differently, from a new plateau or a "higher plane," a place beyond the divisions and fears and resentments that so often bog us down in our daily lives—in Emerson's case, from the perspective of oneness.

Transcendentalism was a movement of expansive imagination. Its goal was audacious: to imagine infinity, and then to write it down. The transcendentalists were master rhetoricians, poet-guru-warriors, who went to war with American common sense. They took aim at assumed limitations and the this-is-what-must-be. They sought to inspire Americans to change their lives so that they might change the world, making it a better, more peaceful, more harmonious, more just place. Nothing is beyond redemption when the imagination expands and leaps beyond the expected in a moment of radical transcendence. Emerson writes from a god's-eye view, from a vast, distant beyond that also is somehow completely this-worldly: "Life must be lived on a *higher plane*. We must go up to a *higher platform*, to which we are always invited to ascend; there, the whole aspect of things changes."[59] Emerson observes the world from the perspective of an individual soul that has transcended division and found its home in the eternal divine wisdom of oneness. It is a glorious place, this view from a star, where the clouds part and the divine reveals itself in all its luminescence, where all suffering ceases, where it is certain that all is and will be well. Seen from this higher platform, oneness is real, and division is but an illusion. Following the Advaita Vedanta of the Bhagavad Gita, Emerson stands firmly, obstinately, patiently on the higher platform of oneness. In "The Over-Soul," he imagines what it might be like to live a life committed to oneness.

Emerson's reading of the Bhagavad Gita shaped his understanding of the possibilities for a transcendentalist rhetoric of oneness, for it revealed new and previously unimaginable and glorious things he could do with language. According to Shanta Acharya, "Indian thought scarcely effected any real changes in the general structure of Emerson's own thinking. However, it provided a reinforcement of certain philosophical tendencies in him while extending his vocabulary."[60] Emerson's expansive and eclectic reading habits make the question of intellectual influence difficult to settle. Clearly, the Bhagavad Gita reinforced Emerson's lifelong tendency toward monism; so, too, did his reading of Plato, Plotinus, Spinoza, Swedenborg, and the Quakers. His journals demonstrate conclusively that he did not find the central teachings of the Gita surprising when he first encountered the poem. Already in the 1820s he believed that the world exists in and through the divine, and that God is the "ground" or the "field" for life (metaphors that Krishna develops in chapter 13 of the Gita). However, Acharya's judgment that Indian philosophy left Emerson's philosophy untouched holds only to the extent that we believe language and thought can be separated. Humans think in language, and so the language we employ will influence our thinking. By extending Emerson's vocabulary—specifically, by providing him with a new rhetoric for God, the "Over-soul"—Indian philosophy, and in particular the Advaita Vedanta of the Bhagavad Gita, helped Emerson to imagine a new rhetoric of God and, consequently, a new way of life devoted to oneness.

Why did Americans need a new rhetoric of God? Simply put, because the old rhetoric was not working. Emerson hoped to persuade his readers to reject the commonsensical picture of God as a bearded patriarch, the God who Michelangelo immortalized on the ceiling of the Sistine Chapel reaching out for Adam. Rather than bring people closer to the divine, like many mystics Emerson believed that this image of God reified separation (notice the distance between Adam and God in Michelangelo's painting) and resulted in great personal pain—the pain of a distance too expansive to bridge, the pain of a longing that will not and cannot be satisfied, the pain of an embrace that is just out of reach. This was a God out of touch.

During Emerson's lifetime, Americans continued to view God as Michelangelo did, as a bearded patriarch. But the paterfamilias's personality changed. In the popular imagination of the early nineteenth century, there was a shift away from the vengeful God on display in Jonathan Edwards's famous 1741 sermon "Sinners in the Hands of an Angry God" to a kinder, gentler father figure who loved his progeny and wanted the best for them. This benevolent God was popularized by the charismatic, Bible-thumping preachers of the Second Great Awakening, a cultural movement that began in the famous "burned-over district" of Western New York in the early 1800s. During the 1820s and '30s, these evangelical preachers completely changed America's theological vocabulary. Emerson, however, rejected both the new and the old pictures of God as old-fashioned and outdated. He called the new God "just another form of antediluvian idolatry."[61] Emerson did not reject God; he rejected the way that most Americans talked about and imagined God. If Americans were to forge a healthy relationship with divinity, they would have to break free from theological common sense and the unfortunate lingua franca of the day. Emerson concluded, emphatically, that only "when we have broken our god of tradition, and ceased from our god of rhetoric, then may God fire the heart with his presence."[62]

On the most important theological matters, most Americans were not self-reliant. In fact, Americans were dependent on pulpit preachers and pushy philosophers to determine their relationship to the divine for them. Americans had ceded their agency to the frock and cowl. Emerson broke from the Christianity of his day because it disenfranchised individual spiritual seekers and prevented Americans from realizing their full potential for inspiration—a word derived from the Latin *inspiratus* and that, in the mystical tradition, means literally "to be filled with the breath of the divine." In his writings, Emerson tends to sound less like an Enlightenment philosopher and more like a mystic calling for a more direct, intuitive relationship to God unmediated by book, ritual, liturgy, or institution. "Why should not we also enjoy an original relation to the universe?" he asked famously.[63] An original relationship between part and whole, between soul and oversoul, between individual and God: this is Emerson's desire. How to rejigger this relationship is his overarching rhetorical goal.

Trained at Harvard Divinity School and ordained as a preacher, Emerson was very much at home in the Protestant, and specifically the Unitarian, vocabulary of his day.[64] Those who are not close readers of the Bible would find it difficult to understand his prose. Antebellum Unitarians questioned the idea of original sin. They denied that the world was fallen. They refused the clad-in-black, doom-and-gloom Puritan ethos that suffering was the surest path to God. In his famous address to the graduates of Harvard Divinity School on July 15, 1838, Emerson began by proclaiming the goodness of nature and the benevolence of universal law. Though he took "common conventions to extremes" in this oration, basically he affirmed Unitarian doctrine.[65] However, in this speech and in essays including "The Over-Soul," Emerson quickly broke with decorum by rebuffing the epistemological sensationalism that most Unitarians adopted from John Locke (1632–1704). Locke was famous for rejecting the idealist argument that knowledge can arise from spontaneous insights of intuition; he held instead that the senses were the only source of knowledge of the world. Like many of his fellow transcendentalists, Emerson rebuked Locke by reaffirming the validity of intuition. When Emerson talked warmly about the wisdom of the "soul" and "the inward eye," this put him at odds with even the more progressive American Unitarians, who tended to be Lockeans.[66] When Emerson announced that "the Moral Nature, that Law of laws," provided "revelations" that "introduce greatness—yea, God himself, into the open soul," he violated American theological dogma.[67] But he was not done. In fact, he told the Harvard graduates that each of them was "a newborn bard of the Holy Ghost"—a statement that was, basically, heresy to most American Christians.[68] Harvard blacklisted him for thirty years after the oration. But the speech struck a chord with many Americans who felt deeply in their hearts that there was more to the world than simple sense experience.

Emerson's quest to develop a new rhetoric of God paralleled reform efforts in India. In the early nineteenth century, Rammohan Roy—who became immensely popular in Europe and the United States for his translations of the Vedas and his work on the Bible, *The Precepts of Jesus* (1825), which read the Gospels through the lens of Advaita (nondualistic) Vedanta—started a doctrinal controversy when he translated the four Gospels from the original Greek into Bengali for the first time. The King James translation of John 1:3 reads, "All things were made by him" [πάντα δι' αὐτοῦ ἐγένετο], but the Greek preposition *dia*, "by," can also mean "through."[69] In line with Advaita Vedanta and the Bhagavad Gita, Roy translated this passage as "All things were made through him," contradicting the official church doctrine of creation by God's command and suggesting, instead, that the world was an emanation of the divine force and that all creatures were *of* God because they *were* God.[70] This was also how Emerson pictured God: not as an agent of creation who lords over his kingdom *by* fiat, but as a power that surges *through* all life.

For Emerson, God is not a father figure to be obeyed but an experience of oneness, connection, and love with all creation. And though this experience transcends rhetoric—it dwarfs the shallowness of "the god of rhetoric" and the "god of tradition"—rhetoric still matters, for rhetoric orients us toward the experience of oneness, coloring how we experience the divine.[71] Emerson believed that language is a manifestation of the divine and simultaneously a means by which people relate to the divine. Emerson treasured the power of words. At its best and most imaginative, language is transcendent; it opens new horizons of meaning and in this way makes new experiences possible. For Emerson, "Words can reveal the parameters of fate and limitation; just as surely, they open spaces beyond these, horizons of new, barely apprehended possibility."[72] Emerson is at his most astute when diagnosing how possibilities get closed through the mindless reiteration of common sense and common words. He is at his most affirmative when he attempts to persuade his readers to reopen these foreclosed possibilities by nurturing the deep human potential for connection and divinity.

Oversoul

Emerson challenged himself to invent a new rhetoric of God that would inspire Americans to see the world and all creation from the perspective of oneness. He invented an entire vocabulary in *Essays: First Series* to achieve this goal. In "Self-Reliance," he calls God "the aboriginal Self," "the divine spirit," "the ever-blessed ONE," "the Supreme Cause," and "the Highest."[73] In "Compensation," he speaks of "the All."[74] In "The Over-Soul," he references "the Supreme Critic," "great nature," "Unity," "the eternal ONE," "the Highest Law," "the Supreme Mind," "the impersonal," "the Maker of all things," "the Divine mind," "the universal soul," "Omniscience," "the great God," "the better and universal self," and, again, "the Highest."[75] He also speaks of God with elemental metaphors, including water, light, and breath. I call this Emerson's *lexicon of oneness*. Emerson was no fan of consistency, and this lexicon is at times confusing, confounding, and contradictory. This is not sloppiness on Emerson's part but a rhetorical necessity, given the nature of oneness. Each term Emerson uses—and sometimes he uses the same term differently from sentence to sentence—describes a distinct aspect of God and a unique way of relating to the divine. If the divine is one and all, then it will have many names; as many names, perhaps, as there are mouths to speak them.

I am interested here in two names Emerson gives God: *oversoul* and *soul*, the latter which Emerson uses mostly (though not exclusively) as a shorthand abbreviation (often with other modifiers, such as *universal*) for *oversoul*. The oversoul represents the divine as a life-giving, life-affirming force that flows through all beings—it is "the divine will, or, the eternal tendency to the good of the whole, active in every atom, every moment."[76] Emerson's oversoul is the soul of the world, its *anima mundi* and first cause. The oversoul infuses every person and every thing with a shared divine essence that is the fountainhead of all sagacity, creativity, genius, morality, emotion, and duty. The oversoul is the source of all goodness in the world, and it is ultimately a force for good, too, if only we learn to heed its quiet insistent urgings. To live an ethical life means communing with the oversoul, becoming filled with its genius, and dedicating oneself to a life of oneness. Ethics for Emerson is a process of mirroring nature, of bowing to the wisdom of the world.

When people commune with the oversoul, they receive an afflatus of wisdom via the inward eye of intuition, and are thus emboldened to behave ethically, to do their duty for the good of the whole:

> The Supreme Critic on the errors of the past and the present, and the only prophet of that which must be, is that great nature, in which we rest, as the earth lies in the soft arms of the atmosphere, that Unity, that Over-soul, within which every man's particular being is contained and made one with all other; that common heart, of which all sincere conversation is the worship, to which all right action is submission; that overpowering reality which confutes our tricks and talents, and constrains every one to pass for what he is, and to speak from his character, and not from his tongue, and which evermore tends to pass into our thought and hand, and become wisdom, and virtue, and power, and beauty. We live in succession, in division, in parts, in particles. Meantime within man is the soul of the whole; the wise silence; the universal beauty, to which every part and particle is equally related; the eternal ONE.[77]

Our day-to-day reality appears to be composed of parts and particles. But what is the true nature of division and succession? Most people experience the world in terms of disjunction and asyndeton, making division the primary ontological reality. Seen from the higher plane of oneness, this is an error, and division an illusion. Emerson portrays the world differently in "The Over-Soul": as a series of connections in which the parts, though real, maintain a synecdochic relationship to the whole. Parts, individuals, souls, are real. And yet these parts are not apart. Pluralities and parts arise out of the transcendental ground of all existence, the oversoul, which means that in reality all things are one.

Synonyms for the *oversoul* include *unity* and *one* because the oversoul contains all individuals and unites every person with all others—it is "a common heart." At the same time, all individuals contain within them "the soul of the whole." The individual soul is not severed from the world, as classical liberals including Locke taught, or separate from God, as many Christians of Emerson's era believed. We are one, and we carry this oneness with us in our hearts. In the Advaita Vedanta of the Bhagavad Gita, it is said that the *atman*, the individual, is an incarnation of *brahman*, universal divinity, and that enlightenment follows from realizing that you are that: *tat tvam asi*. Emerson likewise certifies that the individual *soul* is an incarnation of the *oversoul*, the *individual* of *God*, the *part* of the *whole*. "From within and behind," Emerson concludes, "a light shines through us upon things, and makes us aware that we are nothing, but the light is all. A man is the façade of a temple wherein all wisdom and all good abide."[78] The oversoul is the light that allows us to see; it is also the thing that is seen. It is frame and background and picture. Emerson analogizes the oversoul to the atmosphere. It is invisible, but real. It envelops us totally and completely, and without it, we would not be.

The concept of the oversoul—and the vocabulary that likely inspired the neologism—was in the air during Emerson's day, in widely circulated translations of and commentaries on Advaita Vedanta texts. As we have seen, Emerson attributed his discovery of the Bhagavad Gita to his reading of Cousin's lectures on the history of philosophy in May 1831.[79] However, he was likely exposed to the doctrines of the Bhagavad Gita in the 1820s and '30s not only through Cousin but also through many other popular discussions of Indian thought, including the Hindu reformer Roy's writings, which nudged Americans toward an Advaita Vedanta interpretation of the Gita.[80]

In his translations of the Vedas and Upanishads, Roy rendered *brahman* as "universal soul" and equated "God" with "the soul of the universe" and "the all-pervading soul."[81] Abbe J. A. Dubois's *Description of the Character, Manners, and Customs of the People of India*, published in London in 1817 and Philadelphia in 1818, observed that "Para-Brahma" (in Sanskrit *para* means "over" and "above," and so this is literally "over-God" or "over-the-all-pervading soul") and "Paramatma" (*atman* in Sanskrit means "soul," which is how Roy, Dubois, and others translated it, and so this is literally "over-soul") were the words that Hindus used "to explain the nature and the attributes of the Supreme Being."[82] William Ward's *View of the History, Literature, and Mythology of the Hindoos* (1822) defined *brahman* as "the soul of the world" and "the soul of all creatures."[83] In an 1824 essay, Henry Thomas Colebrooke recounted that in Indian philosophy, individual souls appear numerous but "are identified with the universal being (*Brahme*) in whom all exists," and "the supreme soul (*Paramatma*) is one: the seat of eternal knowledge; demonstrated as the maker of all things."[84] Building on Colebrooke's work, Cousin described *brahman* as "une sorte d'ame du monde" (a sort of soul of the world).[85]

Several scholars point to this widely circulating rhetoric of *paramatman* as the likely source of Emerson's neologism *oversoul*. William Bysshe Stein maintains that Emerson derived his idea of the oversoul from Roy's

Translation of Several Principle Books, Passages, and Texts of the Veds (1832), which included a translation from the Katha Upanishad, one of the principle philosophical sources for the Bhagavad Gita.[86] John S. Harrison speculates that "the name Over-Soul may well have come from the Bhagavat-Gita."[87] Swami Paramananda concludes simply, "'Over-Soul' is almost a literal translation of the Sanskrit word *Param-Atman* (Supreme Self)."[88] Arthur Versluis observes that Emerson's coinage closely translates two Sanskrit words used in the Bhagavad Gita for the transcendental ground of Being: *paramatman*, a word used in the Bhagavad Gita as a synonym for *brahman*; and *adhyatma*, a word used in the Gita to represent the contingent, perishable individual's nature as the participant in and product of *brahman*.[89]

Versluis takes these two words, *paramatman* and *adhyatma* as synonyms, and in the sense of the famous Upanishadic equation of *atman* with *brahman*, this is fair.[90] However, these words serve different rhetorical functions in the Bhagavad Gita. *Paramatman* might best be rendered as the "cosmic soul" and *adhyatma* the "inner soul" of all beings. As the avatar of universal divinity, Krishna claims to be both—he is the cosmic soul that becomes manifested as the inner soul of all creatures. This is precisely the aspect of God that Emerson describes in "The Over-Soul." When he speaks of "Over-soul" or "universal soul," he gestures toward *paramatman*. He repeatedly uses the word *soul* as a convenient shorthand for *oversoul*, and so *soul*, too, points at *paramatman*. At other times, however, Emerson uses the word *soul* to mean something closer to *adhyatma*, which is both the individual as incarnation of the oversoul and the capacity of the reflexive individual "me" to forge a relationship with God: "Ineffable is the union of man and God in every act of the soul."[91] God is at once impersonal (*brahman*) and personal (*atman*), and for Emerson the capacity to behave ethically arises in the act of forging a relationship between the two. Emerson's "soul" represents God in its impersonal life-giving, life-guiding form (the *paramatman*) and also the individual person who is a manifestation of the impersonal—hence, the *adhyatma*, or the "me."

Emerson avers that individuals are composed of two entities, the "me" (or the soul) and the "not-me" (or the oversoul).[92] The individual is the reflexive capacity of a soul to connect to the oversoul, to bring itself into closer alignment with the wisdom of the world.[93] Emerson's most famous essay is undoubtedly "Self-Reliance," but when Emerson speaks of self-reliance, he does not mean rugged—or perhaps, if we are being more honest with ourselves, *ragged*—individualism, the self-made *man* who pulls himself up by his bootstraps and goes it alone (Emerson, as I will explore later, always refers to men in this regard).[94] Freedom in the sense of being independent from the world is a false promise. Instead, Emerson's self-reliance *is a recusant art of breaking free from convention*—from what is expected and demanded by society, from common sense, from normalcy, from decorum, from the commonplace, from stereotypes, from what at the time was called "public opinion."[95] Self-reliance is a practice of learning to think, act, and speak independently, against the crushing weight of centuries of history, tradition, convention, and opinion that teaches people they are separate from the divine and divided from creation. For Emerson, if people are able to lessen the hold of convention over their minds and hearts, they can form a better "me" that is more closely attuned to the divine wisdom of the world.

In "The Over-Soul," Emerson reimagines the individual in line with the Advaita Vedanta of the Bhagavad Gita. The individual is not primarily flesh and bone, mother or father, brother or sister, master or slave. The individual is a capacity, a power, a skill that yokes the soul to the oversoul—the *adhyatma* to the *paramatman*—an ability to see and feel and experience the world as one. For Emerson, every person has the capacity to become an individual by fashioning themselves out of the esources at hand. *The practice of yoga—in the sense that Emerson understood it, "the effort to unite with the deity"—brings the individual into existence.* Oneness is all. Oneness is life. Oneness is the atmosphere. Oneness is discernment. Oneness is the source of right and wrong. Oneness is the deep, clear-sighted percipience that serves as arbiter or "Supreme Critic" of how to act when we come to life's crossroads.[96] Americans will find peace, happiness, and justice only when the soul is brought into harmony with oneness.

It might be difficult for us to understand Emerson's position here because the importance he places on ontology was old-fashioned in his day, and even more old-fashioned in ours. In Plato and in the Bhagavad Gita (to take two examples that were particularly significant for Emerson), truth is found in the world, and ethics involves bringing our conduct into line with a truth larger than the self. Emerson's emphasis on ontology was old-fashioned because the philosophers of the Enlightenment, from Descartes to Kant, emphatically broke with the Platonic lineage of Western philosophy by casting doubt on the ability of humans to know the order of things, if that order even exists. For these thinkers, ontology took a back seat to epistemology, the science of knowing. Humans can never know the thing-in-itself, Kant argued, because we experience the world through an instrument that is limited. Our intellect is "discursive" rather than "intuitive," and so even if the world talks to us, we can't understand it.[97] Though the Enlightenment hastened profound philosophical insights, especially in the area of political philosophy, for many dissidents the Enlightenment propagated a bleak picture of the world as a meaningless and cold place ruled by mechanical laws of cause and effect that did little to satisfy the subtle longings of the heart.

The Romantics, especially in Germany, rebelled against this worldview, against a life marooned from the source, against the Enlightenment picture of existence as a game of billiards. The Romantics affirmed the sacredness of the natural world. They validated the power of human intuition to comprehend this world. And they argued that nature and human feeling provide deep sources of spiritual knowledge and moral insight. It is no coincidence, then, that the Romantics were especially fond of Indian philosophy. Indeed, they prophesied that the arrival of Sanskrit texts in Europe in the nineteenth century would inspire a second Renaissance, much as the arrival of Greek manuscripts and Byzantine commentaries in Western Europe after the fall of Constantinople inspired the first in the fifteenth century. According to Friedrich Schlegel (the brother of A. W., who translated the Gita into Latin), "We must seek the supreme romanticism in the Orient."[98]

Though the oversoul is always present—for the soul always dwells within the oversoul—nevertheless most people find themselves cut off from the acuity it gives, blinded by "the senses," by dualistic social conventions, and by common ways of speaking that make it appear as though "the walls of time and space have come to look real and insurmountable."[99] The practice of yoga in the Bhagavad Gita is concerned with transcending such limitations and seeing the world as one. For millennia, Indian monks have practiced various forms of yoga and meditation that aim at deprogramming and deconditioning the mind so that aspirants can experience the truth of *ekatva*, oneness.[100] These monks are often sannyasis who withdraw from the world and its obligations in order to focus totally and completely on gaining control over their minds and senses.[101] Krishna observes that this is a valid yogic path, but that it will not work for everyone, especially those who have worldly duties to perform.

The first yoga teachers who came to the United States from India in the 1890s quickly recognized that such monastic traditions would never work here, and that if yoga was to have any appeal and benefit for Americans, it would have to be presented as a worldly yoga in action. In *Karma Yoga* (1896), Swami Vivekananda rejected the idea that retreat from the world is somehow more yogic than engagement within it: "It is useless to say that the man who lives out of the world is a greater man than he who lives in the world; it is much more difficult to live in the world and worship God than to give it up and live a free and easy life."[102] He therefore advised his readers that "inactivity should be avoided at all means. Activity always means resistance. Resist all evils, mental and physical; and when you have succeeded in resisting, then will calmness come."[103] Vivekananda recognized that Americans were too much in love with the hustle and bustle of life to abandon it to become meditating nuns and monks. Yoga would have never become as popular as it has if it demanded permanent withdrawal from society. Vivekananda recommended that Americans practice a "muscular" yoga, alongside bodybuilding and the consumption of meat, so they were strong enough to face the world.[104]

The earliest definition of *yoga* in the Rig Veda is "action," in contrast to "rest" (*kshema*).[105] The distinction between a yoga of action and inaction was germane to Emerson's philosophy of oneness, and he touches on these themes in his later essay "Plato; Or, The Philosopher" (1850): "Philosophy is the account which the human mind gives to itself of the constitution of the world. Two cardinal facts lie forever at the base; the one, and the two.—1. Unity, or Identity; and 2. Variety."[106] In this essay, Emerson reiterates the Orientalist distinction between East and West, marking Asia—as represented "in the Indian scriptures, in the Vedas, the Bhagavad Geeta, and the Vishnu Purana"—as a land of quiet contemplation of oneness, and Europe (and by extension, his native United States) as a land of action in a world of variety.[107] "If speculation tends thus to a terrific unity, in which all things are absorbed, action tends directly backwards to diversity."[108] Like the majority of contemporary yogis, Emerson views India as a silent and peaceful land of spiritual purity; he remains blissfully ignorant of India's violent history of sectarian, religious conflict.[109] India was hardly ever a quiet, contemplative place. Emerson contrasts East and West not to extol one and besmirch the other—though he does affirm the superiority of the West here and elsewhere. Emerson's point is to illuminate the central problem of philosophy as he understands it: how to bring an ontology of oneness (which tends toward contemplation and, according to Cousin, quietude) into the world of action. "Oneness and otherness. It is impossible to speak, or to think, without embracing both."[110] Michael Altman notes that Emerson "sought a synthesis of the two, and he found such a synthesis in the person of Plato"—Emerson reads Plato as the philosopher who best synthesizes East and West, India and ancient Greece.[111] But it is not just Plato who solves this perennial philosophical conundrum. In "The Over-Soul," Emerson finds this synthesis between oneness and variety, between contemplation and action, in his reading of the Bhagavad Gita as a philosophy of communication.

Like many philosophers and teachers of yoga who came after him, Emerson imagines a worldly practice of oneness in action. He encourages his readers to touch the oversoul not by sitting quietly but by talking to others: "If we consider what happens in conversation, in reveries, in remorse, in times of passion, in surprises, in the instructions of dreams . . . we shall catch many hints that will broaden and lighten into knowledge of the secret of nature."[112] I take it that by "nature" Emerson means the oversoul. Notice that the first thing that Emerson mentions in this list is "conversation." In Emerson's hands, interpersonal communication becomes a practice of connecting the soul with the oversoul through a radical imaginative act of devotion and daring faith. Emerson advises his readers to commit themselves to a life of oneness by making "all sincere conversation . . . the worship" of the oversoul as it is incarnated in individual souls. If they do this sincerely, with conviction and devotion, they will bring themselves into harmony with the universe and closer to the eternal wisdom of God.[113]

Communication as Yoga

There is a cure for the hollowness of heart you feel, Arjuna, and the cure is yoga: so says Krishna in the Bhagavad Gita. Whenever you feel lost, or unable to face your duty, turn to yoga: so says Krishna in the Bhagavad Gita. And what is this yoga? The Bhagavad Gita describes three paths, or *margas*, of yoga: *bhakti yoga*, the yoga of devotion to God; *jnana yoga*, the yoga of sacred knowledge; and *karma yoga*, the yoga of "actionless action" (*naiskarmya-karma*). Though later Indian yoga traditions understood these paths as distinct and separate, the Bhagavad Gita itself is not so clear—indeed, at times Krishna seems to argue that bhakti yoga accompanies and underlines the other two paths.[114]

Given that Americans are an active people, you might think that Emerson would recommend karma yoga to them. He did not (though Thoreau did). Or you might think, given Emerson's reputation as a pedant, that he would favor the yoga of wisdom. He did not (though the Theosophists did). In "The Over-Soul" Emerson advocates neither karma yoga nor jnana yoga but bhakti yoga, the yoga of devotion and worship. "The simplest person, who in his integrity worships God, becomes God," he announces.[115] Here we must be careful, for Emerson did not understand bhakti in the same way that many Hindus of his day and our own understand it. Emerson distrusted the senses, and he was not prone, as Walt Whitman was, to outbursts of emotion. Emerson was no convert to Krishna worship. The idea of approaching God like the most intimate lover, of loving Krishna like the goddess Radha did, of leaving one's spouse and job and abandoning oneself fully and completely to ecstatic, weeping, heartbreaking devotion, of pledging oneself in marriage to Krishna—none of this is Emerson. However, if we are careful to distinguish the Bhagavad Gita's "intellectual bhakti," which stresses mental concentration, yoga, and meditation, from later Indian traditions of "emotional bhakti" characteristic of the bhakti poets, who, starting with the Tamil Alvars and Nayanmars several centuries after the Gita's composition, celebrated the agony and ecstasy of a life totally abandoned to love of Krishna, then we can recognize in Emersonianism a kind of bhakti yoga—an intellectual bhakti.[116] Though devotion ultimately affects a person's heart, bhakti in the Gita is first and foremost a mental practice of concentration, of seeing the world differently.

In chapter 11 of the Bhagavad Gita, Krishna's dialogue with Arjuna culminates in a revelation of his divine form. This is the ultimate argument by authority, for what is the world of man when compared to the wonder and terror of God! In chapter 12, Arjuna—now convinced beyond a doubt that Krishna is indeed an avatar of Vishnu, God walking on earth, and he should do as God prefers—asks Krishna a question about the practice of bhakti yoga:

> Who knows yoga best—
> Devotees perpetually
> Yoked to you, or worshippers
> Of the eternal Unmanifest?[117]

Is it better, Arjuna asks, to worship God as "the eternal unmanifest" or in his personal form as Krishna? It is possible to attain God through both paths, Krishna answers, though it is difficult for embodied beings to fix their attention on an impersonal divinity, because the mind needs objects on which to focus. For this reason, among others, Krishna counsels Arjuna to focus his attention on, and devote his life to, Krishna.[118]

The Bhagavad Gita's twelfth chapter inaugurates a heated debate in Hinduism. Europeans and Americans during the nineteenth century tended to interpret the Bhagavad Gita through the lens of Advaita Vedanta, and the philosophers who identify with this school prefer the term *nondualist* for their worldview.[119] In Sanskrit, *brahman* is a neuter noun, neither male nor female, and it is the term many Advaitins use to describe the ultimate reality. In the words of Eliot Deutsch, "Brahman, the One, is a state of being. It is not a 'He,' a personal being; nor is it an 'It,' an impersonal concept. Brahman is that state which is when all subject/object distinctions are obliterated. Brahman is ultimately a name for the experience of the timeless plenitude of being."[120] *Brahman* transcends language. To describe this experience—even to label it as an experience—is to limit it. And yet humans crave description, because we relate to the world through language. When describing *brahman*, Advaitins therefore tend to use a rhetoric of denial and negation: they say what it is not, so as not to limit what it is. As the sage Yajnavalkya advises in the Brihadaranyaka Upanishad, "Now, therefore, the description of Brahman:

'Not this, not this' (*neti, neti*); for there is no other and more appropriate description than this 'Not this.'"[121] The language of negation—stating that *brahman* is *not* divisible, that *brahman* is *not* perishable, that *brahman* is *un*thinkable—is meant to safeguard *brahman*'s unqualified oneness while also shielding it from argument.[122] Advaitins hold that a person cannot defend or refute *brahman*; simply, it is.[123]

In the Gita, Krishna uses the synonym *aksara*, which can be translated as "imperishable" or "unmanifest," for *brahman*.[124] And yet, in the same verses that he speaks of unmanifest *brahman*, Krishna personalizes it, telling Arjuna to remember "me" (*mam*):

> Reciting *Aum*, the sole syllabic
> Brahman, remembering me,
> He goes out, goes on to the way
> Beyond, his body left behind.[125]

Long have passages like this baffled Western interpreters—is *brahman nirguna*, without qualities, or *saguna*, with qualities? Is Hinduism monotheistic or polytheistic or both or something different entirely? According to Wendy Doniger, these questions pose little trouble for the actual lived religious lives of most Hindus: "Even when Hindus acknowledge, or insist upon, the ultimate oneness of brahman, or say that all paths lead to brahman, the spirit in which they actually worship the god they pray to, the god they tell stories about, the god they make their art for and about—the god of their religion, as opposed to their philosophy—is seldom if ever brahman, but Shiva or Vishnu or the goddess or, more precisely, a local form of Shiva or Vishnu or the goddess."[126] Philosophers might insist on the inability to characterize the divine—*neti, neti*—but in real life people need a concrete focus for their devotion. Hence, the concept of the avatar: "The down-to-earth Hindus were quick to turn the nirguna question into a saguna answer. Epic and Puranic Hinduism abound in examples of resistance to the nirguna ideal. Avatar is a prime example."[127]

Arjuna's question—Is it better to worship God as manifest Krishna or unmanifest oneness—mattered to Emerson because he recognized that how we talk about God will influence our experience of God and thus our experience of the world. Americans have long understood that when it comes to God, humans are both enabled and constrained by their language. Indeed, this realization is a cornerstone of American philosophy. For Emerson, human history proved that "religion cannot rise above the state of the votary. . . . The god of the cannibals will be a cannibal, of the crusaders a crusader, and of the merchants a merchant."[128] Thoreau concurred: "What man believes,

God believes."[129] So, too, did William James: "The trail of the human serpent is thus over everything."[130] Emerson rejected the contemporary Christian picture of God as like us, only better, a superhuman superhero capable of awesome compassion and awesome violence. He judged the customary Christian rhetoric of God ill fitted to the demands of the moment. He sought to invent a different rhetoric of oneness. He found inspiration in the Bhagavad Gita.

Emerson recognized that most Americans were conditioned to experience separation between themselves and the divine, and so he challenged his readers with an unfamiliar rhetoric of the divine inspired by Krishna's teachings. He rejected any way of speaking about God that creates separation between humans and divinity: "That which shows God in me, fortifies me. That which shows God out of me, makes me a wart and a wen."[131] In place of a God that is outside and above, Emerson invited his readers to imagine the divine as residing in their souls and as the essence of the world we inhabit, a cosmic oversoul that, through a mysterious process of incarnation, becomes our world and ourselves. God is *brahman*, God is oversoul, God is oneness.[132] According to James, Emerson's God is "not a deity *in concreto*, not a superhuman person, but the immanent divinity in things, the essentially spiritualist structure of the universe."[133] As people learn to reconnect soul to oversoul, this divinity offers intelligence, comfort, and genius in the form of "revelations" or "communications" to the intuition, or "the inward eye."[134] "The day of days, the great day of the feast of life, is that in which the inward eye opens to the Unity in things."[135] Today we speak of "gut feelings" and "listening to one's heart." These ideas are explored in Emerson's writings, for Emerson's genius is a genius because they have learned intuitively to hear and heed the divine oneness that is present in all of our souls.

Emerson Americanizes the nondualistic ontology of the Bhagavad Gita. However, on one point he emphatically disagrees with Krishna. Krishna tells Arjuna to worship him. This command is part of Krishna's argument in the Gita against the doctrine of individual responsibility as it was taught by Buddhists, with their theory of karmic retribution.[136] Krishna tells Arjuna to ignore karma. If Arjuna sticks to his social role as warrior and worship Krishna, he can do no wrong. From the Gupta period to the nineteenth century, this advice—to disregard the fruits of one's actions, and love God—justified sectarian conflict and violence by Brahmins (and their allies) against those who refused to follow Vishnu/Krishna.[137] Emerson emphatically rejects Krishna's advice from chapter 12 of the Gita to worship him. However, Emerson's disagreement has less to do with India's violent history and more to do with American psychology. For Emerson, the trouble with Krishna's advice to meditate on or worship "me" is that Americans would imagine the divine to be like themselves, and in the process they would end up worshiping themselves, hence becoming no better than they were at present. Instead, Emerson called on his readers to imagine a different relationship to God, one of "reception,"[138] "influx,"[139] and "communication"[140] with God as the one, the timeless plenitude of being, the oversoul.

Emerson sounds like a good Advaitin here, and he was (better, I believe, in fact, than many historians and philosophers have given him credit for). And yet Emerson was also a good rhetorician, and as an astute student of rhetoric he acknowledges quite clearly the trouble with any impersonal rhetoric of God. Krishna is surely right on this point: it is difficult to form a relationship with something that has no face, body, arms, legs, or voice. A *neti, neti* rhetoric might be philosophically pure, but it is rhetorically weak.[141]

Emerson faced the following rhetorical challenge when interpreting the Gita for Americans: the new American rhetoric of God must be positive—it must say clearly and concretely what divinity is—without falling prey to anthropomorphism, humanity's tendency to imagine God in its image. Emerson knew almost nothing about Hinduism as it was actually lived in India during his time. Nevertheless, he advised Americans to inhabit a devotional space similar to the place that many Hindus made their home. He encouraged Americans to recognize the impersonal, eternal, unmanifest oversoul as the ground of all existence; he also suggested that they actively worship divinity in a manifested form. Recognizing that the path of intellectual bhakti is difficult and requires tremendous discipline, like Krishna Emerson offered an alternative. But his alternative differed from Krishna's. In fact, Emerson *democratizes the doctrine of the divine avatar* by calling on his readers to recognize that the individual soul of another person (their "me") *is* an incarnation of the oversoul (the "not-me") and to worship this transcendent soul in human garb every time they engage in communication.

In "The Over-Soul," Emerson forwards a radically innovative theory of communication as yoga. Practicing communication as yoga is what it means to be committed to a life of oneness for Emerson. "Persons themselves acquaint us with the impersonal," he writes in "The Over-Soul," and that is true especially "in groups where debate is earnest," and also in the most "trivial conversations."[142] "All sincere conversation," Emerson concludes, is "the worship" of divinity in other people.[143] Emerson understands communication as an interpersonal spiritual practice of worshiping the divine soul in another. Too often, in communication with others we forget that they are human and treat them more like objects to be used and manipulated in service of our goals. Communication as yoga involves actively acknowledging that the individual soul is divine, and of the same nature as the universal divinity that animates the world. Other people are not objects; they are gods walking on earth. Though Emerson does not use the word *yoga* to describe his communication ethics, he strongly echoes one practice of yoga in the Gita—the discipline of seeing the divine everywhere, in all things. Both Emerson and Krishna advise their audiences to recognize that the individual *atman*, or soul, is no different than the universal *brahman*, or oversoul. Seeing God in all beings, it becomes possible to meet others on the common ground of oneness, charged by a feeling of divine consubstantiality and at-one-ness with all creation. Humans love to talk, and so it is only natural, Emerson concludes, that we practice such divine vision when conversing with others.

> One mode of the divine teaching is the incarnation of the spirit in a form,—in forms, like my own. I live in society; with persons who answer to thoughts in my own mind, or express a certain obedience to the great instincts to which I live. I see its presence to them. I am certified of a common nature; and these other souls, these separated selves, draw me as nothing can. . . . Persons are supplementary to the primary teaching of the soul. In youth we are mad for persons. Childhood and youth see all the world in them. But the larger experience of man discovers the identical nature appearing though them all. Persons themselves acquaint us with the impersonal. In all conversation between two persons, tacit reference is made, as to a third party, to a common nature. That third party or common nature is not social; it is impersonal; is God.[144]

In our youth, we go ga-ga for those exceptional individuals who stand out from the crowd. We celebrate difference. But as we mature, Emerson attests, we begin to notice the similarities that reside below these apparent differences. In short, we become more attuned to oneness, to the ontological fact that humans share a divine origin and a transcendent essence—that no one is truly alone or separate. Within each soul resides the oversoul, and this divinity is shared by all, though we differ in our awareness of it and the reflexive relationships we have developed with it.

The key to Emerson's interpretation of the Bhagavad Gita is his unique understanding of conversation. Emerson recognized that conversation is perhaps the most humanizing thing that humans do, and for him, conversation *humanizes* by *granting divinity*. If we are devoted to oneness, we will talk to every person we meet as though they are an avatar of the divine, a walking, talking god on earth who is sacred and demands the utmost reverence. We will envision life—not just our own lives, or even the lives of those closest to us, but all lives—as sacred. And if we commit to talking this way—as though we are talking to gods—the result is magic. For Emerson, when we speak with anger and resentment, when we belittle others and push them around like objects in our way, we weaken our words and reveal ourselves to be frauds who have little understanding of the way things could be and ought to be. We can only be at our best, our most persuasive, our most authentic, when we address the divine that resides in others—the impersonal within their personal, the oversoul within their souls—with the respect that it deserves. When we do, we gain tremendous rhetorical power. We also bring ourselves, our own souls, into closer alignment with the oversoul. Speak to the divine, he advises, and the divine has a tendency to answer back.

Emerson shares much in common with nineteenth-century mysticism, spiritualism, and occultism. His vision of communication in "The Over-Soul" is, however, distinct from these trends in American culture.[145] Influenced in large measure by John Locke's psychologism, "which teaches us to see meaning as dwelling in the individual," nineteenth-century spiritualists were concerned with the problem of manifesting an inner soul that was frustratingly opaque to others in communication.[146] Psychologism gives rise to the feeling of mental isolation that so many Americans struggled with then and continue to struggle with today. If my soul is cut off from the world, how can you ever hope to understand me? Emerson reverses the process, making communication about discovery and acquaintance with the oversoul in others that grounds individual identity in a "common nature." The oversoul is always present within the soul, if only we are attuned to it. Communication thus becomes a practice of radical transcendentalist imagination—I imagine you as divine, and then I deliberately choose to address you as though you are divine. In the language of Emerson's Advaita, communication as yoga involves imagining the inner soul of our interlocutors, the *adhyatma*, as the product of the cosmic soul, the *paramatman*, the oversoul. Envisioning you from a higher plane, I practice seeing you as a divine avatar and hearing the same divinity animating your words that animates mine. In this way I transcend our apparent differences and the distance that separates us. In this way I affirm the oneness of being.

When talking with and attempting to persuade others, Emerson argues that it is vital to "act for the soul" by imagining that anyone we speak to is an avatar of God. To converse and deliberate is a chance to devote oneself like a good bhakta to the divine in others. Notably, rather than choose a great political oration or crowd-pleasing public performance as an example to illustrate communication as yoga, he goes smaller, and more intimate. Indeed, Emerson illustrates the practice of communication as yoga by briefly describing a conversation with his son Waldo, who was born in 1836 and was about four and a half years old when *Essays: First Series* was published in 1841. In moments when it was necessary to discipline the headstrong boy, Emerson reports that his superior logic, learning, and strength were useless: "If I am willful, he sets his will against mine, one for one." Like most people, Waldo was obstinate and proud. It was not possible for Emerson to argue his son into better behavior. However, "if I renounce my will, and act for the soul, setting that up as umpire between us two, out of his young eyes looks the same soul; he reveres and loves with me."[147] Speak to the soul, Emerson says, and you will find love, and concord. Speak to the soul, Emerson says, and you will know the oversoul.

Americans have long recognized the power of the mind to shape reality; this is one of the hallmarks of the American worldview. Life is a series of maybes that we turn into yeses and nos with desire, belief, and devotion. Perhaps this is another reason the Bhagavad Gita found such a receptive American audience, for it, too, teaches the transformative power of faith (*sraddha*)—Krishna informs Arjuna that what we believe in has a way of becoming true for us.[148] Emerson understands how closely faith, belief, and truth are bound in determining for us the quality of the universe. There are of course brutal limits to the power of the human mind to shape reality—Emerson calls these limits "fate"—but in many ways life, especially as we live it in our mental movie theaters, is a self-fulfilling prophecy. Those we love are lovable; those we hate are hateful. If we believe that the world is damned and beyond redemption, then it is, at least for us, and the opposite is true as well. "A man is a method, a progressive arrangement; a selecting principle, gathering his like to him, wherever he goes."[149] To practice communication as yoga is to take some control over this mental principle of selection and arrangement, which, Emerson muses, is an unconscious and automatic operation of social conditioning for most people. We have been conditioned not to see the world as it is. To practice communication as yoga is to draw the divine closer and to put oneself in more harmonious relation with the oneness that is.

By connecting the soul with the oversoul, divine wisdom can shine through—and this intelligence is *felt* as much as it is *thought*. Emerson's philosophy of emotions was radical for his time. Employing one of his favorite metaphors for the human experience, water, Emerson writes, "Man is a stream whose source is hidden. Our being is descending into us from we know not whence."[150] Feelings are not subjective personal experiences but are in fact objective forces like a river that rushes down from a distant mountain range and sweeps us away. "When I watch that flowing river, which, out of regions I see not, pours for a season its streams into me, I see that I am a pensioner; not a cause, but a surprised spectator of this ethereal water."[151] It is not that I am happy, but that I experience happiness, which is much bigger than me. No one owns their feelings. Emotions wash over us with little prompting; how we feel is constantly escaping our control.

Krishna demands that Arjuna conquer his emotions by mastering his fears. Emerson teaches something different. He calls on his readers to open themselves to the oversoul, because to commune with divinity is to be emotionally disrupted. Emerson attests that divine revelations—those rare moments when we feel connection to the one, to the expansive, overwhelming plenitude of existence—"are always attended by the emotion of the sublime," an emotion that elevates one's being through a maddening cacophony of mysteriousness, awe, wonder, fear, and joy.[152] In the Western rhetorical tradition, the sublime is an emotional experience that disrupts our habits and forces us to pause in the present moment. The sublime in Emerson invigorates, agitates, invades, entrances, inspires, and empowers. To practice communication as yoga is to bring some control over how we feel by devoting ourselves to oneness and the particular emotions most closely associated with the oversoul, including, especially, love. The active devotion to the oversoul puts us in a position to passively receive its wisdom in the form of "communications" from the divine—communications that are both heard and felt.

The ethics of oneness for Emerson involves opening ourselves to love. Emerson concludes that those who are truly devoted to addressing the soul in others will experience a spiritual expansion of infinite love for their fellow creatures. This is the transformational moment of yoga, of connection between individual and God, soul and oversoul. Love is at the heart of Emerson's vision of politics—not love of country, which can become a restrictive, jealous, conventional love, but love as devotion to the divine in others, the patient, tender, caring love of infinite solidarity. In "The Over-Soul," Emerson gestures toward an unconditional, universal love based in the divine consubstantiality of oneness. To worship the oversoul by practicing communication as yoga will result in "the doubling of the heart itself, nay, the infinite enlargement of the heart with a power of growth to a new infinity on every side."[153] With hearts enlarged to infinity, Americans will see their actions, and the actions of others, from the perspective of the whole, and as a result will be more likely to act out love and charity for, and solidarity with, their fellows, their kin.

"From Within Outwards"

Communication as yoga is an interpersonal practice with ramifications far beyond the individual. Indeed, Emerson believed that practicing communication as yoga could fix the world, one person, one conversation, one relationship at a time. Like his fellow transcendentalists, Emerson saw beyond present evils toward something better. Looking at the world from a higher place, he and his fellow transcendentalist radicals hoped to build a more just world in which slavery did not exist, in which people lived more harmoniously with nature, and in which the wheels of empire were derailed. The transcendentalists believed that even the most intractable social problems could be solved by clear thought and human ingenuity. Yet divergent opinions concerning how best to fix the world split the movement.[154]

Emerson disagreed with his fellow reformers, including Orestes Brownson and George Ripley, who hoped to go straight after social injustice with community pressure. Such grassroots organization had its appeal, but ultimately it meant very little—and would prove ineffective—if it was not rooted in individual change. "Society gains nothing whilst a man, not himself renovated, attempts to renovate things around him," Emerson wrote.[155] Margaret Fuller explained that the chief goal of the transcendentalist poet warriors was "to quicken the soul, that they may work from within outwards."[156] *From within outwards:* this is the path to social justice—not because self-transformation automatically transforms the world, like ripples from a pond-tossed stone, but instead because no meaningful political and social change is possible without self-transformation. Only by first transforming ourselves to transcend habit and convention can we experience the most transformative emotion of them all—love. And once we do, everything becomes sacred.

It is easy when reading Emerson to focus on the "within" and forget the "outwards." In "The Over-Soul," Emerson contends that the effects of practicing communication as yoga will radiate outward from the individual, altering society and its politics. Emerson frames many of America's problems as the result of wrongheaded assumptions about individuality. Having adopted the philosophy of liberalism from the founders, Americans believed then—and many of us continue to believe today—that individuals came into the world fully formed and ready-made. Born autonomous, cut off from a fallen world, and isolated by impenetrable psychic barriers from their fellows, Americans better go it alone if we desire happiness. Americans are heroes, masters of the outer and inner universe, including their minds, their hearts, and their destinies. And yet for Emerson, true independence, in the form of the "possessive individualism" taught by early liberal philosophers including Locke and Hobbes, is ontologically impossible.[157] The soul is an incarnation of the oversoul; we suffer, and are weakened, when we forget that we are one and stop seeking connection with the one. Communication as yoga is a civic practice, then, because it challenges the illusion of independence. Talk to the soul in others, and see what happens to yourself. See what thoughts and emotions come over you. If you pay attention, you will see that you are not cut off from the divine—it is always there. Nor are you so cut off from others, as your culture has led you to believe.

Emerson declares that we will view life from a new plane—our worldview will be expanded—if we dedicate ourselves to oneness and practice communication as yoga. We will find eloquence, power, peace, and genius: "Behold! their speech shall be lyrical, and sweet, and universal as the rising of the wind."[158] For Emerson, a genuine commitment to oneness soothes and empowers:

> The simplest person, who in his integrity worships God, becomes God; yet for ever and ever the influx of this better and universal self is new and unsearchable. It inspires awe and astonishment. How dear, how soothing to man, arises the idea of God, peopling the lonely place, effacing the scars of our mistakes and disappointments![159]

If we are devoted to oneness in our interpersonal interactions, we will experience a "better and universal self"—*better* because it will be happier, having overcome the godforsaken, heedless illusion of loneliness fostered by liberal individualism, and more *universal* because it will recognize its divine kinship with all other living creatures. Humans squabble and fight and kill when they forget their connection to the one. Emerson describes the oversoul as the "Supreme Critic" concerning our errors and "the only prophet of that which must be."[160] Those who are devoted to the oversoul are changed, for the oversoul demands that people consider their actions in the context of the universal. Devotees to oneness will not be so easily divided from their fellow human beings; they will question any political or social practice that cuts them off from the source, or that puts them at each others' throats. This, at least, is Emerson's hope. And, in many ways, during the long nineteenth century, it also became America's hope.

2

Cosmos

Was the greatest of American poems, Walt Whitman's *Leaves of Grass*—first published in 1855 and revised for the rest of Whitman's life, with a ninth and final "deathbed" edition appearing in 1891–1892—influenced by the Bhagavad Gita?[1] Emerson thought so. He labeled Whitman's poetry "a remarkable mixture of the Bhagvat Ghita and the *New York Herald*," lauding it for combining the cosmic vision of the Gita with the scandalous sensationalism typical of the penny press.[2] Whitman died in 1892 with a copy of J. Cockburn Thompson's 1855 English translation of the Bhagavad Gita tucked under his pillow—which I take to be strong evidence that he treasured the book.[3]

In spite of Emerson's testimony, scholars cannot agree on this point, and the evidence is unclear.[4] When the two eloquent, democratic loafers met for the first time in 1856, Thoreau purportedly asked Whitman if he had read the Gita and other Indian philosophical works. Whitman replied, "No, tell me about them."[5] This might have been an honest admission of ignorance; or (more likely, in my opinion) it was the ornery Whitman poking a little fun at the haughty Thoreau and his famed erudition. In Whitman's 1888 essay "A Backward Glance o'er Travel'd Road," he mentioned "the ancient Hindu poems"—presumably the Mahabharata and the Ramayana—as among the many "embryonic facts" of *Leaves of Grass*.[6] It is likely that Whitman was familiar with the Gita simply by being attuned to cultural currents. Surely he knew the Gita from reading Emerson and Thoreau. In "A Passage to India," a poem celebrating the human capacity to connect with distant, far-flung others through railroads and steamships and telegraph cables and electrical currents that made a giant planet seem just a little smaller, Whitman described India as a land of personal inspiration. His poetry, he claimed, was inspired by "the far-darting beams of the spirit" from India whose soul "soundest below the Sanscrit and the Vedas."[7] Like Emerson before him, he took poetic inspiration from the literature of mysticism and the perennial philosophy; and, also like Emerson, he was a philosopher of oneness, the poet of rapport. So it was only natural that he engaged with many of the Gita's central themes, even if he rarely mentioned the divine song itself.[8]

Whitman (1819–1892) had the highest of aspirations. He hoped to invent a new religion: "I, too, following many and follow'd by many, inaugurate a religion."[9] In mid-nineteenth-century America, this was not the outlandish claim that it might seem today, for a number of new religions were founded at this time. Whitman's goal was not to found a church, with rituals and dogma; this is not what he meant by religion. Instead, he hoped to change the American worldview by writing poetry that addressed the deepest questions of human being, the eternal questions, the questions that we cannot help but ask ourselves at twilight while watching the sun set behind the hills over yonder, as day gives way to night and the stars twinkle gently overhead with a promise of celestial brilliance and, if we're lucky, transcendence. When Whitman said he wanted to found a religion, I hear him saying he hoped to create a new American ontology—not an ontology that lives only in books, an ontology written by scholastics for scholastics; not a bespectacled ontology but one that breathes, an ontology that fires the heart and permeates one's entire being, an ontology that is felt as much as it is thought, an ontology that Americans can put their faith in and surrender their hearts to. This philosophy would pull people into its orbit like a magnet; its expression would be like a camp revival meeting. People would weep and wail and faint and nothing would ever be the same.

"Whitmanism," as one prominent critic dubbed it, was a religion of oneness.[10] Whitman was not the first American to pronounce an ontology of oneness—he followed Emerson in this regard. However, what made Whitman unique was that he based his religion on a mystical, meditative experience he'd had in his mid-thirties, in which he achieved "cosmic consciousness": "a consciousness of the cosmos, that is, of the life and order of the universe."[11] Profound were the effects of this experience on Whitman. Transported to the fabled higher plane, he achieved "rapport" with the divine—and looked differently at everything, and everyone. Filled with divine energy, feeling the pulse of all things, Whitman experienced the universe as an interconnected whole, infused by divinity, bound in body, breath, and purpose. He saw humanity gathered around one big table, united in common purpose, and knew that all would be well. Whitman described his experience in the following terms:

Swiftly arose and spread around me the peace and knowledge that pass all the
art and argument of the earth,
And I know that the hand of God is the promise of my own,
And I know that the spirit of God is the brother of my own,
And that all the men ever born are also my brothers, and the women my sisters
and lovers,
And that a kelson of the creation is love,
And limitless are leaves stiff or drooping in the fields,
And brown ants in the little wells beneath them,
And mossy scraps of the worm fence, heap'd stones, elder, mullein and
poke-weed.[12]

This wonderful experience revealed to Whitman that Emerson was right about the nature of the oversoul, though Whitman preferred different words for this reality—he called it "All," "kosmos," "ensemble," and a host of other terms that composed his own personal lexicon of oneness. Rather than emphasizing that the divine oneness is *over* us, which might be misconstrued to imply hierarchy and, perhaps, disconnection, Whitman suggested repeatedly that the divine is part of us and we of it. Divinity is the all, it is everything, it is us, and everything that is "not us," too. And while Emerson spoke of the relationship between soul and oversoul as one of container and contained—we are "filled" with the divine—or as a prism—the divine light shines through us—Whitman preferred to speak of finding "rapport" with the all.[13] This is the feeling that the universe has our back, and it arises, Whitman contends, when we recognize the truth that all things are one. In such moments, we become "lit with the Infinite."[14] Though full rapport is "rare," everyone has the capacity to experience it. They need only develop their innate capacity for meditation, which the German Romantics called "intuition," which Emerson called "the inward eye," and which Whitman called "soul-sight."[15] Cosmic consciousness is the feeling of being at one with the universe, and Whitman's poetry is a record of the rich rapport he developed with the all. At times, Whitman the poetic narrator directly addresses the all, sometimes as a friend, sometimes as a lover, calling it closer, begging to feel its touch and hear its words. At other times, Whitman the individual seems to dissolve into the background and it is the all itself that addresses the audience through Whitman's pen, with ink kissed by the cosmos.

The truth of oneness is right there, waiting to be seen; but the reality is that people have stopped looking for it, so consumed are they by the profit motive. And so on every page Whitman reminds his readers of the ontological reality of the all by modeling his own devotion to oneness.[16] At the end of one of his many long lists detailing the motley cast and characters of New York City life, from opera singers to duck hunters to painters, farmers, businessmen, social reformers, philosophers, young mothers, and emancipated slaves, Whitman reflects:

> And these tend inward to me, and I tend outward to them,
> And such as it is to be of these more or less I am,
> And of these one and all I weave the song of myself.[17]

The song of myself is a song of all, a canto of connection, a celebration of cooperation, and a deep recognition that all lives are shared, as are all fates. In Whitman's poetry, oneness does not exclude the many; it enlivens, enriches, and emboldens individuals who are tied together metaphysically on a common path they walk on a common earth while living a common life.

For Whitman, like Emerson, living a life devoted to oneness has everything to do with how we communicate with our fellows. But there are differences with Emerson, too, two of which are absolutely critical to the history I narrate in this book. The first is that Emerson and Whitman were drawn to two very different expressions of Vedanta that were in turn inspired by two very different readings of the Bhagavad Gita. Emerson interpreted the Gita through the lens of nondualistic Advaita Vedanta, and he articulated a transcendentalist yoga inspired by Advaita—a position that, we will see in the next chapter, grew more extreme after the publication of "The Over-Soul" in 1841. Whitman was also a devoted proponent of oneness, but his philosophy is much closer in spirit to Bhedabheda Vedanta, a philosophy that charts a middle path between Vedantic dualism (*dvaita*) and nondualism (*advaita*) by incorporating elements of both.

Bhedabheda is a compound of two Sanskrit words: *bheda*, meaning "difference or distinction," and *abheda*, meaning "nondifference or nondistinction."[18] Bhedabheda Vedanta holds that the soul is both similar to and different from God.[19] "Just a fragment of me in the living world becomes a life," Krishna explains to Arjuna.[20] In Bhedabheda Vedanta, oneness (*abheda*) is the truth and all souls are manifestations of the eternal *brahman*, but souls are not identical to *brahman*, and the precise nature of this relationship is beyond human understanding. Bhedabheda Vedanta affirms the reality of the material world and also the fact of difference (*bheda*), for while souls are manifestations of the universal, they are unique in how they manifest the divine oneness. Though the Advaitic interpretation championed by Emerson's contemporary Rammohan Roy (and a host of later Vedantins inspired by Swami Vivekananda) became the most popular interpretation of the Bhagavad Gita in the United States and Europe, there is a good argument to be made that the Gita is at its heart a Bhedabheda text.[21] Certainly, Bhedabheda Vedanta is much closer to Whitman's position in *Leaves of Grass* than Emerson's Advaita;

and, as I will show over the following chapters, when it comes to determining what it means to live a life committed to oneness, this is a difference that makes a difference.

Whitman recognizes and celebrates diversity—and this leads to a second divergence from Emerson. For Emerson, oneness is an ontological state to be discovered, whereas for Whitman oneness is also an ontological reality that individuals can and ought to reproduce through their speech and action in the broken, zugzwang world that we have created for ourselves: "A song make I of the One form'd out of all."[22] Practicing an ethics of oneness for Whitman means more than mirroring nature. To behave ethically people must be actively committed to oneness in all facets of their lives, acting with all urgency to make oneness real in the realm of convention, habit, and everyday life. I read *Leaves of Grass* as a poetic model for what it means to live a life committed to oneness. In particular, Whitman models three practices that prototype such a life: first, he commits himself to using a lexicon of god terms that express oneness rather than division; second, he practices communication as yoga, adopting a mode of addressing others that emphasizes ontological consubstantiality and shared divinity; and third, he cultivates an emotion, gratefulness, that is conducive to oneness. By describing these practices, in this chapter I explore the ontology of Whitmanism as an ethics of oneness.

The God Terms of Oneness

Philosophers have long assumed that life cannot be lived without certain fixed reference points, or "first principles," that give it significance and purpose. Life demands "ontological orientation."[23] To know oneself is to know where one stands in the world. It is to place oneself on a map, a philosophical map whose orientation is defined by considerations of the good.[24] What we assume to be the point of life—to be good—shapes our hopes, our dreams, our fears, and our habits. Though certain contemporary theorists of "public reason" attempt to disallow it, talk of the good is foundational to democratic politics.

Of course, philosophers disagree about the origin of the good: Does it come from the stars or the social world into which we are born?[25] This was a particularly contentious debate during the nineteenth century. For Whitman, it is the duty of poets like himself to awaken Americans to the true meaning of democracy by talking "first principles"—namely, what is good: "The poets of the kosmos advance through all interpositions and coverings and turmoils and stratagems to *first principles*."[26] Whitman's conception of the good is based on the ontology of oneness—oneness is good, as is the experience of cosmic consciousness of oneness. About "the central divine idea of All," he muses: "I say he has studied, meditated to no profit, whatever may be his erudition, who has not absorb'd this simple consciousness and faith."[27] "The latent eternal intuitional sense . . . is *sine qua non* to democracy," he concludes, "and a highest widest aim of democratic literature"—including poetry like *Leaves of Grass*—"may well be to bring forth, cultivate, brace, and strengthen this sense, in individuals and society."[28] For Whitman, a democratic life is a mystical life that nurtures people's capacity for cosmic consciousness.

A good is no good if it cannot be articulated. What a particular culture understands to be good is on display in its "god terms," "the terms to which the very highest respect is paid."[29] A god term is "a secular summarizing term" whose role is "analogous to the over-all entitling role played by the theologian's word for the godhead."[30] These terms pull us toward them by their rhetorical gravity. God terms give the good a rhetorical form so that it can provide direction and orientation. God terms give voice to our unvoiced ideals and direction to our wanderings, so that they are not aimless. God terms bring the good before our eyes. These terms demand *dedication*, of time, of money, of energy, and, in the most extreme cases, of life itself.[31] Take these terms away, or corrupt their meaning, and we are like wanderers in the desert with no map.

Whitman positions oneness as the metaphysical foundation of democracy, and he employs a number of god terms to capture the ineffable experience of rapport, including *All*, *rondure*, *ensemble*, *mélange*, and *kosmos*. What is notable about Whitman's vocabulary is that he uses language that, as much as possible, pushes against boundaries and divisions, rhetoric that curates an experience of at-one-ness with the world. His words leap right over all the walls, metaphorical and real, we construct to make ourselves feel more secure in an uncertain world. This language is meant to evoke a state of oneness, a divine goodness that knows no bounds.

In the dialogue *Phaedrus*, Plato argues that it is necessary to invoke the good in moments when truth alone is not enough to persuade.[32] Whitman's poetry flowers from a mystical experience of rapport with the divine. He assumes as a metaphysical truth what this experience has revealed to him, that all is divine because all is one. Diversity is real, but absolute separation is an illusion. We are one. He does not seek to persuade his readers of this truth; he simply states it. However, as Plato recognizes, the truth alone does not always have the power to set us free. It is often necessary to create an appetite for the truth by framing it as good. Whitman does precisely this in his poetry. To inspire his readers to change their lives, he describes separation as the cruelest illusion, the root of suffering and unhappiness. The path to overcoming this illusion is to work diligently to develop one's capacity for cosmic consciousness and a direct experience of oneness. He reports that the experience of rapport with "the mystic unseen soul" results in "happiness, knowledge, not in another place but this place, not for another hour but this hour."[33] Seeking rapport, for Whitman, is the proper way to pursue happiness, and we can find rapport only if we devote ourselves to oneness. This in turn entails a change in the language we use on a daily basis, which is why Whitman dedicates himself to employing a number of god terms of oneness in his poetry whenever possible.

Reality constantly eludes our ability to represent it. Still, language is our first and surest throughway into the world. Whitman admits that words cannot capture or engender an experience of oneness: "I do not know it—it is without name—it is a word unsaid, / It is not in any dictionary, utterance, symbol."[34] Nevertheless, words are what we have, and words can prepare us for this experience not by goading, but through *devotion*. Whitman agrees with Krishna's teaching in chapter 17 of the Gita: "Yo yat shraddhah sa eva sah," "as a person's faith is, so are they"; in other words, that which we place our faith in has a way of becoming true for us, for the faithful are habituated to seeing what we want and expect and hope to see.[35] In his poetry, Whitman actively models how Americans might devote themselves to oneness. Whitman's devotion is a fierce determination to use the language of oneness as much as possible, whenever possible, even in situations where custom makes it seem awkward or inappropriate or off base or ineffective. Devotion here means placing one's faith in the language of oneness and fully abandoning oneself to this language, making it a part of oneself, as much as one's arms or legs or heart.

Advaita Vedanta became incredibly popular in the United States during Whitman's lifetime; and as we saw in chapter 1, Advaita prefers not to describe *brahman*, the transcendental ground of all existence, but instead to signify what it is not.[36] To say what *brahman* is is to create a mental picture of *brahman* that limits *brahman*, because by definition all mental pictures are limited. Most Advaitins say that *brahman* is not-two, or nondualistic—not that it is one. I call this *negative definition*, saying what something is not, as opposed to *affirmative definition*, saying what something is. Whitman was not an Advaitin, so he was never boxed in by Advaita's apophantic theology and its insistence on negative definition. Interestingly enough, a number of avowed Advaitins also refused the tactic of negative definition. Notably, beginning with Swami Vivekananda in the 1890s, many of the Indian gurus who taught Americans yoga through the lens of Advaita Vedanta were quite effusive, creative, and concrete in defining the nature of *brahman*, often making copious use of familiar Western philosophical reference points in their descriptions. Take, for instance, Swami Abhedananda (1866–1939), who followed Swami Vivekananda as the head of the New York Vedanta Society. In his 1905 book *Vedanta Philosophy* the swami explained that

> the universal substance was called "Substantia" by Spinoza. Herbert Spencer calls it the "Unknowable." It is the same as "Ding an sich," or the transcendental thing-in-itself of Kant; Plato named it the "Good." It is the "Over-Soul" of Emerson; while in Vedanta it is called "Brahman," the absolute substance of the universe, the infinite and eternal source of matter and mind, of object and substance. This substance is not many but one. It is the universal energy, the mother or producer of all forces. . . . This is monism.[37]

Negative definition works best when an audience is already familiar with the topic under discussion. It's likely that Swami Abhedananda and others adopted the tactic of affirmative definition because both the concept and the experience of *brahman* were unfamiliar to their American audiences, and so these audiences needed mental pictures to get started along the path of yoga. It's also likely that Americans, as an incredibly practical people with little taste for abstract metaphysical thinking—one of the markers of United States history is its "evasion" of philosophy[38]—demanded concrete images of *brahman* from the gurus. Though Advaita caught on in America, it was a modified Advaita that defined the undefinable. This was a game at which Whitman proved particularly skilled.

Whitman's lexicon of oneness is one of his greatest poetic legacies. He understood the importance of describing oneness with a concrete, robust, vibrant vocabulary of god terms that would come alive in his readers' minds and fire their imaginations. Whitman's lexicon is earthly, and it expresses a deep ecological awareness that roots people to the natural world in a mystical, cosmic fusion with all creation. Whitman uses the word *rondure*—a gracefully round object—to conjure the beautiful totality of the earth that encompasses all life and that makes life possible: "Behold the great rondure, the cohesion of all, how perfect!"[39] *Rondure* implies cohesion and connection, as does *ensemble*. "I will not make poems with references to parts," Whitman writes. "But I will make poems, songs, thoughts, with reference to ensemble."[40] In French, *ensemble* means "together"; in English, an ensemble is a musical group of people playing or laughing or singing in harmony. When Whitman uses the word *ensemble* in his poetry, it evokes how much stronger, how much more beautiful and powerful and evocative we are when we act together. *Ensemble* is meant to be a reference point—it refers to our ontological state. In "Laws for Creations," Whitman promulgates the following law:

"All must have reference to the ensemble of the world, and the compact truth of the world."[41] We do not stand alone or apart. We stand together, interconnected, as manifestations of oneness and members of the earthly *ensemble*.

Humans are like waves in the ocean, to use an image that Whitman enjoys and that is common in the mystical tradition.[42] No ocean, no waves. Whitman uses the French word *mélange*, a mixture or medley, also in reference to the ocean: "Mélange mine own, the unseen and the seen, / Mysterious ocean where the streams empty."[43] Each of us is an embodiment of unseen infinity, of beautiful totality, of terrestrial luminescence. Most of us make our lives in reference to parts, but Whitman instead models how to create a life with the language of oneness. By adopting these god terms, Whitman reinforces the truth that was revealed to him in his moment of cosmic consciousness: from oneness we emerge and to oneness we return, like a stream to the ocean.

Famously, Whitman introduces himself to his readers in *Leaves of Grass* as "Walt Whitman, an American, one of the roughs, a kosmos."[44] The etymology of *kosmos* is ancient Greek. From Homer's *Iliad* to Plato's *Timaeus*, the word represented "order," as in the fixed expression *kata kosmon*, "in good order." For the ancient Greeks, "the term denotes order and beauty, even more specifically the beauty resulting from order, the beauty that is still implied today by an activity that derives its name from the word—'cosmetics.'"[45] For Pythagoras, *kosmos* represented "the encompassing of all things (*he ton holon periokhe*)."[46] The universe, the cosmos, was for him a beautifully ordered, harmonious whole. Plato's Socrates argued, repeatedly, that the good life could be found by imitating the divine order of the universe, of the cosmos.[47]

The Prussian geographer and explorer Alexander von Humboldt popularized the word in his four-volume *Kosmos: A General Survey of the Physical Phenomena of the Universe* (1845). For Humboldt, nature was cosmos, "an harmoniously ordered whole," and "the most important consequences of physical researches are therefore these:—To acknowledge unity in multiplicity; from the individual to embrace all."[48] Cosmos represents unity in diversity, which for Humboldt was spiritual as well as physical. For Whitman, the word *kosmos* represents oneness, the interconnected whole of which everyone is a part. At the same time, Whitman uses the word *kosmos* with an indefinite article—he is "a kosmos." The person who is *a* kosmos is devoted to what the god term *kosmos* represents. This person desires a direct experience of oneness. They strive to be at one with the universe, in tune with its natural interconnectedness, attuned to the cosmetic beauty of existence, and consubstantial with all living beings. By flagging himself as one of the "roughs," Whitman acknowledges his material reality as a citizen and a member of the democratic masses. Whitman was disturbed by the excessive violence and brutality of other roughs, however, and so pairing *rough* with *kosmos* was a rhetorical move meant to signify spiritual uplift.[49] In Whitman's poetry, this god term is a constant reminder to his readers that they are the walking, talking incarnations of divine order. The one who is a kosmos is devoted to oneness, and prepared to dedicate time, and energy, to this constitutive good.

Note that many of the words in Whitman's lexicon of oneness are foreign, sourced from ancient Greek (*kosmos*) and French (*ensemble*, *mélange*, and perhaps *rondure*, probably a misspelling of the French word *rondeur*, "round," that corresponded to Whitman's pronunciation of that word[50]). Why does Whitman import so many foreign words to describe oneness? A simple answer is that he, like most poets, loves language, all language. Though he was invested in creating an American poetry written in American English for an American audience, he understands that, to be of any value, an American language cannot be insular and isolationist; it must be a polyglot tongue, a language of the world. As such, there is an ethical lesson in his multilingual lexicon of oneness. For Whitman, we need all the world's languages and linguistic resources to capture the experience of cosmic consciousness. A true lexicon of oneness would be *a global project*, because oneness is an experience common to humanity, no matter what language is used. No one people or culture owns oneness, and no one language can capture it. A true lexicon of oneness breaks narrow mental and political conventions by cutting across all borders, including time and place.

Language is hierarchal, and god terms function by influencing the meaning of associated and subordinated words. Richard Weaver writes, "All of the terms in a rhetorical vocabulary are like links in a chain stretching up to some master link which transmits its influence down through the linkages."[51] Weaver celebrates (and also fears) the power of god terms to condense a number of attitudes in a word or phrase that might diverge if more specific language were used. Whitman understands god terms slightly differently. Rather than rely on these terms to work their rhetorical magic on the individual, pulling them north and south, east and west, hither and thither, this way and that, he actively devotes himself to oneness and all it represents—because what we devote ourselves to has a way of becoming real for us.[52] The language we use naturally follows from our beliefs, but that language also has the power to actively shape our beliefs. To reinforce oneness rather than division, and make the world appear as a manifestation of the all, Whitman practices a conscious, deliberate care for the language he uses. The god terms of oneness become the master links in his poetry, the keywords that give meaning to all of his other words, binding his vocabulary together into a life story with a coherent arc from here to there through now. Even when he was forced to utter divisive words—and such words are inevitable, the words of dissent, confrontation, and conflict—these words were subordinate to, and influenced by, the god terms of oneness.

Devotion (bhakti) is one of the three paths of yoga Krishna describes in the Bhagavad Gita. To understand what Whitman is up to in *Leaves of Grass*, we must be careful to distinguish the rhetorical devotion to a lexicon of oneness from the "magical voluntarism"[53] that came to be closely associated with the New Thought movement of the 1880s and '90s, a movement Whitman (and Emerson before him) helped inspire. The New Thought movement (which I will discuss in more detail in chapter 6) taught the virtues of positive thinking: think good thoughts, and the universe will respond in kind with health, happiness, and success, regardless of material conditions.[54] But of course if a person devotes themselves to financial wealth, wealth is not guaranteed (unless they be Midas, and we all know how that turned out). However, if a person actively devotes themselves to wealth, this devotion does change how they see the world—everything becomes about profit, and people, and the earth itself, become exploitable means to this end. Whitman counters the greediness of his own culture by modeling total devotion to oneness, pursuing it at every corner, worshiping it at every opportunity, praising it without qualification.

Communication as Yoga

Whitman's poetry is ripe with images of dissemination—leaves fall, seeds are scattered in the wind, and so on—but it also contains a number of deliberative set pieces. Interpersonal dialogue is important to Whitman because in face-to-face conversation he meets actual living, breathing, embodied human beings who are imperfect and flawed, who laugh and cry and yell and shout. Too often democracy is conceptualized in the abstract. Whitman makes democracy personal. Every time he meets another person on the road, in the pub, or around the park, he transforms the encounter into an opportunity to devote himself to their divinity by picturing their soul as a unique and sacred manifestation of the all. For Whitman, every interaction is a chance to practice addressing another person as an essential, inevitable, invaluable part of the divine cosmos.

At times, this practice takes the form of a rosy determination to engage others convivially. In "Song of the Open Road," Whitman makes the following pledge: "I think whatever I shall meet on the road I shall like, and whoever beholds me shall like me, / I think whoever I see must be happy."[55] Amiability is not always easy, so at times this is enough for Whitman. Often, however, he asks much more of himself, pledging to hold others in the same high esteem that he holds himself, allowing that they, too, might be heroes and heroines acting the lead in their own dramas that are constantly unfolding out of our sight. In his poetry, Whitman practices picturing the people he meets as proof of divine goodness. To practice communication as yoga involves viewing others as immortal and divine, as avatars of the divine walking on earth, who can never be fitted into simple boxes and categories of identity because, in reality, they are transcendent. "I am the mate and companion of people, all just as immortal and fathomless as myself, / (They do not know how immortal, but I know)," Whitman writes in "Song of Myself."[56] Whitman promises to meet everyone on the ground of divine equality—"I think some divine rapport has equalized me with them," he reports.[57]

> Each of us inevitable,
> Each of us limitless—each of us with his or her right upon the Earth,
> Each of us allow'd the eternal purports of the earth,
> Each of us here as divinely as any is here.[58]

Equality is the way of things. Equality is the wisdom of the world. When we are in rapport with the universe, we understand deep in our hearts that all beings are equal in their divinity. To live a life committed to oneness involves recognizing that everyone has a right to exist on the earth and that everyone deserves respect and love, because we are all avatars of the all. Most Americans of Whitman's day recognized the importance of addressing the divine with reverence. Whitman extends such respect to everyone that he meets while running errands or just loafing about. In his poetry, Whitman models a total commitment to address others as divine, to speak from a place of connection, a common source, and a common life.

Whitman likely adopted this practice from the description of communication as yoga in Emerson's essay "The Over-Soul." As we saw in chapter 1, in this essay Emerson instructs his readers in the basic lessons of the Bhagavad Gita: that the individual soul is divine, and that Americans ought to practice seeing the divinity in all creatures at all times. Emerson frames every conversation, every interaction, as an opportunity to "see how the thing stands in God."[59] "All sincere conversation," he observes, is "the worship" of the oversoul in the form of another human being.[60] "Persons themselves acquaint us with the impersonal. In all conversation between two persons, tacit reference is made, as to a third party, to a common nature. That third party or common nature is not social; it is impersonal; is God," he states—not the Christian God who sits in judgment, but the oversoul, which gives life to all.[61] Emerson reports that in his experience, addressing others with dignity and devotion invites them to respond in kind. Whitman takes up this challenge in his poetry, meeting strangers on the common ground of divine consubstantiality—but with a crucial difference.

In her brilliant, pathbreaking work of feminist social criticism, *Woman in the Nineteenth Century* (1845), Margaret Fuller (1810–1850) raises a piercing question about the Emersonian practice of communication as yoga: Is it truly universal and open to everyone, or to men only? Cataloguing the many boneheaded, stereotypical beliefs that relegated women to second-class status in nineteenth-century American culture, she observes:

> There exists in the minds of men a tone of feeling towards women as towards slaves, such as is expressed in the common phrase, "Tell that to women and children," *that the infinite soul can only work through them in already ascertained limits*; that the gift of reason, man's highest prerogative, is allowed to them in much lower degree; that they must be kept from mischief and melancholy by being constantly engaged in active labor, which is to be furnished and directed by those better able to think, &c. &c.[62]

Fuller draws attention to the fact that for men—and she does not exempt her many male transcendentalist friends here, including Emerson, with whom she founded the *Dial* and with whom she had a number of epistolary battles about gender politics—there were limits to women's access to the oversoul.[63] Indeed, she implies that in an American public culture dominated by men, there were ingrained sexist assumptions about women's inferiority, irrationality, and immaturity that marked the female soul as inferior to a man's. That, in the minds of men, women had at best but imperfect access to divine revelations. That, in short, in the minds of men, women could touch infinity only through "already ascertained limits." Fuller here raises a serious ethical concern about Emerson's rhetoric of oneness and his vision of communication as yoga. Indeed, she suggests that the rhetoric of oneness might well be just another gendered rhetoric of oppression wrapped up in fancy metaphysical garlands.

When I first read this passage in *Woman in the Nineteenth Century*, I was gobsmacked. How could anyone think that a person's access to the divine would be limited by their gender? On further reflection and after much contemplation, I now realize that I should have been gobsmacked at the fact that I was gobsmacked by Fuller's words, not at the words themselves. Of course the rhetorics of oneness would be colored by patriarchal assumptions, because almost all rhetorics in American history are colored by patriarchal assumptions! Why would oneness be any different? And once Fuller pointed it out, I saw the very thing she saw, that damning assumption in the minds of men about the "limits" of women, at play in Emerson's "The Over-Soul." In this essay Emerson repeatedly speaks of "man" and uses the masculine pronouns: "Ineffable is the union of man and God in every act of the soul. The simplest person, who in his integrity worships God, becomes God; yet for ever and ever the influx of this better and universal self is new and unsearchable."[64] Could Emerson really be thinking only of men here? He never explicitly argues that women are excluded from divine revelation, but he never says that they are included, either. Moreover, his vision of interpersonal conversation—which he explores in his essay "Friendship," and which he argues in "The Over-Soul" is one path to the experience of divine oneness through the practice of communication as yoga—*is* gender exclusive. For Emerson, conversation and friendship happen between men. Both practices are characterized by exclusively "manly" virtues.[65] Conversation between friends "treats its object as a god, that it may deify both"—but what if it deifies men exclusively?[66]

Here is one place where I judge Whitman's vision of communication as yoga light years ahead of Emerson's. Whitman is explicit that women are equal to men. As he writes in "Starting from Paumanok," a poetic introduction to the major themes of *Leaves of Grass*: "And I will show of male and female that either is but the equal of the other."[67] During the 1850s Whitman became good friends with several prominent women's rights activists, including Abby Hills Price, Paulina Kellogg Wright Davis, and Ernestine L. Rose; and in *Democratic Vistas*, his post–Civil War treatment of democratic theory, he prophesied that the success, or failure, of women's rights would prove the ultimate success, or failure, of democracy itself: "Democracy, in silence, biding its time, ponders its own ideals, not of literature and art only—not of men only, but of women."[68] Women are not sideshow characters in Whitman's poetry. Women are real, embodied beings, with dreams and desires that are equal in worth to men's.

Whitman espouses sexual equality. He envisions a time when women will be liberated from oppressive Victorian attitudes toward the body.[69] His poetry extols men and women "raised to become the robust equals," but this will only happen, he testifies, when "the idea of the women of America" is "extricated from this daze, this fossil and unhealthy air which hangs about the word *lady*."[70] In the land of *The Scarlet Letter*, long has sex been synonymous with sin; Whitman rejects such prudery, which he associates with an aristocratic European genteel culture that had no place in an America forging its own unique democratic future. When a number of mostly male critics denounced the 1860 version of *Leaves of Grass* for shocking indecency and Whitman for peddling sexually explicit filth, a number of prominent women spoke out in his defense.[71] Whitman dreamed of sexual liberation; he also demanded equality for women in the occupations in which they were most likely to suffer from invisible, everyday oppression in a patriarchal society like the United States:

> The wife, and she is not one joy less than the husband,
> The daughter, and she is just as good as the son,
> The mother, and she is every bit as much as the father.[72]

The divine oneness does not exclude any genders, races, or sexualities—Whitman rhapsodizes a "spirituality" and "theology" that is common to "humankind" (and not just "mankind"); his is a oneness of "the All" that rests on "the idea of All."[73] This rich, magnanimous allness excludes no one, and in his poems, women have just as much access to the divine as men. Whitman's practice of communication as yoga can and ought to happen when *any* two or more people converse, no matter their gender, their race, or their sexuality.

Whitman's poetry is inclusive and cosmic in a way that Emerson's rhetoric is not. He creates space for love in many forms. His democratic poems celebrating male friendship, especially the "Calamus" poems, are queer poems of love between comrades:

> Yet underneath Socrates clearly see, and underneath Christ the divine I see,
> The dear love of man for his comrade, the attraction of friend to friend,
> Of the well-married husband and wife, of children and parents,
> Of city for city and land for land.[74]

Many of Whitman's queer admirers in both the United States and England read phrases like "the dear love of man for his comrade" as a "textual wink," a rhetorical nod to them in coded language that his straight readers would likely miss, a subtle acknowledgment that he saw them and loved them, for he was one of them, too.[75] Whitman never married, and historians agree that he was queer—a 1997 biography by Gary Schmidgall is titled *Walt Whitman: A Gay Life*, and John Marsh's 2015 study is titled *In Walt We Trust: How a Queer Socialist Poet Can Save America from Itself*.[76] Whitman's English readers, including Edward Carpenter and Oscar Wilde, "thrilled to his ennobling portrayal of male love as an island of purity amid the moral filth of the larger world," and Carpenter in particular cited Whitman frequently in his activist writings calling for an expansive, vibrant, open democracy that actively embraced love of all forms.[77] Whitman is the champion of true democracy, for he recognizes that exclusivity destroys democracy. Democracy dies at the hand of beliefs or politics or stereotypes that prevent people from joining the ensemble because of who they are or who they love. Democracy must always strive toward oneness, which for Whitman means striving toward inclusion and allness.

In *Leaves of Grass*, Whitman follows Emerson's advice in "The Over-Soul" to treat every conversation as an opportunity to address the divinity in others. Emerson's essay, I argued in the previous chapter, is a significant touchstone in American thought because it democratized the Bhagavad Gita's doctrine of the divine avatar. Rather than worship Krishna or any one avatar of the divine allness, Emerson calls on his readers to worship all people as though they are avatars of the divine. Whitman further democratizes Emerson's democratization of the Bhagavad Gita's doctrine of the avatar by insisting that everyone is equal—no matter their gender, their sexuality, or, as we will see in the following two chapters, their race—in their capacity to see and know and speak to the divine. Whitman puts no limits (which are arbitrary anyway, derived from social convention) on who is and is not included in the all. Everyone is included in the ensemble. Cosmos embraces all.

In *Leaves of Grass*, Whitman describes his daily meditation as he sonders around Manhattan and Brooklyn:

> Why should I wish to see God better than this day?
> I see something of God each hour of the twenty-four, and each moment then,
> In the faces of men and women I see God, and in my own face in the glass;
> I find letters from God dropt in the street, and every one is sign'd by God's name,
> And I leave them where they are, for I know that wheresoe'er I go,
> Others will punctually come for ever and ever.[78]

This is one of the most beautiful passages in Whitman's long poem, and it has been the subject of much scholarly commentary. I interpret this passage differently than does the communication scholar John Durham Peters. There is much wisdom to be found in Peters's erudite book *Speaking into the Air: A History of the Idea of Communication* (1999), but I differ from him on how best to interpret this passage. Peters's general thesis is that Western culture is much too enthralled with Platonic images of dialogue, and so we judge all forms of communication as if two or more people are talking in person. And yet most communication takes the form not of Socrates sitting on the agora steps or under the shade of a plane tree talking with his interlocutors, but of dissemination—of seeds scattered in the wind, to use the model of communication from the synoptic Gospels that Peters prefers. Communication is rarely about me saying something and you responding; instead, it is about me broadcasting messages of longing into the world and waiting, often with longing, anxiety, and a twinge of agony, for a response that might never come.[79]

This passage from Whitman's *Leaves of Grass* is significant for Peters, then, because it mentions letters dropped in the street, not people talking face to face. Through this passage and a few brief comments on Emerson, Peters concludes that the American transcendentalists transcended the assumption that the best communication is face-to-face communication. Whitman, he expostulates, overcomes the dialogic need to "restrict the reception of a message to one recipient," and does not fall prey to "the pathologies unique to the person-to-person ideal" of communication.[80] "Whitman expresses the older wisdom of dissemination: a letter written to one is written to all," Peters insists.[81] Peters reads Whitman as a fellow liberal (on a par with St. Augustine and John Locke) who believes in an isolated, distinct self cut off from the world, struggling to make his ideas known to a public that might well misunderstand.[82] While Whitman recognizes the dangers of "miscommunication" and the possibility that a message might get lost in the mail, he doesn't care—and Peters applauds him for his daring commitment "to live ethically and joyously without any assurance of secure channels."[83]

Of course, Whitman does mention walking around the city streets seeing letters to God dropped in the street, which sounds like pamphlets dropped—disseminated—from a dirigible flying high over head, audience nonspecific and unknown, addressed to one and all. That is indeed one way to imagine a rhetoric of oneness: as a general message to a universal audience. I think that's an exceedingly weak rhetoric, however, and it's certainly not Whitman's poetic project, which is much more intimate than Peters acknowledges—more intimate, in fact, than liberal political theorists convinced that people are ontologically isolated from the world and psychically isolated from each other probably *can* acknowledge. Whitman's message is universal, but it is also interpersonal. Democracy happens in relationships. So, too, does enlightenment. This is the secret to Whitman's ethics of oneness: oneness should guide our interactions with others, and if it doesn't, then it has little value, even if it is the truth.

What matters most for Whitman is not that there are letters from God dropped in the street. There are letters from God everywhere, little reminders and tokens of oneness all over the place, if only we learn how to spot them. What matters most to Whitman is what we do with the oneness we find when we meditate. What matters most, in short, is how we express oneness in our interpersonal interactions, how we let oneness guide our relationships with others. Cosmic consciousness is not something that can be broadcast from loudspeakers. It is found in the quiet, intimate moments between me and you and us, in the junctures where bodies meet and voices intermingle and the cicadas hum in the background. Time and time again, Whitman's poetry describes his communicative interactions with friends and strangers.

His poetry is not Platonic dialectic, with questions and answers leading the participants toward the transcendence of a higher truth; but it is not a social media post written for whoever might read it, either. What is significant about this passage from *Leaves of Grass* is the way of looking at the world that Whitman models for his readers. The street scene is an opportunity to practice yogic meditation, the single-minded focus on the divinity of all things. Notice that Whitman mentions seeing God in every hour of the day, in the faces of the men and women he meets, and in his own face, too. The letters dropped from God in the street are not "dead letters"—how could they be? They are reminders of oneness amid the hustle and bustle of city life, and Whitman leaves them lying there on the ground without longing or agony, but with absolute certainty that they will be well received by other spiritual seekers, others who are on the path toward rapport. In this passage, Whitman models what it means to practice communication as yoga.

I read this luminescent passage in two ways, as report and advice. Whitman recounts his own experience of the world, and in the process he models for his readers how they might experience the world. He describes his own spiritual practice of addressing the divine in others when he speaks to them—this is communication as yoga. In his poetry, he reminds his readers that they, too, can engage with others this way. He disseminates a message of oneness in print in order to promote a recognition of oneness in dialogue. Like the letters dropped in the street, he drops letters on the page as a reminder that his readers need not experience the world as a place of division and hatred, as they are habituated to do. Hatred is just as much a habit as love; why should we judge the one inevitable, the other a luxury? Why make hatred our cultural baseline? Whitman's poetry resounds with the soothing message that it is possible to experience the world differently than we are accustomed to. Finding a letter dropped in the street might jolt a person out of autopilot (or what rhetorical scholars call *doxa*, our common, habitual ways of going about our days). Whitman's words, too, jolt—this is how his poetry works, in jolts and bolts of lightning insight. Democratic rhetoric is often addressed to the aspects of people that are the weakest and ugliest, to their resentment, hatred, and greed. Whitman models a very different way of interpersonally engaging with others. In his poetry, he addresses the part of people that is capable of love, affection, and gratefulness, the part that reaches out for connection and identification and cooperation, the expansive part that recognizes the beauty and wonder of existence.

After experiencing cosmic consciousness, Whitman reports feeling a divine oneness without boundary or limitation. The trouble, for him (and for all mystics), is to translate this experience of oneness into language, which is inherently dualistic. In his poetry, Whitman attempts to do what many philosophers deem impossible—to describe a universal community without division, a solidarity that does not exclude, a friendship without an enemyship, an us without a them.[84] Most philosophers believe that all talk of oneness will inevitably lead to division, for all pictures of "us" also create an excluded "them." The most common metaphors for human community are based in blood or family; these metaphors are more elemental than modern patriotic metaphors like the nation or the flag that serve much the same function. The elemental metaphors of blood and family are rhetorically powerful in large measure because they are exclusive. It is "our" heritage, "our" blood, "our" family, not "yours." It is only natural, when we talk of sharing the same blood or of being kith and kin, to look askance, with suspicion and perhaps hostility, on those who do not share our blood or who are not part of the family. This is the first step along the path to enemyship, to tribalism, to xenophobia, to jingoism, to know-nothingism, to violence, to war.

Can the elemental communal metaphors be saved? It might be possible to extend these metaphors to include more and more people, making them less exclusionary and more universal. But at some point, these metaphors get stretched to the breaking point and lose their power, because this power is derived from a sense of belonging to something that others are banned from. Rather than admit defeat and resign himself to a restrictive democracy committed to enemyship, Whitman shifts the conversation away from *theory* toward *practice*, from attempting to craft a message that will appeal to a universal audience toward modeling how his readers might forge better relationships with the people they encounter as they go about their days. It bears repeating: democracy happens in relationships, and it is by changing our relationships that we will save democracy (or let it perish). Whitman illustrates a truly local democracy in his poetry, suggesting that democracy is found in how we engage with the people we meet every day.

It is easy enough to talk about exclusion on a theoretical level, though it is undoubtedly true that the history of democracy, like the history of humanity more generally, proves the timeless lure of enemyship.[85] The human mind seems primed to divide the world into friends and enemies. Perhaps this is rooted in a survival instinct inherited from our distant evolutionary past. However, this tendency toward division, toward suspicion, toward disbelief and distrust is a blueprint for disaster in the contemporary world of massive armies and efficient killing machines. Whitman knew this well, having lived through the Civil War. He recognized that the only place individuals can confidently intervene in democratic culture is in our interpersonal relationships. That to which we devote ourselves has a way of becoming real for us. And so Whitman models how to devote ourselves to oneness in our relationships. This devotion is not abstract or intellectual. It is real and practical: it involves addressing everyone he meets as divine, to see the divine in his most intimate friends, in total strangers, and even in those who treated him like an enemy.

Whitman repeatedly addresses friends and enemies and strangers alike as "brothers" and "sisters."[86] In his poetry, these terms are not exclusionary. He does not create a boundary between family and nonfamily, those who are kin and those who are not. Everyone is kin in the moment of address. Whitman stretches words such as *brother* and *sister* to their breaking point, but in his poetry they do not break, because his poetry is a record of hundreds, even thousands of interpersonal interactions that accumulate to form a life and a lifetime printed on the page. It could be argued that Whitman tackles one democratic dilemma by inviting another. Indeed, many philosophers assert that rhetorics of oneness are dangerous because they tend to erase difference by demanding that everyone look, act, and speak the same.[87] Though he calls on his readers to devote themselves to oneness as democracy's ontological foundation, Whitman avoids this potential trap of oneness. Devoted to cosmos, "the diverse shall be no less diverse, but they shall flow and unite—they unite now."[88] In Whitman's poetry, devotion to oneness acts as the ground on which citizens can stand together when it comes time to argue, to judge, to debate, and to draw the lines that make politics work.

Whitman models how a person devoted to oneness manages difference by making space for everyone in his poetry—people who the grandest poets of his day, Wordsworth and Longfellow, would never think of addressing in their odes. Whitman plays no games of normal and abnormal. "Rejecting none, permitting all,"[89] runaway slaves, prostitutes, farmers, mothers, children, dockworkers, common workers, the deformed and the sick, the poor and destitute—all have their place at the table, for all are embodied gods; all souls are avatars of the all in unique clothing.

> This is the meal pleasantly set . . . this is the meat and drink for natural hunger,
> It is for the wicked just the same as the righteous . . . I make appointments with all,
> I will not have a single person slighted or left away,
> The keptwoman and sponger and thief are hereby invited . . . the heavy lipped slave is invited . . . the venerealee is invited,
> There shall be no difference between them and the rest.[90]

Whitman's famous (or for many literary critics, infamous) catalogues in "Song of Myself" draw the motley characters he meets together into a community. The similar grammatical structure of these lists keep them from being random collections of disconnected characters. The lists serve an equalizing function, bringing the high level with the low, rich with poor, men with women, white with black, North with South, East with West. Whitman's lists invert common social hierarchies by emphasizing the divine unity underlining diversity. He envisions deeper ties binding people than blood, tradition, or ancestry—concepts that can, under the right circumstances, fuel rhetorical division. Oneness excludes no one, for oneness encompasses all. To practice communication as yoga means affirming the divine interconnectedness of all beings, and then letting this affirmation guide speech and action. It means addressing all audiences and all beings with the dignity due to gods.

The Poet of Gratefulness

According to William James, Whitman's poetry is dominated by the emotions of *ontic wonder* and *existential gladness*. His words shine "with his own love of comrades, with his own gladness that he and they exist."[91] When James says "gladness," I hear "gratefulness."

I say gratefulness, and not gratitude, because for most of Western history, gratitude has been closely associated with indebtedness.[92] The contemporary positive psychologist Robert Emmons observes that to be grateful "is to feel indebted."[93] Gratitude is "an acknowledgement of debt."[94] Though the exchange of gifts and debts is often assumed to be the foundation of human community, such exchange, I argue in my book *The Art of Gratitude*, is a cancer eating away at the health of democratic communities, for it transforms gratitude into an economic exchange that tends to nurture anger and resentment in those who are put in debt.[95] Drawing us into an economic logic of compensation, tit for tat, quid pro quo, the debt of gratitude makes life a transaction and as such cannot put us in the right frame of mind to experience oneness, which is why Whitman recognizes no debts in his poetry. Gratefulness, in contrast, is the emotional experience of being moved by thanksgiving for the miracle of life, and Whitman repeatedly invokes this emotion because it is most closely associated in the mystical traditions with insight into divine oneness.[96] Gratefulness points toward an embodied existential earthly ethics.

I can think of no literary text that dramatizes the dangers inherent to a culture of indebtedness better than the Mahabharata. The authors of this Indian epic were interested in how gratitude becomes weaponized, and this is a theme that Krishna also discusses in the Bhagavad Gita. At times, Krishna presents the battle at Kurukshetra as God's plan, but the Mahabharata makes it clear that the war is in fact the product a cascade of bad decisions and miscalculations made by characters against their own interests and the interests of a common good because of various debts of gratitude they assume. Duryodhana—the firstborn Kaurava son, Arjuna's cousin, and the five Pandava brothers' primary antagonist—is a master at controlling others through patronage. By bestowing his immense inherited wealth upon his fellows, he wins their allegiance in return. He is like a mob boss: one good turn deserves another is his motto. During his youth, Duryodhana began preparing for the inevitable conflict over succession with the Pandava brothers by establishing an army of supporters bound to him by obligations born from gifts given:

> . . . he was busy
> weaving a network of alliances,
> a secret coterie made up of men
> bound to him by ties of obligation;
> men of ill will, who felt themselves shut out
> from the gilded circle of the Pandavas.[97]

He successfully ensnared a number of prominent figures in his net, including the family patriarch (Bhishma) and the family's primary combat teacher (Drona). In the midst of a heated deliberation about the shrewdness of a preemptive war with their cousins, Arjuna's brother and the rightful king Yudhishthira reflects that Duryodhana had grown mighty through the imposition of a series of debts of gratitude:

> Think—his wealth is almost without limit.
> Many kings who bowed to us before
> are now rallying to Duryodhana.
> Our cousin has distributed such wealth
> and privileges that he is surrounded
> by strong allies. Bhishma, Drona and Krupa,
> although they love us equally, are conscious
> of whose food they are eating. In this end,
> their skill and their celestial weapons will be
> deployed in the service of Duryodhana.[98]

Having some familiarity with the Mahabharata and being an astute student of Western philosophy, Emerson recognized the problem with the debt of gratitude in his essay "Gifts": "It is not the office of a man to receive gifts. How dare you give them? We wish to be self-sustained. We do not quite forgive a giver."[99] A giver is not to be forgiven, because with the gift comes a debt that binds. And, indeed, in many yoga traditions, one of the basic spiritual practices is *aparigraha*, which is often translated as "not grasping" or "not possessing" but which can also mean something like "self-reliance." Swami Vivekananda explained in *Raja Yoga* (1896):

> Not receiving any present from anybody, even when one is suffering terribly, is what is called Aparigraha. The idea is, when a man receives a gift from another, his heart becomes impure, he becomes low, he loses his independence, he becomes bound and attached.[100]

It is easy to take *aparigraha* too far and deny the basic reality of human interconnectedness—indeed, this is a problem with many yogic traditions, which seek a kind of independence from material reality that is impossible. But the impulse here is a good one that, it seems to me, aligns with an actionable ethics of oneness—not to be drawn into debt relationships with others that will force us to act as though the world is not one. Indeed, while many philosophers and sociologists argue that the exchange of gifts and debts is the glue that holds all communities together, from the perspective of Whitmanism, such relationships are deeply problematic when they become exclusionary, unequal, and exploitative.

The Bhagavad Gita has much to say about gratitude.[101] You can tell a lot about a person's character, and their rapport with oneness, by how they give to others. Krishna singles out charity as an opportunity to practice an ethics of oneness, and he demands that Arjuna reconsider what it means to be grateful as part of his yogic training. There are those who give not out of charity (*dana*) but from a destructive desire for domination over others. Like Duryodhana, these people use their tremendous wealth to throw parties, put on festivals, and stage rituals—not for the good of the community, but to increase their fame and renown.[102] They give, not to benefit others, but to control, to enslave, to own them.[103] Like Duryodhana, these people view gratitude as an instrument of power. In contrast, Krishna prompts Arjuna to look at life in the context of the whole, and to understand that the quality of one life cannot be detached from the quality of all lives. Arjuna must recognize a common goodness rooted in the divine oneness of being, and give without hope of return, for the benefit of all.

In the traditions of the Bhagavad Gita and Plato and the Stoics, spiritual practice is concerned largely with emotion. This is because we humans see the world through the lens of our emotions. The world does not look the same to us when we are angry and when we are grateful. Our feelings are, first and foremost, somatic.[104] As we are affected through our five (or for many yogis, six) senses by others and the world, we feel; contemporary scholars designate these feelings as "affect." Affect is extradiscursive: it exceeds representation. And yet people make sense of the somatic experience of affect by labeling it with the language of emotion. Emotion provides us with a language for processing and attempting to shape how we feel. While it is true that emotion tries to capture something that is uncapturable about the body, and that affect always troubles the labels we put on it, nevertheless, how we label and describe our affective experiences of the world can shape these experiences.[105] Cultivating an emotion means using rhetoric to reframe the experience of being affected by the world.

Whitman is the poet of gratefulness. He observes that life itself is good, and so long as people are alive, they need not despair, for they can find happiness and freedom from suffering.[106]

> It seems to me that everything in the light and air ought to be happy;
> Whoever is not in his coffin and the dark grave, let him know he has enough.[107]

Gratefulness is an emotion of contentment . . .

> I exist as I am, that is enough,
> If no other in the world be aware I sit content,
> And if each and all be aware I sit content.[108]

. . . but it is not a feeling of isolation. *Leaves of Grass* is an inventory of all the people, places, things, and activities that make Whitman grateful. The "I" that speaks is not self-contained or cut off from the world (as liberalism imagines the individual to be); it is deeply interconnected with the world (though not identical to it). Whitman's "I" and his "you" are physically and spiritually connected—"for every atom belonging to me as good belongs to you"—because both are composed from the divine oneness.[109] This fact makes Whitman happy. He reports feeling gratefulness, appreciation, gladness for everyone he meets, for they, like him, are divine, and they, like him, are born from and embraced by the all.

Whitman's poetry deifies people but deconstructs the liberal individual, who, according to philosophers including Thomas Hobbes and John Locke, comes into the world fully formed and ready-made, apart from society and the world, and whose job is to gain as much property as he might possess, for his worth is proved by his wealth.[110] With his epic lists of motley characters, with his vibrant, tactile talk of clothes and shoes and food, with his description of houses and other dwelling places, with his warm words about the earth, Whitman radically reimagines what it means to be an individual: an individual is never self-made, and wealth proves nothing. To be an individual is to be supported, because life is not possible without assistance. Delving deeply and honestly into biology or history (two of Whitman's favorite subjects), we quickly realize that true autonomy is impossible. The living need help—the aid of the sun and everything that grows from its beneficence, the aid of cooling rains and the rivers that bring water down from the mountains, the aid of the bacteria that colonize our bellies and digest our food for us, the aid of antibodies that fight off disease, the aid of friends and family and benefactors and educators and laborers who provide laughter and education and muscle. This does not make us weak; it makes us human.

Whitman's practice of gratefulness in *Leaves of Grass* involves recognizing and delineating the many forms of help, obvious and invisible, that allow him to live his life. Americans are not habituated to doing this. We are good at cataloguing our possessions, but bad at noticing the props that keep us upright. Astutely, Whitman asks: "Shall I make my list of things in the house and skip the house that supports them?"[111] Whitman is determined not to skip the house—the house, here, symbolizing the buttressing that supports life and everyday democracy. The house, in short, is the all. In *Leaves of Grass*, living a life of oneness means recognizing that as individuals we are deeply interconnected with other humans and the rest of the natural world. I think Whitman cultivates gratefulness more than any other emotion because this emotion naturally leads toward a worldview that emphasizes connection. Looking at the world through grateful eyes, it is easier to focus on that which supports us and to notice our inherent ontological interconnectedness with the world we inhabit. Through grateful eyes, we see that we are a part of, and not apart from, the all.

The Advaita Vedanta interpretation of the Bhagavad Gita dominated American engagement with Indian philosophy during the nineteenth century, but it was not the only Indian spiritual tradition that Americans were exposed to. During the late nineteenth century, Buddhism also became popular, especially after the publication of Edwin Arnold's free verse poem *The Light of Asia; Or, The Great Renunciation: Being the Life and Teaching of Gautama, Prince of India and Founder of Buddhism*. First published in London in 1879, it was reprinted in Boston in 1880 and went on to sell between five hundred thousand and one million copies in the United States.[112] Arnold's book was no doubt so popular because it emphasized the striking parallels between the lives of Shakyamuni Buddha and Jesus Christ, and indeed, Americans came to know Buddhism as just one more expression of the perennial philosophy. The *philosophia perennis* highlights eternal questions concerning the human condition. The trouble with perennialist thinking is that it has a tendency to erase what is distinctive about a particular religious or spiritual tradition.[113]

Both Emerson and Whitman's philosophies are true to the Bhagavad Gita in that they are soteriological. They aim at a particular goal—call it rapport or enthusiasm or cosmic consciousness or enlightenment—and they invite people to change their lives by talking up the value of this goal, which will ease suffering, promote happiness, and nurture love. Though many forms of yogic meditation are influenced profoundly by Buddhism, Buddhist meditation tends not to be so directive. In the Buddhist practices of "mindfulness" that have become popular today, meditation is about nurturing the human capacity for present-minded, nonjudgmental awareness of things as they are.[114] When practicing mindfulness, a person does not attempt to still the mind, but instead notices the stillness that already exists below thought and the noisy mind. Mindfulness does not judge or attempt to fit experiences into a narrative or a literary form. It is not captured by memory or projection. Instead, it is about noticing what is happening right now, whatever that might be. When Whitman talks about his appreciation for other animals, he, too, models a mindful way of engaging with the world:

> I think I could turn and live with animals, they are so placid and self-contain'd,
> I stand and look at them long and long.
>
> They do not sweat and whine about their condition,
> They do not lie awake in the dark and weep for their sins,
> They do not make me sick discussing their duty to God,
> Not one is dissatisfied, not one is demented with the mania of owning things,
> Not one kneels to another, nor to his kind that lived thousands of years ago,
> Not one is respectable or unhappy over the whole earth.
>
> So they show their relations to me and I accept them,
> They bring me tokens of myself, they evince them plainly in their possession.[115]

Whitman admires other animals because they are not beholden to the past or conditioned by stories about how they should act or who they should be. They do not know capitalism or consumption or possession. They simply are. Sitting with the other animals, noticing how they walk on the earth, Whitman is able to shake off one of the great lies of human culture, that humans are separate from other animals and the earth and are in fact their masters. These animals bring him "tokens" of himself; they reveal their fundamental kinship by reminding him of a quiet side of himself long neglected. One consequence of mindfulness meditation is that people begin to notice and appreciate the interconnectedness of life, its "interbeing."[116] And the feeling that is most often awakened by simply sitting with things as they are? Gratefulness. In this emotional state, Whitman attests, it becomes possible to recognize that we are not alone, that we are in fact incarnations of the divine, that we are at one with the universe and interconnected with all living beings.

Whitman's poetry exudes existential gratefulness. He is grateful for his own existence and for the existence of everyone, because the existence of "I" and "you" is intertwined. Whitman reminds us that life itself is good, even if our lives are not. He focuses on what he has—lungs to breathe, feet to walk, a mouth to laugh and talk and sing and argue—and then looks on the world with gratefulness for how it supports his embodied being and yours, too. The world does not discriminate; it gives freely to all. It is people who discriminate. Whitman's gratefulness is an ontological emotion, because it concerns being. He does not see people as the givers and bearers of debt, but as collaborators in building a common life committed to oneness. Whitman addresses his audience as divine by repeatedly expressing how glad and grateful he is that his fellows exist, how much he is in love with them:

> We thought our Union grand and our Constitution grand;
> I do not say that they are not grand and good—for they are,
> I am this day just as much in love with them as you,
> But I am eternally in love with you and with all my fellows upon the earth.[117]

Such gratefulness does not stop with people. Whitman expresses gratefulness for plants and animals and the natural world around him, which also collaborate in the ensemble that composes this great mysterious baffling thing we call life. For Whitman, gratefulness is an emotional pathway to oneness.

Soteriology

Whitman's poetry models an unabashed devotion to an ontology of oneness. In *Leaves of Grass*, he extends a hand to his readers, calling them friends, comrades, "camerados," and he bids them to join him in his commitment:

> Camerado, I give you my hand!
> I give you my love more precious than money,
> I give you myself before preaching or law;
> Will you give me yourself? will you come travel with me?
> Shall we stick by each other as long as we live?[118]

Whitman's poetry at times reads like a travelogue, documenting his journeys into the world and the mystical beyond. In "Song of the Open Road," Whitman invites his readers to imagine the universe as a road and a highway. Repeating the cry of "Allons!"—"let's go!"—Whitman urges us to travel hand in hand with him on a cosmic journey around the broad circle of the world, through past and present and into the future, through misery and joy, through war and peace, to find a truth that cannot be pinned down in words, a truth beyond mocking and discouragement, a truth that will set us free:

> Allons! whoever you are come travel with me!
> Traveling with me you find what never tires.
> The earth never tires,
> The earth is rude, silent, incomprehensible at first, Nature is rude and
> incomprehensible at first,
> Be not discouraged, keep on, there are divine things well envelop'd,
> I swear to you there are divine things more beautiful than words can tell.[119]

When he swears like this—and in his enthusiasm Whitman often utters such full-throated vows—he speaks from experience about a freedom, a joy, a divinity that is just out of reach but that can, with small changes, be touched. Whitman never offers a step-by-step guide to rapport. What he does in his poetry is model what it means to live a life committed to oneness, the type of life that prepared him for his achievement of cosmic consciousness. To describe this life is also to create an alluring picture of human potential, and Whitman repeatedly tempts his readers with this possibility in his poems. Whitman's poetry is inspired by the idea that if people take him by his hand and actively devote themselves, like he does, to oneness in language, they will begin to the see the world as though it is one (because in reality it is). A spiritual change follows a change in rhetorical habit. Talk differently, he suggests, and the world will be different. Infinity is but a few god terms away.

But to most of us, as we are right now, infinity is off limits because of how we have chosen to live our lives—because of our "frivolous sullen moping angry affected disheartened atheistical" ways.[120] The transcendentalists recognized that most people, most of the time, habitually accommodate themselves to public opinion and the truths of *doxa*, or convention. This is what Emerson rebelled against in his famous essay "Self-Reliance": *truth as veridiction*, people bowing down to expectation, convention, and public opinion.[121] Whitman likewise flouts unthinking habit. He insists that it is possible to challenge, and defeat, the rule of convention. It is possible to break from social norms and fashion a new self, a new way of living, in line with a new truth. Indeed, if we did not have the capacity to change our behaviors, *the capacity to be otherwise*, then morality and responsibility would be metaphysically impossible. This is why Kant calls it a "metaphysics" of morality—if humans did not possess some degree of freedom and autonomy, some ability to reflect on their actions and say yes, this is right, or no, this is not right, then morality would be nonsensical, just another type of cruel optimism.[122] And, indeed, for Whitman the individual is real and autonomous in the sense that they have the capacity to change their lives, but this autonomy is developed in and through communication and community with others. We exist as a part of the world, not apart from it, and our sense of who we are as individuals is a constant negotiation with the world we live in. We become individuals by reflecting on our reactions to the world and, perhaps, by determining to act differently in the future. This capacity for autonomous reflection on our place in the interconnected world is what individuality means.

It is not yet clear what we shall be. As individuals we could always be different than we are now. But why would we want to be different? To change is hard work; it is much easier to submit to routine. What is the motivation for undertaking the hard work of spiritual practice? Why on earth would anyone look deeply into their present conditioning (what in the yogic traditions is called *samskara*) and attempt to change their ways of relating to the world? Because they believe that such a change will bring happiness, joy, tranquility, and, ultimately, salvation. The motivation to change one's art of living is *soteriological.* One does not undertake the extreme discipline of spiritual practice for its own sake.[123] Spiritual practice is the means to realizing salvation in this life (and not the next).[124] The promise of salvation—the promise that suffering might end and that happiness might be found, after so many years of frustrated pursuit—offers people the motivation for spiritual practice.

I have spoken about Whitman's rhetoric in this chapter, but of course his poetry is not rhetorical in the conventional sense. In the preface to the first edition of *Leaves of Grass*, published in 1855, he explains the poet's vocation:

> He is no arguer . . . he is judgment.
> He judges not as the judge judges but as the sun falling around a helpless thing.[125]

Whitman's primary purpose is not to persuade. His poetry records what delights him, what touches and revolts him, what gives him pause and inspires wonder. Generally, he does not plead or shout or coax. He does not argue for or justify his divine vision. He simply bears witness to the experience of the all, and in the process of bearing witness and recreating this experience in language, he invites his readers to have the same experience. Whitman rarely makes demands of or petitions his readers, telling them directly what to do or how to behave. However, there is a motivational logic behind his words. Whitman speaks of the joy and peace found in cosmic consciousness in order to inspire his readers to that state, and he then models one way to live a life devoted to oneness. The many tempting pictures of emancipated experience that Whitman sprinkles throughout his poetry are inspirational—they are meant to cheer his readers toward the path to enlightenment.

How Whitman portrays the end goal of cosmic consciousness is important, for he makes it so alluring that it might inspire his readers to undertake a spiritual change. Equally important about Whitman's poetry is how he models what it means to live a life committed to oneness. If his readers begin speaking with the god terms of oneness, if they begin practicing communication as yoga, if they begin to cultivate gratefulness rather than many of the more common democratic emotions, and—as we will see in the next chapter—if they begin to practice the deification of the body, they may or may not experience cosmic consciousness, but they will certainly contribute to the larger project of recreating the ontological truth of oneness in the contingent human world of action and desire.

All mystical traditions aim at a fundamental change in being. In many traditions, this change is sudden, like a flash of lightning. For Whitman, the change is more gradual, like water smoothing a stone. As people walk the procession toward the all, they gain new freedoms found in the form of an enriched ethical capacity for awareness and reflection. They learn how to look deeply at their own conditioned patterns of responding to the world, and how to bring a change to their lives so that they are not mere vessels for the inherited traumas and biases and stereotypes and errors of their culture. Whitman aspired to create a religion of democracy. I will describe Whitman's vision of democracy in more detail in chapter 6, but for now it is worth noting that on the question of democracy, Whitman is clear: democracy is enriched by anyone who pursues cosmic consciousness, *even if that consciousness never comes*. By working toward cosmic consciousness and living a life devoted to oneness, people gain the peace and freedom that Whitman describes as following from cosmic consciousness—even if this experience never happens. Rapport is won slowly, gradually, over time, in conversation with others; in life, not apart from it.

3

Bodies

Our everyday experience of the world as a place of diversity and variety is the most persuasive counterargument to a philosophy of oneness. It is said that we can never step into the same river twice, and indeed, the world appears to be constantly changing. Travel outside your narrow bubble and you will invariably meet people with different customs who speak a different language and who live different lives with different priorities. How can reality be one when difference is so clear, so omnipresent, so real? This is a metaphysical problem, and also an ethical challenge. In this chapter, I argue that, to be ethical, philosophies of oneness must treat difference as a *reality* and not an *illusion*. To make my case, I put Emerson and Whitman in dialogue on the question of the body. At times, both Emerson and Whitman waxed poetic about the immortality of the soul and flirted with doctrines of reincarnation.[1] Both taught an American Vedanta. But on the question of the body, they arrived at vastly different positions that illustrate the radically divergent possibilities for how a person might live a life committed to oneness.

After the publication of *Essays: First Series*, Emerson's philosophy grew more severe in its insistence that material reality is identical to the oversoul; this is the position of Advaita (nondualistic) Vedanta. Because the individual soul is equivalent to the universal oversoul, the body becomes irrelevant to Emerson. Death is an illusion. When dealing with death, it can be helpful to become a philosophical idealist, as Emerson claimed to, and say clearly, with otherworldly serenity and no tremble in your voice, that death is not real, that no one really dies, that the soul is immortal and the body just old clothes that are cast aside when they are no longer needed. But when building an actionable ethics of oneness, death must be real, and it must make us tremble and weep, or else life itself can cease to matter. A oneness that denies the divinity of the body or that downplays the sacredness of the individual is a powerful justification for violence and slaughter. This means that philosophers of oneness must sing the body electric, as Whitman does.

Indeed, in his poetry Whitman repeatedly bears witness to the physical body, treating it as an embodiment of divinity that is both the same and not the same as the oversoul. Whitman denies the dualism between body and soul so common in Western philosophy. He deifies the body as a manifestation of divine oneness that is also unique and special. Advaita Vedanta teaches that the body is an illusion; Whitman rejects this premise, adopting a position much closer to Bhedabheda (identity-in-difference) Vedanta. This school of Vedanta recognizes the reality of the material world and contends that while the individual, with body and soul, is a manifestation of the divine, it is not equal to the divine but is somehow unique. Bodies are real, they are divine, they are sacred, they can die—and when they do, something real is lost. This leads Whitman to an ethics of oneness that seeks to enrich and emancipate bodies. As I read Whitman on the divine body, I daydream about how different the Bhagavad Gita would read if Krishna, too, sang the body electric!

Caducous

Emerson published *Essays: First Series*, which included his seminal essay "The Over-Soul," in 1841. In the coming years he continued to work through and elaborate on the implications of his philosophy of oneness. In 1844, Emerson borrowed and read James Elliot Cabot's copy of the first full English translation of the Bhagavad Gita, Charles Wilkins's *Bhăgvăt-Gēētā, or Dialogues of Krēēshnă and Ărjŏŏn*, which was originally published in 1785. In 1845, after months of writing to booksellers in Europe, Emerson finally purchased a personal copy of Wilkins's *Bhăgvăt-Gēētā*, along with Horace Hayman Wilson's translation of *The Vishnu Purana* (1840) and Henry Thomas Colebrooke's *Miscellaneous Essays on Indian Philosophy* (1837), a subtle and comprehensive discussion of Indian thought.[2] From this point forward, Emerson's reading lists titled heavily toward Indian philosophy. "When India was explored, and the wonderful riches of Indian theologic literature found, that dispelled once and for all the dream about Christianity being the sole revelation,—for, here in India—there in China, were the same principles, the same grandeurs, the like depths moral and intellectual," he wrote in his journal.[3] The Gita, he concluded, was "majestic" and useful; it spoke "more to our daily purpose than this year's almanac or this day's newspaper."[4]

Emerson saw oneness everywhere. He believed in a timeless, universal philosophical truth, a *philosophia perennias*, which he hoped to bring home to America in his essays.[5] He explained that he looked to Indian philosophy with great enthusiasm because he saw in texts like the Bhagavad Gita an eloquent articulation of this perennial philosophy that could be extremely useful for Americans if properly reframed and updated for the present.[6] "All philosophy of east and west has the same centerpiece," he surmised in his 1850 essay "Plato; Or, The Philosopher": "In all nations, there are minds which incline to dwell in the conception of the fundamental Unity. The raptures of prayer and ecstasy of devotion lose all beings in one Being. This tendency finds its highest expression in the religious writings of the East, and chiefly in the Indian Scriptures, in the Vedas, the Bhagavat Geeta, and the Vishnu Purana. Those writings contain little else than this idea, and they rise to pure and sublime strains in celebrating it."[7] Emerson loved Plato, but here it is telling that in introducing Plato to his readers, he quoted not from Plato but from the Bhagavad Gita and the Vishnu Purana. Emerson surmised that it was likely that Plato learned his philosophy on "eastern pilgrimages," for Emerson was certain, just as Victor Cousin, the French philosopher who influenced his interpretation of the Bhagavad Gita, was certain, that the genius of the Greeks originated in India.[8] Beginning with *Essays: First Series* in 1841, Emerson's lectures and essays from the next three decades explore what it means to be committed to a life of oneness.

In January 1842, tragedy struck. On January 24, Emerson's little son Waldo, "the apple of his father's eye and his constant companion," came down with a severe case of scarlet fever. After fighting the illness for three days, the boy died on January 27.[9] He was only five years old. The Emerson family never fully healed.

In contemporary America, we hide death and would rather not discuss it. In Emerson's time, it was unavoidable. It hit you in the face, repeatedly, every day. Tuberculosis took scores, as did childbirth, putrid sanitation, war, and a number of wasting plagues that have since been eradicated. To take just one example: today we have tetanus shots to prevent what happened earlier that horrible month of January 1842, when Henry David Thoreau's older brother John cut himself shaving and died several days later from lockjaw, leaving the younger Thoreau in shambles. Life in nineteenth-century America was a daunting dance with death. As hard as it might be to believe, Emerson and the transcendentalists described cemeteries as "schools of life" where people could learn to deal with death, and they advised their readers to visit the graves of the dead often in order to build up a tolerance toward loss.[10] A general, widespread cultural stoicism does not mean that death was any easier to cope with, however. We can't all be Seneca. Little Waldo's death tested Emerson, personally and philosophically.

In 1844, Emerson published *Essays: Second Series*, based on talks and lectures that were given around the time of little Waldo's death. These essays read more darkly than the previous volume of essays. Emerson is less cheerful and upbeat. Some scholars believe that Waldo's tragic death explains the somber tone of *Essays: Second Series*, in which death is a central theme. "Grief too will make us idealists," Emerson concludes in "Experience," the second essay in *Essays: Second Series*.

> In the death of my son, now more than two years ago, I seem to have lost a beautiful estate,—no more. I cannot get it nearer to me. If tomorrow I should be informed of the bankruptcy of my principal debtors, the loss of my property would be a great inconvenience to me, perhaps, for many years; but it would leave me as it found me,—neither better nor worse. So it is with this calamity: it does not touch me: some thing which I fancied was a part of me, which could not be torn away without tearing me, nor enlarged without enriching me, falls off from me, and leaves no scars. It was caducous. I grieve that grief can teach me nothing, nor carry me one step into the real nature. The Indian who was laid under a curse, that the wind should not blow on him, nor water flow to him, not fire burn him, is a type of us all. The dearest events are summer-rain, and we the Para coats that shed every drop. Nothing is left us now but death. We look to that with a grim satisfaction, saying, there at least is reality that will not dodge us.[11]

We know, from his letters and the recollections of friends and family, that Emerson grieved terribly for his son. He was no different from any parent in this regard. In a letter to Margaret Fuller, he wondered, "Shall I ever dare to love anything again?" His wife, Lidian, observed that little Waldo's death nearly broke her heartsick husband: "How intensely his heart yearns over every memento of his boy I cannot express to you. Never was a greater hope disappointed—a more devoted love bereaved."[12] The heart never heals from such loss. Yet two years on, in his public philosophy, at least, Emerson adopted a different perspective on things, choosing to view his son's death through the lens of Advaita Vedanta. Calamity does not touch him—he does not grieve for his son—because death is an illusion, and the soul, in its connection to the oversoul, is immortal. "What opium is instilled into all disaster!"[13] His son was "caducous," a word botanists used during the nineteenth century to describe leaves that fell early, before the end of summer, without damaging the tree.

When Emerson says that grief makes all people idealists, he means that one way the wounded broken heart manages its woe is by viewing what has been lost as illusory. Through some magical cosmic power—Emerson would later adopt the Sanskrit word *maya* to describe this power (though as we will see in chapter 5, he only began to use this word later, after *Essays: Second Series*)—the true reality, the oversoul, the divine oneness, came to appear on earth as an individual named Waldo; but this individual was never real in the sense that the oversoul is real: "Dream delivers us to dream, and there is no end to illusion."[14] Nature makes us her "fools" by deceiving us that there are independent individuals who live and die.[15]

In *Essays: Second Series* and subsequent works, Emerson strengthens the weak monism of "The Over-Soul" into a more extreme position consistent with Advaita Vedanta that views individuality and difference as *delusions* that obscure the true reality of a oneness beyond description. Following little Waldo's death, Emerson's oneness grows more severe. He doubles down on the doctrine that there is no "I," there is no "mine," there are no sons or daughters, brothers, sisters, wives, husbands, friends, enemies. All is one. In his reflections on his son's death, Emerson speaks as a good Advaitin. This is no mere speculative indifference to death. Emerson models how to make this indifference real. The Emersonian manages loss by transforming life itself into an illusion, a summer rain that cannot tickle the skin.

In "The Over-Soul," Emerson challenged his readers to seek out the headwaters of the eternities by seeing and addressing the divine in all people. This is the practice of communication as yoga. In the following years and decades he continued to work out what this meant in practice, and, increasingly, it meant looking past the embodied individual, the person living in the here and now with concrete feelings, dreams, and vulnerabilities, the person enmeshed in relationships and on whom so many others depend, the person with a body so strong and frail, toward something distant and more real. "We are amphibious creatures, weaponed for two elements, having two sets of faculties, the particular and the catholic."[16] Emerson continued to use the rhetorical weapons of the particular, nouns and pronouns, in his prose, and so the illusion of individual identity persists. Such is the nature of language. However, as he aged, Emerson adjusted his instrument to observe the general, to sweep the heavens in the blink of an eye. The individual remained but as a palimpsest, a quirk of grammar. It, too, was caducous.

Relationships and Other Fictions

Laser-focused on the all, the one, the oversoul, the particular became less important to Emerson in his later years. This is a danger of monistic philosophies, especially those that trope the world as a oneness born out of spirit in which bodies specifically, and matter more generally, are illusions, tricks of the deluded, deceived mind. Emerson encourages his readers to worship the divine as incarnated in fellow humans. However, the soul, which is immortal, necessary, and catholic, seems to matter more to him than the human body, which is perishable and accidental. Like many Advaitins, Emerson values the active principle of divinity—its verbing power to incarnate, to flow—more than the container that is filled, the noun that is verbed. Quoting the Vishnu Purana, Emerson observes, "The words I and mine constitute ignorance."[17] Relationships, people, attachments, bodies, emotions, everything that makes us human: it is all an illusion. To cling to names and forms, to markers of individual identity, to people, to partners, to children, is to reinforce an illusion that prevents us from seeing things as they are.

The people closest to Emerson—including his most brilliant interlocutor and conversation partner, Margaret Fuller, and his wife, Lidian—repeatedly accused him of being a cold and distant friend, and this might explain why.[18] Committed to addressing the personified impersonal in others, Emerson himself became the impersonal personified, a personality lost to the surrounding infinity of all things. Uttering the mystic's curse, Emerson complained, "Our relations to each other are oblique and casual."[19] Though he heard his wife's remonstrations, he excused himself philosophically: "We are not very much to blame for our bad marriages. We live amid hallucinations."[20] Though the true Emersonian walks *among* people, he is not *of* them. He is perfectly apart.

Oneness is not gendered. Sanskrit is a highly gendered language, but the word *brahman* is a neuter noun that has no gender. The English word *oneness* has no gender, either. If oneness were gendered, it would be twoness, or threeness, or manyness, not oneness. Nevertheless, our everyday experience of oneness is mediated by our culture's often-unquestioned assumptions about gender (and race, and sexuality, and class). Margaret Fuller pointed this out. Every bit the intellectual equal of the most prominent Boston Brahmin intellectuals, including Emerson, Fuller fought for equality between men and women in all spheres, including the male public world. In the "Conversations" she hosted in Boston in the late 1830s, in her work as the cofounder and first editor in chief at the *Dial* in the early 1840s, and in her literary criticism for the *New York Tribune* in the mid-'40s, Fuller battled to dismantle the system of gender relations that marked a woman's place as the private household, and that portrayed women as too fragile and hysterical to play a role in public life. In her landmark 1845 book *Woman in the Nineteenth Century*, published three years prior to the first woman's rights convention in American history at Seneca Falls in 1848, Fuller took aim at what historians call the "cult of true womanhood" or the "cult of domesticity," which taught that good American women embodied virtues including servility and domesticity and thus prepared them for a life of "drudgery."[21] Fuller rightly identified "the belief that woman was made *for man*" as the most prominent barrier to equality.[22] Woman was not made for man, nor was man made for woman. People were people, and they deserved to grow, to thrive, to unfold whatever talents might reside in their natures: "What woman needs is not as a woman to act or rule, but as a nature to grow, as an intellect to discern, as a soul to live freely and unimpeded, to unfold such powers as were given her when we left our common home."[23]

Fuller was a preeminent transcendentalist, but she did not fall head over heels for the Bhagavad Gita or Advaita Vedanta like many of her male colleagues.[24] *Woman in the Nineteenth Century* explodes with references to Greek and Latin mythology and history, proving Fuller's deep learning and making the general absence of Eastern philosophy all the more conspicuous—but perhaps not surprising. The Mahabharata portrays a world of macho, hypermasculine male warriors preening and posturing and killing for prestige and renown; women live their lives mostly in the background, coming to the foreground primarily to tempt men sexually, to mourn their dead warrior husbands, and, after the apocalypse at Kurukshetra is complete, to commit mass suicide, throwing themselves on their dead warrior husbands' funeral pyres, a practice known as *sati*.[25] Like nineteenth-century America, this was a world in which *woman was made for man*.[26] The Gita itself is a dialogue between two men, with no women's voices represented. Krishna demands that Arjuna act *loka-samgraha*, for the common good of society.[27] This is, however, a common good as understood by warrior kings and enacted in the name of the kingdom's women and children. In one of the Bhagavad Gita's cruelest moments, women become the instruments of Krishna's desire to punish those who have sinned—for he describes how he places the worst criminals into "hexed demonic wombs" in order to ensure their pain and suffering in future rebirths.[28]

As a woman, Fuller knew firsthand the relational labor—the drudgery—that women were expected to perform in the background with nary a complaint so that the men in their lives could become public actors. As a woman, she was well aware that relationships are real—because relational labor was demanded of her, and because she often lacked the relational support from her male peers that would have allowed her to unfold her prodigious literary powers in the male-dominated world of culture and letters.[29] As a woman she was well aware that bodies were real, because men were constantly telling her and her American sisters that it was their bodies—their frailty, their emotions, and the purported inability of their rational faculties to control these emotions—that prevented them from participating in politics and public life.

When Emerson said that bodies and relationships were unreal, he spoke from a position of great privilege, for it meant that no one was using his body as an excuse to bar him from pursuing his individual duty, or *svadharma*; and it also meant that he was completely blind to how his literary success was enabled by the very same relational support he marked as an illusion.

Heeding Fuller's warning, we must be on guard to ensure that oneness does not gloss over injustice, including the unequal demands society places on differing groups of people and the corresponding possibilities that are or are not opened to them. Oneness cannot become just another rhetoric of injustice—a turbo-charged, divinely backed sanctification of the status quo that excludes based on assumptions about gender, race, sexuality, and class and that reinforces whatever present hierarchies exist. If it does this, then it has no value. To prevent this, oneness must recognize, acknowledge, and directly confront injustices, including sexism and racism—as Krishna tells Arjuna, stand up! To me, this means that any viable ethics of oneness must acknowledge the reality of individuals, the sacredness of bodies, and the significance of relationships that make life possible.

"The world is awaking to the idea of union, and these experiments show what it is thinking of. It is and will be magic. Men will live and communicate, and plough, and reap, and govern, as by added ethereal power, when once they are united," Emerson writes in "New England Reformers," the closing missive of *Essays: Second Series*.[30] Emerson means something specific, particular, and quite peculiar by "union" here: he means the voluntary coordination of men who are filled with the genius of the oversoul but are perfectly apart from each other (I do not read the gendered language as a mistake or a general marker of "humanity" here, for in both series of essays Emerson insists that friendship and community happen between males). These men are not entwined and never touch. This is union as joyous anarchy, the perfect synchronization of truly independent, self-reliant parts in touch with a common source:

> The union is only perfect, when all the uniters are isolated. It is the union of friends who live in different streets or towns. Each man, if he attempts to join himself to others, is on all sides cramped and diminished of his proportion; and the stricter the union, the smaller and more pitiful he is. But leave him alone, to recognize in every hour and place the secret soul, he will go up and down doing the works of a true member, and, to the astonishment of all, the work will be done with concert, though no man spoke. Government will be adamantine without any governor. The union must be ideal in actual individualism.[31]

One in reality, separate in illusion: the individualism Emerson speaks of is a reverse liberalism. Emerson denies that men—I speak here of men because Emerson speaks of men; it is a union of male "friends," not of "brothers and sisters"[32]—come into the world independent and autonomous. For Emerson, men grow up fully immersed in a sea of common sense and convention, and so they must strike out heroically to find truth by practicing self-reliance. This truth is a truth of connection between a man and the divine, between soul and oversoul, but it is not a truth of interconnectedness between men based in shared happiness and grief or common cause. Emerson does not reject the world; he does not call for *sannyasa*, or renunciation; he does not tell his readers to act like turtles and withdraw themselves into their hard shells. He advocates an engaged life of devotion to shared divinity. This is a life of action, a worldly life, a life of communication and community; but the worldly action is aimed at escaping the world's delusions. Emerson calls for transcendence: first, for transcending the conventions that prevent men from being individuals; and second, for transcending the illusion of individuality itself that prevents men from realizing a truer, nondual perspective on life. This is the chief mystery of Emerson's philosophy—to affirm the divine means rejecting many of the things that make us human: "I grieve that I cannot grieve."[33] The Emersonian craves immortal oneness, the unchanging reality underneath the world of impermanence, and finds it. But at what cost?

"Brahma"

There is a direct line from Emerson's meditation on his son's death in "Experience" to his famous 1857 poem "Brahma." Emerson began tinkering with the poem in 1845; he composed the final version in 1856; it was published in the inaugural issue of the *Atlantic Monthly* in November 1857, just a few months after the devastating Supreme Court decision in the case of *Dred Scott v. Sandford* (a case that had everything to do with bodies) that catapulted the young nation toward an unimaginably bloody civil war—a war that snuffed out the futures of so many young men of his son Waldo's generation.

"Brahma" is the apotheosis of Emerson's Advaita.[34] In *Emerson and Asia* (1930), Frederic Ives Carpenter observed—apparently without irony, but certainly not without hyperbole, that "Emerson's poem 'Brahma' probably expresses the central idea of Hindu philosophy more clearly and concisely than any other writing in the English language—perhaps better than any writing in Hindu literature itself."[35] (I know at least three Hindus who would quibble with this comment). Setting aside the argument over who said it best,

Emerson's "Brahma" expresses, in four terse stanzas, ideas central to Advaita Vedanta:

> If the red slayer think he slays,
> Or if the slain think he is slain,
> They know not well the subtle ways
> I keep, and pass, and turn again.
>
> Far or forgot to me is near;
> Shadow and sunlight are the same;
> The vanished gods to me appear;
> And one to me are shame and fame.
>
> They reckon ill who leave me out;
> When me they fly, I am the wings;
> I am the doubter and the doubt,
> And I the hymn the Brahmin sings.
>
> The strong gods pine for my abode,
> And pine in vain the sacred Seven;
> But thou, meek lover of the good!
> Find me, and turn thy back on heaven.[36]

This arcane poem keeps many secrets. The readers of the *Atlantic Monthly* were perplexed. According to one Emerson scholar, "No single poem ever mystified its readers more. Probably no poem ever will. It will always remain an enigma to the Western mind."[37] The *New York Times* trashed the poem in a review titled "Emerson Travestie" as "an exquisite piece of meaningless versification, that no sooner is it read than the desire to parody it becomes irresistible."[38] Emerson deserved praise, for "a poem in which no one can find a meaning, must be acknowledged a very great success. None but a man of genius could have produced such an exquisite piece of nonothingism."[39] Parodies begin popping up in the pages of the *New York Times* and other rags almost immediately.

Not everyone was so mystified. The editor of *Graham's Magazine* explicitly and correctly tied the poem to the Bhagavad Gita's doctrine that "God is all things, one being and one substance, or all beings and all substances."[40] Indeed. To solve one of "Brahma's" enigmas, it is helpful to put Emerson's poem in conversation with one of its chief philosophical sources, the Bhagavad Gita, on the question of the true nature of reality. Of course, Advaita Vedanta is somewhat cagey on this question. In Advaita, "the world then is not real, but it is not wholly unreal."[41] The nature of reality depends on one's perspective. For Advaitins, "the world is an illusion only on the basis of an experience of the Absolute. The world cannot be an illusion to one who lacks that experience. Empirical reality, in other words, is transcended only absolutely. Only from the viewpoint of the infinite does everything but itself appear as without substance, without independent reality and value. In short: 'there is no reason to call the world unreal before the knowledge of the oneness of the Atman (has been attained).'"[42] The world is not real (*sat*, or "that which is"), but it is also not unreal (*asat*, or "that which is not"). What, then, is the world? The phenomenal world in Advaita has an "apparent or practical reality" (*vyavaharika*)—the world exists in order to teach us the difference between what is real and what is not.[43]

Once a person has achieved the higher plane of insight into the true nature of things, they see the world for the illusion that it is, a fever dream of plurality and multiplicity and change that masks the truth of divine oneness. Krishna instructs Arjuna:

> What is unreal cannot come to be.
> What is real cannot not be.
> Two conclusions. Those who see true
> See the truth in both.[44]

For those who have grasped the truth, for those who have seen the true nature of divine oneness, what is unreal—what is subject to change and decay—is false; and what is real—what is eternal and unkillable—can never not be.

Emerson learned many things from Advaita Vedanta. His innovation in reading the Bhagavad Gita was to democratize devotion through the spiritual practice of communication as yoga. God is for him beyond description and anthropomorphism. And yet God is everywhere, in everything, in all of us. To transcend division and enemyship and resentment, Emerson called on his readers to attend to divinity in its everyday guise of their fellow citizens, to address their fellows—or at least their fellow men—as walking, talking incarnations of the divine. In "The Over-Soul," he proclaimed that this practice would create a more loving, compassionate world. I grant that this is one possibility of communication as yoga; addressing others as divine will encourage people to treat their fellows as sacred and worthy of respect. Such address might promote peace: *ad bellum purificandum*. But there is another possibility, a darker possibility, a terrible possibility—one that the Gita explores and the Mahabharata expounds: that addressing others as divine can actually fuel violence, that communication as yoga is the most effective war rhetoric imaginable.

In the Bhagavad Gita, Krishna advises Arjuna to do his duty:

Better your own dharma, botched,
Than someone else's dharma practiced well.
Better death in your own dharma!
Another's dharma carries danger.[45]

With these verses, Krishna teaches Arjuna the doctrine of *svadharma*, one's personal dharma or duty. Every person has a duty to perform. Doing this duty is virtue; ignoring it—or even worse, performing another's duty instead of your own—is vice. Do your duty, Krishna demands, and fret not about consequence. If a person does their duty, they are not touched by the stain of karma; they are not individually responsible for the consequences of their actions; they are free from evil. In the Mahabharata and the Bhagavad Gita, *svadharma* is intimately related to one's *varna*, or class. Arjuna's *svadharma* is the duty of the Kshatriyas, the warrior class, to fight and defeat the enemies of the kingdom and protect its people.[46] Krishna reproaches Arjuna for neglecting this duty as a warrior, and for attempting instead to perform the duty of a renunciate monk.[47] Though his duty is personal, Arjuna has no freedom to decide what this duty is. It is determined for him by his rank in society.

To persuade him to fulfill his duty as a Kshatriya, Krishna teaches Arjuna about the immortality of the soul and the unreality of the body:

Someone who imagines this a killer,
Someone who believes that this is killed—
Neither of them knows
This cannot kill and cannot be killed.

It is not born and does not die at any time
And, having come to be, will never cease to be.
Birthless, undying, constant, before time, this
When killed inside the body is not killed.

A man who knows the indestructible,
Eternal, birthless, imperishable this—
In what way, Partha, does he
Cause the killing? Who is it he kills?[48]

To persuade Arjuna to kill his cousins and teachers and bring victory to the Pandavas, Krishna teaches him that the body is an illusion, time-bound and destined to pass. The immortal soul, however, never dies. It cannot be killed. To destroy the body is not to destroy the soul. God cannot be killed, and we are all God. Both oversoul and soul are immortal. And so Krishna calls on Arjuna to kill, because killing is not really killing, for that which is real cannot not be, and that which is unreal never was.

Henry David Thoreau loved the Bhagavad Gita nearly as much as Emerson did. He borrowed Emerson's copy and trucked it with him to Walden Pond in 1845, where he reported that each morning, "I bathe[d] my intellect in the stupendous and cosmogonal philosophy of the Bhagvat-Geeta."[49] In Thoreau's imagination, during each day he spent in the woods reading the Gita, "the pure Walden water [was] mingled with the sacred water of the Ganges."[50] The Gita spoke to Emerson's desire to articulate a philosophy of oneness. Thoreau was a vitalist who reveled in diversity. He was not as committed to monism as Emerson, and so the Gita spoke to him differently, as both a guide to inward, meditative experience and as a manual for right action, or karma yoga—action that is ethical because it springs from a proper understanding of one's duty.[51]

Thoreau finished a draft of his first book, *A Week on the Concord and Merrimack Rivers* (1849), while living at Walden Pond. Given that he read the Bhagavad Gita meditatively each morning, it is unsurprising that Thoreau quickly turns his attention to the poem in *A Week*. He wholeheartedly recommends the Gita to his readers: "I would say to the readers of Scriptures, if they wish for a good book, read the Bhagvat-Geeta, an episode to the Mahabharat," for "the reader is nowhere raised into and sustained in a higher, purer, or rarer region of thought than in the Bhagvat-Geeta."[52] However, true to his ethics of nonviolence, Thoreau emphatically rejects Krishna's central argument for war: "Kreeshna's argument, it must be allowed, is defective. No sufficient reason is given why Arjoon should fight. Arjoon may be convinced, but the reader is not."[53] Krishna asserts that it is Arjuna's duty to fight, but "the duty of which he speaks is an arbitrary one. When was it established? The Brahmin's virtue consists in doing, not right, but arbitrary things."[54] As far as I know, Emerson never questioned Arjuna's duty, though he, like Thoreau, found abhorrent the Indian idea of caste, or *jati*, that European and American readers believed predestined Arjuna, the greatest of Kshatriyas, to fight, and kill, his relations.[55] For Emerson, caste was just another convention that frustrated self-reliance. Unlike Thoreau, however, Emerson tacitly endorsed Krishna's words about killing—for he expressed these very sentiments in the first verses of "Brahma."[56]

Writing in the aftermath of World War II as a veteran of that war, Perry Miller, one of the founders of the discipline of American studies, raised the obvious objection to Emerson's poem: "Life was exciting in Massachusetts of the 1830s and 1840s; abolitionists were mobbed, and for a time Mr. Emerson was a dangerous radical. . . . But by and large, young men were not called upon to confront possible slaughter. . . . Thus it seems today that Emerson ran no great risk in asserting that should he ever be bayoneted he would fall by his own hand disguised in another uniform, that because all men participate in the Over-Soul those who shoot and those who are shot prove to be identical, that in the realm of the transcendental there is nothing to choose between eating and being eaten." After the war, these doctrines became distasteful:

> It is hardly surprising that the present generation, those who are called upon to serve not merely as doubters and the doubt but also as slayers and slain, greet the serene pronouncements of Brahma with cries of dissent. Professors somewhat nervously explain to unsympathetic undergraduates that of course these theories are not the real Emerson, much less the real Thoreau. They were importations, not native American growths. They came from Germany, through Coleridge; they were extracted from imperfect translations of the Hindu scriptures, misunderstood and extravagantly embraced by Yankees *who ought to have known better*—and who fortunately in some moments did know better. . . . The doctrines of the Over-Soul, correspondence, and compensation seem nowadays to add up to shallow optimism and insufferable smugness.

"Fortunately, no one is compelled to take them seriously," Miller concludes. If Americans want serious philosophy, a serious transcendentalism worthy of the present moment, they must ignore Emerson's "undiscriminating eclecticism which merges the Bhagavad-Gita, Robert Herrick, Saadi, Swedenborg, Plotinus, and Confucius into one monotonous iteration." Miller here voices an unfortunate scholarly consensus about Americans' engagement with Indian philosophy: we should know better, and stick to serious scholarly sources, like Locke and Kant. This is the casual Orientalism that looks down on any attempt to find resources for democracy in traditions that do not originate in Athens. I can testify, from personal experience, that such Orientalism is very much alive in the academy today.[57]

Even at his most arrogant, however, Miller broaches a valid question: If we want to prevent war, shouldn't we turn away from Emerson's reading of the Bhagavad Gita and look to a different Emerson than the mystic dreamer poet warrior who wrote "Brahma"? But verily, this is impossible. Contrary to Miller and the other nervous university professors he mentions, anxiously shuffling their lecture notes and muttering Orientalist curses as they try to explain away Emerson's strange affinity for Advaita to their students, there is no other Emerson apart from the essayist of mystical oneness. This is my most serious worry about Emerson's oneness: by symbolizing God as a universal, eternal oneness that envelops all things and gives them life, by elevating the soul in importance over the body, does Emerson not devalue life, which is fragile and perishable? There is an ironic nihilism that accompanies the jubilant assertion of immortality in Emerson's "Brahma," an ancient nihilism that negates the value of life in the here and now by affirming the value of eternal life. If we are not careful, I fear that we will find that to pronounce individual identity an illusion is to court catastrophe.

Divine Bodies

In his later years, Emerson took Advaita Vedanta to its most extreme logical conclusion, announcing that only the oversoul is real and hence that plurality and individuality are illusions, the product of divine magic. No one lives and no one dies; no one kills, and no one is killed; there is only the soul, which is immortal, and indestructible. The individual lives on in grammar, but loses the capacity to breathe, to bleed, to bend, to break, to die, to matter. I worry that as he articulated something akin to an American Advaita, Emerson compromised the dignity of the embodied individual. Emerson testified that the practice of communication as yoga has the potential to change the world. If addressing the divine in others means talking to that which is immortal and ignoring the rest, however, then this yoga can quickly become sinister. This is another area where Whitman's ethics of oneness represents an advance on Emerson. Whitman's poetry is based on a joyous contradiction: the divine is imperishable, but the perishable body is somehow just as divine as the immortal soul. Whitman does not resolve this paradox; he simply sits with it in contemplation and then explores it in his poetry.

Emerson was an early and committed champion of Whitman's poetry. After the first edition of *Leaves of Grass* dropped in 1855, Emerson composed "what has become the most famous letter in American literary history," an unsolicited, scintillating review that commended Whitman for writing of "incomparable things said incomparably well."[58] This is precisely the type of review that all authors dream of, a review from a noted cultural authority that single-handedly puts a book on the map. Never one to shy away from self-promotion, Whitman used the review without Emerson's consent (along with three self-authored anonymous reviews of his own book!) to promote the second edition of *Leaves of Grass* in 1856.

Whitman loved and admired Emerson from afar. During the early 1850s, "my ideas were simmering and simmering," he told a friend, "and Emerson brought them to a boil."[59] Whitman saw himself as "The Poet" Emerson described in *Essays: Second Series*, the transcendent wordsmith who would speak a better world into existence. Poetry, according to Emerson, is "the activity which repairs the decays of things."[60] Emerson prophesied that the great American poet, once he arrived on the scene, would feel "the ethereal tides to roll and circulate through him. . . . He is caught up in the life of the Universe, his speech is thunder, his thought is law, and his words are universally intelligible as the plants and the animals."[61] Whitman believed himself to be this poet. At times, it seems that Emerson believed Whitman to be this poet, too. However, the two disagreed about the more salacious passages in *Leaves of Grass*.

In 1860, while preparing the third edition of *Leaves of Grass* for publication in Boston, Whitman and Emerson took a stroll through Boston Common. Emerson advised Whitman to cut the sex poems from the "Enfans d'Adam" section that offended censors. Whitman refused, arguing that there would be no book left if he did. Scholars sometimes read this conversation—which stuck with Whitman until his dying days—as a disagreement in which Emerson revealed his prudishness and priggishness, only to be rejected by Whitman, the champion of free love. This might be true, but I read it somewhat differently: as a disagreement over the place of the body in a philosophy of oneness.

Whitman built his poetry on Emersonian bedrock. However, he never made the extreme turn toward Advaita Vedanta that Emerson undertook in his later years. Whitman taught a "soft monism" in line with Bhedabheda Vedanta, in which there is only one substance, divinity, but that substance has an infinite number of expressions. There are many leaves of grass, but it is all grass.[62] Whitman does not deny the reality of individuals or their value. The poet's perspective is cosmic:

> He sees eternity less like a play with a prologue and denouement,
> He sees eternity in men and women, he does not see men and women as
> dreams or dots.[63]

When we wake up to the mystery of who we are, we recognize that we are so much bigger than our egos. There is something eternal in us all. Finding rapport with this deep source of insight is the surest route to happiness and peace. And yet, the acknowledgement of eternity does not lead Whitman to downplay the significance of the individual human experience, as Emerson tended to. Whitman does not see people "as dreams or dots." It is the body that keeps Whitman's oneness grounded in material reality and prevents him from reiterating, intentionally or not, the Bhagavad Gita's argument for war. "All comes by the body, only health puts you rapport with the universe."[64]

The democratic mystic cannot disregard the body. The true poet sings songs of body and soul: "I am the poet of the Body and I am the poet of the Soul."[65] One of Whitman's most resonant metaphors for describing the relationship between the individual and the divine, the soul and the oversoul, is material and visceral: he describes the divine as the "pulse" of the human heart.[66] To tune in to one's pulse is to listen to the divine as it lives inside us and pushes blood and oxygen through our veins, giving us life. The body is the route to the all. It is through our bodies that we achieve rapport. Recognizing the divinity of the body, and treating it as divine, is a necessary spiritual practice toward achieving cosmic consciousness.

In the interest of achieving divine rapport, Whitman gently urges his readers to see the body differently than they are accustomed to. Beginning with Plato and the Sophists, it became common in the West to speak about human nature as separated into *soma* (body) and *psyche* (soul)—a distinction that the earlier epic poets, including Homer, did not make.[67] Once sundered, Greek philosophers treated the soul as far more important than the body. This hierarchy persisted into Whitman's day in many forms, including in Christianity, Enlightenment philosophy, and philosophical liberalism. Christianity inherited many ideas from Platonism, including the idea that the eternal soul is superior to the perishable body, the site of carnal sin. Doubling down on Cartesian dualism, many philosophers of the Enlightenment tended to view people as little more than brains on a stick. Early liberal thinkers maintained Christianity's suspicion of the body.[68] Indeed, the liberal founders of the United States saw the body as a problem to be managed, for they viewed the body as the source of destructive emotions and unquenchable urges that keep people from thinking rationally and behaving lawfully.[69] Against every one of these dualistic traditions, Whitman rebels. Those who aspire to cosmic consciousness must overcome all dualisms, including the dualism between the body and the soul. Only then will the experience of oneness, of the all, become available. In his poem "I Sing the Body Electric," Whitman models how to do this: by deifying the body.

Upholding the ancient hierarchy of body and soul he inherited from his beloved Plato, Emerson imagined the soul as the agent that uses the body for its ends.[70] To defend oneness, Emerson could not rely too heavily on such dualistic discourses, however, and so he denied the reality of the body by marking it as a kind of illusion. For Emerson, all is soul. Whitman, too, forwards an ontology in which everything is one, but he resists the urge to elevate the ideal over the real, the immaterial over the material. Reality, he contends, is *embodied soul*, the divine all come to life in real breathing heaving sweating laughing bodies that are unique manifestations of divine oneness.

The Body Electric

In "I Sing the Body Electric," his beautiful, poetic encomium to the body, Whitman pivots quickly back and forth between description of the interconnected oneness of reality to interrogative questions meant to prompt his readers to question their commonsensical yet wrongheaded assumptions about that reality. He asks several such questions at the advent of the poem:

> Was it doubted that those who corrupt their own bodies conceal themselves?
> And if those who defile the living are as bad as they who defile the dead?
> And if the body does not do fully as much as the soul?
> And if the body were not the soul, what is the soul?[71]

Answering this last question, Whitman takes a courageous stand against philosophical dualism by affirming that the body is the soul, that the soul is the body, and that both are divine. And, he seems to suggest, in spite of our culture's many twonesses, we already know this, if only we would take a moment to pause, look around, and consider.

The next time we are around those we hold most dear, Whitman urges us to pay attention to how we feel. Are we not closer to God when we are with those we love, because we are more ourselves, and because our bodies are more at peace? That the touch of our loved ones—a handshake, a hug, a pat on the back, a kiss, a kind word spoken softly into the ear—can calm our minds and fire our hearts is the definitive argument against philosophical dualism. The divinity of the body is proved by the poignancy of proximity. To defile the body, to live an unhealthy life, is to "conceal" oneself—by which Whitman means to conceal a person's soul sight and thus that person's intuitive connection to the divine. The body is the pathway to the soul because it *is* the soul. This is probably why Whitman expresses perplexity that there are prohibitions against exhuming corpses and defiling the dead, but not prohibitions against defiling the living body. To say that the body is a temple does not take it nearly far enough. The living are gods walking on earth.

Whitman calls on his readers to view the body—the bodies of the people they meet, as well as their own bodies—as "sacred":

> The man's body is sacred and the woman's body is sacred,
> No matter who it is, it is sacred. . . .[72]

Though this word, *sacred*, was as common during Whitman's day as it is during our own, to understand what Whitman is up to in "I Sing the Body Electric" we must recognize that when he uses this word, he is engaged in a little rhetorical rebellion against convention. The scholar of world religions and yoga Mircea Eliade contends that all religion is founded on a distinction between sacred and profane: "Man becomes aware of the sacred because it manifests itself, shows itself, as something wholly different from the profane." Eliade designates this act of manifestation "hierophany," when "something sacred shows itself to us." The religious person desires to spend as much time as possible in the presence of the sacred. For certain mystics "who have a religious experience all nature is capable of revealing itself as cosmic sacrality. The cosmos in its entirety can become a hierophany."[73] This is precisely Whitman's project, to expand the domain of sacredness so far that the concept of the profane loses any power to tarnish the body. In founding his own religion, Whitman attempts to stretch religion to its breaking point, past which distinctions and dualisms lose their power to persuade.

Whitman's use of *sacred* is contrary to Christianity, which denies that bodies are divine and demands that the sacred be carefully guarded from the profane.[74] Whitman rebels against anyone who would keep the sacred secret or sequestered from public view. Bodies are common and worldly, but this makes them no less sacred, no less holy, no less divine. By insisting that the body is "sacred," Whitman's poetry comes into direct conflict with the beliefs and rhetoric of what Eliade famously calls the "modern nonreligious man"—in short, *the atheist*. This figure has always been present, lurking on the outskirts of official discourse, but it burst forth onto the scene in the eighteenth and nineteenth centuries due to what has been called the "nova effect," the explosion of a number of religious, ethical, spiritual, and scientific vocabularies that called Christian orthodoxy into question. Westerners during this period experienced "a spiritual super-nova, a kind of galloping pluralism on the spiritual plane."[75] The simplistic story of "disenchantment" or "secularization" that many philosophers and sociologists spin about the nineteenth century is incorrect: it is not that science supplanted religion and spirituality, but instead that humans invented a number of new doctrines that could give their lives meaning, such that they did not have to be Christian to live a meaningful or ethical life.[76]

Christianity's hold on America's imagination and on its public discourse began to crack during the decades preceding and following the Civil War. The major Christian churches had difficulty responding to advances in nineteenth-century science, especially scholarship in evolutionary theory, biology, and geology that challenged the biblical account of creation. The churches also struggled to respond to new hermeneutical scholarship that read the Bible as a collection of disparate historical texts and not a divinely inspired, unified work. Emerson and many other transcendentalists viewed Jesus as a morally exemplary individual, but not as the one true son of God (because everyone is God's son or daughter).[77] The mid-nineteenth century was, according to one historian, "the golden age of freethought."[78] A majority of Americans remained Christian, but atheism and its associated belief systems (agnosticism, deism) surged.

According to Eliade, the atheist "regards himself solely as the subject and agent of history"; he "refuses all appeal to transcendence."[79] In the United States, atheism takes many forms.[80] At its most brutal is a greedy capitalism whose devotion to profit transforms human bodies (and the world in which they make their home) into commodities to be exploited. There is nothing sacred to such capitalism; it has no religion other than profit. This destructive, blind avarice is sometimes supported, sometimes opposed by a cold, rational scientific materialism that pictures life as little more than cells and molecules combining in orderly, predictable, observable ways. And, of course, there are those who turn to atheism because they genuinely believe that religion is an opiate of the masses that stunts people's capacity to think independently and take responsibility for the lives they live and the earth on which they live them.[81] There is a courage and dignity in this atheism that is completely lacking in its capitalist cousin.

Emersonian transcendentalism and Whitmanism also proliferated in this golden age of freethinking, for "before the Civil War most spiritual seekers abandoned the church and turned for inspiration to some combination of Emersonian transcendentalism and non-Western religious writings and traditions. From the 1860s on, many turned as well to Walt Whitman's *Leaves of Grass*."[82] Neither Emerson nor Whitman were atheists, however. They both believed in God—God as oneness, as oversoul, as *brahman*, as the all—and they both believed that religion was essential for living an ethical, democratic life. In Whitman's words, "At the core of democracy, finally, is the religious element."[83] Whitman rejects any philosophy or politics or ethics that does not begin in religion, because religion is based in an experience of the sacred. However, unlike many religions, Whitman's religion—his ontology—denies a stark division between sacred and profane. He rebels against atheists of all stripes who desacralize the body, for, he fears, to deny the sacredness of the body is the first step toward the creation of undemocratic hierarchies that lead to discrimination, exclusion, and violence. And on this point Whitman is emphatic: active participation in such hierarchies—putting oneself above another, exploiting another, marking another body as disposable—will make it impossible to achieve cosmic consciousness. Abusing others might lead to material success, but it will never lead to spiritual enlightenment.

Sacred bodies walking on earth. Life, Whitman announces, is a "procession."

> The man's body is sacred and the woman's body is sacred,
> No matter who it is, it is sacred—is it the meanest one in the laborers' gang?
> Is it one of the dull-faced immigrants just landed on the wharf?

> Each belongs here or anywhere just as much as the well-off, just as much as you,
> Each has his or her place in the procession.
>
> (All is a procession,
> The universe is a procession with measured and perfect motion.)[84]

For Whitman, a man's body and a woman's body are equally sacred. One is not better or superior. Both are equal, for all bodies are sacred. Likewise this is true of those bodies commonly excluded from polite society and the democratic polis. The body of the laborer is sacred. The body of the immigrant—marked as different, disparaged as "dull-faced"—is sacred. The body of the slave is sacred. Whitman's ethics of oneness stands against any discrimination rooted in assumptions about gender, class, and nationality. He stands strongly against xenophobia and the racist anti-immigrant discourses common during his day (and, unfortunately, our own). Each individual has a place in the *procession.*

In "I Sing the Body Electric," Whitman does not use the word *procession* to signify evolution; nor does he use it to signify metempsychosis, as it was sometimes used in the occult literature of his day (often with the image of a procession of souls climbing up Jacob's ladder to heaven).[85] Instead, Whitman means a procession of people walking together down a common path toward rapport. What unites this motley crew is the path, and the fact that each of us must walk this path for ourselves in our own bodies (though we often do so hand in hand with those we love). At times, Whitman grounds oneness in shared substance—we are all divine. Here, he grounds oneness in a shared journey—we are all on the path toward realizing our divinity. Everyone has an equal claim to this path toward cosmic consciousness. It exists for one and all, rich and poor, men and women.

To cement the democratic nature of the path, Whitman asks his readers more searching, piercing questions designed to provoke self-study:

> Do you know so much yourself that you call the meanest ignorant?
> Do you suppose you have a right to a good sight, and he or she has not right
> to a sight?
> Do you think matter has covered together from its diffuse float, and the soil is
> on the surface, and water runs and vegetation sprouts,
> For you only, and not for him and her?[86]

Provocations such as this are a cornerstone of Whitman's poetry. In *Leaves of Grass*, Whitman dares his readers to play the role of both Krishna and Arjuna. He poses difficult questions about egotism and entitlement and privilege and invites them not to shy away from offering honest answers. Whitman wants his readers to feel deeply and think critically, to be open enough with themselves that they can admit when they cannot justify their actions based on anything more than *argumentum ad populum*. Answer these questions about the body electric honestly, Whitman seems to suggest, and you will recognize that there are no good arguments for discrimination or hierarchy. Answer these questions honestly, Whitman seems to suggest, and you will find democracy.

And that brings Whitman to slavery. Perhaps the starkest division in Whitman's America was the line between white and black. Though it is hard for many Americans to admit, this has always been a strategic division in our nation. A number of historians have proven that slavery was not a "peculiar institution" that survived American independence for idiosyncratic reasons. In the nineteenth century, slavery was not some fossilized relic of a distant, unfortunate past. On the contrary, many political leaders deemed slavery essential to the foundation and civic health of the United States. Why? Because slavery served to unify and to pacify white Americans who had little in common other than their "whiteness." In the absence of an enemyship premised on the antagonism between white and black, it was feared that white Americans would fight among themselves (especially given the massive disparities between rich and poor) or with the government. Well into the nineteenth century, no matter how badly they had it, no matter how violent their resentments might be, white Americans could bond over the fact that at least they weren't slaves. European colonists invented racist discourses during the 1600s to justify slavery, and even after the Thirteenth Amendment was ratified in 1865, officially banning slavery, and after the Civil War ended, these racist discourses lived on, for they had become deeply ingrained in American politics, law, and popular culture.[87] Enemyship held the white republic together in the absence of other, healthier forms of shared purpose and communal identity.

When he traveled to the United States in the 1830s to get a glimpse of a democracy emergent, Alexis de Tocqueville (1805–1859) suggested that most Americans were too individualistic to see the crucial role that racist rhetorics played in their democracy.[88] Moreover, he identified a strategic denial at the heart of American racism that most Americans also failed to notice. Building on Tocqueville's argument in *Democracy in America*, the political theorist Jack Turner observes that individualism and white supremacy were intimately linked during the nineteenth century. The rising culture of individualism shattered many of the old hierarchies of the European genteel tradition by which people derived value, resulting in profound and widespread insecurities over status and success. This insecurity at times was productive—it drove Americans to build voluntary associations that collectively harnessed their individual energies to remake the world. More often than not, however, this insecurity encouraged white Americans to embrace racism and defend slavery; or, if not to defend it outright, to at least passively accept it (which, Thoreau ventures in his essay "Civil Obedience," amounts to the same thing[89]). Turner writes, "Personal insecurity amid democratic flux drives individuals to merge their identities with that of an exalted group. . . . One of the functions of antiblack racism in Tocqueville's America was to assure the white individualist that he was not a slave, that he was indeed free, independent, and self-sufficient. Yet the only way he could maintain this self-conception was by evading his own dependence on structures of racial hierarchy and representation."[90] White Americans were free, it was said, because they were not slaves. But this belief birthed a new and noxious form of dependence, one that many Americans were blind to then, and which we continue to be oblivious to today. *To the extent that white Americans must exclude, dehumanize, and abuse other races to prove our value and self-worth, we are not free.* Racism is not strength. Racism is weakness. This is one reason it is so hard for white Americans like myself to talk about our country's history of white supremacy—for to acknowledge the role that rhetorics of white supremacy play in American life is to admit our own weakness.

The Declaration of Independence proclaimed that "all men are created equal." According to the political philosopher Danielle Allen, "On the subject of equality, no more important sentence has ever been written."[91] This sentence is a harbinger of a bright future, but also a marker of a dark past. For the majority of Americans that Thomas Jefferson dismissed when he wrote these timeless words—that is, *all women and all men who were not "white"*—American history has been a long battle for inclusion in the equality that is promised by our founding documents. Whitman made the journey that many other Americans made during the mid-nineteenth century, from proslavery to "free soil" to anti-slavery; and indeed, he opposed slavery, repeatedly, in *Leaves of Grass*.[92] When a runaway slave shows up at his door, Whitman's narrator in "Song of Myself" openly defies the Fugitive Slave Act of 1850 and does not return the man to the slave masters, as required by federal law. Instead, Whitman takes him in and helps him mend before sending him further north along the procession toward freedom:

> The runaway slave came to my house and stopt outside,
> I heard his motions cracking the twigs of the woodpile,
> Through the swung half-door for the kitchen I saw him limpsy and weak,
> And went where he sat on a log and led him in and assured him,
> And brought water and fill'd a tub for his sweated body and bruis'd feet,

> And gave him a room that enter'd from my own, and gave him some coarse clean clothes,
> And remember perfectly well his revolving eyes and his awkwardness,
> And remember putting plasters on the galls of his neck and ankles;
> He staid with me a week before he was recuperated and pass'd north,
> I had him sit next me at table, my fire-lock lean'd in the corner.[93]

Whitman keeps his rifle close to hand not to protect himself—had he feared the man, he would not have given him a room that entered from his own—but to protect the man from those who might chase him down and return him to shackles.

Whitman does not argue directly against slavery or racism in "I Sing the Body Electric." Instead, he defies racist rhetorics of white supremacy that sought to stoke disgust at the sight of the black body by marking it as subhuman, simian, ugly.[94] He does this by calling on his readers to bear witness to the bodies of slaves, to really look at them and see them, *to observe their beauty and strength.* "A man's body at auction," Whitman begins stanza 7 of the poem; "a woman's body at auction," he continues in stanza 8. He confronts his readers with descriptions of actual physical bodies on the auction block, worth far more than even the richest person could pay. He describes their muscles and bones, tendons and nerves. Their veins pulse with "the same red-running blood!" Their hearts beat with the "passions, desires, reachings, aspirations." Bearing witness, he directs his readers to see these bodies as divine, composed of the same materials as their own, to see these men and women as heroes, models of strength, the mothers and fathers of future generations, scions of "countless immortal lives with countless embodiments and enjoyments."[95] Whitman grounds his ethics of oneness in an ontology of shared substance. Our bodies are basically the same, Whitman concludes, for they are equally godly:

> Have you ever loved the body of a woman?
> Have you ever loved the body of a man?
> Do you not see that these are exactly the same to all in all nations and times all over the earth?
>
> If any thing is sacred the human body is sacred,
> And the glory and sweat of a man is the token of manhood untainted,
> And in man or woman a clean, strong, firm-fibred body, is more beautiful than the most beautiful face.
> Have you seen the fool that corrupted his own live body? or the fool that corrupted her own live body?
> For they do not conceal themselves, and cannot conceal themselves.[96]

In his description of the slaves at auction, Whitman brings together his twin discourses of oneness. Though their bodies are of a different color than his, they are made of the same divine materials. They pulse with the same divine energy. Moreover, these people are on the same journey as everyone else, and like everyone else, they have an equal claim to this path. This is why their strength matters, and why Whitman calls attention to it—for tremendous strength and vitality are required to walk the path toward cosmic consciousness. The soul sight is not for the faint of heart. For a slaveholder, the strength of slaves might prove that they are destined for a life of toil. For Whitman, the slaves' bodily health proves they are ready to walk the path to cosmic consciousness, boldly, without fear.

Everything Whitman says about the bodies of others is true, too, of his own body. Look deeply at your body; touch it from head to toe, and see its strength and its health, know that it is divine, one of many divine bodies walking on this earth in a global procession toward enlightenment. This is an additional, fourth spiritual exercise that Whitman models for his readers in his poetry, *the deification of the body*. According to one of his admirers, Whitman was one of the great nineteenth-century "heroes of the enfranchisement of the body."[97] Whitman does not argue that all bodies are divine. He simply states this as fact, suggesting that if Americans want to experience the intuitive insight of cosmic consciousness—if they want to talk with God—then they will mark all bodies as divine, too. To sing the body electric is to recognize the sacredness of one's body and the bodies of others and then to actively devote oneself to this sacredness in all interactions.

Whitman's deification of the body corrects a profound deficiency in Emerson's ethics of oneness; but Whitman, too, has his own excesses that need to be acknowledged. Indeed, Whitman's descriptions of slaves and slavery reveal yet another hazard implicit to rhetorics of oneness. In "I Sing the Body Electric," the narrative trajectory moves from outside in, from the other to the self—the bodies of others are divine, and so, too, is my own. I suspect that Whitman organized his poem this way in order to counteract the egotism of his culture. Whenever I teach this poem, however, my students tend to reverse the direction of poetic enlightenment, reading it like good Emersonian transcendentalists, from within outward. They begin with themselves, with attempting to see their own bodies as divine, and then they move on to a practice of seeing the bodies of others as divine. This is only natural. And yet in my experience as a professor and a meditation teacher, moving from self to other in this way has a tendency to flatten experience and make it seem like *consubstantiality*—literally occupying the body of another individual—is a possibility. This is a dangerous assumption, but one that Whitman shares.

Because my body is divine, and your body is divine, then you must feel what I feel, you must assume what I assume, and, conversely, I can perfectly understand your experiences, no matter how foreign from my own.

Whitman himself encourages such a reading of oneness at times. Because you and I share the same divine atoms, the same divine consciousness, the same divine souls, "what I assume you shall assume."[98] Whitman assumes that whatever he finds significant will be of significance to others, too—that they will find the same joy he finds in smelling a flower, for instance, or petting a cat. This is incorrect. Nothing matters inherently. Humans make things matter through their rhetoric. But this is not so bad as those moments in "Song of Myself" where Whitman imagines himself literally becoming others and experiencing their joys and pains:

> I am the hounded slave, I wince at the bite of the dogs,
> Hell and despair are upon me, crack and again crack the marksmen,
> I clutch the rails of the fence, my gore dribs, thinn'd with the ooze of my skin,
> I fall on the weeds and stones,
> The riders spur their unwilling horses, haul close,
> Taunt my dizzy ears and beat me violently over the head with whip-stocks.
>
> Agonies are one of my changes of garments,
> I do not ask the wounded person how he feels, I myself become the wounded person,
> My hurts turn livid upon me as I lean on a cane and observe.[99]

Whitman does not ask the wounded person how he feels—he becomes the wounded person, and the other's pain and dizziness become his own. As a nurse during the Civil War, he of course had plenty of opportunities to practice such *livid turning*. This is not empathy or sympathy; it is radical consubstantiality, the art of literally turning into another person, of occupying their place in the cosmos, of becoming someone else. In esoteric yoga philosophy, this is known as the practice of *parkaya pravesh*, and it is an example of black magic, the purview of sinister yogis.[100] For Whitman, there is nothing sinister about it—it is a natural consequence of cosmic consciousness, of becoming one with the universe and all beings. Livid turning follows from singing the body electric. "I am the man, I suffer'd, I was there," he intones.[101]

The trouble is that Whitman wasn't there. He was not the slave. He can act with compassion toward the runaway slave—and should—but he cannot become the slave. He does not know the feeling of being hunted, of never feeling safe, of constantly being on guard. As a white man he does not know what it means to be black in America in the way someone who is black knows what it means to be black in America, and neither do I. Recognizing this limitation need not lead us to the bleak and desolate land of solipsism or psychologism, to the belief that we are cut off from the world or that we can never truly understand another person's joys and pains. Sympathy, empathy, and understanding are possible, and necessary. And yet Whitman's flights of fancy into the bodies of others demonstrate that the ethics of oneness requires a hefty dose of humility lest it become a philosophy of universalist arrogance. The ethics of oneness must be grounded in the understanding that while it is possible to expand the perspective from which we see the world, nevertheless we will always see that world from a perspective. The ethics of oneness cannot be an ethics of sameness. Whitman is at his best when he refuses to collapse differences into sameness, when he recognizes that others' experiences are incommensurate even though they share the same divine scaffolding, when he himself is humble in his divine vision.

Grief and Its Expression

Perhaps Whitman learned the practice of communication as yoga straight from the Bhagavad Gita, where Krishna calls on Arjuna to treat everyone as divine; but he almost certainly encountered it in Emerson's essays, and Emerson himself learned it from the Gita. I trace this lineage because it demonstrates the many divergent paths that monistic philosophies of oneness can take. Krishna teaches oneness in order to argue for war without enemyship. Whitman's oneness is a gospel of peace and connection without enemyship. By marking the body as sacred, Whitman undercuts the case for war that Krishna so eloquently and passionately makes in the Gita. Indeed, it's hard to imagine a war rhetoric that admits the sacredness of the body—for war is based on dehumanization, on the marking of bodies as disposable. Had Krishna sung the body electric, I think that things would have gone down very differently at Kurukshetra, for he wouldn't have been able to convince Arjuna to fight. The first principle of war rhetoric is to frame the enemy as less than human, as savage, as a dirty rat or flea, as a cancer or a plague, so that they are easier to kill and in fact must be killed if we are to survive.[102] Interestingly enough, the converse is also true: to mark the enemy as divine and eternal, to celebrate them as a walking talking embodiment of the unkillable *brahman*, can also serve as powerful war rhetoric. Whitman's framing of the body as sacred and real thus corrects a crucial error of Emerson's thought. To live an ethical life of oneness, democratic citizens must sing the body electric.

And this means, finally, learning how to mourn. After his son's death, Emerson felt tremendous grief, and it reinforced his already-present inclination toward an idealism that encouraged him to mourn by announcing that death is an illusion. Whitman did not allow himself such idealism. In Whitman's ethics of oneness, *grief* is a sister emotion to *gratefulness*. Both are grounding emotions, pulling us back to earth when our philosophies of oneness float us off into the clouds. For Emerson, oneness was a perspective achieved by ascending to a "higher plane." Whitman loves the view from such a pinnacle—at times he sets up camp there, looking down on creation from the mountain peak or the orbit of a dancing star—but in general his oneness is more grounded, more earthy, more visceral and concrete and real. Whitman's poetry creates an atmosphere of gratefulness for life, of reverence and wonder at the eternal mystery of being. Gladness draws Whitman's attention, and his readers', to the interconnectedness of the all, for it encourages us to notice the sprawling support infrastructure that makes life possible. *Leaves of Grass* is also marked by tender moments of grieving. It's okay to grieve, Whitman reassures us. Even though the body and the soul are in some mysterious way eternal, something real is lost when a brother or a sister in being dies. Those who die are not caducous.

Grief drew Emerson even closer to the Bhagavad Gita. Emerson allowed himself to become Arjuna and to be convinced by Krishna's words, such that these words poured forth from his pen in a new language for a new audience in a new culture in his poem "Brahma." Like Krishna, Emerson recognized that there is power in emotion—the power to inspire us to act but also to throw us off balance, to divert us from what must be done. Repeatedly in the Bhagavad Gita, Krishna instructs Arjuna to master his emotions, to set aside his compassion and grief, to overcome his fear and resentment, to fix his mind on his duty, and to fight. This is no time for Arjuna to engage in "anticipatory grief" for his cousins and teachers and friends, no time to mourn them (mourning being the outward expression of grief):

> Mighty-armed Arjuna,
> Even if you think this
> Born forever or forever dead,
> You should not mourn for this.
>
> For what is born a death is sure
> And sure a birth for what is dead.
> Over this inevitable meaning
> You are not to mourn.[103]

Yogis are supposed to be completely balanced, no matter what happens in life. "In success or failure, stay the same," Krishna tells Arjuna. "It's said that equilibrium is yoga."[104] *Samatva*, equilibrium or evenness of mind, is yoga. As Patanjali testifies in his Yoga Sutra (a text popularized in the United States in the late nineteenth century by the Theosophical Society and Swami Vivekananda), the yogi is "not afflicted by the dualities of the opposites" such as hot and cold or pain and pleasure or grief and joy.[105] Looking at life from a higher plane, taking refuge in transcendent oneness, and knowing that nothing truly lives or truly dies because the soul is immortal, the yogi has learned how to master change. The mind's tornadoes are nothing to the yogi. Life's vicissitudes are nothing to the yogi. Nothing throws the yogi off balance. Why mourn, Arjuna, when there is nothing to mourn? Grief is a natural human emotion; however, for Advaita Vedanta, it is based in delusion.

There is power in grief. Krishna recognizes this, and his philosophy is designed to teach Arjuna to block this emotion so that it does not again bring him to his knees. If Arjuna grieves his opponents, he will not fight. Think of their eternal souls, Krishna therefore advises. If you understand the true ontology of oneness, you will recognize that their bodies might perish during the war but their souls never die. So why grieve? Why mourn? There is no reason!

There is freedom in yoga, the freedom to act. But we must ask, What are the costs of such freedom?

There is power in grief. To grieve is to remember. To grieve is to honor. To grieve is to treat with reverence a life lived in and through a body. To grieve is to feel an absence—not just to acknowledge it, but to feel it deep in one's heart. To grieve is to meet change and loss and tragedy with respect and sadness. If Arjuna grieves, he cannot fight. Grieving is not the job of warriors and yogis in the Bhagavad Gita; the yogi knows oneness, feels eternity, and fights. After the war is over, the surviving men of the Mahabharata tell stories, spin parables, and talk philosophy in order to justify the conflict and process their emotions. The goal is to cut the ties with "the wheel of death and rebirth."[106] Philosophy is the work of men. Grieving is women's work. And, indeed, the book of the Mahabharata that immediately follows the doomsday conflagration at Kurukshetra is titled "The Book of the Women." In her feminist retelling of the Mahabharata, *The Palace of Illusions* (2008), the contemporary novelist Chitra Banerjee Divakaruni transforms this book from a scene of helpless, will-less women weeping and wailing over the bodies of their dead husbands and children into a story of strong women taking charge and exercising their agency to make the world a more just place.[107] Divakaruni's Panchaali and Gandhari and Kunti and Subhadra are not pawns in a man's story but agents who see a wrong—the terrible mistreatment of women who no longer have their husbands to defend them after the war—and step up to right it. The justice they seek (and the peace they find) is rooted in the recognition of loss, the very thing that Krishna refuses Arjuna in the Gita. And the very thing that Emerson refused himself after his son's death.

But not Whitman. "When Lilacs Last in the Dooryard Bloom'd," one of the poems Whitman wrote in honor of President Lincoln after he was murdered, is a magisterial, mystical poem of wonder and grief and awe that begins with a shock. Spring arrives; the lilacs bloom, fragrant and beautiful; and at this optimistic moment of rebirth and renewal, when humanity can finally take a collective sigh of relief that we have survived another winter and the time has come to thaw, Whitman mourns, and thinks of death:

> When lilacs last in the dooryard bloom'd,
> And the great star early droop'd in the western sky in the night,
> I mourn'd, and yet shall mourn with ever-returning spring.[108]

This is a jarring juxtaposition, especially for a poet who, according to William James, "owes his importance in literature to the systematic expulsion from his writings of all contractile elements."[109] Here the great poet invites us into paradox. Spring, symbolized by fragrant lilacs, contains within it the seeds of change and decay; the bird's song, a harbinger of spring, and life, is a thrilling lament. As he looks at the beautiful blooming lilac bush, Whitman remembers a lost love: "And I thought of him I love."[110] The poem ends with a battle scene, armies arrayed, trumpets blaring, flags flying, bodies lying on the ground. Perhaps it is a battlefield from the Civil War; perhaps it is Kurukshetra. Ultimately it doesn't really matter, for in this case the poet does not root his musings to a particular time or place. After the war ends, Whitman grieves for those who have passed. But as he grieves he recalls the lilacs and the bird songs, knowing that they persist somewhere and also here, in his memory, and he is grateful for the time he has now. Grief does not lead him away from the battlefield and up a mountainside in search of fresh air and a better view. Grief inspires him to walk the battlefield, to remember, to mourn, and to honor. Grief draws Whitman closer to his fellows and to the world. It fires his gratefulness for what remains. For Whitman, the key to grief is how it is expressed. Does mourning lead us toward oneness and human interconnectedness, or away from it? And how? Does grief encourage us to deny the reality of life, or affirm it? Whitman's grief orients him toward oneness, with the highest respect toward the embodied individuals of the world who walk on distant battlefields, violets on their lapels, bird songs in their hearts.

4

Two Visions

Not I, not any one else can travel that road for you,
You must travel it for yourself . . .

You are also asking me questions and I hear you,
I answer that I cannot answer, you must find out for yourself.
WALT WHITMAN, "Song of Myself"

There is a delightful contradiction at the heart of Walt Whitman's *Leaves of Grass*—a contradiction, perhaps, that also characterizes the American mystical tradition more generally. Mystical experience is personal. As Whitman observes, cosmic consciousness is not something that someone else can have for you; it is a path you must walk for yourself, a question only you can answer. However, most people, in the state we currently find ourselves in, are incapable of this meditative experience of oneness. Too long have we been blinded by habit and convention, by everyday routines that condition us to experience the world as a place of division, separation, "duelity," and competition rather than as an integrated, unified whole bound in shared divinity. We have been out of joint with the universe for so long that we've forgotten what rapport feels like. And so we need a teacher or a guide to help us, someone who, because they have walked the ground themselves, can give us a map of the mystical terrain, someone who will take our hand and show us the way. The teacher tells us what to pack, how to prepare, and what to expect along the journey. The teacher also tells us which mountains to climb and in what order. This, then, is the contradiction: mystical experience is a personal journey, but it is based on a common map that others have provided to us, one that, we know from psychological studies of priming and self-fulfilling prophecies, will determine to a large extent what we experience on our trek.[1] Though we must achieve rapport for ourselves, the experience we have of oneness will invariably be influenced by the teachers we speak to, the poets we read, the friends we consult, and the philosophers we query as we prepare for our sojourn. Meditation remains a personal experience, but this experience is molded by impersonal factors that are outside our personal control. At times, even infinity is shaped by human motivations.

The Bhagavad Gita seems to admit as much. In chapter 17, Krishna—who takes on the role of Arjuna's teacher, guru, and *yogacharya* in the poem—testifies to the power of faith (*sraddha*), instructing Arjuna that a person's faith will shape what they consider to be true and how they see the world:

> Truth takes on the shape of
> Each man's faith, Arjuna.
> Man is made of faith.
> As his faith is, he is.[2]

In the 1855 translation by J. Cockburn Thompson that Whitman owned and annotated and kept under his pillow at the time of his death, Krishna observes, "Mortal man, who is gifted with faith, is of the same nature as that (being) on whom he reposes his faith."[3] Thompson admitted that he struggled with the complex Sanskrit grammar of this passage, though, he mused, invoking the example of demons, or Rakshasas: "The sense is clear enough. . . . If a man worship the gods, whose nature contains a predominance of goodness, his own nature will contain a like predominance. If he worship the Rakshasas, and rely on them, his nature is a bad one, and so on."[4] In many yoga traditions, including the Gita, *sraddha*, faith, is a gift from the gods that sustains seekers on their spiritual journey, helping them confront and overcome doubt (*samshaya*).[5] According to Krishna, what we hold to be true will be shaped by our beliefs, our expectations, and our desires. If we have faith that the world is this way rather than that, then the world tends to look this way rather than that. As we believe, so the world becomes, *for us*. If we have faith in oneness, then the world might begin to look like it is one. If we have faith in oneness, then moments of connection become more salient and instances of disconnection lose their vitality. The future is conditioned by faith. Faith has a way of proving its own verification, as William James once said.[6]

Many mystics testify that the moment of enlightenment transcends words. Perhaps Advaitins do believe that oneness is beyond argument, as the scholars say.[7] But the Bhagavad Gita is a complex pastiche of many philosophies included in an epic narrative, the Mahabharata, that is intended to be a cultural encyclopedia holding the wealth of all Indian knowledge, with all its glorious paradoxes and inconsistencies—and it's not clear Krishna believes that the experience of oneness is beyond argument. If the truth of oneness is in fact beyond argument—if there were no case for oneness—there would be very little to say on the matter, and neither this Bhagavad Gita nor the other Indian classics would exist. And yet Krishna spends the first ten chapters of the Gita attempting to convince Arjuna of the truth of oneness.

At the beginning of chapter 11 of the Bhagavad Gita, Arjuna finally admits he is convinced by Krishna's arguments. He thanks Krishna for his "kindness," for teaching him "the highest secret"—that the many-splendored world of variety is in fact one, that individuals, who on the surface appear separate and alone, are interconnected incarnations of divine oneness.[8] Now, desiring an unmediated vision of God, Arjuna petitions to see Krishna's divine form (the *vishvarupa* or *virat-swarup*). Krishna grants him his wish, only to have Arjuna look on his divine form with a dumbfounded expression and a blank, uncomprehending stare.[9] And then Krishna remembers—Arjuna cannot see his true cosmic form as he presently is:

> But you can't see me
> With this, your own eye . . .
> I'll give you a divine eye.
> Look at my majestic yoga![10]

Here, *yoga* means the power of revelation. Through his "majestic yoga," Krishna, the "prince of yoga" (*yogesvara*) shows Arjuna the true majesty of oneness. There is a reason this revelation comes in chapter 11 rather than chapter 1—at the outset of the dialogue, Arjuna is not ready for it. Krishna had to prepare him by teaching him how to meditate and to properly devote himself to God. Krishna also has to convince Arjuna that he wants to see the divine form, for the suggestion here is that only those who actively desire to see God will see God. And even then, Arjuna is not able to see Krishna as he truly is. First he has to be granted the gift of a divine eye.

I've always found it jarring that in his first aborted attempt at revealing his divine form to Arjuna, Krishna tells him to look upon the splendor of God and also to see "whatever else you wish to see!"[11] Is it really a divine vision if Arjuna sees whatever he wishes to see? This seems more like a daydream and less like a true glimpse of reality. Now I recognize Krishna's words as a profound commentary about hermeneutics, the science of interpretation, for he addresses the relationship between faith, belief, and experience. Under normal circumstances, humans are incapable of experiencing divine oneness in its totality. As such, Krishna understands that Arjuna's experience of oneness will be shaped by his faith, his desires, his fears, and his expectations, by how he wants and needs to experience infinity. As his teacher, Krishna provides Arjuna with a map to the world of oneness and actively works to shape his experience through the construction of this map. As the prince of yoga, Krishna has the power to highlight certain aspects of oneness while downplaying others. In a sense, Krishna is the author of Arjuna's vision. What Krishna shows Arjuna is aimed at achieving the larger rhetorical goal of the Gita—that is, convincing the great warrior to fight in the battle at

Kurukshetra. Any description of oneness, any attempt to bring oneness before the eyes, will influence how those who hear it, see it, seek it, and attempt to embody it. And this is Whitman's connection to the Bhagavad Gita that I most want to highlight in this chapter.

The divine vision of chapter 11 is the centerpiece of the Bhagavad Gita. A transcendent vision of oneness is also at the heart of Whitman's *Leaves of Grass*, especially his poem "Salut au Monde!" In this poem, Whitman attempts something that Emerson never attempted, that to my knowledge had up to that point rarely been attempted in American literature and letters (and rarely has been attempted since): he puts oneness into words.[12] I admire this as one of Whitman's greatest poetic achievements. Whitman does the impossible, expressing the inexpressible. In *Leaves of Grass*, Whitman takes up Emerson's challenge in "The Poet" of using language—which is inherently a medium of division—to repair "the decays of things" by capturing an experience that is beyond division, that is beyond language itself, a moment of rapport with the divine ground of existence.[13] We should stop and dwell on Whitman's divine vision because *to talk of oneness is to orient an audience toward this experience*. To describe the nature of oneness, which is beyond words, with words is to shape the audience's beliefs about the nature of oneness and hence how they will attempt to live a life committed to oneness. This is rhetoric at its most powerful, its most grandiose, its most subtle.

First Vision

What did Arjuna see when he saw the all?

To understand what Arjuna saw requires stepping back for a moment and looking at the rhetorical structure of the divine vision, which requires walking back one step further and briefly discussing the narrative structure of the Mahabharata itself (of which the Bhagavad Gita is a central chapter). The Mahabharata is a product of an oral culture that foregrounded the question of the narrator. Tales are told by people, and every narrator puts their own personal, idiosyncratic spin on things. The epic openly advertises its own complex composition. The work presents itself as a creation of Vyasa, whose name in Sanskrit means "the composer" or "the divider." Vyasa was one of the original Vedic rishis; he is also a character in the Mahabharata who keeps the plot moving (let us say that he is *genetically involved* in the events that unfold). Supposedly, after composing his epic history of the war at Kurukshetra—in some later versions, including Peter Brook's famous stage play and film from the 1980s, with the assistance of the elephant god Ganesha, who breaks off one of his tusks to use as a quill to write down the divine verses—Vyasa teaches the Mahabharata to five of his students, who then travel around the world reciting it for diverse audiences (and not just for humans). The implication is that the version we have is just one of five Mahabharatas, and that, theoretically at least, there might be others out there that present matters somewhat differently. Take everything with a grain of salt, in other words.

The version of the Mahabharata we know is narrated by Vyasa's student Vaishampayana to King Janamejaya, who is Arjuna's great-grandson, on the occasion of a snake sacrifice, many years after the war, and long after the original Pandava brothers and their wife, Draupadi, died. The Mahabharata is a textbook example of polyphony, for as the story unfolds, multiple voices compete for time and attention.[14] Indeed, even as Vaishampayana recites the story, other narrators emerge to put their own spin on things. Chapters 5 and 6 of the Mahabharata, which include the Bhagavad Gita, are spoken by the blind king Dhritarashtra's charioteer, Sanjaya. Earlier in the Mahabharata, Sanjaya had also been awarded the divine eye, *divya-drishti*—in his case by Vyasa, not Krishna—and he uses this ability to see the distant events of the war as they unfold and to report them to the king.

This context is vital to understanding the divine vision of the Bhagavad Gita, because in chapter 11 there are at least three narrators who speak: Sanjaya, reporting to Dhritarashtra what Arjuna sees and how Krishna explains this vision to him; Arjuna, reporting what he sees; and Krishna, explaining to Arjuna the meaning of what he has seen.[15] Sanjaya's report emphasizes that Krishna is diversity in unity and the unity underlining diversity. Indeed, Sanjaya's verses provide good evidence for the Bhedabheda Vedanta interpretation of the Gita—he says repeatedly that what Arjuna sees is *an-eka*, "not one" or "many." The all is the manyness of oneness. He then observes that Arjuna sees "the cosmos whole / Divided in many ways" in Krishna's body.[16] Arjuna describes his awesome vision of Krishna as the all, but he admits that he doesn't understand what he sees. As a human being, he is simply incapable of comprehending divinity in all its glory. Krishna explains what Arjuna's vision (and also Sanjaya's vision) means in terms that Arjuna can understand. Here, Krishna takes on the role of spiritual guide and also rhetorician, for his purpose is to actively shape Arjuna's experience of infinity so that he is persuaded to do what the narrative demands of him—fight and defeat his cousins.

Gifted divine vision temporarily, Arjuna struggles over seventeen verses to narrate what he sees. He views the universe in Krishna's body—arms and legs, eyes and mouths, infinite in every direction. Refracted like light through a prism, Krishna is everything, and everything is Krishna. God is all, and yet somehow more. Sun and moon for eyes, Krishna's mouth is the sacred fire that eats the Brahmin's oblations. Krishna is the sun, heating creation with his brilliant warmth. Krishna is space and time, all-encompassing and all-consuming, infinite and unchanging, without beginning, middle, or end. Krishna—who was once a local village deity—is here elevated to the great god Vishnu, adorned with crown, mace, and chakra, standing ready to guard the eternal dharma. The many lesser gods gather to worship Krishna and are part of him. Great yogis and prophets praise him and are part of him. All the classes of beings look on in astonishment and are part of him. *Hare* Krishna! Hail Krishna!

And then the vision turns dark, and violent.

> Your mighty form—its many mouths and many eyes,
> Its many mighty arms, many thighs and many feet,
> Many bellies, many harrowing tusks—seeing this,
> The worlds are shaking—so am I!
>
> A multicolor blaze that touches the sky,
> Mouths agape, and vast and blazing eyes—
> I see you, and my inner self is shaking!
> I find no calm or courage, Vishnu!
>
> Seeing these harrowing tusks of yours
> In mouths that resemble the fires of time,
> I have lost my direction, I can't get to shelter!
> Lord God, home of the moving world, have mercy![17]

Arjuna sees his foes at Kurukshetra—his uncle Dhritarashtra's one hundred sons, his cousins the Kauravas, alongside his teachers Bhishma and Drona, and his mortal enemy Karna—enter Krishna's flaming mouths to be crushed and broken, crushed up, and spit out by God himself:

> Swiftly they enter your mouths
> With those fearsome, those harrowing tusks!
> Some of them I see with mashed heads
> Stuck between your teeth![18]

Like moths to a flame, Arjuna sees warriors—armies—planets—solar systems—all of creation—drawn to Krishna's mouth to be devoured. Krishna is life; Krishna is death. "Namaste to you, best of Gods! Mercy!"[19] Arjuna bows to him in fearful worship, though he admits that he doesn't understand what he has seen.

Over the course of three vivid shocking jaw-dropping verses Krishna explains:

I am Time. I make worlds die.
I have come here to annihilate worlds.
All these warriors, stationed in opposing ranks:
Even without you, they will cease to be.

So stand up. Get your glory.
Beat your enemies. Enjoy a thriving kingdom.
I have struck them down already.
Archer, simply be my instrument.

Drona, Bhishma, Jayadratha,
Karna, and others, too. War heroes. Killed
By me. Now you kill. Do not tremble!
Fight! You'll beat your rivals in the joy of battle![20]

These are the verses that came to J. Robert Oppenheimer's mind when the first atomic bomb exploded over the Trinity test site in New Mexico in 1945 (he recalled Krishna's words from a slightly different translation—"I am become death, the destroyer of worlds"). Oppenheimer knew the Bhagavad Gita well, and it helped steel his nerves against the guilt he felt as he spearheaded the effort to build this new and almost unimaginably powerful weapon of destruction. For Oppenheimer, the Gita served as "an anodyne for the pangs of conscience."[21] In the context of the Mahabharata, this is exactly the purpose that Krishna intends his discourse to serve. It is meant to rebut Arjuna's argument that the war is immoral and to mollify his frayed nerves so that he is prepared to fight.

Many scholars and pandits read the Gita as disconnected from the larger narrative.[22] These three famous verses challenge this interpretation, however, for Krishna specifically mentions characters from the Mahabharata in explicating himself to Arjuna. And these verses are not some diversion within a much longer discourse—Krishna needs only three verses, *these three verses*, to explain to Arjuna the true nature of God, and these verses all directly address the critical plot point of the Mahabharata; namely, that Arjuna is the greatest warrior of the age and he refuses to fight, though he must. These three verses prove that the divine vision of the Bhagavad Gita is not free of the needs and demands of the narrative in which it takes place.

Notice here that Krishna is actively working to shape Arjuna's experience of oneness, both in what he reveals to him (the death of his opponents, four of which he mentions by name) and what he does not (all the widows wailing over the bodies of their dead husbands after the apocalypse, or the fact that the Pandavas' children will be slaughtered during and after the war, or the Pandavas' eventual ignominious deaths on a snowy mountainside, or

Krishna's own tragic death after being cursed by the matriarch of his adversaries), and then in how he explains and justifies what Arjuna sees. Meditation is not a formless, directionless, meandering exercise in the Gita. It is highly scripted and carefully orchestrated. The meditation Krishna teaches Arjuna is soteriological, for it aims to achieve the ultimate state of *samadhi*, absorption of the *atman* into the *brahman*, the one into oneness.[23] To learn to meditate, one must study with a teacher (in this case, Krishna), who instructs the pupil (in this case, Arjuna) how to experience the truth. Krishna teaches Arjuna what to see as he meditates, and tells him how he should feel, carefully curating his experience in order to achieve a particular outcome—to get Arjuna to fight. And so he informs Arjuna that God, acting as Time, has already destroyed his opponents, including the four war heroes he invokes. From a cosmic perspective, Arjuna's enemies have already been vanquished by Krishna, the annihilator of worlds. Even without any action on Arjuna's part, they are all dead. All that is left for Arjuna is "merely" (*matram*) to become Krishna's "instrument" (*nimitta*) and to enjoy the battle.

The narrative of the Mahabharata is a composite that grew and changed over many centuries. Perhaps this explains why characters are certain of something in one chapter only to forget it in the next. At times Arjuna is positive that Krishna is an avatar of Vishnu. Other times he seems confused about this fact. At times even Krishna himself seems to forget that he is God. But Krishna's importance to the outcome of the war is never doubted: "Wherever Lord Krishna is, there, surely, will be virtue, wisdom—and victory!"[24] Understanding this, at a pivotal moment before the war Arjuna and his cousin Duryodhana (the haughty, brawny, firstborn bulldozer who leads the enemy Kauravas), go to Krishna's home in Dwarka to petition his support for their respective sides. They find Krishna sleeping. Having arrived first, Duryodhana sits down by Krishna's head, and Arjuna by Krishna's feet. When Krishna wakes, he informs the cousins that both are dear to him, and that he wishes to support both sides in the conflict. Krishna has an unbeatable army of a million hardened, well-drilled soldiers. One cousin can have the troops; the other can have *him*, but only as an adviser, for he refuses to lift a hand in battle against those he loves (he will come close to violating this rule several times during the ensuing paroxysm). Because Krishna saw Arjuna first, he lets him choose, over Duryodhana's protestations that he is older and that he arrived first and so *he* should get to choose. Duryodhana gets what he wants anyway, for Arjuna chooses Krishna. Duryodhana leaves Dwarka thinking Arjuna a moron for choosing one man over a million. With shiny new toys to add to his already superior army, Duryodhana is certain that he is unbeatable. But Arjuna, Krishna, and the audience know better.

From a narrative standpoint, the four enemy warriors that Krishna mentions by name in his explication of Arjuna's divine vision—Bhishma, Jayadratha, Drona, and Karna—are particularly significant, for they are the soldiers who pose the greatest threat to Arjuna, and hence to the victory of the Pandavas.[25] To understand the full rhetorical power of how Krishna frames Arjuna's divine vision, it is worth taking a moment to briefly tell each of these four warriors' stories. Bhishma acts as patriarch and guru to both the Pandavas and the Kauravas. He is literally invincible, for due to an extreme austerity, the gods grant him a boon that he can choose the moment of his death. Debts of gratitude have godly power, and because he ate Duryodhana's salt, as the Mahabharata says, Bhishma is compelled to support his side during the war. Bhishma becomes the first fearsome commander of Duryodhana's army, and with this unbreakable genius in charge, the Kauravas successfully repel the Pandava assault, inflicting heavy losses on their opponents. Beaten badly by his stratagems, the Pandavas go to Bhishma at night, asking how he can be defeated. Bhishma—compelled to fight for the wrong side in the conflict—orchestrates an elaborate ruse involving a reincarnated cross-dressing hermaphrodite warrior who, due to an ancient vendetta, was granted a boon by the gods that could hasten Bhishma's downfall. Eventually Bhishma is felled by a reluctant, crestfallen Arjuna, but really Bhishma is responsible for his own death. In the other three cases, however, it is Krishna who is responsible for the death of Arjuna's opponents, even when Arjuna or others kill them.

After Arjuna's son Abhimanyu is killed in battle, Arjuna vows that by the next nightfall he will cut off the head of one of his son's murderers, the Sindhu King Jayadratha.[26] When Jayadratha learns of Arjuna's vow, he hides behind enemy lines, always a step or two ahead of Arjuna's crazed pursuit. Krishna becomes anxious—if Arjuna fails and breaks his vow, the gods will curse him to eternal damnation. Vows are taken very seriously in the Mahabharata. And so Krishna pledges to "resort to yoga" to make it seem as though the sun has set, when it in fact is still high in the sky, to get Jayadratha to let his guard down.[27] He does, and Arjuna aims his majestic weapon Pashupata at the unknowing and defenseless Jayadratha, lopping his head clean off.

Drona, too, gets decapitated. After Bhishma is incapacitated, Drona takes over control of Duryodhana's forces. Drona served as the primary combat teacher of both the Pandavas and the Kauravas, and he is a formidable warrior in his own right. Like Bhishma, he fights for Duryodhana not out of love—Arjuna is his favorite pupil—but due to a debt of gratitude. Drona is so fearsome in the field that not even Arjuna can hurt him, though it is clear that Arjuna does not desire to hurt his teacher and so he is not trying his hardest. "Come, Arjuna," Krishna urges at one point, "things are serious. What we need is rather less scruple, much more stratagem."[28] And so Krishna devises a plan. Krishna is certain that Drona will lose the will to fight if his son, Ashvatthaman, is killed. At the moment it is not possible for the Pandavas to slay Ashvatthaman, and so Krishna instructs Arjuna's brother Bhima to kill a nearby elephant who happens to share the name Ashvatthaman. Bhima murders the elephant, and the Pandavas call out, "Ashvatthaman is dead!" Badly shaken by this terrible news, Drona stops fighting and queries the eldest Pandava, Yudhishthira, who is known for his unflinching honesty, if it is true that his son is dead. He replies, "Ashvatthaman is dead!" though he is thinking of the elephant, not Drona's son.[29] In some versions of the Mahabharata Yudhishthira mutters under his breath, "It's an elephant," but this does not assuage his conscience, for he knows that he is lying—and his lie proves effective, coming as it does from the mouth of a *dharmaputra*, the son of virtue who supposedly never lies. Drona drops his weapons and refuses to fight any further. Reclining on his chariot, he "composed himself in yoga, in profound meditation. As he sat, seemingly still alive, his soul was liberated from his body and traveled to the domain of the blessed."[30] Unaware that Drona has given up the battle, one of Arjuna's compatriots raises his sword triumphantly and severs Drona's calm and placid head from his body.

Karna's story is a tragedy that transcends time, far sadder to me at least than anything invented by Sophocles or Shakespeare or Melville. Karna is the eldest Pandava brother—in the unfolding telenovela, there are really six Pandava brothers, not five! Karna is in fact the rightful heir to the throne, though he does not learn this fact until it is too late, and the Pandavas do not learn this fact until Karna is dead, felled by his brother's hand. Raised by humble charioteers, Karna is a mighty warrior, the son of the sun god, Surya, who matches his brother Arjuna's skill arrow for arrow. Famed for his charity, a debt of gratitude proves his downfall. When he first emerges into the narrative, Karna is dissed and mocked by the Pandavas for his low status. In this moment of clever scheming, Duryodhana sees a golden opportunity and takes Karna in, lavishing him with gifts and material support and titles that Karna is then obligated to repay with his life. Karna is not blameless. He is driven by status anxiety, resentment, and hatred, and he participates in one of the Mahabharata's most shameful episodes, the disrobing of Draupadi.[31] As the narrative unfolds, however, he repeatedly proves himself to be a tragic hero, and for many of my Indian friends, he (along with Krishna, of course) is the true hero of the Mahabharata.[32]

Before the war begins, Karna pledges to Arjuna's mother—his mother—Kunti, that though he is coming for Arjuna, he will not hurt her other four sons; it is only Arjuna, who so often mocked and insulted him, that he will kill. That way, whether he or Arjuna lives, whether he or Arjuna dies, Kunti will be left with five healthy sons. Karna fights valiantly on Duryodhana's side against his brothers. He possesses a weapon, a gift from the chief of the gods, Indra, against which there is no defense; he marks it with Arjuna's name. To spare Arjuna, Krishna tricks Karna into using this weapon on Arjuna's nephew, the beloved Rakshasa Ghatotkacha. After he dies, the Pandavas wail and mourn, but Krishna is jubilant. He exclaims to Arjuna:

> The spear of Indra was his last advantage
> and now it has been spent! Ghatotkacha
> was created to be the instrument
> of Karna's downfall. But make no mistake,
> it will not be easy to overcome him
> even now. You must do as I tell you:
> there will come a moment, as you fight him,
> when his chariot wheel will stick in the ground.
> Disregarding all the rules of warfare,
> you must kill him when I give the sign.[33]

He reassures an incredulous Arjuna:

> By means of stratagems like this, I have worked
> For your good, and for the good of Earth.[34]

During the final climactic scene, the wheel of Karna's chariot gets stuck in the ground. His charioteer, Shayla, is a double agent who has been secretly working for his downfall—the ersatz son of a charioteer condemned by an ersatz charioteer!—and he refuses to help Karna at this crucial moment. So Karna dismounts the chariot and attempts to pull the wheel from the earth's greedy maw. Observant of the rules of war, which forbid attacking an unarmed man with his back turned to the battle, Arjuna lowers his bow. But Krishna commands him to stand up and fight. This is the climactic moment. It has all been leading up to this. "Don't let up now! Karna is your hate-filled enemy. Kill him while you can."[35] Arjuna shoots him in the back. Karna dies, realizing that dharma, righteousness, is of no help to him when Krishna is determined that he fall.

According to Sanjaya, after hearing Krishna's three verses explaining the truth of life and death in a world of divine oneness, and heeding his command to kill his enemies who, from a god's-eye view, are already dead, Arjuna kneels and addresses Krishna "in a terror-struck stutter." Praising Krishna in the highest as the highest, Arjuna apologizes over the course of eleven additional verses for any offense he might have caused in the past when he addressed Krishna merely as a "friend" and not as the Lord. And then he pleads for a return to normalcy. Divine sight is just too much. Please, please return to your familiar form, please, please, stop speaking in your cosmic booming voice, Arjuna pleads, please, please. Heeding Arjuna's desperate plea, Krishna returns to being Krishna, happy, smiling, kind Krishna. "Be free of fear again, and in high spirits," Krishna says.[36] Chapter 11 ends with Krishna reminding Arjuna just how special this divine vision is. Scholarship, austerities, charity, sacrifice—none of these traditional Brahminical practices can successfully petition God to reveal himself. Only the purest devotion to Krishna makes it possible to see the true face of oneness.

The Bhagavad Gita lists fearlessness (*abhaya*) as the first virtue of a noble life.[37] Studying the Bhagavad Gita in India, I heard numerous teachers say that the reason Arjuna is afraid during this scene is because he erroneously views himself as an "I" who is separate from the divine oneness. In Advaita Vedanta, fear (*bhaya*) is the product of division, of the wrongheaded belief that I am separate from the all, that someone or something is opposed to me and wants to harm me (nothing does), or that I have something that can be taken from me (nothing can be). Viewing himself as a lonely individual opposed to his enemies and apart from God, Arjuna feels the fear of isolation and alienation born from opposition. Swami Dayananda Saraswati argues that "Arjuna is going to be frightened by what he saw because he did not include himself."[38] "If you are everything, who is to be frightened by what? Only from a second thing can there be fear—*dvitiyat hi bhayam bhavati*. And there would be no second thing if he had included himself."[39] Saraswati concludes, "There cannot be a source of fear because you can only be afraid of something other than yourself."[40] Arjuna should have recognized that he, like his enemies, was already dead, that he was only a temporary, illusionary manifestation of divine maya, of Krishna's divine play. On a cosmic level it is God who acts, so what do the actions of little lowly humans matter? What is there to fear? What is there to hate? We are all one, we are all already dead, devoured by a hungry god.

Of course, I can think of many other explanations for Arjuna's fear. The dialogue between Krishna and Arjuna starts when, just as the battle is about to begin—right at the peak of the collective inhale before the war trumpets blare and the conches sound, before the first bodies fall to the ground—Arjuna drops his bow and has a panic attack that brings him to his knees. He is overcome, his body wilts; he will not fight. Many readers of the Bhagavad Gita forget that at this point, even in his frazzled state, Arjuna is able to make an eloquent and moving case against war that boils down to this: isn't it against dharma to kill one's relatives and teachers? It is easy to encode the moment when Arjuna collapses as an expression of weakness. I see it rather as an illustration of profound thoughtfulness. Martha Nussbaum points out that Arjuna asks two questions at this moment in the story. The first is "the obvious question"—namely, what should he do? Should he fight or not? This is an obvious question, for while the answer is fraught, it is clear that the question must be answered in the context of the story. The second is "the tragic question"—namely, are any of the choices that Arjuna can make free of moral wrongdoing?[41] Krishna advises Arjuna to act out of duty without concern for the consequences of his actions. At this point, though, Arjuna cannot help but focus on the consequences of killing his friends and family and all the moral hazards that follow from such action. Wouldn't it be better to retire to the forest than to participate in fratricide? Arjuna, the greatest warrior of his age, a soldier who has fought and won countless battles, begins to doubt that it is possible to behave ethically in war.

The Mahabharata was composed at a moment when Indians were arguing about the proper duties of kings—should they be great warriors or peace-building ascetic renouncers devoted to *nivritti*, the contemplative life?[42] The Mahabharata in general is ambivalent about warfare. The Gita is less so. The Mahabharata repeatedly raises tragic questions about war, and to ensure that these questions are not glossed over, the narrator often has the characters stop whatever they are doing to sit down and deliberate the justness of war.[43] And yet, when Arjuna creates the opening for such a conversation at the beginning of the Gita, Krishna immediately shuts down the discussion by demanding that Arjuna focus on the obvious question (should he fight or not) rather than the tragic question (can he make a choice that is morally good). As Nussbaum observes, Arjuna asks the question of whether any action he can take is morally acceptable, but "Krishna, by contrast, either simply fails to see the force of the question altogether or recommends a policy of deliberately not facing it, in order to better get on with one's duty."[44]

Arjuna crumbles on the battlefield the moment that he begins to doubt that he can act morally, whichever path he chooses. Krishna attempts to redefine the situation so that Arjuna will stop contemplating the consequences of his actions and instead focus solely on his duty as a warrior. Krishna makes argument after argument to convince Arjuna that he should willingly, even joyfully, participate in the slaughter. He needs ten chapters to convince Arjuna that Krishna is God and that therefore Arjuna should do as he counsels—Arjuna should fight. Krishna plays his ultimate rhetorical trump card in the eleventh chapter, his *argumentum ad mysterium*, the argument by divine revelation. Here he reveals his cosmic form and commands Arjuna to fight in a booming astral voice that must have assaulted all Arjuna's senses and fried his nerves. Wouldn't this cause fear?

When your dearest friend—someone who has been with you through thick and thin—reveals that he is Vishnu, God walking on earth, and shows himself as a monster with tusks instead of teeth and infinite mouths that grind up the soldiers assembled all around him, wouldn't this cause fear? Perhaps Arjuna felt fear at the close of the divine vision because he was not allowed to explore the tragic doubts he felt, deep in his heart, about the war? Perhaps he felt fear because he suspected that his actions would be morally suspect no matter what he chose to do? Perhaps he felt fear because he realized that no matter what decision he made, his hands would be dirty? Perhaps he felt fear because he recognized that morality demands consideration of the consequences of our actions, and Krishna forbade such consideration with his teaching of actionless action? Perhaps he felt fear because he felt deliberately blocked—he wanted a conversation about the morality of war, and instead got a lesson in duty from God? Perhaps he felt fear because he worried that fighting would be contrary to dharma and might in fact be ethically wrong, but, commanded by God, he felt he didn't have a choice but to behave as he was told? Perhaps he felt fear because he felt coerced? Trapped? Bamboozled? Perhaps he felt fear because he realized in this moment that what he had always thought of as dharma was not set in stone but could, in fact, be redefined by lordly fiat?[45]

Second Vision

What did Walt Whitman see when he saw the all?

Whitman repeatedly asks himself this question in his poem "Salut au Monde!," a beautiful, expansive poem that I read as Whitman's venture to describe his mystical experience of cosmic consciousness as he sat in rapport with the universe. This poem is Whitman's divine vision, his soul sight put into words; it is his analogue to the eleventh chapter of the Bhagavad Gita. Like the Gita, the poem is structured as a dialogue, but here, Whitman talks to himself—he plays the roles of both Krishna and Arjuna:

> O take my hand Walt Whitman!
> Such gliding wonders! such sights and sounds!
> Such join'd unending links, each hood'd to the next,
> Each answering all, each sharing the earth with all.[46]

The essence, the beating heart, the central uplifting message of *Leaves of Grass* is found in this opening stanza. Whitman imagines the poet as a guide who takes a friend by the hand and personally leads them into the dazzling wondrous world. There are sights and sounds to be enjoyed—the world is full of delights and gourmandises, *à la vôtre!*—but it is the poet's job to repeatedly return his friend's focus to the many unseen unities at work amid the spectacle. See the "unending links" that hook this to that! Notice how each is connected to all! Watch how each of us impacts those around us and vice versa! Observe that no one is alone, for each of us shares the earth with all! In this poem, Whitman again models his devotion to oneness. Oneness is all, and Whitman worships and celebrates it. By reaffirming the ontological truth of oneness as Whitman understands it and has experienced it, these verses act as a call for his readers who have not experienced oneness—or who have experienced something very different in their lives—to join hands with the poet in the project of actualizing oneness in a world of division, strife, and conflict.

"What widens within you Walt Whitman?"[47] Arjuna looks at Krishna and sees the universe in his body. Whitman, however, instructs himself to see the universe in his own body, not in the body of an external deity. He is not an isolated individual, severed from the world, an independent, self-made man. Even in the state of rapport, Whitman retains his capacity for awareness and his ability to notice and judge, but as he becomes sensitive to the reality of the all, Whitman becomes conscious of himself as an emanation, an avatar, or, to use his preferred term, an *eidolon*, of the divine all.

The word *eidolon* in ancient Greek meant "phantom" or "ghost," a spirit double of a person that haunts the living, like the eidolon of Helen of Troy in Homer. Plato claimed that such fanciful images were mental delusions, but in the drama of ancient Greece, and perhaps also in the popular religion of the time that such drama reflected, they were imagined to be real.[48] Indeed, in Euripides's plays, Penelope found herself locked in battle against eidolons of the dead Clytemnestra and Helen.[49] Whitman gives the word a more positive and cosmic meaning. In his short poem "Eidolons," an eidolon is the image that a person builds of themselves out of the materials provided by the all:

> Ever the mutable,
> Ever materials, changing, crumbling, re-cohering,
> Ever the ateliers, the factories divine,
> Issuing eidolons.
>
> Lo, I or you,
> Or woman, man, or state, known or unknown,
> We seeming solid wealth, strength, beauty build,
> But really build eidolons.[50]

The "factories divine"—the mutable, changeable, malleable materials of earth and atmosphere—provide us with the raw materials from which we fashion our lives. Americans like to believe that we build wealth, strength, and beauty through our individual initiative, that we are self-made; but really we are sculptors building an image of ourselves out of orbic clay. No clay, no individual; no oversoul, no soul; no all, no each. "The real I myself" is an eidolon fix'd and forg'd from our perception of the way things are and should be.[51] And the ways things are? The all? Far transcending human comprehension, and residing beyond the limits of language, it, too, is an eidolon. Every picture we forge of oneness is a projection, "a round full-orb'd eidolon":

> The noiseless myriads,
> The infinite oceans where the rivers empty,
> The separate countless free identities, like eyesight,
> The true realities, eidolons.
>
> Not this the world,
> Nor these the universes, they the universes,
> Purport and end, ever the permanent life of life,
> Eidolons, eidolons.[52]

Whitman repeatedly describes his experience of cosmic consciousness as beyond language, beyond argument, beyond rhetoric, beyond thought: "I am charged with untold and untellable wisdom, I am silent, I require nothing further."[53] A true mystic, Whitman believes that meditation transcends language. However, in "Salut au Monde!" he also seems to grant that our mental images, or eidolons, of what such an experience should consist of will shape that experience for us. We project finity onto infinity so that it becomes comprehensible to our finite minds. Even the true realities are eidolons, for we perceive them through human eyes.

Advaita Vedanta recognizes this as a vexing metaphysical problem—to talk of oneness is to limit oneness, which is why Advaitins prefer *neti, neti* rhetorics that signal what reality is not rather than attempting to define what it is. In *Leaves of Grass*, however, and especially in "Salut au Monde!," Whitman views the fact that language orients us toward infinity as a rhetorical advantage that a great poet can leverage to change a reader's experience of the world. Indeed, Whitman recognizes that talk of oneness is inherently *moral*—a word I use here fully cognizant of its Latin root, *mores*, or what is appropriate and inappropriate in a given situation. Morality is intimately related to decorum. It is about knowing and following rules of conduct so that we behave as is expected. Talk of oneness is moral, then, because such talk shapes our expectations of what an experience of oneness might consist of and how we should experience it. This is the motivation behind poems like "Salut au Monde!": by describing oneness with a series of rich images, rather than simply saying what it is not, Whitman seeks to shape his audience's expectations and experiences of the all. With his poetry, Whitman provides his readers with orientation, a map to the unnamable, unutterable mysterious terrain of the infinite world.

In the state of cosmic consciousness, fully aware of himself as an eidolon of the all, the world widens within Whitman: "Within me latitude widens, longitude lengthens."[54] "Within me zones, seas, cataracts, forests, volcanoes, groups," he writes.[55] From birth, his being—like all beings—was fashioned out of earth and sky and wind and fire, but in this moment Whitman glimpses his true nature. His breath is the wind that rings the hot equator, his blood the world's waves and rivers, his body its mountains and soils, his voice the sounds of infants crying and people chatting in all the world's languages. His life becomes the gentle arc of the sun rising over the horizon and sinking back again. Like everyone he is divine, for God is found in the wind, and in the fire, in the earth and the sky.

"What do you hear Walt Whitman?" Whitman hears the world's voices—"the workman singing," "the sounds of children and of animals early in the day," "fierce French liberty songs," "the Arab muezzin," "the cry of the Cossack," "the wheeze of the slave-coffee as the slaves march on," "the Hebrew reading his records and psalms," "the rhythmic myths of the Greeks," "the strong legends of the Romans," "the tale of the divine life and blood death of the beautiful God the Christ," "the Hindoo teaching his favorite pupil the loves, wars, adages, transmitted safely to this day from poets who wrote three thousand years ago"—and he knows that his own voice is composed from the same sounds as these voices, the same nouns and verbs, the same praise and blame, the same songs and laments, the same commands and jeers, a sometimes sad, mostly joyous cacophony of life lived in countless ways. What Whitman hears shatters any felt pretense for xenophobia and jingoism. No one would accuse Whitman of being unpatriotic—he believed deeply in the red-white-and-blue, in the unique mission of the United States, the City on a Hill, the nation that would prove the worth of democracy or its downfall. But what he hears levels and equalizes. All the world's wisdom is worthy of attention, as are all the mellifluous voices. And whether we hear these voices or not, they are ours. Each answers all.[56]

"What do you see Walt Whitman?" In seven stanzas, Whitman recounts what he sees during his divine vision. Nearly every one of these more than one hundred verses begins "I see . . ." And Whitman sees everything. He sees the geography of the world, its great mountains, waterways, deserts, and ice fields; he sees the world's history, its empires rising and falling; he sees the religions of the world, including Christianity and Hinduism, born on the Ganges in "the place of the idea of the Deity incarnated by avatars in human forms," growing into and out of the world's great myths and stories; he sees "the cities of the earth and make myself at random a part of them"; he sees the people of the world, from all classes and climes, all races and genders, even the outcasts and those that others label "defective."[57] All of this he sees as a part of himself, and of everyone else, too.

> My spirit has pass'd in compassion and determination around the whole earth,
> I have look'd for equals and lovers and found them ready for me in all lands,
> I think some divine rapport has equalized me with them.[58]

He sees everything—he sees himself—and is compelled to offer salutations: "And I salute all the inhabitants of the earth."[59]

Here the vision breaks off, and the poem changes from a report into an address. "You whoever you are!" Whitman begins, and then in series of hortatory verses he personally addresses the people he has seen in his vision, ending with an expression of well wishes, a love letter to all from all:

> Health to you! good will to you all, from me and America sent!
>
> Each of us inevitable.
> Each of us limitless—each of us with his or her right upon the earth,
> Each of us allow'd the eternal purports of the earth,
> Each of us here as divinely as any is here.[60]

From his experience of cosmic consciousness, Whitman derives the following moral lesson: "each of us" deserves dignity and respect, "each of us" has a *right* to the earth and a *right* to feel rapport, "each of us" is just as welcome here as anyone else, because "each of us" is divine. In the divine, Whitman sees democracy. Whitman's vision of oneness acts as the ultimate ontological justification for human rights, and for the rights of the nonhuman, too. Everyone is divine, everyone is sacred, everyone is worthy of respect, because everyone, though unique, is constantly fashioning themselves out of the divine orbic materials of oneness. Whitman's divine vision is, like Arjuna's, a projection that is designed to create an image, an eidolon, that becomes real the more passionately we attempt to enact it and make it real in our everyday conversations. Whitman here crafts an eidolon of America, an ideal image of how American democracy should be, of what America would look like were it committed to oneness.

In colloquial French, *salut* means "hey" or "hello," so the poem's title "Salut au Monde!" literally means "Hello to the world!" In medieval French, however, the word *salut* had religious connotations related to the concept of salvation—a nuance that Whitman most likely knew from his travels to New Orleans and French Catholic Louisiana. And so the poem's title might also be translated "Salvation to the world!" The salvation of the world is to be found in a direct experience of divine oneness. This experience changes a person's worldview, for while individuality remains, there is no longer separation. Each of us is connected—at first blush by links and hooks, but, peering more deeply into the true state of things, by matter, spirit, and purpose shared. For Whitman, to "see" and "behold" is to *salut*—to rejoice, and be glad, for when a person has had the divine vision of cosmic consciousness, when they've experienced rapport, they see that salvation can only be found in common with others. "Each answering all, each sharing the earth with all." Salvation can only be found in the world, because each of us is a part of the world, not apart from it.

There is one verse in "Salut au Monde!" in particular that illustrates the profound difference between Whitman and Arjuna's experiences of the all, and the subtle difference, too, between Whitman's poetry and Emerson's philosophy. In the midst of describing his vision of the world's geographies, which grow in and out of himself, Whitman observes:

> I see the battle-fields of the earth, grass grows upon them and blossoms and corn[61]

Krishna shows Arjuna the divine vision to persuade him to fight on the battlefield at Kurukshetra, the field of the Kurus, the field of dharma. Whitman, too, experienced war—he served as a nurse on the front lines of the American Civil War, and the war profoundly affected him. Working in the medical tents, talking with the wounded and dying, this restored Whitman's faith in humanity, and in democracy.[62] Whitman does not shy away from the bellicose. He also composes poems of war—he calls them "Drum Taps," poems of shot and steel—but these are not cosmic poems; they are poems of manly nationalism, not rapport. "Salut au Monde!" is a poem of peace, for in his divine vision Whitman arrives at a realization that countervails war: like the Gita, Whitman sees shared divinity in all people, yet he interprets this as a call to affirm human equality based in the common dignity of all people and their shared right to walk on the earth. "Salut au Monde!" is a poem of the deepest respect for the embodied human being. Whitman frames his divine vision as an opening to peaceful cooperation and cohabitation of the earth.

The Gita precedes war.[63] Whitman's poem both chronologically precedes the Civil War (it was originally composed in 1856) and thematically follows this and all wars.[64] His emphasis is not on the soldiers in formation but on the aftermath of battle, on the "new birth of freedom" (to adopt President Lincoln's famous phrase from the Gettysburg Address) that the sacrifices of war make possible. He implies that what matters most about war is what grows from the scene of horror and tragedy. Oneness is an ontological reality that we recreate in every word we speak, every glance, every deed. How people choose to enact oneness matters. It can be the difference between heaven and hell on earth. This is why divine visions like Whitman's are essential to an ethics of oneness. Such visions shape our expectations concerning infinity, and will, in turn, shape our conduct as we pursue the type of experience that the soul-sighted masters—those who have experienced cosmic consciousness directly—speak of. Whitman's divine vision in "Salut au Monde!" is orbic, for it addresses being human on all its dharmic battlefields: the intrapersonal, the interpersonal, the social, the political, the military. By drawing our attention to the grass, flowers, and crops growing on the battlefield, Whitman encourages us to recognize the violent legacy of humankind and then, rather than indulging it as righteous or inevitable, to make something healthy, nourishing, and peaceful from it.

Whitman meets war at the edges of language. If people are truly one, as Vedanta, Emerson, and Whitman teach, then why do we erroneously view ourselves as isolated and alone, separated from, and in competition with other people, and cut off from the divine source? It is language that makes us appear separate. The towering twentieth-century literary critic Kenneth Burke was certainly no Advaitin, but he recognized that language tends to separate humans from our "natural condition."[65] Adopting the Christian vocabulary that was more comfortable to him, Burke goes so far as to analogize language to original sin.[66] Language is dualistic. It is based on distinction, negation, and division. Every term implies its antithesis and what it is not. Humans are the "inventor of the negative"—the creators of twoness.[67] War, according to Burke, is ultimately a disease of language, goading us toward what I like to call "duelity."[68] Its cure is better words---a more transcendental language. The malady of enemyship must be treated by rhetorical genius, *ad bellum purificandum*.

Humans live a double life, one foot in language, one foot seeking a reality transcendent. Emerson called our condition "double consciousness."[69] There is our everyday life of language use, in which we cleave and categorize and create distinctions. We name to master the world, but in the process we cut ourselves off from the source. "Whilst thus the world will be whole, and refuses to be disparted, we seek to act partially, to sunder, to appropriate," Emerson states.[70] Then there is the meditative life of communion with the divine ground of all existence, with *brahman*, or the oversoul—the "Unity" and "common heart" "within which every man's particular being is contained and made one with all other."[71] In his later years, Emerson adopted a strong monism that portrayed the divine life as the true life, and life in the material world, the world of language and rhetoric, as a kind of illusion, or maya. Succession, division, part, particle; subject, verb, object—this was all of a lesser reality for him. The only true reality was the soul, the whole, the eternal one.

Whitman built his poetry on the metaphysical foundation of Emersonism, but he refused to jettison the body as a site of divine revelation, and he emphatically refused to abandon individuality to illusion. "I will not make poems with reference to parts," Whitman attests. "But I will make poems, songs, thoughts, with reference to ensemble."[72] *There is something unethical about any philosophy of oneness that denies the individual.* Whitman is emphatic—he will not disregard or disparage the individual, who is worthy of the utmost dignity and respect: "I swear nothing is good to me now that ignores individuals."[73] He vows, however, to place the individual within its proper context, the part within its whole, each leaf of grass within the field. Only then will the disease of war be cured, for it is individuals, living on long-abandoned battlefields, songs of long-forgotten wars ringing in our heads, who will fix our broken world by embodying oneness. We cannot wait for some genius to arrive and save us. We must get in touch with our own capacity for genius and save ourselves.

Emerson mentions blades of grass twice in his essays. In "Self-Reliance," an essay that resounds with the militaristic imagery of a battle against convention, Emerson notes that most people are too "timid and apologetic" to be themselves.[74] The modern individual "is ashamed before the blade of grass or the blowing rose. These roses under my window make no reference to former roses or to better ones; they are for what they are; they exist with God to-day. There is no time to them. There is simply the rose; it is perfect in every moment of its existence."[75] People should be more like these roses. These blossoms do not postpone or remember; they are fully centered in the present. The rose is a rose, nothing more, nothing less; a blade of grass is grass, nothing more, nothing less; neither frets that it is not a tree or a cow. To the extent that people can learn to heed "the sanity and the authority of the soul," to the extent that they can connect with the oversoul and the divine all, they will find the contentedness of grass and rose.[76] Grasses and roses here act as models of human conduct. In "New England Reformers," leaves of grass serve as a caution against human hubris: "All the men in the world cannot make a statue walk and speak, cannot make a drop of blood, or a blade of grass, any more than one man can."[77] There are limits to what people can do to fix the world. In the end, there is only acquiescence.

Battlefields like Kurukshetra and Gettysburg are part of the human experience, which is surely why Whitman reports being transported to a battlefield in his divine vision. No vision of the all would be complete without war, without tragedy, without brave soldiers burning on the funeral pyre, without flag-draped coffins, anonymous graves, and wailing widows and widowers. This, too, is part of the human experience. Yet in "Salut au Monde!" Whitman does not mark war as inevitable; nor does he celebrate war as a chance to win glory and renown. He does not use his divine eye to transform himself into a divine instrument of vengeance against his enemies. He does not tell himself that everyone is already dead. He does not absolve himself of responsibility for how his weapons of the particular (in this case, words rather than arrows) might wound others. It is the ethical responsibility of the poet—of any language user, really—to recognize that words have consequences, that they not only alter our relationships to others and to ourselves but to the all. In his poetry, Whitman wields words for good rather than ill, to nourish rather than harm, to promote connection rather than refine disconnection, to cultivate gratefulness rather than resentment.

Whitman derives a different moral from the battlefield than the lesson that Krishna teaches Arjuna on the battlefield. Battlefields are omnipresent in human culture. It is impossible to see a battlefield and not see what it represents. I have visited both Gettysburg and Kurukshetra; these sites resonate with symbolism and stories. Indeed, both sites demonstrate the desperate human need to tell stories to make sense of atrocity and the unbounded human capacity to make meaning from suffering. For Krishna, the battlefield is a field of dharma and justice, and an opportunity for Arjuna to achieve glory. For Whitman, the battlefield is field that grows flowers and crops and people. (Leaves of grass are Whitman's chosen metaphor for individuals.) In the aftermath of war, the focus must be on what type of people grow from the battlefields of the world, what lessons they learn, and whether or not they treat people with the dignity due to limitless, inevitable individuals sanctified by the divine.

In chapter 13 of the Bhagavad Gita, the mind is repeatedly compared to a field. What is true of war is true, too, of the divine vision that frames war—what matters most is what grows from such a vision, the uses to which such visions are put, how they condition and prod and prompt people to experience the world and their fellow beings. Does meditation encourage us to grow flowers and corn and a better self? Or more death and destruction?

Whitman's poetry celebrates "the One" that comes from "All." His poetry models how people might change their behaviors and actions to make oneness a reality—which also means, for Whitman, making democracy a reality.

Talking Oneness

From the perspective of Vedanta and many mystical traditions, including the American traditions of Emersonianism and Whitmanism, it is wrong to say that humans fabricate oneness, because oneness is always present. Oneness can be neither created nor destroyed. Oneness is reality, it is life and breath, the wind and the waves, the divine pulse of all things. Our national motto, *e pluribus unum*, "out of many, one"—a phrase memorialized on our federal letterhead and on the national currency we carry around in our pockets and purses—gestures toward a political aspiration premised on an ontological absurdity. Oneness cannot emerge from manyness. Oneness is the ground, the field, the foundation for variety. There can be two or three or four only because there is one. From oneness—from the oversoul—from cosmos—from the all—people are born into lives of diversity and difference and discourse. Rhetoric is the art of making one into many. Molded by biology and culture and wind and sun and family and language and experience, we blossom in unique ways. Whitman's poetry models how to recognize difference, to acknowledge and honor it, without forgetting that multiplicity grows from oneness. The same divine energy animates all life.

Metaphysically it would be more true to the way of things to redefine our national motto as *ex uno plures*, "out of one, many." Now this is a motto for life! And yet, when contemplating oneness, Whitman describes it both as an ontological reality and a human achievement. Make no mistake, Whitman assures us: to live is to create. We are always building something—we are building the world we inhabit—from eidolons ancient and new. Acknowledging life's active, creative passion is healthy, for it keeps us from sitting on our hands. In "Salut au Monde!," Whitman describes the all; then, directly addressing his readers, he envisions everyone working together hand in hand to build a democratic world of oneness on the battlefields of the past. We do not create this democracy out of thin air, he insists. We construct it on the foundation of, and from the materials provided by, the all.

To recognize oneness as a human achievement is to invite a consideration of the difficult, tragic questions that must accompany all political action. What does it mean to build a world of oneness—and can this oneness be moral? There are myriad lexicons of oneness, and a good number of these are toxic. A language of oneness is noxious to the extent that it perverts the ontological reality of interconnectedness by smuggling in a divisive, exclusionary agenda under the cover of conjunction. If we interpret *e pluribus unum* to mean, simply and rightly, that we are stronger together, then this phrase is a worthy aspiration in spite of its ontological questionability. But if we interpret it to mean that we must all look and be and act the same, then we will see just how quickly oneness wrongly conceived becomes unethical. The most common languages of oneness cling to one element of social and political life—a color, a flag, a symbol, a story—and elevate it to preeminent status, asking everyone and everything to conform to this reality. Here, one thing among many becomes THE ONE THING. This oneness makes demands. It petitions. It exhorts. It builds walls. It constructs prisons. It punishes those who do not obey. It is the tyrannical oneness of kings and bullies and would-be dictators. Whenever a person speaking the language of oneness tells an in-group of people that they are superior to others and marks other groups as inferior or impure or invaders or unclean or ugly or evil, this is a toxic perversion of oneness. For Whitman, a oneness that bullies us into denying the lived reality of oneness-in-difference and difference-in-oneness, that forces us to conform to some arbitrary banner of identity, that is grounded in fear, is not the true oneness without a second.

True oneness does not suppress difference. Whitman's vision of oneness in "Salut au Monde!" makes space for the allness of oneness. He allows for no arbitrary judgments of superiority and inferiority, no inside and outside, no top and bottom, no inclusion and exclusion—for what is there to exclude, and how? Life is composed of a common substance; it is born from the divine energy that pulses through one and all. This acknowledgement becomes the basis for Whitman's democratic ethics, as we will see in chapter 6. The ethics of Whitmanism is a practice of respect for difference couched in new norms of social interaction that are based in the certainty of oneness. This ethics is embodied in a handshake, a kind word, a nod of acknowledgement and recognition that you, too, are worthy, whoever you are, that you, too, belong, that you, too, are a miracle. When Whitman talks about oneness as a human achievement, this is the goal—to build a world that is true to oneness, in which people practice an inclusive humane democratic ethics of compassion.

We are well versed at turning our backs on oneness. Many of our most basic social and political structures are built on principles of separation and division. How are we to remediate this situation? In *Leaves of Grass*, Whitman jumps straight past political argumentation and disputation and speech-making. He is playing an entirely different game. His purpose is to take something that is multidimensional and capture it in two-dimensional words that explode in the reader's imagination in 3D technicolor. He does not issue moral commandments. He does not instruct his readers to love their neighbors. He creates a picture of reality, a vision of the divine, that he then offers to his readers as an invitation to be different than they are now, to change their lives to better align with the cosmos.

Talk of oneness is inherently rhetorical, and we get good at what we practice.

5

Genius

The faith that stands on authority is not faith. The reliance on authority measures the decline of religion, the withdrawal of the soul.

EMERSON, "The Over-Soul"

Was Emerson an authoritarian? The opponent of convention and routine, the champion of self-reliance, the scourge of the secondhand, Emerson seems steeled against such a charge. To rely on the authority of another in spiritual matters, Emerson repeatedly concludes, is folly. And yet, according to Christopher Newfield's controversial argument in *The Emerson Effect: Individualism and Submission in America* (1996), though it seems a strange turn from self-reliance to submission, in the end they are two sides of the same coin for Emerson. Newfield highlights a dark side to Emerson's writings. When Emerson champions self-determination, his discussions of this virtue are often accompanied by soliloquies praising submission to authority. Moreover, according to Newfield, Emerson's persistent talk about the virtues of submission and acquiescence habituates Americans to practices that are congenial to authoritarianism.[1] People get good at what they practice, and if this practice of passivity, or *acquiescence*, is misplaced—if people submit to the wrong thing or the wrong guru—catastrophe can be the result.

Was Emerson an authoritarian? Emerson consistently celebrated heroism, and the answer to the question depends on how we interpret Emerson's theory of "genius." When a person overcomes convention and their soul is reunited with the oversoul, the result is genius. In Emerson's philosophy, *genius* is both a person and an action. The enlightened person is a genius (noun), but genius (verb) is also something that the enlightened person enacts—"genius is the activity which repairs the decays of things."[2] At times, Emerson speaks about genius as though it is singular and embodied in a great man (for Emerson, it seems to be always a man): "Let a man fall into the divine circuits, and he is enlarged. Obedience to his genius is the only liberating influence."[3] When this genius arrives on the scene, Emerson implies that he will be so impressive that his words will be undeniable; the heavens will part, the sun will shine, trumpets will sound, bugs and birds will sing hymns, and the air will sizzle with the electricity of true wisdom embodied in the flesh. Liberation is found only in "obedience to his genius." This is Emerson at his most "authoritarian," for he seems to grant the genius the prestigious position of spokesperson for the oversoul, with all this position's inherent, magnificent power.[4]

Was Emerson an authoritarian? At times, Emerson speaks about genius as though it is a collective resource that lives in the oversoul and to which everyone shares access because, ultimately, all souls are connected: "We see the world piece by piece, as the sun, the moon, the animal, the tree; but the whole, of which the sea are shining parts is the soul. Only by the vision of that Wisdom can the horoscope of the ages be read, and by falling back on our better thoughts, by yielding to *the spirit of prophecy which is innate in every man*, we can know what it saith."[5] Genius, Emerson often suggests, is not a difference of kind but of intensity. "Genius is religious," he concludes, "it is a larger imbibing of the common heart. It is not anomalous, but more like and not less like other men."[6] Whether genius is someone we need to follow or a capacity we need to draw out of ourselves—whether genius is individual or collective—is ultimately a difference that makes all the difference. The first position hastens a kind of spiritual authoritarianism, and its potential ethical ramifications are severe. The second position also has ethical consequences, especially on how Emerson imagines a spiritual democracy based on the metaphysics of oneness. If genius is a shared resource, then citizens are obligated to learn how to access it; if genius is an individual achievement of great power, then citizens are obligated to learn how to discern true genius from false, lest they be led astray.

Was Emerson an authoritarian? In this chapter, I address this question by tackling the problem of genius in Emerson's philosophy. This topic bears directly on his contribution to a theory of what I will call *everyday democracy*—not the grand democracy of high French political theory, nor the televised democratic melodrama of American elections, but the quiet, commonplace, even banal democracy that happens all the time on a local scale when we talk with, and listen to, our fellows guided by the virtues of equality, dignity, and respect. Emersonianism is a worldview; it is a map to a life of oneness. In the following pages, I trace the contours of this map, focusing on the consequences of Emerson's vision of genius on democracy. Ultimately, I conclude that the question of whether genius is individual or collective is an unresolvable tension in Emerson's philosophy, because Emerson himself never makes up his mind about the conflicted, contested status of genius.

Was Emerson an authoritarian? Though it would be nice to close the debate about whether or not Emerson was an authoritarian by saying, with certainty, that this or that is what Emerson believed, keeping the question open has its advantages. Indeed, the matter of authority is central to any spiritual or religious tradition that chases the ultimate human questions concerning the nature of reality and the soul and its salvation, and, as such, it should always be a topic that is discussed openly, critically, and democratically. Surely Emerson is right—the faith that rests on argument by authority is not faith; the teacher or guru is suspect who says this is so because I say so, or because tradition or lineage demands that it be so. There are many geniuses in the world; many more, in fact, than Emerson would allow. Some are true, most are not. Any ethics of oneness must be, at a minimum, about learning the difference.

Maya

In the 1850s and 1860s, Emerson became enamored with the Advaita Vedanta theory of "maya," or divine illusion. In the Advaita Vedanta texts familiar to Emerson, maya signified the illusion—and in fact the delusion—that the world is not one. Maya is the concept that Advaitins developed to explain away the apparent contradiction at the heart of their philosophy: that though the world is one, it appears as many. In the Mahabharata and the Bhagavad Gita, maya also represents the creative power of supernatural beings like Krishna to alter the world and how it appears to humans. In the Bhagavad Gita, Krishna claims to act *mayaya*, by the power of maya, "magic" or "illusion," to make the world appear as a place of change and variation when it fact it is eternal, unchanging, and one.[7] Epistemologically, the word *maya* means "error"—it is the mistake that humans make when they fail to see oneness. Ontologically, maya is the creative, magical, mysterious power of *brahman* and its avatars including Vishnu and Krishna to make the world whirl and spin and dance. Why does *brahman* do this? Why is there life at all? Emerson does not touch these questions, for which Advaitins have many and no answers. Emerson, however, does put a hopeful spin on a potentially depressing theory (if life is but an illusion, then what's the point?). True to his goal of developing an affirmative philosophy, in the end Emerson's philosophy of maya is profoundly upbeat.

From the Vishnu Purana, Emerson learned that the Hindu goddess Yoganidra was the sorceress of maya (the goddess of illusion was known by many names, including both Yoganidra and Maya).[8] In his essay "Illusions," originally composed for the lecture scene in the early 1850s and published in *The Conduct of Life* (1860), Emerson has this to say about Yoganidra:

> I find men victims of illusions in all parts of life. Children, youths, adults, and old men, all are led by one bawble or another. Yoganidra, the goddess of illusion, Proteus, or Momus, or Gylfi's Mocking,—for the Power has many names,—is stronger than the Titans, stronger than Apollo. Few have overheard the gods, or surprised their secret. Life is a succession of lessons which must be lived to be understood. All is riddle, and the key to a riddle is another riddle. There are as many pillows of illusion as flakes in a snow-storm. We wake from one dream into another dream. The toys, to be sure, are various, and are graduated in refinement to the quality of the dupe. The intellectual man requires a fine bait; the sots are easily amused. But everybody is drugged with his own frenzy, and the pageant marches at all hours, with music and banner and badge.[9]

Here, Emerson alludes to his famous 1838 Divinity School Address at Harvard, in which he juxtaposes the false sapience of the church against the true wisdom of the world. In this oration, Emerson recounts how one day, sitting in a pew, listening to a preacher drone on endlessly about some topic or other, he looked out the window and watched the real teacher—nature—rain lessons down upon the snow-dappled heads of the cold shivering people shuffling down the street: "Men go, thought I, where they are wont to go, else had no soul entered the temple in the afternoon. A snow storm was falling around us. The snow storm was real; the preacher merely spectral, and the eye felt the sad contrast in looking at him, and then out of the window behind him, into the beautiful meteor of the snow."[10] In his earliest lectures and sermons, in his first book *Nature* (1836), and in essays including "The Over-Soul" (1841), Emerson expresses his faith that humans are equipped to read the mystic language of nature, written in tree, rock, and star.[11] This faith underlines the American "nature religion."[12] The belief that nature has lessons to teach us, that there is a truth out there, is one reason Americans repeatedly return to bathe in the forests that built our ancestors' homes.

In "Illusions," Emerson takes his readers on an eclectic tour de force of world mythology—in addition to Yoganidra, there is the shape-shifting Proteus, the all-knowing old man of the sea, who will reveal his secrets only when gagged and bound; Momus, the masked personification of satire, ridicule, and blame, who was banished from Mount Olympus for incessantly mocking the Olympians; and the legendary king Gylfi, who is "beguiled" in Norse myth. These mythological figures shadow Emerson's sunny optimism. Now he begins to doubt that nature is so easily read. Perhaps the snow is simply another illusion, no different than the preacher's cliches. The Titans deposed their father, Uranus, the god of the sky; Apollo, the golden-throated god of prophecy, could literally interpret the mysteries of nature—but these mighty mythic figures were no match for Yoganidra's maya. This passage leaves Emerson's readers with little hope that we can ever escape from the riddle. If we do break out, we are promptly presented with a new riddle. The circles of illusion constantly expand to encompass life. Did his reading of Vedanta lead Emerson to become a pessimist?

In a word, no. About maya, Emerson is not pessimistic. Emersonianism continues to be inspired by the central virtues of "cheerfulness and courage": "We may come to accept it as the fixed rule and theory of our state of education, that God is a substance, and his method is illusion. The eastern sages owned the goddess Yoganidra, the great illusory energy of Vishnu, by whom, as utter ignorance, the whole world is beguiled."[13] Note the shift in Emerson's rhetoric of God—a shift that many later Emersonians emulate. God is substance, reality, oversoul. But here, God is also a person who acts with intention and purpose. God's goal (here Emerson adopts the Vaishnavite practice of addressing God as a person with a proper name, as a *he*, as Vishnu) is *education*. God's preferred pedagogy is to become Yoganidra, the dark priestess of maya, illusion. Though the tone of "Illusions" is pessimistic, in his journal Emerson is more upbeat: "The doctrine of the Imagination can only be rightly opened by treating it in connection with the subject of Illusions. And the Hindoos alone have treated this last with sufficient breadth in their legends of the successive Maias of Vishnu. With them, youth, age, property, condition, events, persons, self, are only successive Maias, through which Vishnu mocks & instructs the soul."[14] Maya is a trial, a classroom, a textbook of divine instruction that constantly challenges people to see things more clearly: "As we refine, our checks become finer. If we rise to spiritual culture, the antagonism takes a spiritual form."[15] Vishnu's goal is not to bury people in a snowstorm of illusion. By tempting us with many shiny things—baubles and bait, parades and parties, badges and banners, which never deliver the joy they promise—he seeks to inspire us to seek self-reliance and the higher plane of existence.

In his 1870 book *Society and Solitude*, Emerson offers the following summary statement of his philosophy:

> But what a force of illusion begins life with us, and attends us to the end! We are coaxed, flattered, and duped, from morn to eve, from birth to death; and where is the old eye that ever saw through the deception? The Hindoos represent Maia, the illusory energy of Vishnu, as one of his principle attributes.

> As if, in this gale of warring elements, which life is, it was necessary to bind souls to human life as mariners in a tempest lash themselves to the mast and bulwarks of a ship, and Nature employed certain illusions as her ties and straps. . . . *Seldom and slowly* the mask falls, and *the pupil* is permitted to see that all is one stuff, cooked and painted under many counterfeit appearances.[16]

Emerson uses the word *pupil* to describe the human condition. People are pupils, souls incarnated on the earth out of the oversoul in order to learn the truth of existence. In *Essays: First Series,* overcoming counterfeit convention and experiencing the true oneness of all things required tremendous effort and steely discipline. But here, Emerson seems to suggest that liberation is coming for us all, eventually: "Seldom and slowly the mask falls."

This is a slow process, and it is also precious—all humans are pupils of maya, but *seldom* is it that the mask of illusion falls for an individual. Emerson thus echoes Advaita Vedanta, which teaches that the experience of true meditation is exceedingly rare.[17] *Samadhi* requires tremendous commitment (*abhyasa*) and, at times, ridiculous feats of mental daring. The Upanishads liken the path of seeing beyond maya to walking "a razor's sharp edge."[18] At the close of chapter 11 of the Bhagavad Gita, Krishna tells Arjuna that his vision of the divine form is privileged:

> This Form of mine you saw
> Is hard to see.
> Even Gods are always
> Hoping for the sight of it.[19]

Though Emerson is optimistic that humans are capable of seeing through maya to the truth of things, he follows Krishna in recognizing that it is the rare individual—a true singular genius—who sees beyond illusion. We are all pupils, but that does not guarantee that we all learn.

Emerson's choice of snow as a metaphor for illusion is particularly apt. Emerson loved water metaphors. Water gives life (human beings are mostly water) while definitely, unequivocally, unquestionably proving our powerlessness. Without water, we die. And even a few inches of rushing water are strong enough to knock a grown person down. The divine fills us like water filling a cup; divinity rushes into us like a river born from some distant, speechless alpine mountain range. Most people do not willingly go out into the snowstorm, however. When it snows, they seek refuge, inside, in the warmth. If life's illusions are like the first drops of rain after a boiling summer afternoon, releasing petrichor perfume into the air, who would ever seek freedom? But if illusions are snow? To think of illusion as snow is to recognize the need to come into the warmth, into truth's incandescence.

Not long after he finally added a copy of Charles Wilkins's translation of the Bhagavad Gita to his personal library in 1845, Emerson pledged to make a subtle but significant change to Advaita Vedanta as he would proclaim it to Americans. He wrote in his journal: "Emancipation from existence, they say, is the Indian beatitude. I think it intends emancipation from organization."[20] Emerson would have nothing of the world-denying ascetic tendencies that many travelers to India reported were common to its yogis. Emerson sought to bring Advaita home to this world as a philosophy of emancipation from "organization," which here is used as a synonym for "convention" and "public opinion."[21] Convention is the enemy, because it prevents people from accessing their innate capacity for genius that is found in the connection between the individual soul and the universal oversoul: "There is a certain wisdom of humanity which is common to the greatest men with the lowest, and which our ordinary education often labors to silence and obstruct."[22] From time to time, this wisdom comes over us through no doing of our own, brightening our days, teaching us the virtue of "infinite hope": "The soul lets no man go without some visitations and holy-days of a diviner presence."[23] Emerson employed a rhetoric inspired by Advaita Vedanta to call on people to become self-reliant and to realize their connection to the oversoul by practicing communication as yoga. Maya offered a divine warrant to his mission. The world is an illusion, but it is a "purposive" illusion.[24] For Emerson, it takes a truly special person to deliberately and purposely overcome maya and access genius—and when this person does, he (again, for Emerson it is almost certainly a "he") "shall destroy trust by his trust" and shatter social conventions through the sheer power of his truthful words.[25]

People are bound by illusion and fate, but they are graced with the power, the agency, the drive to push their limits and test fate.[26] Human life unfolds at the crossroads. We live in a world that is at times cruel and unjust. "Nature is no sentimentalist,—does not cosset or pamper us. We must see that the world is rough and surly, and will not mind drowning a man or a woman; but swallows your ship like a grain of dust."[27] Fate exists to teach: "'Tis the best use of Fate to teach a fatal courage," a lesson Americans could learn from India: "The Hindoo, under the wheel, is as firm."[28] The existence of genius proves that people can achieve self-reliance. Effort, discipline, practice—all matter. But in the end, illusions are snow, and people naturally shun the snow in search of warmth. Eventually the mountains will thaw, and life is like a rampaging, rushing, raging river in the spring that sweeps away those who slip in. There is a direction to the world. We are pupils. Life is a classroom. God is the teacher. The world exists to set us free. And so, in the end, we had better trust the world.

Self-Reliance and Duty

From the 1830s to the end of his life, Emerson was remarkably consistent that the greatest enemy to humankind is convention.[29] Convention is maya enacted through human hands. The trouble with convention is that it reinforces illusions of separation and frustrates people's attempts to access genius. All around him, for all his life, Emerson observed friends and family members, acquaintances and strangers, determined to decorously conform to social norms, conventions, and expectations at the expense of independent thought. Emerson believed that above all other rhetorical arts democracy values *decorum*, the ability to fit in. This is the first rule of American democracy—survival of the fittest. Public opinion rules the day: "Most men have bound their eyes with some or another handkerchief, and attached themselves to some one of these communities of opinion. This conformity makes them not false in a few particulars, authors of a few lies, but false in all particulars. Their every truth is not quite true. Their two is not the real two, their four not the real four; so that every word they say chagrins us, and we know no where to begin to set them right."[30] Ben Franklin told the readers of *Poor Richard's Almanac* that if they wanted to find success and esteem, they shouldn't rock the boat, because outcasts and rebels were rarely successful: "Singularity in the right, hath ruined many; Happy those who are convinced of the general Opinion."[31] For Emerson, Americans took this advice much too seriously.

People want to fit in, to be liked; and so their progress toward freedom and emancipation is stunted by a slavish devotion to public opinion. Driven mad by popularity, most people act for others, striving for their esteem. Against the grain, Emerson pledges to do his duty:

> My life is for itself and not for a spectacle. . . . What I must do is all that concerns me, not what the people think. This rule, equally arduous in actual and in intellectual life, may serve for the whole distinction between greatness and meanness. It is the harder, because you will always find those who think they know what is your duty better than you know it. It is easy in the world to live after the world's opinion; it is easy in solitude to live after our own; but the great man is he who in the midst of the crowd keeps with perfect sweetness the independence of solitude.[32]

"Each man has his vocation. The talent is the call," Emerson muses, and "by doing his own work, he unfolds himself."[33] "God will not have his work made manifest by cowards," he also states. "A man is relieved and gay when he has put his heart into his work and done his best; but what he has said or done otherwise, shall give him no peace. It is a deliverance which does not deliver. In the attempt his *genius* deserts him; no muse befriends; no invention, no hope."[34] Here, Emerson speaks of genius as a shared resource—it is the wisdom of the world, the divine mind as inscribed on the rocks and rivers and branches and faces that make up the world. This wisdom is over us but it also lives in our souls, providing guidance and insight. If we allow it to fill us up, we will be changed, and so, too, will the world. And yet convention shrouds circumspection. It blocks intuition. It muffles the subtle urgings of the oversoul, closing us to genius. To the degree that we become self-reliant and independent, to the degree that we have the courage to say no to what others demand and want from us, to the degree that we do our own duty and not what others think we should do, we liberate genius and bring ourselves closer to the oversoul.

In "Self-Reliance," Emerson echoes the Bhagavad Gita—specifically, Krishna's advice to Arjuna concerning the performance of duty:

> Better your own dharma, botched,
> Than someone else's dharma practiced well.
> Better death than your own dharma!
> Another's dharma carries danger.[35]

With these verses, Krishna teaches Arjuna the doctrine of *svadharma*, one's personal dharma, or duty. Every person has a duty to perform. Doing this duty is virtue; ignoring it—or even worse, performing another's duty instead of your own—is vice. In the *charamasloka* (the central, foundational verse) of 2.48, Krishna tells Arjuna:

> Fixed in yoga, do your work
> Relinquishing attachment, Wealthwinner.
> In success or failure, stay the same.
> It's said that equilibrium [*samatva*] is yoga.[36]

Most people act out of desire, but to do so creates bondage. Krishna teaches Arjuna (addressing him here with one of his many nicknames, Wealthwinner) the virtues of *nishkama karma*, action without desire. Krishna advises Arjuna that if he performs his duty, acting with *samatva*—equanimity, equableness, and indifference to outcomes—he will be not touched by the stain of karma or consequence; he will be free from all evil. There is no need to ask tragic questions about the war, no need to consider the moral consequences of fighting. Krishna tells Arjuna to focus on the task at hand, and to do what is demanded of someone of his social class. Indeed, in the Mahabharata and the Bhagavad Gita, *svadharma* is derived from one's *varna*, or class. Arjuna's *svadharma* is the duty of the Kshatriyas, the warrior class, to fight and defeat the enemies of the kingdom and protect its people. Krishna reproaches Arjuna for neglecting this duty as a warrior, and for attempting instead to perform the duty of a renunciate monk. Though his duty is personal, Arjuna has no freedom to decide what this duty is. His duty is conventional. It is determined for him by his rank in society.

Emerson also instructs Americans to do their duty, but his concept of duty is quite different than the Gita's. In fact, Emerson attempted to liberate *svadharma* from its ties to any class system by arguing that each individual has the duty to determine their individual duty for themselves. Society cannot tell a person what they should do. There is no genius in convention. Each person must listen to the soul and learn to trust their hearts. Emerson holds a doctrine of individual responsibility that only partly squares with Krishna's philosophy in the Gita. Krishna tells Arjuna to put his faith in him and act without concern for the consequences of his actions (namely, killing his family). Moreover, Krishna is emphatic that Arjuna has no individual responsibility to determine his duty for himself; it is determined for him, by his rank in society. For Emerson, Americans are individually responsible for determining their duty, and then they must live with the real and immediate consequences of their actions. Duty (Emerson called it "right action") proves the truth of the law of karma (Emerson called it "compensation").[37] "You cannot do wrong without suffering wrong," Emerson concludes, and "the law holds with equal sureness for all right action."[38] Emerson teaches that the consequences of our actions matter—but, it must be noted, they matter only for their effect on ourselves and our ability to commune with their oversoul, not for how they touch others or impact the world in which we live. This is a profound limitation of Emerson's ethics of oneness.

Krishna purports to release Arjuna (and all other devotees who love him) from karma. Emerson is steadfast that there is no escape from compensation. This is so because the universe is a synecdoche. We draw all our powers, all our life force, all our wisdom not from convention, but from the oversoul. Every wrong action throws up a roadblock between the individual soul and the oversoul; to do wrong is thus to suffer wrong. Wrong action closes the container lid, preventing the individual from being filled with genius. An immediate question arises: How do we know if an action is wrong if not by following convention and heeding decorum, by looking to others and gauging their reactions to our behavior—which, according to liberal moral theorists including Adam Smith, is how people learn right from wrong?[39] We know, Emerson attests. We know deep in our hearts, deep in our souls, because the individual soul is a part of but not apart from the whole, the universe, the oversoul, a force that is working tirelessly and without fail to push us toward the good. "The universe is represented in every one of its particles. Every thing in nature contains all the powers of nature. Every thing is made of one hidden stuff."[40] "Res nolunt diu male administrari," he admonishes, "things refuse to be mismanaged long."[41]

Emerson invokes stories from Greek, Roman, and Indian mythology to prove what he believes humans have long known: that the universe is moral, and people are, too, for we are built from the intelligent, ethical, vibrant matter of the universe. Studying the world's great stories, one sees "a plain confession of the in-working of the All, and of its moral aim. The Indian mythology ends in the same ethics."[42] Karma—compensation—retribution—concerns the relationship between part and whole, person and God, soul and oversoul: "What we call retribution is the universal necessity by which the whole appears wherever a part appears."[43] When a person fails to do their duty, they will be punished; not in some otherworldly hell by imaginary devils, but in this world, here and now, by the devil of separation from the source—"the intellect is at once infected, so that the man ceases to see God whole in each object."[44] In Emerson's essays, punishment means the frustration that follows from having the path to genius closed by wrong action. To avoid such punishment and continue progressing along the path toward enlightenment, Emerson urges his readers to determine for themselves their duty, and then to do it without hesitation or concern for the consequences of their actions on others or the world around us.

This is a radical doctrine, for American philosophy tends to be concerned with consequences more than anything else.[45] In *Pragmatism* (1907), William James attempts to do away with abstract metaphysical speculation by suggesting that only those philosophical debates that have immediate and real practical consequences are worth having. For James, truth is not a hidden property of nature, waiting to be dis-covered, but instead something that humans ascribe to actions, beliefs, and statements that prove beneficial. He argues that "truth is *made*, just as health, wealth and strength are made, in the course of experience."[46] American philosophy involves a particular "orientation" or "attitude": "the attitude of looking away from first things, principles, 'categories,' supposed necessities; and of looking towards last things, fruits, consequences, facts."[47] For James, it is the consequences of a belief in action that prove its truth.

James uses the same word, *fruits*, that Krishna uses in the Bhagavad Gita (in Sanskrit, *phala*). Yet Krishna instructs Arjuna to do exactly the opposite, to look away from last things, fruits, consequences, toward first things, including one's duty and the ontological reality of oneness (*ekatva*):

> The action alone is your mandate,
> Never the fruits at any time.
> Never let the fruits of action goad you.
> Never get attached to your inertia.[48]

As an aspiring yogi studying the Gita in both the United States and India, I learned this *sloka* by heart, for it is said to encapsulate the essence of karma yoga and the core message of the divine song—act, with purpose and vigor in the right, and worry not about how others view you or whether or not your action is materially successful. Teach, not for awards or recognition, which are rare and never guaranteed (and highly political), but for the love of teaching. Write, not for esteem, which may never come, but to share knowledge because it is good. Give, not to get a return, but to share. Love, not for profit, but because it brightens the world. If we read the battle in the Bhagavad Gita strictly as an allegory, privileging the divine song's setting on *dharmakshetre*, the field of dharma, and supposing that the subject of the Gita is not really war but human psychology, then this practice of karma yoga can be revolutionary. However, the moment we remember that we do not live exclusively in our minds but in the world where our actions impact others, often in ways we cannot predict or foresee—a fact that the Gita acknowledges, setting the dialogue on the field of dharma and also on *kurukshetre*, the physical battlefield at Kurukshetra—then this practice of acting without concern for the consequences of one's actions becomes ethically dubious. We don't have to devise complicated methodologies for weighing the pros and cons of an action to understand that consequences matter. Even the most apparently uncontroversial ethical duties can lead to unethical outcomes if applied mindlessly.

Countless Americans have measured their philosophy against Krishna's words concerning duty, and the Indian gurus who came to the United States to teach Americans yoga beginning in the 1890s made the Bhagavad Gita a cornerstone of their presentations—Swami Vivekananda, Paramhansa Yogananda, Maharishi Mahesh Yogi, Swami Prabhupada, and B. K. S. Iyengar all spoke eloquently and often about the Bhagavad Gita's karma yoga, as does contemporary neoliberal spiritual healer extraordinaire Deepak Chopra. However, despite all the love, the Gita's doctrine of karma yoga marks one place where the poem is not so easily absorbed into American culture; for in America, with our overarching cultural emphases on *practicality* and *usefulness*, we hold closely to the fruits of action and we judge the ethics of an action by its consequence. This is also one place where Emerson's philosophy is not so easily absorbed into the lineage of American pragmatism. Indeed, on the question of consequences, Emerson takes the side of the Gita. For him, the truly self-reliant person "cumbers himself never about consequences."[49] "The effect of every action is measured by the depth of the sentiment from which it proceeds," he says, suggesting that the virtue of an action depends entirely on a person's connection to the oversoul.[50]

Arjuna need not worry about the fruits of his actions because he acts in line with duty without desire, and so his actions are necessarily ethical. Emerson's self-reliant individual can ignore consequences because he has learned how to access the genius of the oversoul, and, becoming a vessel for its deep eternal wisdom, he knows with certainty how to act: "I desire not to disgrace the soul. The fact that I am here certainly shows me that the soul had need of an organ here. Shall I not assume the post?"[51] Emerson commits to assume the post, and he promises his readers that if they do the same, they will find new and great and tremendous power. This is the promise of genius: once a person is filled with the divine, they can do no wrong, and they need not worry about consequences, for they know what is right in their hearts. Once a person is filled with the divine, there is nothing left but to trust. Trust yourself, Emerson teaches, for "with the exercise of self-trust, new powers shall appear."[52] "What your heart thinks great is great. The soul's emphasis is always right."[53]

Emerson seems not to admit the possibility of theodicy, of knowing what is right and still doing what is wrong. The oversoul is no trickster or evil genius. Ethics is based on a transformative mystical experience on a higher plane that completely changes a person's mind, heart, and soul, such that they cannot help but behave ethically. Emerson employs a number of words to describe the moment in which the soul reconnects with the oversoul—the moment of enlightenment—including *revelation*, *agitation*, *passing through*, *mingling*, *communication*, *connection*, *abandonment*, *invasion*, *enthusiasm*, *reception*, *ecstasy*, *trance*, *prophetic inspiration*, and even *insanity*.[54] All these words connote a state of becoming passive to divinity. When describing the relationship between the soul and the oversoul, Emerson prefers a *prism model*—the divine light shines through us—a *container model*—when the soul comes into contact with the oversoul, it is filled with divine wisdom—and a *breathing model*—"when it breathes through his intellect, it is genius."[55] When the soul is illuminated or filled or expanded by the oversoul, it gains a picture of "the whole" and is granted the gift of genius. Old things pass away. Temples fall. Past and future dissolve into an eternal present. The divided and scattered masses return to the center. The clouds part. All is made sacred by an experience of oneness.

Before I began my serious study of Emerson's writings, I (like many readers, I'm guessing) misunderstood Emerson as a propagandist of the Protestant work ethic and the "Ben Franklin principle."[56] At times Emerson reads like the most passionate spokesperson for individualism and Whig economics. He has been described as the forerunner of twentieth-century individualist capitalism, liberal conformism, and "weird" "hucksterism."[57] Though Emerson champions individualism, he is also a critic of classical liberalism, which teaches that the individual predates society and arrives into the world fully formed, with natural rights that must be protected from others, and from government. For Emerson, individualism is not a fact; it is an achievement. Insofar as it views the individual as self-possessed and self-caused, Emerson judges the liberal project misguided from the start.

Emerson teaches an active practice of becoming passive. Indeed, it is ironic that in an essay called "Self-Reliance," Emerson actually preaches a radical doctrine of spiritual dependence. Humans exist, he concludes, in a "condition of universal dependence."[58] We live in the oversoul, and "the ardors of piety agree at last with the coldest skepticism,—that nothing is of us or our works,—that all is of God. Nature will not spare us the smallest leaf of laurel. All writing comes by the grace of God, and all doing and having."[59] Reading Emerson closely, the stereotypical picture of self-reliance as rugged individualism, as the self-made man, as anyone who pulls themselves up by their bootstraps and goes it alone, no longer looks right. Sentence by sentence this picture dissolves into something much fuzzier and more mysterious. Reading Emerson closely, self-reliance becomes something altogether different: a first step toward a new life rooted in the certainty of cosmic optimism and divine wisdom.

Acquiescence

In the 1830s and '40s, Emerson located the seed of political change in *self-transformation*—in what the ancient Greeks called *askesis*, the care of the self, what the German Romantics called *Bildung*, self-development or self-realization, and what Americans in the early nineteenth century dubbed "self-culture."[60] In the 1850s and '60s, Emerson continued to preach the importance of self-culture, but he balanced his emphasis on individual discipline with a gospel of trust and letting go. In certain strands of Indian thought, the concept of maya was closely related to the concept of *fate*—to the idea that goddesses control human destiny by spinning fate into a "life thread" (a concept the ancient Greeks shared).[61] For Emerson, *fate* meant acknowledgment, abandonment, and acquiescence—*acknowledgment* that the true agent is the oversoul, and that any agency we have as humans is derived from this source; *abandonment* of any worries and fear we might have over the state of the world; and *acquiescence* to divinity, for the world is not neutral, but actively works toward the good of all and the liberation of the individual from illusion.

Emerson repeatedly celebrates the virtues of acquiescence in his essays. According to the *Oxford English Dictionary*, the English word *acquiescence* is derived from the classical Latin verb *acquiescere*, a compound verb consisting of the prefix *ad* (to or toward) and the verb *quiescere* (to be at rest).[62] *Acquiescere* means "moving towards a state of rest."[63] In medieval Latin, *acquiescere* came to entail an active recognition of a power greater than oneself, a Logos supreme to which one would pay tribute and in the name of which one ceded political agency in order to achieve spiritual completeness (hence Calvin's *acquiescere in scriptura*).[64] Retaining this sense of coming to rest (*ad* + *quiescere*), I would suggest that acquiescence is an apt descriptor for Emerson's philosophy of oneness. Emerson reimagines the nature of the divinity in which we rest—it is not the Christian God, but the oversoul—and yet the dynamics of submission, of humbling before the Lord, remain the same.

To the end, Emerson was a good reader of the Bhagavad Gita. Conceding just how difficult it is to achieve enlightenment through the prescribed paths of meditation, scholarship, and right action, in the final chapter of the Gita Krishna offers Arjuna—and by extension, all readers of the Gita—an out:

> Mind on me, to me devote yourself,
> Sacrifice for me, to me make reverence,
> And it's to me that you will come—
> I promise you—because you're dear to me.
>
> Relinquish all your dharma.
> Come shelter in me,
> And I will free you
> From all sins. Never grieve.[65]

For many later schools of Hinduism, these verses represent the essence of the Gita. Krishna states his love for Arjuna, and then Arjuna, reciprocating this love, devotes himself totally and completely, without qualification or reservation, to Krishna, and as a consequence is liberated. These verses are surprising, for they shift the responsibility for liberation from Arjuna to Krishna, from soul to oversoul, from humans to the divine. Richard Davis observes: "After strongly supporting duty as the foundation for detached or selfless action throughout his earlier teachings, Krishna seems to allow an antinomian escape clause for the true devotee who takes refuge in God alone. In the end, Krishna takes responsibility for granting liberation to Arjuna, or to anyone completely devoted to him."[66] Emerson echoes this antinomian theme of liberation through submission. By taking refuge in the divine oversoul, people need not fret about ethics or morality or social reform, for they will know, deep in their hearts, that all will be well.

To the end, Emerson was a cosmic optimist. He believed, as so many Emersonians after him have believed, that the world has a way of rising up to meet our actions and to put itself beneath our leaping feet—that, in spite of human efforts, our pros or cons, the world always rights itself. In 1841, he wrote, "Thus is the universe alive. All things are moral. That soul, which within us is a sentiment, outside of us is a law. We feel its inspiration; out there in history we can see its fatal strength. . . . Justice is not postponed. A perfect equity adjusts its balance in all parts of life. . . . The dice of God are always loaded. . . . Every secret is told, every crime is punished, every virtue rewarded, every wrong redressed, in silence and certainty. What we call retribution is the universal necessity by which the whole appears wherever a part appears."[67] In 1860 he wrote, "In the world of morals, Fate appears as vindicator, levelling the high, lifting the low, requiring justice in man, and always striking soon or late, when justice is not done. What is useful will last; what is hurtful will sink."[68] Emerson's message is consistent across the decades: Trust the soul, and all will be well. Protest and agitate, seek reform if you will, refuse to be complicit in injustice; petition, prod, and plead. But in the end, all you can really do is worship the oversoul, and get out of its way.

To the end, Emerson framed acquiescence as the heart of ethics and an ethics of the heart. "The lesson," he wrote in 1841, "is Be, and not seem. Let us acquiesce. Let us take our bloated nothingness out of the path of the divine circuits. . . . The object of the man, the aim of these moments, is to make daylight shine through him, to suffer the law to traverse his whole being without obstruction."[69] And in 1860, he wrote, "Let us build altars to the Blessed Unity which holds nature and souls in perfect solution, and compels every atom to serve an universal end. . . . Let us build altars to the Beautiful Necessity, which secures that all is made of one piece; that plaintiff and defendant, friend and enemy, animal and planet, food and eater, are of one kind. . . . Let us build to the Beautiful Necessity . . . which rudely or softly educates him to the perception that there are no contingencies; that Law rules throughout existence, a Law which is not intelligent but intelligence,—not personal nor impersonal,—it disdains words and passes understanding; it dissolves persons; it vivifies nature; yet solicits the pure in heart to draw on all its omnipotence."[70]

No good writer tells the same story over and over again. Emerson's thought continued to develop and mature after *Essays: First Series*, and we should expect nothing less. However, Emerson never wavered from the central insight of “The Over-Soul,” an insight inspired by Krishna’s commandment to Arjuna in the Bhagavad Gita to become his “instrument.” As Emerson wrote, “All reform aims, in some one particular, to let the soul have its way through us; in other words, to engage us to obey.”[71] People are agog with reform; they strive and stress to improve the world around them. Emerson agreed that it was important to do all that a person could to not be complicit in injustice (and he himself took action against slavery).[72] Beyond that, people could do what their talents allowed. They could strive to reach the higher plane of oneness and access the deep resources of genius. But in the end, all will be well, regardless of what is done. The easiest path to peace, then, is to acquiesce, and to leave reform to the universe—for what is the power of a soul when compared to the power of the oversoul? Even Arjuna’s power—even the power of all the armies on the earth—pales in comparison to Krishna. Where Krishna is, there, too, is victory. It is best, then, to move our “bloated nothingness” out of the way—to try less, and allow more.

Spiritual Authoritarianism?

I admit that, if you twist and turn Emerson’s philosophy enough, forgetting his teachings on self-reliance and ignoring certain rhetorical safeguards that he puts in place, there is something to the argument that he laid the foundation for a kind of spiritual authoritarianism, though Emerson himself would have disavowed any such politics. Emerson does say that, in general, people are much too troubled about the state of the world. We need not worry so much, because the oversoul is actively working for the good of all. True knowledge of oneness hastens peace. Sometimes the best thing we can do is get out of its way. “Let us acquiesce. Let us take our bloated nothingness out of the path of the divine circuits,” he observes, for “the whole course of things goes to teach us faith. We need only obey.”[73] Notice here that Emerson is not arguing—as an authoritarian would argue—that we must obey a person, a prophet, a politician, a philosopher king, a guru, or a messiah. No, we must obey the oversoul. We must acquiesce to the wisdom of the world. The hitch, of course, is that many people, prophets, politicians, philosopher kings, gurus, and messiahs derive their authority from the argument that their extraordinary experiences grant them the extraordinary authority to speak extraordinary words on behalf of the divine. As extraordinary spokespeople for the true ontology, they then demand that we spiritual plebeians acquiesce to their genius. Americans are generally well-meaning, but we are not known to be the most discriminating people. The gullibility of Americans who fall for confidence men and other flimflam artists was a common theme in nineteenth-century American literature, from Melville's *Confidence Man* (1857) to L. Frank Baum's *Wizard of Oz* (1900).[74] The words of genius, backed by an otherworldly experience that cannot be questioned, and that are supposedly sanctioned by divinity, are some of the most powerful words that can be uttered. If we place our faith in the wrong person, one whose god terms sound sweetly of honey but in reality are poison, who can portend the catastrophe that might result? Surely we must admit that this is a possibility, and a dangerous one in any democracy.

Emerson did not have the same religious-like attachment to democracy that has long characterized American culture. For Emerson, there were higher gods than democracy. He admitted that Americans were temperamentally suited to democracy: "Democracy is better for us, because the religious sentiment of the present time accords better with it."[75] However, he doubted the wisdom of assembled masses, and he refused to speak the language I've elsewhere dubbed *demophilia*, the love of democracy, that closely accompanied the rise of democracy in the United States.[76] "Democracy is morose, and runs to anarchy, but in the state, and in the schools, it is indispensable to resist the consolidation of all men into a few men," Emerson announced.[77] Democracy checks a dangerous political tendency toward tyranny, but it has its own dangerous tendencies, too.

For Emerson, democracy's greatest sin is that it stifles independent thought and destroys self-reliance. Emerson expressed a lifelong distrust of democracy because, he believed, it elevates convention and public opinion to the status of gods. Convention and conformity are blindfolds, masking the true nature of reality: "Liberation of the will from the sheaths and clogs of organization which he has outgrown, is the end and aim of this world."[78] Democracy errs insofar as it refuses to celebrate the heroic individual who, transcending convention, reconnects with the genius of the oversoul and in the process gains great power. Democracy errs insofar as it celebrates *the masses*—the group, the community, the crowd, the public, the agglomerate, the multitude. Americans wax eloquently about individualism, but when it comes down to it, they are conformists. Their eleventh commandment is: do not think.

In his essays from the 1840s and '50s, Emerson repeatedly expressed his craving for independent thought and free discussion. He railed against "the god of tradition" and "the god of rhetoric," against a staid and stodgy rhetoric that stilted Americans with its slavish devotion to tradition and practices centuries old.[79] For Emerson, it was the duty of the lecturer, the essayist, the poet, the genius to affirm the true oneness of all creation while resisting attempts at achieving union through convention in the world of appearance. Emerson disagreed with his rhetoric professor at Harvard, Edward Tyrrel Channing, about the proper place of oratory in a democracy. According to Channing, democracy rendered irrelevant the podium thunderbolts who shook the very earth with their words. In the United States, Channing said, no longer did the great speaker stand above the people; now he stood among them: "In the ancient republics, the orator might control the audience, but now we see the audience controlling him."[80] In democracies, the speaker does not control the audience, the audience controls the speaker. The job of the speaker is to conform. In the United States, the orator "can no longer be a despot, either to save freedom or destroy it. He is not the important personage he once was. He is fortunately less able to do harm, and less needed to do good."[81] Democracy no longer needs the singular genius, because it places its faith in the collective genius of the people. *Vox populi, vox Dei*—the voice of the people is the voice of God.

Emerson judged this vision of democratic rhetoric complete and utter folly. The people were not wise; collectively they were stupid, and the types of public speaking that they acclaimed were worthless. "A public oration is an escapade, a noncommittal, an apology, a gag, and not a communication, not a speech, not a man," Emerson fretted.[82] "It is the vice of our public speaking that it has not abandonment," he concluded, employing a word, *abandonment*, that he frequently used to signify the connection between soul and oversoul.[83] Emerson pined for a better rhetoric, a true rhetoric based in divine revelation: "What is it we heartily wish of each other? Is it to be pleased and flattered? No, but to be convicted and exposed, to be shamed out of our nonsense of all kinds, and made men of, instead of ghosts and phantoms. We are weary of gliding ghostlike through the world, which is itself so slight and unreal. We crave a sense of reality, though it come in strokes of pain."[84] What we heartily wish for is truth, and to be moved by genius. Emerson's vision of democratic rhetoric affirmed his hope that a true genius would arise on the scene, a great man (again, for Emerson it was certainly a man) who pierces the veil of maya and then persuades others of the truth of oneness by embodying it so completely, so totally, that the earth cannot help but move under his feet.

It's an ancient dream: we are born with eternal truths in our hearts just waiting to burst forth if only we could find the words. But the words don't come. For Emerson, the mark of genius is the ability to find the words. The genius has deciphered the language of being—the words of the world—and pronounces them for all to hear. "I dare not speak for it. My words do not carry its august sense; they fall short and cold," Emerson admits. "Only itself can inspire whom it will, and behold! their speech shall be lyrical, and sweet, and universal as the rising of the sun."[85] Unlike his rhetoric professor at Harvard, who downplayed the role of great speakers in democracy, Emerson took it for granted that reform would issue forth from daring geniuses who, standing on a "higher plane" or "higher platform," had the courage to speak truthfully, convention be damned.[86] When Emerson speaks of a "higher platform," his words carry a double meaning—he alludes to a cosmic vista and also to a rostrum, a podium, a pulpit far above the crowd from which the orator educates his audience in the truths of oneness.

Emerson concludes his 1844 lecture "New England Reformers" with the following message:

> Suppress for a few days your criticism on the insufficiency of this or that teacher or experimenter, and he will have demonstrated his insufficiency to all men's eyes. In like manner, let a man fall into the divine circuits, and he is enlarged. Obedience to his genius is the only liberating influence. We wish to escape from subjection, and a sense of inferiority,—and we make self-denying ordinances, we drink water, we eat grass, we refuse the laws, we go to jail: it is all in vain; only by obedience to his genius; only by the freest activity in the way constitutional to him, does an angel seem to arise before a man, and lead him by the hand out of all the wards of the prison.[87]

Here, Emerson dismisses many of the reform efforts of his times. Americans are misguided to believe they can fix the world by eating and drinking differently or practicing civil disobedience. The only hope is genius. This position—to fix the world, we must *wait for the genius to come and save us*—is not an atypical view of social reform. In fact, it's something like a cultural fallback position, a kind of deus ex machina wishful thinking that we invoke in those desperate, frustrating moments when we don't know how to fix the wicked problems we face. Punt the problem down the road, and trust that something or someone better and smarter than us will fix it! For Emerson, the genius repairs the world by reconnecting that which has been separated. Language is a manifestation of the divine, and simultaneously a means by which we relate to the divine. The alphabet brims with divine energy. Rhetoric is the art of making use of this energy to remake the world. The genius's words resonate with all the power of the universe, for they fully harness the divine energy that makes letters and words and sentences and paragraphs and arguments and societies and worlds.

Simple sentences sell us short. Emerson treasures the power of words, which is one reason he never makes his prose easy on his readers. Language, he believes, should open up new horizons of meaning, rather than closing them off with definiteness and unambiguity. Every time I encountered the pivotal passage from "New England Reformers" quoted above while writing this book, I found myself struggling with the ambiguity of Emerson's words about genius. Is the genius he mentions individual, or collective? Is it the possession of a great man, or a universal resource all citizens are obligated to pursue? Are Americans required to acquiesce to the words of genius—that is, to the mighty words of guru-orator-poet; or, are Americans obliged to acquiesce to the words of genius—that is, to the wisdom of the oversoul gleaned through meditation? The ethical ramifications of Emerson's words change depending on the answer. If when Emerson says that liberation lies in "obedience to *his* genius" he is referring to the exceptional "man" from the previous sentence who has fallen into divine circuits and, filled with the divine, becomes genius, then it raises serious ethical questions about Emerson's philosophy of oneness. Though Emerson often fantasized about reinventing society as a joyous anarchy of earnest spiritual seekers who form a union of perfect isolation, this passage might describe a kind of *spiritual authoritarianism* in which the masses bow down to the mystical gravity of one who has seen the truth who speaks "*from within*, or from experience," rather than "*from without*, as spectators merely."[88] This genius speaks from experience and moves masses through the sheer gravity of his presence, and those around him have little choice but to be uplifted. Indeed, the genius "has a power which society cannot choose but to feel."[89] In many essays, Emerson reminds us of the virtues of acquiescing to the oversoul. Here it is possible that he advises us to acquiesce to the spokesperson for oversoul, the genius of oneness.

Philosophies of oneness seem to be particularly susceptible to the problems of what I have called, in an article written with William Saas, "acquiescent rhetoric."[90] Following the guidance of ancient authorities including Cicero, we in the West have traditionally understood rhetoric as the art of persuasion. It surely is that. Yet it is high time we recognize that not all rhetoric is aimed at winning assent. Oftentimes, rhetoric aims to achieve a bored shrug of the shoulders and a casual "whatever." Oftentimes, rhetoric aims to get our passive acceptance rather than our active support. Oftentimes, the goal of rhetoric is acquiescence as authorities tell us, *don't worry, we've got this*, just go about your everyday business, leave the big decisions about your salvation to us, pay no attention to the man behind the curtain. Acquiescent rhetoric aims to disempower citizens by cultivating passivity and numbness in the face of authoritarian action and commands. Acquiescent rhetoric corrodes democracy by encouraging citizens to abandon control over their lives to the authorities that be. To fix this situation, we must carefully probe its origins, however surprising or unexpected they might be; and that includes taking a close, critical look at Emerson's theory of genius like I have done in this chapter.

That is not the end of the matter. In fact, Emerson radically reimagines the civic role of democratic citizens, and in so doing he also describes a powerful check on the ability of the genius to wield oneness for nefarious ends. To fulfill their dharma as human beings, Emerson contends that people must attempt to overcome the maya of convention by practicing self-reliance and communication as yoga. Only in this way can they access the collective wisdom of genius and know the truth of oneness. This is general obligation; it applies to all human beings. Yet citizens in democratic cultures have another, more specific dharma. Indeed, if people are to fulfill their *svadharma* as democratic citizens of the United States, they must perform a second duty: they must learn to become *critical genius hunters*.

Emerson insists that there are not two classes of people—leaders and followers, gurus and students, geniuses and stupid people, the few and the many. "I do not believe in two classes," he states. "I believe not in two classes of men, but in man in two moods, in Philip drunk and Philip sober. I think, according to the good-hearted word of Plato, 'Unwillingly the soul is deprived of truth.'"[91] When people are drunk, they do not see things as they are, which is why we often speak of reckoning as a kind of "sobering up." People who are drunk on maya see only illusion. Emersonianism is sobriety. And it is a practice open to all. The divine "comes to the lowly and simple; it comes to whosoever will put off what is foreign and proud; it comes as insight; it comes as serenity and grandeur."[92] All philosophies rest on faith, and Emerson's faith is that human beings naturally crave the truth—all people, high and low, want to see things as they are, not just as they appear. Given the choice between illusion and lucidity, people will choose truth every time: "Nothing shall warp me from the belief, that every man is a lover of truth. There is no pure lie, no pure malignity in nature. The entertainment of the proposition of depravity is the last profligacy and profanation. There is no skepticism, no atheism but that. Could it be received into common belief, suicide would unpeople the planet."[93] If people really believed that there is no truth, if people really believed that nature is a force for evil, then there would be no point in going on living. But we continue to live, and we continue to search for the answers to the eternal questions we feel deep in our hearts.

Emerson's greatest contribution to the history of American yoga is, I believe, also his greatest contribution to everyday democracy: he democratizes the divine avatar of the Bhagavad Gita by encouraging people to address everyone they meet as an incarnation of the divine. This is the bhakti, devotional practice of communication as yoga. Emerson was not in the business of writing self-help books—he never offered a step-by-step how-to guide to enlightenment—and communication as yoga is one of the few spiritual exercises he prescribes in his essays for seeing the truth of oneness. Speak to others as though they are divine and experience "the doubling of the heart itself, nay, the infinite enlargement of the heart with a power of growth to a new infinity on every side."[94] Speak to others as though they are divine, and the divine appears, as if by magic. Speak to others as though they are divine, and know the truth of infinity, a truth beyond words. At times, Emerson practically guarantees that this practice will lead to genius: "The simplest person, who in his integrity worships God, becomes God."[95] At other times, he is more skeptical—after all, the mask *seldom* falls. So what else are we to do if we crave the truth? We are obligated to seek out worthy teachers who know the difference between reality and illusion, between truth and convention, and can instruct us in the art of true knowledge—or what in the Gita is called *jnana yoga*.

What is the mark of a worthy teacher? In a word, genius. A worthy teacher experiences the oversoul and the oneness of all things, and has made it their purpose in life to practice connection rather than separation. And how do we spiritual seekers who are just beginning to sober up know genius? The geniuses who experience oneness are changed, and their spiritual elevation is clear to those who know what to look for:

> The soul that ascends to worship the great God is plain and true; has no rose-color, no fine friends, no chivalry, no adventures; does not want admiration; dwells in the hour that now is, in the earnest experience of the common day,—by reason of the present moment and the mere trifles having become porous to thought, and bibulous of the sea of light.[96]

The genius is simple, in speech and dress and desires. The genius doesn't care about social esteem, about powerful friends, about great adventures, about money. People who care about what others think of them naturally engage in flattery and puffery to win esteem. The genius refuses to flatter, and speaks only the truth.[97] "Souls like these make us feel that sincerity is more excellent than flattery."[98] The genius does not dwell on the past or talk constantly of the future. The genius is fully present. The genius is not distracted by the trifles and baubles of maya; the genius is not distracted, period—for in all phenomena the genius sees the oversoul ("trifles having become porous to thought"). The genius is "bibulous," a word that meant both "spongy" and "excessively fond of drinking" during Emerson's day. The genius is a sponge for divinity, and drinks its nectar with great relish and joy. Most of all, the genius treats others with the respect due to gods: "Souls such as these treat you as gods would."[99] Of course this makes sense, for the genius became a genius by practicing communication as yoga. The words of genius are power—but according to Emerson, the genius wants nothing. The genius craves neither power nor followers nor profit. And so where is the danger of spiritual authoritarianism?

Americans are not always the best judge of character—read Emerson's brilliant contemporary Herman Melville for a series of case studies in gullibility, stereotyping, bad optics, and good intentions gone wrong. We are what we practice. The argument that Emerson was an authoritarian rests on the claim that Emersonians get good at acquiescing to the oversoul and its spokespeople, and, being no better judge of character than other Americans, are primed to acquiesce to false geniuses, including political elites, capitalist robber barons, and spiritual charlatans, whose outsized power, influence, and money is no proof of their virtue. I think that Emerson recognized this as a potential danger, and he recognized, too, that there is no easy, foolproof way to prevent false prophets, malevolent gurus, and would-be demagogues from seizing on our good faith and our spiritual needs. Anytime people gather, there is danger of manipulation; but this does not mean we shouldn't gather (or that we could avoid gathering). It is asking too much of Emerson to solve the problem of democratic manipulation. It is enough that he recognizes it as a problem that any mystical philosophy of oneness must address, so that we can, too.

For Emerson, citizens have a duty as citizens to seek out geniuses and to learn what we can from them. Though it might seem like a contradiction that Emerson opposes convention and then establishes one, his is a duty to challenge duty as it is defined by society. It is a convention to challenge established convention. This is not a practice of blind obedience, of spiritual authoritarianism, for Emerson is emphatic that the faith that rests on authority is not faith. The teacher-student relationship is based on a worthy respect won from rhetorical challenge: "When we see those whom [the oversoul] inhabits, we are apprised of new degrees of greatness. From that inspiration the man comes back with a changed tone. He does not talk with men with an eye to their opinion. *He tries them*."[100] Once we become aware of the existence of genius, even though we have only felt it ourselves in fits and starts and random moments of divine visitation, we can begin to test others to see if they have achieved it. If they flatter, move on. If they demean, move on. If they speak in arcana, move on. If they are arrogant, move on. If they sneer, move on. If they lord their knowledge over us as a form of power, move on. If they engage in enemyship, move on. If they speak in high dudgeon, move on. If they attempt to impose a debt of gratitude, move on. If there are dollar signs where their pupils should be, move on. If they offer to walk the path in our place, move on. If they take away the power to consent and dissent, move on. But perhaps they pass the test, and so we learn what we can from them, treating it not as gospel but as assistance as we walk our path. True genius is religious, but it would never build a church to itself.

Recall that for some commentators Emerson is the founder of American yoga. Emerson believes that genius is necessarily a force for good; the idea of abusing genius seems completely foreign to him. It should not be foreign to contemporary Americans. Most yogic traditions in India tend to emphasize the guru-student relationship. A master guru takes the student under his or her (but mostly his) roof, providing careful, one-on-one apprenticeship and training. I do not deny that there are good and worthy teachers out there—I have studied with a few—but the translation of the guru model to the United States has created a perfect context for abuse (which, unfortunately, I have also experienced firsthand). If the guru uses their status for good, to promote oneness, respect, and human dignity, then that is one thing. Sadly, however, there is a long record in the United States of gurus and would-be gurus abusing their students emotionally, psychologically, financially, physically, and sexually for personal gain.[101] The amount of pain that has been caused by bad gurus is beyond calculation. This is why many contemporary American yogis and yoga teachers, myself included, are reconsidering the appropriateness of the guru model in the United States in the twenty-first century.[102]

None of this is Emerson's fault, and to blame him for our cultural disorders would be a grave deflection that lets the rest of us off the hook.[103] Investigating Emerson's philosophy of oneness does reveal something important about the ethics of oneness, however. There is a great danger in all those who claim to speak as vessels or prophets of the divine. The words of those who speak from within the oversoul are difficult to refute, and they are particularly appealing to those who suffer mightily. We must remember that all words about infinity are shaped by human motivations. The genius remains a human being, and when we hear a "genius" speak, we should always keep at least one eye and one ear open. The words of a guru, a leader, or a spiritual teacher must be judged by how their vision of oneness is enacted on the battlefield of life. Does this philosophy inspire us to create a better democracy and a better world? Does it help us build healthier, more collaborative and respectful relationships with others—all others—who also happen to walk on this earth?

We have now seen how Emerson puts oneness into practice; in the next, final chapter we will see what Whitman has to say on the matter. "Allons!" as Whitman would say. Onward, let's go! Let's see how Whitman's philosophy of oneness meets the challenges of everyday democracy.

6

Democracy

> Democracy is a name for a life of free and enriching communion. It had its seer in Walt Whitman.
>
> JOHN DEWEY, *The Public and Its Problems*

Seer, prophet, genius: Walt Whitman is the mystic poet of democracy. "We have frequently printed the word Democracy. Yet I cannot too often repeat that it is a word the real gist of which still sleeps, quite unawaken'd."[1] Democracy is a god term, perhaps the highest god term, of American culture; but to Whitman, we use this word casually and carelessly, without understanding its true power. For Whitman, the word *democracy* resonates with concerns sempiternal. What he means by democracy, however, is not what most of us mean when we speak those fateful four syllables. Democracy is not primarily about voting or policy debate. Democracy is a communal, relational way of life that teaches citizens how to develop their capacity for cosmic consciousness, their "soul-sight," "the latent eternal *intuitional* sense" that connects them to the divine source of existence.[2] The purpose of democracy is to facilitate rapport—a meditative, yogic experience of being at one with the universe and all beings.

People see the world as a place of separation and conflict because that is what they are habituated to seeing. Yet there is a part of us that cries out for connection, that longs to feel united with the world and those around us, that says, in a tiny but insistent voice, there is more to life than material acquisition. Whitman speaks directly to that part of us in his poetry, which the German Romantics call "intuition," which Emerson calls "the inward eye," and which he himself calls "soul-sight." "There is, apart from mere intellect, in the make-up of every superior human identity," he proffers,

> a wondrous something that realizes without argument, frequently without what is called education, (though I think it the goal and apex of all education deserving the name)—an intuition of the absolute balance, in time and space,

> of the whole of this multifarious, mad chaos of fraud, frivolity, hoggishness—this revel of fools, and incredible make-believe and general unsettledness, we call *the world*; a soul-sight of that divine clue and unseen thread which holds the whole congeries of things, all history and time, and all events, however trivial, however momentous, like a leash'd dog in the hand of a hunter.[3]

Intuition, or "soul-sight," is the "root-centre for the mind."[4] For Whitman, the goal of democracy is to develop one's soul sight and to experience oneness in a transcendent moment of cosmic consciousness. In such a moment, we overcome foolishness and unsettledness and make-believe and see things as they are, not as a jumble of disordered elements but as a unified whole. There is balance; the congeries is one. It's not possible to argue oneself into such consciousness—here Whitman differs from Plato and the Neoplatonists, who placed their faith in dialectic as a path to enlightenment. Whitman muses, "I do not know it—it is without name—it is a word unsaid, / It is not in any dictionary, utterance, symbol."[5] Soul sight does not respond to book learning or "education." And yet Whitman implies that true education, worldly education, aims at nurturing soul sight. This is the type of education that happens outside the schoolroom, while walking alongside and talking with others. The type of education that happens in a democracy.

According to the most influential American philosopher of the twentieth century, John Dewey, Whitman was the "seer" of democracy. Through the lens of cosmic consciousness, Whitman discerned a truth that lent support and sanction to democracy, and, for the rest of his life, he committed himself to defending and promoting democracy in both poetry and prose. And what did Whitman see? He described oneness manifesting itself as political equality, giving democracy a warrant and a justification that was beyond question. Whitman styled himself a prophet of cosmic democracy.

For Whitman, democracy is not primarily about voting or about stump speeches or about two political parties duking it out for control over government. Partisanship is a dualistic distraction; democracy's concerns are more elemental. In a long explanatory footnote in *Democratic Vistas* (1871), his postwar paean to the power of democracy to bring peace and prosperity to an aching, broken nation, Whitman observes:

> Standing on this ground—the last, the highest, only permanent ground—and sternly criticizing, from it, all works, either of the literary, or any art, we have peremptorily to dismiss every pretensive production, however fine its esthetic or intellectual points, which violates or ignores, or even does not celebrate, the central divine idea of All, suffusing universe, of eternal trains of purpose, in the development, by however slow degrees, of the physical, moral, and

> spiritual kosmos. I say he has studied, meditated to no profit, whatever may be his mere erudition, who has not absorb'd this simple consciousness and faith. It is not entirely new—but it is for Democracy to elaborate it, and look to build upon and expand from it, with uncompromising reliance.[6]

What do we see in meditation? The *central divine idea of the all*, which suffuses and gives purpose to the cosmos and sanction to democracy. Of all the virtues, equality is most closely associated with democracy.[7] The all unites the multiples and connects the disconnected, granting our commonplace reality a degree of equality. Whitman grounds democracy in the deep ontological equality of oneness. Multiplicity is real, but what we share is much deeper than what divides us, for we are bound in body and breath. In truth, we are one. We share atoms and air, we share the earth, we share a common divinity. We are brothers and sisters in the all, a cosmic ensemble, joined on an orbic procession from oneness through variety back to oneness. If we can somehow realize this oneness in the world of variety, in this hour, not some other, our lives will be infinitely enriched. Whitman defends democracy because in a moment of meditation he saw the truth of oneness, and democracy is the politics best suited to elaborating oneness in the bustling, booming social world of conflict and drama that we call home.

Whitman grounds democracy in ontology and also in ethics. For Whitman, it is ethically good for people to develop their capacity for meditation, and democracy is the best form of government because it respects *spiritual equality*. Whitman's poetry positions the shared human capacity for mystical insight at the very heart of democracy. For Whitman, soul sight is no respecter of persons. Everyone, no matter their race or gender or class or nationality, has the capacity to experience oneness. In this way meditation is democratic. Intuition, or soul sight, is an indispensable ingredient for democracy: "The latent eternal intuitional sense . . . is *sine qua non* to democracy."[8] We should pause for a moment to reflect on the magnitude of these words. In Western philosophy, when something is sine qua non, it is a necessary condition. Oxygen is sine qua non for life as we know it; without oxygen, we die. For Whitman, without the capacity for intuition into divine oneness, democracy dies. Why? Intuition—soul sight—provides people with a glimpse of oneness, which is the true argument, the one true irrefutable justification, for democracy. In moments of rapport, when we espy oneness and feel ourselves in tune with the universe, we understand that it is impossible for people to be isolated from, and buffered against, the world.[9] An experience of oneness shatters many of our guiding philosophical assumptions about the separation and isolation of individuals. Moreover, because everyone possesses this capacity, soul sight naturally equalizes humanity—and the innate need to cultivate our intuition, to find out if there is a deeper truth to life, to find liberation from suffering and freedom from pain, is what draws people together into the relationships and communities from which we build democracy.

Democracy is premised on the possibility of, and is concerned with facilitating, rapport with the divine. Indeed, for Whitman the purpose of democracy, and the poets who sing of it, is to develop individuals' soul sight: "A highest widest aim of democratic literature may well be to bring forth, cultivate, brace, and strengthen this sense, in individuals and society."[10] The modus operandi of democracy and its literature is to cultivate the soul sight of citizens. Today, meditation is popular, perhaps even mainstream, but sometimes we view it as a hobby or something to do in our free time when we need a break from our real jobs and responsibilities. For Whitman, meditation is our real job—it is the real work of citizenship. There is no higher purpose. "That mystic baffling wonder alone completes all."[11]

The Bhagavad Gita is a direct call to action. Krishna tells Arjuna what to do, and, as we saw above in chapter 4, he marshals the strongest possible peremptory argument to make his case. Chapter 11 of the Gita is the ultimate argument from authority: Krishna reveals his true nature as God, and who can argue with God? Krishna is more didactic than Whitman (perhaps as God this is his privilege). Though inspired by the Bhagavad Gita, Whitman is not so imperious. Whitman's poetry is a record of his delights and joys as he savors life. His rhetoric is an invitation to his readers to take his hand and discover if they, too, can find the same happiness in life that he has found. He is not interested in rallying anyone for any particular cause. He does not debate, he models.

Whitman was not a self-help author. He never crafted a step-by-step guide titled something like "How to Find Divinity amidst the Chaos" or "Finding Democracy in a Dualistic World." In this final chapter, I attempt to infer from Whitman's writings what he might say if he were calling people to action, if he did tell us, as Krishna tells Arjuna, to stand up and fight for what is good. I ask, what advice does Whitman have for us about how to live a life committed to oneness? How does he advise us to meet the challenges that such a life poses, in all its beauty, in all its ugliness, and ultimately in all its perplexity? And, finally, what are the ethical consequences of committing ourselves to living the type of life that he recommends?

Consider this chapter a textually grounded thought experiment that uses Whitman's poetry as a springboard to dive deeply into the problems and challenges of everyday democracy from the perspective of his ethics of oneness. I begin by confronting one of Whitman's smartest critics and attempting to detangle his oneness from the teachings of the New Thought movement. I then turn to a description of two major schools of contemporary democratic theory to see what Whitman might have to say about their claims. Inspired by Whitman's words in "Song of the Open Road"—"Now I re-examine philosophies and religions, / They may prove well in lecture-rooms, yet not prove at all under the spacious clouds and along the landscape and flowing currents"[12]—I propose in this final chapter to take his philosophy on the road and see what difference it might make to us as we face the realities of everyday democratic life. Let us see if Whitman and his oneness are up the challenge!

Healthy-Minded Delusions?

Whitman died in 1892, and when it came time to reflect on his cultural legacy, William James (1842–1910) gave Whitman the prophet of oneness poor marks as an ethical thinker.[13] James did not believe that Whitman invented a viable philosophy. James disagreed with Whitman on the most basic ontological question of whether the world was one or many. Indeed, James was then, and remains today, one of America's greatest and most eloquent defenders of multiplicity—he called our world a "pluralistic universe."[14] But James had a big heart and a curious mind, and he was loath to rule out any philosophical position before it had been thoroughly tested in experience. He did not dismiss Whitman's position by default or *ex ante facto*, as so many philosophers during his day and ours do. He judged it by its consequences. From his perspective, it was a beautiful, cosmic failure.

In *The Varieties of Religious Experience* (1902), James set out to capture the personal experience of the religious believer, which he speculated fell in line with one of two schemata. There are the "healthy-minded," who see the world as fundamentally good and who actively minimize consideration of evil, or simply dismiss it as illusion; and then there are the "sick souls," reborn Puritans who believe that the world is fallen and who are obsessed with evil, disease, and death. With their "sky-blue" outlook on life, with their tendency to wander about "in a grateful admiration of the gift of so happy an existence," the healthy-minded appear much happier than the sick-souled, whose "morbid-mindedness" often leads to anhedonia, depression, disillusionment, and other forms of world sickness.[15] And yet in truth, the healthy-minded's happiness is only skin deep. It is weak, and shallow, and impotent, for it comes too easily. True happiness must be won from the jaws of the dragon.

James marked the "joy-destroying chill" that sick souls feel as a necessary preliminary step along the path of spiritual development.[16] People judge their lives as most meaningful, he believed, when they are confronted by challenges and obstacles that prevent them from realizing their deepest ideals and commitments.[17] For James, the meaning of life is found in the struggle, at the crossroads, in "the everlasting battle of the powers of light with those of darkness."[18] The religion of the sick soul prepares people for the scuffle, and in fact validates it with religious significance. The world is fallen. It is our job to redeem it, and we will likely fail, so let us be humble in our aspirations and savor sweetly our hard-won happiness. The religion of healthy-mindedness doubly fails us, then. By blasting the world in bright light, it overexposes the chiaroscuro space where shadows dance; in so doing, it leaves us ill equipped to meet the impersonal brutality of the world. Healthy-mindedness is all well and good when things are going well, when the world seems to rise up to meet us halfway—but what of those moments when the shadows come and everything falls apart? When depression and anxiety overwhelm us? When we or our loved ones get sick? When the earth shakes, when the forest goes up in smoke, when a funnel drops from the tornadic sky, when the rising, rushing muddy river overwhelms the sandbags?

For James, the first and most important philosophical question, the question that had to be answered before all others, was this: Is life worth living? Each person had to answer this question for themselves. James believed that people feel that their lives hold significance only when they are struggling to overcome some present obstacle that is blocking their achievement of a personal ideal. Life's significance is found in good old-fashioned American pluck and grit, in "fidelity, courage, and endurance."[19] By marking the world as fundamentally good and denying the reality of evils to be overcome, the religion of healthy-mindedness makes life insignificant. The great error of the healthy-minded is their tendency to ignore evil, or to dismiss it as illusion. They say, "It is Avidhya, ignorance!"[20] James believed that healthy-mindedness—here, a healthy-mindedness grounded in Indian thought, for in yoga philosophy, *avidya* means "ignorance" or "error"—was no match for life. This religious worldview "breaks down impotently as soon as melancholy comes."[21] Though it might make people superficially happy, "healthy-mindedness is inadequate as a philosophical doctrine, because the evil facts which it refuses positively to account for are a genuine portion of reality, and they may after all be the best key to life's significance, and possibly the only openers of our eyes to the deepest levels of truth."[22]

Healthy-minded religion is as old as religion. It has had many American apostles. But to James there was no question who its prophet was: "The supreme contemporary example of such an inability to feel evil is of course Walt Whitman."[23] Whitman's poetry was healthy-minded silliness scrawled on the page. For James, "Walt Whitman owes his importance in literature to the systematic expulsion from his writings of all contractile elements. The only sentiments he allowed himself to express were of the expansive order; and he expressed these in the first person, not as your mere monstrously conceited individual might so express them, but vicariously for all men, so that a passionate and mystic ontological emotion suffuses his words, and ends by persuading the reader that men and women, life and death, and all things are divinely good."[24] Whitman had no time to dwell on the negative, because his job was to cheer his readers on, to encourage them to be grateful for life and to urge them to make the most of their opportunity on earth. It was not quite that he was unaware of evil. Instead, he chose to turn his back on evil in order to focus completely and totally on the good. In one of the most oft-quoted lines ever written about Whitman, James concluded: "He is aware enough of sin for a swagger to be present in his indifference towards it, a conscious pride in his freedom from flexions and contradictions."[25]

Whitmanism was a small church, but James stated that he personally knew many people who pledged their lives to this homegrown religion. Whitman "has infected them with his own love of comrades, with his own gladness that he and they exist."[26] In framing Whitman as the prophet of healthy-mindedness, James relied on an account written by one of Whitman's devotees and closest friends, Richard Maurice Bucke (1837–1902). Bucke's *Cosmic Consciousness: A Study in the Evolution of the Human Mind*, published in Philadelphia in 1901, set out to explore the history of "cosmic consciousness," which is, "as its name implies, a consciousness of the cosmos, that is, of the life and order of the universe."[27] James equated Bucke's cosmic consciousness with the mystical experiences of Buddhists and Indian yogis, yet Bucke preferred more local examples.[28] One was Emerson's "The Over-Soul"; another was Whitman's poetry.[29] Bucke professed that "no man who ever lived liked so many things and disliked so few as Walt Whitman"—and Bucke offered a long description of Whitman's fondness for flowers that James quoted as evidence that he was little more than a naive lover of nature.[30] Whitman's love of life, his refusal to speak badly of anyone, his belief that the world was fundamentally good, his desire to cheer others on, was for Bucke a direct result of Whitman's enlightenment: "Walt Whitman is the best, most perfect, example the world has so far had of the Cosmic Sense."[31] The key, for Bucke, was that Whitman was "lit with the infinite" (to use Whitman's own words)—Whitman had a mystical experience of rapport, and from that point forward he knew with soul sight that everything was one and the divine was all.[32] From that point forward there was no soil in which soul sickness could take root, no doubt or fear, no aloneness.

James judged mysticism, like all things, by a pragmatic, "empirical" test: "Its fruits must be good for life."[33] James's critique of Whitman in *Varieties* boils down to this: following a mystical experience of cosmic consciousness, Whitman was so perpetually overcome with gratefulness for life that he was unable—and more important, his religion was unable—to deal with evil, which, whether or not we close our eyes to it, is real. "Let sanguine healthy-mindedness do its best with this strange power of living in the moment and ignoring and forgetting, still the evil background is really there to be thought of, and the skull will grin in at the banquet."[34] Whitman's poetry, in short, is not up the challenge of life. It is a failure.

Is this judgment correct? Perhaps unsurprisingly, as a healthy-minded, tenderhearted, democratic mystic with transcendentalist and Whitmanite proclivities, I believe that it is not. But not only that, I believe that James's critique in *The Varieties of Religious Experience* is deeply unfair to Whitman.

At-One-Ment: Mind Cure and the New Thought

According to James, the New Thought movement, which originated in the 1840s in New England and exploded in popularity in the 1880s and '90s, was the most popular example of the religion of healthy-mindedness in American culture at the turn of the century. James dubbed New Thought "the mind-cure movement," capturing its fundamental tenet, that all bodily illnesses are caused by improper, diseased thinking, and therefore can be cured by changing our minds.[35] According to James, it was Whitman who was responsible for unleashing mind cure on the world. About this he was clearly wrong—a quick perusal of the books and pamphlets of New Thought authors demonstrates that they cite Emerson repeatedly and go to great lengths to tie their philosophy to his; rarely do they invoke Whitman. Why was James so wrong about this? Because he saw something he didn't like in the mind-cure movement, and, employing the logic of guilt by association, he attributed it to another philosopher that he tended not to like, Whitman.

In *Power through Repose* (1891), Annie Payson Call (1853–1940) lamented that Americans suffered from "Americanitis," a complex of nervousnesses and overexertion that broke the backs of even the mightiest men and women.[36] She prescribed a daily practice of "true concentration" in which people sit alone in repose from the world. After quieting the mind and body, softening the muscles, and slowing the breath, she advised, her readers should cultivate positive thoughts about themselves and the world—thoughts that would undoubtedly materialize if only they concentrated hard enough.[37] For the New Thought movement, thoughts were real, and matter—including the body—was an illusion subject to thought manipulation. "There is no matter," the popular reformer Emma Curtis Hopkins (1849–1925) told her students. "There is no sensation in matter. . . . There is no sin, sickness, or death. . . . All that we perceive as matter or reality," she concluded, "is permeable to the ever-flowing power of thought."[38] To heal one's body, it was necessary to change one's thinking. Assume that one is well, and claim health rather than sickness, for "all life is from within out."[39] In practical terms, mind cure meant turning away from so-called "negative" thoughts, from anxiety, worry, fear, and sadness, and instead cultivating the positive. Many Americans found that practicing New Thought made them feel better. James himself received mind-cure treatment several times between 1887 and 1909 for insomnia, depression, anxiety, and angina.[40] But did their recovery last, even when things got tough? And did mind cure truly fix the world, as it promised to do? James was skeptical.

New Thought is the homegrown American meditation movement.[41] Its proponents invited Americans to pause their pursuit of happiness for a moment and turn inward. "A mind floating in a chaotic sea of thoughts, without a ruling aim and positive ideal, is like a rudderless ship, at the mercy of winds, waves, and breakers," wrote Henry Wood (1834–1909) in *New Thought Simplified* (1903).[42] This was the state that most Americans found themselves in (and, I might add, continue to find themselves in today)—they were rudderless ships at sea during a mental hurricane, completely at the mercy of convention and public opinion because they hadn't ever learned how to concentrate and to meditate. Wood continued: "The heart and essence of the New Thought can be most readily acquired by what is known as 'going into the silence.' No amount of intellectual study can reveal that which only can come through spiritual perception and feeling."[43] Americans were so focused on external goals and markers of success that they had forgotten to look inward at the quality of their minds and study the impact of their thoughts on their lives. To find health and happiness, Americans had to "go into the silence" and ask, What effect was their stress, their worry, their fear, their anxiety having on their health and their life journeys?

This was the hard work of self-study, the real work of life, and no one else could do it but individuals themselves. "Life is a problem which has for each an individual solution," Horatio W. Dresser (1866–1954) wrote in *The Power of Silence* (1895). "No one can wholly solve it for us or take from it the element of personal responsibility. It has its own particular history and meaning in each individual case."[44] To do the work, Americans had to gin up the courage to face the noisy silence of their busy minds. Only then could we determine if we were living our individual duties, the truth of which we would feel deep in our hearts. "Have I ever devoted time and reflection—alone with my deepest self—to realize the full bearing of the profoundest and sublimest truths of life? Have I ever made them my own and actualized them in daily life, or is there still a schism between theory and practice?"[45]

Building on the maxim that "what we dwell upon we become, or at least grow like," Wood's popular book *Ideal Suggestion through Mental Photography* (1893) offered the following suggestions for meditation:

> FIRST.—Retire each day to a quiet apartment, and be alone IN THE SILENCE.
>
> SECOND.—Assume the most restful position possible, in an easy-chair, or otherwise; breathe deeply and rather rapidly for a few moments, and thoroughly relax the physical body, for by suggestive corresponds this renders it easier for the mind to be passive and receptive.
>
> THIRD.—Bar the door of thought against the external world, and also shut out all physical sensation and imperfection.
>
> FOURTH.—Rivet the mind upon the "meditation" (left-hand page), and by careful and repeated reading absorb its truth. Then place the "suggestion" (right-hand page), at a suitable distance from the eyes, and fasten them upon it for from ten to twenty minutes. Do not merely look upon it, but wholly GIVE YOURSELF UP TO IT, until it fills and overflows the entire consciousness.
>
> FIFTH.—Close the eyes for twenty to thirty minutes more; behold it with the mind's eye, and let it permeate the whole organism.
>
> SIXTH.—Call it into the field of mental vision during every wakeful hour of the night.
>
> FINALLY.—If disordered conditions are chronic and tenacious, there need be no discouragement if progress is not rapid, nor if "ups and downs" occur. Absorb the ideals REPEATEDLY, until no longer needed. The cure is NOT magical, but a NATURAL GROWTH. Ideals will be actualized in due season.[46]

In New Thought, meditation—or "mental photography," to use Wood's apt phrase—involved contemplating a text with a positive, uplifting philosophical message (printed on the left-hand page of *Ideal Suggestion*) with one-pointed focus and then memorizing short affirming mottos (printed on the right-hand page) that were designed to bring harmony to the mind, health to the body, and courage to the spirit. These mottos included "I AM SOUL," "I AM NOT BODY," "I AM PART OF A GREAT WHOLE," "I AM FREE," "I am one with the Infinite Spirit of Life," and "Dear everybody, I love you."[47]

The New Thought movement was eclectic, and its jolly proponents took inspiration from the mystical traditions from both the East and the West; there are striking parallels to, and evidence of the influence of, Indian philosophy generally and the Bhagavad Gita specifically on New Thought.[48] But no influence loomed larger than Emerson. Dresser observed simply that when it came to New Thought, "we associate the name of Emerson with its spiritual teachings."[49] "Perhaps no other modern seer has emphasized the full-orbed vision so strongly as Emerson," Wood announced, for Emerson taught a "law of mutuality" that boiled down to the basic lesson: "There is but one."[50] The proponents of New Thought believed that the Gilded Age's gospel of rugged individualism actively harmed Americans, for this individualism boxed people into an antagonistic relationship with their fellow citizens and with the world. The New Thoughters countered individualistic common sense by citing Emerson: the world is one, and once the mind is stilled it cries out for this oneness, like a child for its parent. New Thought appeals "to those deeper feelings which find their reason in our relationship to the great Over-Soul."[51] "The essence of the New Thought is found not only in the good of all things but in their oneness," Wood concluded. ". . . Brush away superficialities, and each soul is a miniature of the 'Over-soul.' "[52] Sitting alone in silence, "there is soul-contact with the Parent-Soul, and an influx of life, love, virtue, health and happiness from the Inexhaustible Foundation. There is growing *at-one-ment*, and something of the divine beauty and perfection is photographed upon the human soul."[53]

According to the popular contemporary author Mitch Horowitz, during the late nineteenth century "positive thinking entered the groundwater of American life. It became the unifying element of all aspects of the American search for meaning. The shapers of positive thinking fundamentally altered how we see ourselves today—psychologically, religiously, commercially, and politically. Their story is the backstory of modern America. Peer into any corner of current American life, and you'll find the positive-thinking outlook."[54] Positive thinking—mind cure—the religion of healthy-mindedness—New Thought—is the air we breathe, the water we drink as Americans. The trouble with New Thought, according to Horowitz's careful and astute analysis, is not that it is hokum; self-suggestion is without question one of the most powerful forces in the world. The trouble is that New Thought quickly developed into *the prosperity gospel*, for the second generation of New Thought gurus taught Americans that just as they could create health by altering their thoughts, so, too, could they create wealth through "the law of attraction" (known today as "the Secret").[55] There were great fortunes to be won, but Americans lost something significant when New Thought became just another way to pursue happiness through material gain—they lost the Emersonian sense of dependence on the divine oneness for all life's blessings, and hence the humility to be found in a grateful appreciation of true interconnectedness. Emerson is clear: Americans who pursue happiness by accumulating wealth and esteem are misguided. Greed is never the answer (unless the question is what makes us suffer). The proper way to pursue happiness is to become a vessel for the divine, for such an experience results in *personal* as well as *political* salvation. In the decades after Emerson's and Whitman's deaths, New Thought became less about opening the self to the divine and more about nurturing the awesome, unequaled power of thought to conquer the world. New Thought became American hubris, another way to laud the rich for their success and to blame the poor for their poverty.

Though the mind curers talked up Emerson's influence, they often failed to grasp his central spiritual exercise of communication as yoga. Separated by decades, New Thought recognized many of the same personal and social problems that Emerson did. According to Wood, "For the lack of the sense of a larger organic connection, the world struggles and suffers. Each one views his own life as a thing by itself, and thus he closes himself to the influx of the Universal."[56] "Instead of opening its vision upon a fundamental oneness, the body politic is severed into fragments, and, each thinks its interest opposed to all the others," he deduced.[57] Emerson advised Americans to attune themselves to the fundamental oneness of all beings through social interaction. By practicing addressing the divine in other people even when those people are horrible and nasty, even when they act like enemies, Americans open themselves to the divine in their lives. New Thought reverses the process. First, people must retreat from the world, to a private room or apartment where they can sit quietly. Then, by practicing contemplation and "mental photography," people change how they think, and magically the world is different. Picture the world as one—"All in one, and one in all"—and concentrate deeply enough on this desire and it will become true.[58] When it comes to oneness and democracy, New Thought seems less like a self-fulling prophecy and more like circular logic. If Horowitz is right and the religion of healthy-mindedness has infused all aspects of American life, does this not mean that our culture is based on a fallacy, the error of logic that rhetorical scholars since ancient Rome have dubbed petitio principii, the fallacy of begging the question? Assume the conclusion to be true, and so shall it be!

For James, the most severe fault of New Thought was that it actively shunned talk of evil, and now we can see why it did. To speak of evil was to introduce disharmony into the mind and bring evil into the world. To contemplate evil was to invite it into the house of the mind, like an uninvited guest. It was far better to think only of good. According to Wood, "We must refuse mental standing-room to discord, and by right thinking call into existence a wholesome and inspiring environment. Think no evil, and have eyes only for the good. Optimism is of God, and it stimulates and attracts its possessor along the upward road towards the ideal and the perfect. Pessimism creates and multiples unwholesome conditions, and galvanizes them into apparent life."[59] Urging his readers to memorize and repeat the motto "I MAKE HARMONY," Wood suggested that they also sit in silence and contemplate the following message:

> There are invisible threads which connect us with every object which makes up our environment. Vibrations are ever passing over these connections, backward and forward, and it is for us to control their purpose and quality. Every star, sun, person, circumstance, and principle is exchanging messages with us. The dispatches we send are echoed back in duplicate quality. Love for love, antagonism for antagonism, pain for pain. Everything bears the aspect that we give it. Love gilds every object upon which we project it, and its sheen is reflected back in rays of golden light. By its magic, stumbling-blocks become stepping-stones. Love "thinketh no evil," and I follow its example. I create a harmonious environment by projecting thought only of the good. God created all things good, and in the kingdom of my own consciousness I will do the same. I will think only harmonious thoughts, and thereby make harmony. All is good.[60]

Oneness is real, and it is good. Evil has no reality. It is an illusion conjured by the mind. Casting the individual in the Emersonian role as pupil to the oversoul, Wood counseled his readers to think of evils as stepping-stones, not stumbling blocks: "All so-called evils and disordered are existent as conditions, but have no reality as entities. Conditions and educational experiences serve their purpose and come to an end, but all true verities are eternal, because they are divine."[61]

New Thought demonstrates one of the many trajectories that oneness assumed after the deaths of Emerson and Whitman. From the late nineteenth century forward, mind cure has proven a potent influence on American culture. When the first yogis (including Swami Vivekananda) came to the United States and breathed in the American air, they inhaled mind-cure doctrines that they then exhaled in their yoga instruction. The earliest American yoga was a creole that combined Advaita Vedanta with mind cure, Emersonism, Whitmanism, and Theosophy.[62] Indeed, the vocabulary of New Thought infuses Vivekananda's yogic treatises including *Raja Yoga* (1896) and *Karma Yoga* (1896), and also the work of his successors, Swami Abhedananda and Swami Paramananda.[63] The popular Chicago author and attorney William Walker Atkinson (1862–1932), writing under the pseudonym Yogi Ramacharaka, published a series of early twentieth-century bestsellers teaching a New Thought–inspired yoga and meditation for mental calm and material success.[64] And the Iowa-born Pierre Bernard (1875–1955), who styled himself "Oom the Omnipotent" and taught hatha yoga to early twentieth-century celebrities and socialites, blended Vedanta, tantra, and New Thought into his asana practices (he was also one of the first in a long line of male yoga teachers to be dogged by sex scandals and charges of assault).[65]

Via the New Thought movement, the ethics of oneness—and the increasingly popular practice of yoga—took on a decidedly healthy-minded cast in the early twentieth-century United States. But let us be clear: this determination to think only positive thoughts and to deny the reality of evil, the idea that thinking something makes it real—none of this is Whitman. It is hardly Emerson, either, though the New Thoughters went to great lengths to trace their concepts back to Emerson's writings. James might be right to be suspicious of the New Thought treatment of evil, but he is certainly wrong to pin his opprobrium on Whitman. Whitman's poetry is healthy-mindedness par excellence; but as we will see in the following pages, he does not deny the reality of evil or conflict or injustice. In fact, it is in rising to meet these challenges that Whitman's philosophy of oneness and his cosmic democracy proves its mettle.

Deux Democracies

Walt Whitman represents a problem for scholars of American democracy.

American scholars tend to fall into two camps when studying democracy.[66] The first camp is *antifoundationalist*.[67] Antifoundationalism was a response to the Civil War. Louis Menand observes that "the outcome of the Civil War was a validation, as Lincoln had hoped it would be, of the American experiment. Except for one thing, which is that people in democratic societies are not supposed to settle their disagreements by killing one another. For the generation that lived after it, the Civil War was a terrible and traumatic experience. It tore a hole in their lives."[68] In their postbellum reflections, it was only natural that Americans wondered what caused the Civil War and how such a war could be prevented in the future. Many American philosophers concluded that, at bottom, it was a war over ideas. While many of these ideas were noxious—in particular, the argument that slavery was necessary, useful, and morally just because white bodies were superior to disposable black bodies—what was worse was the tendency, especially pronounced in times of heightened cultural division, for ideas to harden into ideologies that no persuasion, no argument, and no rhetoric can touch. This is when ideas become dangerous. The Civil War proved that democracy dies when people cling so closely to their ideas that they are willing to kill their fellow citizens for them.

During the formative years of the United States, the founders aspirationally framed the Constitution as an engine of deliberation. Indeed, they argued that the Constitution would ensure the stability of the republic by creating an institutional structure for promoting deliberation among the best, most well-educated Americans about the nation's future. In the early nineteenth century, deliberative ideals spread unevenly through American culture. In the years leading up to the Civil War, popular deliberation repeatedly broke down into racist taunts, resentful bromides, conspiracy theories, enemyship, and ever worsening cycles of reciprocal, Hatfield and McCoy–style violence. Citizens brawled and rioted and massacred each other out on the plains, a congressman beat another congressman with a cane, and, eventually, armies clashed, wiping out entire families and communities and towns with gruesome new weapons of rusty death. In the postbellum years, many philosophers—especially those who came to be known as the American pragmatists—attempted to stave off future conflicts by renewing the promise of America's deliberative culture and teaching Americans to view their ideas, their beliefs, and their truths differently: with skepticism and humility.

Truth, the pragmatists taught, does not come from some external, transcendent source on high. There is no such thing as "intuition," as Romantism, Emersonianism, and Whitmanism taught. Soul sight is stupidity. The words of preachers and prophets are of no help when it comes to determining what is true and what is not. Moreover, no truth is beyond question, no matter how true it might feel in our hearts, because human nature is limited and fallible. In his foundational essay "The Fixation of Belief" (1877), Charles Sanders Peirce (1839–1914) demands that Americans recognize that uncertainty is an existential, and not merely a cognitive, condition.[69] There is no certainty in life. Every choice we make might be wrong; we simply have no way of knowing before the fact. No life is constructed on unshakeable foundations. All lives are built on sand that is perpetually shifting. The pragmatists hoped that if Americans could recognize this, then they might be more humble in their politics, thereby preventing future wars—because war is a disease of the most extreme arrogance. The pragmatists also hoped that if Americans would genuinely struggle with the realities of existential uncertainty and human fallibility, it would lead them to seek out new opportunities to cooperate and deliberate with others, because the truths we build together, through communication, will be better—that is, better adapted to meet the demands and confront the challenges of the world we live in—than any we might conjure up alone, sitting in meditation or contemplation.

The pragmatist John Dewey (1859–1952) remains the most influential voice of antifoundationalism in American philosophy. Just as it was customary for philosophers of Dewey's generation to cite Emerson and Whitman and sometimes Jefferson, Lincoln, or Tocqueville in their writings, today it would be almost unheard of to write about American democracy without invoking Dewey.[70] At a time when many American intellectuals were bewailing the stupidity of the masses and extolling the merits of expert rule, Dewey defended a democracy rooted in the everyday needs and concerns of citizens on the local level. He extolled the wisdom of citizens, especially when gathered in deliberation. Indeed, for Dewey, democracy was located in local communities and there was magic in communication. "Of all affairs communication is the most wonderful," he wrote, for communication "is a wonder by the side of which transubstantiation pales."[71] Dewey was an antifoundationalist who taught that everything people believe to be true is rhetorical, meaning that people build their truths through interaction and conversation with others. The world is a random cascade of contingencies and unintended consequences that people must band together to manage. Both Emerson and Whitman assumed the absolute truth of oneness. Dewey allows for no such assumption—for him, to assume that anything is true beyond question is the first step along the path toward conflict, violence, and war. Some truths are better than others, but all truths are subject to revision as our knowledge grows and as circumstances change.

Dewey teaches that truth is socially constructed, contingent, perspectival, and fallible.[72] This lesson about ontology applies equally to politics. Democracy is the optimal form of government because it promotes deliberation, leading to the creation of better truths and, hopefully, a more intelligent public opinion. In the Deweyan tradition, there are no *ends* outside of democracy that justify the *means* of democracy, which include consultation, conference, persuasion, and discussion.[73] Instead, the means of democracy are considered to be good in themselves, and they constitute the ends that we collectively pursue, even if those ends are unclear when we start communicating. Democracy is the justification for democracy. The Deweyan antifoundationalists are skeptical of religion, for religious leaders offer false certainties. Pragmatists actively attempt to banish metaphysics to the dustbin of history.

The second camp of scholarship I call *democracy as dissent*. This camp is as old as democracy itself, and, in many ways, it is the polar opposite of antifoundationalism—for while pragmatists picture democracy as an alternative to war, dissenters tend to view democracy as war by other (generally rhetorical) means. The English word *democracy* is derived from the classical Greek *demokratia*, which means "popular government" or "the power of the citizens" (a compound of *demos*, the native adult males of the polis, and *kratos*, power, sovereignty, rule). In classical Athens, it was widely assumed that this power, this *kratos*, was the power of the disenfranchised poor banding together to resist the oppressions perpetuated by the wealthy and powerful. From classical Greece to republican Rome to Renaissance Italy to Enlightenment-era England to the founding period of the United States, philosophers and statesmen viewed the antagonism between rich and poor, the few and the many, as the primary social division.[74]

Following the Civil War, many Americans continued to view politics through this lens, especially those angry midwestern rebels who dubbed themselves "Populists" and fought to redeem their nation's broken democratic promises of a more equal life in a Gilded Age of glaring material, political, and social inequality. As I argue in my book *The Politics of Resentment* (2015), this idea—of democracy as a populist force by which resentful people come together to resist injustice—has long shaped how people in the United States, both proponents and opponents, have viewed democracy. For dissenters, the democratic playbook is clear: the poor, the demos, the many, the 99 percent, *the people* band together in anger and resentment to challenge the rich, the 1 percent, the prominent, and the well-connected—those who would be lords of the whole world. In the millennia-long history of conflict between rich and poor, democracy does not mean voting or governing; it means dissent. "Democracy exists only in the presence of dissent."[75]

The democracy-as-dissent camp is driven by a deep-seated feeling that we live amid oppression, that everything we take to be true is an imposition of powerful interests looking to dupe and detain and derail us. Freedom is a lie, happiness a trick, your smile a ploy, oneness an assertion of hegemony. It's all just culture industry. There is a war going on, just beneath the surface of polite social interactions. Put your ear to the ground and you will hear it. There are many varieties of democracy as dissent, but most share the belief that democracy exists *in reaction to* perceived wrongs as a grand coordinated gesture of refusal, a brilliant, collective *no*. Dissenters tend to celebrate reactive emotions, including resentment and anger and outrage, for these emotions are the most effective at raising consciousness and moving people to action.[76] Dissenters tend to be skeptical of any democratic or rhetorical theory that foregrounds identification, consensus, common ground, agreement, and consubstantiality as a hypergood. For dissenters, such ideals occlude power disparities and the subtle operations of hegemony. There can be no common good, because what "we" want and what "they" want are incommensurate. The stakes are high. Dissenters call on Americans to recognize that democracy is war by other means, and to learn how to fight their battles tactically, rhetorically, to best their enemies with words—the strongest, most piercing words in our arsenal.

Walt Whitman represents a problem for democratic theorists, then, because he articulates a vision of democracy that is not simply different from these two camps of scholarship—it seems completely antithetical to them. "Democracy," Dewey stated, "had its seer in Walt Whitman."[77] What Whitman saw in democracy is not what Dewey saw. In fact, what Whitman saw in democracy is so strange, so confounding, so paradoxical that, I would wager, it stretches the boundaries of believability for most contemporary scholars of democracy.

Why Deliberate?

Why should scholars of democracy pay attention to Whitman? Whitman's poetry has inherent interest as an influential moment in the history of American democracy.[78] But more than this, democratic theorists, political philosophers, and rhetorical scholars should pay attention because the utter oddness of Whitman's philosophy of oneness when compared with contemporary democratic theories invites us to reflect on our scholarly assumptions. Reading Whitman's poetry has inspired me to ask new questions about the models I've inherited for understanding and studying democracy, and after reading Whitman, I better understand the range of possible democratic experiences. Democracy is far wider and more mysterious than we think. In the end, I believe that Whitman's poetry of oneness might help us manage the challenges, tragedies, and disappointments of democratic life in those moments when antifoundationalism and democracy as dissent prove limited in their application. I therefore conclude this chapter by discussing how Whitman's *cosmic democracy* speaks to antifoundationalists' and dissenters' particular blind spots.

Following the Civil War, the antifoundationalists concluded that ideas become dangerous when they are beyond question, when citizens put so much faith into them that they are willing to sacrifice, fight, and die for them. Accordingly, pragmatists including Richard Rorty and Stanley Fish teach us to approach ideas with a degree of ironic detachment, quietly and subtly winking at all truth claims.[79] Whitman derived a very different lesson from the Civil War. In *Democratic Vistas*, he contended that democracy requires a metaphysical foundation—the ontology of oneness—in order to prevent Americans from devolving into the types of divisions and partisan infighting that fueled the war. The trouble for Whitman was not that Americans were too committed to the truth of their ideas; it was that they were committed to the wrong ideas.

Whitman was one of many astute Americans who recognized that while the Civil War had passed into memory and legend, nevertheless the potential for war lingered, especially in a divided, dueling world. Many American politicians looked to enemyship to put the nation back together and promote peace and concord—at least, between white Americans (hence, the Spanish-American War of 1898). Today we continue to live in a world shaped by enemyship. Whitman envisioned a more collaborative future that prized peace over war and friendship over enemyship. Whitman encouraged his readers to treat everyone—no matter their race, their gender, their class, religion, nationality, or sexuality—as divine. His philosophy of oneness did not actively seek to erase differences; instead, it sought to sanctify all lives in order to avoid the active exclusion and dehumanization of whole groups of Americans. Whitman challenged the individualistic bias of American culture—the doctrine of possessive individualism and the old trope of "the American Adam"—by stressing the deep interconnectedness of bodies and brains and souls on a procession toward cosmic consciousness.[80] Based on his mystical experience of at-one-ness with the universe, Whitman marked equality as the metaphysical foundation of oneness and taught a gospel of interdependence: "For every atom belonging to me as good belongs to you."[81] This is a gospel of peace. If all bodies are sacred and everyone is interconnected, war loses its most persuasive justifications.

Obviously, by grounding democracy in a metaphysics of oneness, Whitman's poetry stands opposed to antifoundationalism in important ways. However, Whitman provides something to those who prize deliberation as an end in itself—he offers citizens *a reason to deliberate*. One of the crucial features of democracy is that it brings people together to talk.[82] Democracy only works if citizens are well practiced in talking, laughing, arguing, singing, and deliberating with their friends as well as strangers.[83] Instead of viewing democratic deliberation as an inherent good, as many pragmatists do, Whitman contends that we talk, discuss, and argue with others to learn to develop our ability to see the divine in everyone and the interconnectedness of apparently disparate beings. We deliberate to work through our differences and strategize over how to handle shared problems, and also to practice certain skills that will develop our soul sight and prepare ourselves for cosmic consciousness. We deliberate, in short, to become better attuned to oneness. Whitman transforms democracy into a gymnasium by providing people with a strong motivation to practice talking and deliberating with others. For Whitman, by multiplying the opportunities for practicing communication as yoga, democracy also multiplies the possible sites of enlightenment: a street corner, a local pub, a produce market, a coffee shop, a park, a living room, a boardroom are democracy's ashrams. Every time we open our mouths and our ears is a chance to experience things as they really are, as one.

Whitman challenges the way many scholars study democracy by asking, What is the motivation for citizens to deliberate together, to talk to strangers, to form publics and counterpublics, and to put in the hard work necessary to be good citizens? Simply repeating the old mantra that citizenship is both a right and a responsibility, as most Americans have been taught since at least middle school, is not nearly enough. Whitman represents a tradition that neither defines humans as political animals nor sees politics as an end in itself. Democracy is a means, not an end, for him. He believed that for democracy to work, it requires a metaphysical warrant, a soteriology to light a fire in our hollow hearts. That goal is cosmic consciousness. We practice democracy to feel the comfort of oneness. Our neoliberal, capitalist culture rips the individual out of the whole and demands that we experience the world as though we are apart from it, not a part of it. Democracy is a chance for reintegration, for returning the part (ourselves) back to the all. Those who experience the rapport of oneness find peace. And the experience of oneness provides metaphysical backing to a democratic argument for world peace.

Generally, democratic theorists are uncomfortable talking about salvation, being, and the good—*and for good reason*. We live in a pluralistic world, after all, and so to broach such questions is to bring potentially violent disagreements to the foreground, where they are liable to explode into conflict. Rorty labels all religious talk, including talk about salvation, a "conversation stopper."[84] Of course, such talk need not shut down deliberation, but it is tricky, and handling religious controversy requires a skill set that most people simply have not yet developed. Many democratic theorists are skeptical of spiritual and religious talk, fearing that it is really a mask for oppression. There is no question that metaphysical and soteriological arguments have traditionally acted as cover for the proliferation of bourgeois and neoliberal values, which is why some scholars are critical of such claims.[85] However, we cannot divorce Whitman's poetry from his soteriology or his metaphysics, and I believe it is worth reconsidering the costs of divorcing democracy from such matters, as many scholars typically do.

In the Deweyan pragmatist tradition, democracy is a good in itself—it is a means that generates its own ends. Truly, then, the only cure for the ills of democracy is more democracy. Yet I wonder if democracy has any magic left to inspire us to be better than we are today. I hope that it does. However, it is worth asking, alongside Whitman, What is the point of democracy? For Whitman, if people are not working toward some life-changing goal, then it is doubtful that they will put in the work necessary to become good citizens. That goal is cosmic consciousness. Everyone has this capacity; yet people can only develop it through interaction with others. The lasting value of

Whitmanism is not just enlightenment, however. If rapport happens, if people are able to transcend convention and common sense and to experience the elemental rapport of at-one-ness with all creation, then great. Such an experience is wonderful and life-enriching. But Whitmanism does not demand the achievement of such an experience. The lasting value of Whitmanism is also found in the skills and lessons people learn while developing their soul sight and seeking cosmic consciousness by practicing communication as yoga. Through such practice, we will become good democratic citizens and capable ethical actors whether or not we ultimately experience enlightenment.

Whitman's poetry models how citizens can learn to be better communicators prepared to undertake the challenges of democratic life. However, it would be a mistake to divorce the means from the end. In *The Sermon on the Mount According to Vedanta* (1963), Swami Prabhavananda writes, "In every religion you will find two principles: there is the ideal to be realized and there is the method of realization."[86] To understand Whitman's vision of democracy, we must keep these two principles in mind: the ideal or goal (cosmic consciousness), and the method of realization (spiritual practices like communication as yoga and the deification of the body). Whitman posits a soteriological goal (wrapped up in a metaphysics inspired by Bhedabheda Vedanta and Emersonianism) and frames spiritual practice as a means to a much higher end—namely, the peace that is found by experiencing rapport with the universe. By dedicating ourselves to the spiritual transformation necessary to experience cosmic consciousness, people are changed for the better. Take this end away and there is no motivation to change, and no real reason to behave ethically. To use an analogy that is common in the perennial philosophy: the motivation for why people climb a mountain is to reach the top, but it is what people learn about themselves as they prepare to make the journey and as they place bootprint after bootprint up the path that truly matters. For Whitman, we misunderstand democracy if we make it solely about voting or governing. Whitman reimagines democracy as a path up the mountain of enlightenment.

Infidelity and Heedlessness: A Cosmic Vocabulary for Democracy and Dissent

For Whitman, democracy is the best form of government because it is guided by the virtue of equality. Equality, for Whitman, means oneness, and oneness is a revelation of equality. For Whitman, then, democracy is superior because it is most closely attuned to the ontological truth of oneness. It is democracy's job—and by extension, the job of democracy's philosophers and poets and orators—to "elaborate," to cultivate, to develop the intuitive sense that all people possess, so that they can experience oneness and know, without question, the truth of democracy. What this democracy will look like in practice, Whitman does not, will not, in fact cannot, say. For him democracy seems to mean the creative power of a multitude of people, thrown together by circumstance, to create unique patterns, communities, and ways of being that are contingent, unpredictable, and often beautiful in their own way. How we work together to develop our soul sight is up to us to determine democratically.

Whitman's *cosmic democracy*, if I may call it that, is driven by the belief that no life is intrinsically more valuable than any other, because everyone is divine. No bodies are disposable, because all bodies are divine. More radically, cosmic democracy is invested in ensuring that everyone has access to a good life, because, again, everyone is divine, and ultimately life is lived in common. Everyone has the capacity for soul sight, and it is democracy's job to ensure that everyone has what they need in order to develop their cosmic consciousness. Because we are enriched by the wisdom and insights of our fellows, to restrict a person's (or a group of people's) soul sight is to weaken us all. In "Song of Myself," Whitman heralds a radical definition of democracy:

> I speak the pass-word primeval, I give the sign of democracy,
> By God! I will accept nothing which all cannot have their counterpart of on the same terms.[87]

According to one of Whitman's admirers, when he gives "the sign of democracy" he means "the sign of equality"—for equality is the "password" of democracy, its not-so-secret pin code.[88] Whitman's poetry is a celebration of "the body electric," of real embodied souls with hopes and dreams and fears and resentments, who suffer joys and tragedies, who laugh and cry and love, who are common in their divinity but uncommon in personal dreams and experiences. At the bottom of this human drama is the divine foundation of oneness. For Whitman, democracy at its best attunes us to our shared existence of a common life. Americans celebrate the Declaration of Independence, not of Interdependence; we know the allure of autonomy. And yet Whitman constantly reminds us that no one goes it alone, and so he expresses his thankfulness with long catalogues of all the motley characters who were, he affirmed, as much a part of himself as his eyes or hands or bones: "Of these one and all I weave the song of myself."[89]

In *Leaves of Grass*, Whitman takes up the mantle of the democratic poet, whose job, whose "highest widest aim" is "to bring forth, cultivate, brace, and strengthen" the soul sight of citizens, individually and collectively.[90] Whitman seeks to empower people toward communal, cooperative world-building by grounding democracy in ontological connectedness. We are all in this together. Life is a shared procession.

Whitman's poetry grounds democracy in the truth of oneness, a truth that is at once "physical, moral, and spiritual." Whitman recognizes that democracy emerges in the tender, honest, often desperate insight that our agency as individuals is severely limited, and that we need others to live, and to live well. Industry is a virtue, but individual initiative and hard work can take us only so far. We might strive for self-reliance in the Ben Franklin style of going it alone, we might wish to live a strenuous life, we might wish to pull ourselves up by our bootstraps; but this is impossible.[91] To manage the opportunities and challenges presented by the world in which we live, we must act together. Agency is communal, and an individual life is really a shared life of association with others.[92] Democracy is sanctified by the ontological reality of oneness. Democracy is demanded because as spiritual seekers our soul sight is housed in bodies that are at once remarkably strong and ridiculously fragile and frail. We are radically open to the world in which we live. To sing the body electric is to praise the body's strength and acknowledge its beautiful, tragic frailty. We like to believe that we are in charge of nature or biology, but all it takes is one pandemic to show us who's boss. Life involves a cascade of risks. Democracy is one way that we work together with others to mitigate these risks and cultivate our strengths so that we might face the challenges of a shared life together. Democracy grows from human vulnerability. As such, it must constantly fight against the human tendency toward what I call "oneness panic"—the deep existential fear that can follow from realizing just how interconnected human lives are to each other and the natural world in which we live.

In his more introverted moments, Emerson suggests that the more vulnerable people are—the more they acknowledge the often harsh realities of bodily life in the material world, the realities of gain and loss, the slings and arrows of fate and fortune—the more they will recognize that they need each other, and as a consequence the less self-reliant they will be. Whitman concludes the opposite. There is no need to transcend material reality, to find perfect isolation even in the moments when we are with others. Life in the material, phenomenal world is not maya, illusion. It is real. We should not turn away from our vulnerability. We must turn toward it and face it squarely, together. Whitman emphasizes human interconnectedness and our abiding reliance on the support of others. In so doing, he also enriches the democracy-as-dissent scholarly framework.

Democracy is a politics of contestation—no one, certainly not Whitman, would deny this fact. Democracy blossoms from the need to solve problems that are bigger than any one of us; it is based on the belief that, in general, we are smarter in groups than we are alone. Any time people gather to discuss problems, there also will be disagreement over how best to solve them (and controversy, too, over whether a problem is in fact a problem in the first place). One of the great challenges of democracy is to keep this contestation from spiraling out of control into faction, schism, and hateful, resentful violence. The inevitability of disagreement and the inherent rowdiness of people gathered need not lead us to what the ancient Greeks called *misodemia*, the fear and hatred of democracy, which is how the founders of the United States felt about democracy.[93] For democracy to work, citizens need training in rhetoric. Democratic citizens must learn how to prevent politics from becoming open warfare by developing the skills necessary to talk with and listen to those people with whom they disagree. We must learn how to build trust.[94] One of the foundational rhetorical habits of democracy concerns how we view those with whom we disagree. According to Kenneth Burke, "The progress of human enlightenment can go no further than in picturing people not as *vicious*, but as *mistaken*."[95] It makes no sense to talk to monsters. If our antagonists are vicious or "evil," the only path forward is to destroy them; but if they are mistaken, they can be redeemed, through rhetoric and argument.[96]

Democracy should not be a rubber stamp of authority. Democracy should be disruptive. Democracy should be a way for people to voice their displeasure with the way things are and to call out instances of injustice as we witness and experience them. Democracy is how we challenge those who deny oneness or who seek to profit by stoking oneness panic. Democracy does not erase battle lines. Contemporary citizens of the United States live on a *dharmakshetre* that is also a *lokatantrakshetre* (a democratic battlefield).[97] At times the most democratic thing to do is to stand up and fight! The great challenge of democratic politics, then, is to preserve a space for dissent while transforming potentially violent conflicts into discussions that can be negotiated with argument and deliberation rather than fists and guns. Rhetorical scholars have given substantial consideration to how we might do this. The best solution we have come up with is to say that every act of democratic dissent must be coupled with a rhetorical affirmation of the interdependence of adversaries.[98] We must address our opponents as human beings rather than objects, and we must remember what we share even as we draw our disagreements out into the open.

This is the trouble with the democracy-as-dissent perspective—it tends to view disagreement as war, and downplays or eliminates entirely the space of commonality, identification, and interconnectedness between opponents. If the opposing sides in a controversy share no common ground, there is no hope for resolving a conflict aside from the triumph of one over the other. Rather than an argument, we get a fight; rather than persuasion, we get coercion; either way, democracy becomes an invitation to violence.[99] Whitman's poetry addresses this challenge by offering a strong affirming gesture of interdependence—he encourages people to approach everyone, even those with whom they disagree, with the inherent worth and dignity due to divine beings—while still preserving the disruptive gesture that is at the heart of democratic politics.

Whitman's practice of an embodied communication as yoga models how to approach everyone—even those with whom they disagree—as divine, and to argue with sympathy, understanding, and love. For Whitman, people are not inherently *evil*; they are *mistaken* about the ontological order.[100] In short, they are marked by *infidelity*, an august term of great symbolic power in Whitman's poetry.[101] The English word is derived from the Latin *infidelis*, "not keeping faith," "treacherous," "disloyal," and *infidelitas*, "faithlessness" and "inconstancy." For Whitman, infidelity is a lack of faith in the divine oneness and the unity of all things. This lack of faith is, for him, the pinnacle of danger, for it destroys democracy.

In his poetry and prose, Whitman associates infidelity with *mocking*, with *scorn*, with *negligence*, with *disdain*, with *irreverence* for the living and the dead, with *alarmism*, with *solipsism* and self-centeredness, with *obedience* to myths, public opinion, and class, with *flippancy* and slavishness to fashion, with the elevation of *pecuniary gain* above all other goals, with *doubt and gloom*, with *superciliousness*, and with *nihilism*.[102] In "By Blue Ontario's Shore," one of Whitman's most cosmic poems, he describes a culture tending toward infidelity and the great poet's heroic battle to uphold oneness in the face of cultural entropy—"the years straying toward infidelity he withholds by his steady faith."[103] When he charges people with "infidelity," Whitman does not posit an innate, fixed character trait (such as "evil") that defines a being rotten to its core. Instead, he calls attention to a person's behavior and how they interact with others. Evil concerns being; infidelity is about outlook and action. In American Protestant traditions it is common to accuse people of being evil, but according to Whitman it would be better to say that people behave as infidels, for while the only option for managing evil is to fight and hopefully defeat it, infidelity can be corrected by the kind words and gestures of the faithful. Whitman's democracy rests on faith: faith in oneness, and faith that those who do not recognize oneness can be brought around to see the light. This, then, becomes the poet's task.[104]

Whitman's words are a constant reminder, and a perpetual celebration, of oneness—of the ontological fact that we are all in this together, for better and for worse, because each of us is a manifestation of the all. In Whitman's cosmos, those who deny oneness behave unethically. Again, for Whitman, such people are not inherently *evil*, though they are clearly capable of doing awful things; they are *mistaken* about the true nature of reality, for they are habituated to acting as if they are rugged individuals.[105] And so they are *infidels*. To call people who have so thoroughly imbibed the conventions of possessive liberalism and rugged individualism that they have forgotten oneness "infidels," as Whitman does, is a powerful rhetorical retort. However, I worry that this word has been so completely colored by its associations with the "clash of civilizations" thesis (that Islamic fundamentalism and the Western liberalism are somehow locked in an epic struggle for the future of civilization, Jihad vs. McWorld) and misplaced Western anti-Islamic sentiment (as well as misplaced Islamic anti-Western sentiment) that it cannot serve as a spur to communication as yoga in the way that Whitman imagined. Moreover, this word is for my taste too close to the Sanskrit term *mleccha*, which traditionally marked anyone who did not speak Sanskrit (or love Krishna, or, today, identify as a Hindu nationalist) as a "barbarian." Consequently I prefer a different term for such *avidya*: *heedlessness*. And though it is true that Whitman does not use the word *heedlessness*, I believe this word is very much in the spirit of his poetry.

When invoking the word *heedless*, I follow one of my other favorite poets, Norman Fischer, who in his "Zen inspired" translation of the Christian Psalms speaks not of "wickedness" or "evil" but "heedlessness"—Psalm 1:6 thus becomes "What you see is always lovely and remembered, / But the way of heedlessness is oblivion."[106] The trouble with the rhetoric of evil for Fischer is that it denies a person's potential for change and growth while condemning that person to eternal damnation. Moreover, to say that one's opponents are evil is to close off any need to talk to them or attempt to understand them. Evil shuts down thought and self-inquiry. The rhetoric of evil creates an environment of enemyship that makes the expedient question of what to do now all too easy: the proper response to evil, as we know from decades of horror films, is to kill it. Though today we toss this word around flippantly, *evil* is a term of great rhetorical power that, in many ways, runs counter to the spirit of both Whitmanism and democracy.

The accomplished yogi, according to the Bhagavad Gita, sees the divine in all people and the oneness of all things. According to Whitman, this is true, too, of the accomplished democratic citizen. To call someone evil is to deny this divinity. Consequently, the battle for democracy is not a fight against evil but against *avidya*, the ignorance of interconnectedness. People act heedlessly, announcing their *avidya*, when they deny the divinity of others' bodies, when they neglect human interconnectedness, and when they pit themselves against others in order to dominate and destroy them. To me, the term *heedless* retains much of the rhetorical force, and the democratic potential for critique, of Whitman's "infidelity" without that word's baggage. Indeed, the charge of heedlessness is a call to dialogue and discussion in the way that the condemnations of "evil" or "infidel" are not. No matter where they are from or what they believe, anyone can act heedlessly. Moreover, to charge someone with heedlessness is not a life sentence—this charge implies that the person *could* be persuaded to be heedful, that they could be brought around to seeing oneness. *The ethics of oneness, supported by a rhetoric of heedlessness, reframes the very purpose of democratic speech and democratic life.* Inspired by Whitman, I understand democratic rhetoric as speech that aims to communicate oneness so that we can manage our shared vulnerability. This understanding of democratic rhetoric is also inspired by the Bhagavad Gita and the curious fact that it has two settings—it is set on a physical battlefield (*kurukshetre*) as well as a psychological, ethical battlefield (*dharmakshetre*). The Gita recognizes that we make our lives on a battlefield of conflicting potentials—the potential for oneness, and the potential for division. Whitman recognizes this, too. For him, democracy is the *dharmakshetra.*

What to do when faced with hate? Whitman's answer to this question is grounded in his metaphysics of oneness and the practices he models that attune us to the feeling of at-one-ness with all beings. Whitman is a poet of affirmation; he rarely employs the rhetoric of blame. His "polytheistic democracy" is tolerant of most ways of being and speaking.[107] He reserves his animus for those people who deny "divine rapport" and the interconnectedness of all beings, for those heedless people who position themselves above their fellows in order to exploit them: "Of all the dangers . . . there can be no greater one than having certain portions of the people set off from the rest by a line drawn—they are not privileged as others, but degraded, humiliated, made of no account."[108] Whitman employs a number of powerful metaphors, including "the tyrant," "the menacing one," and "the scorner," to depict the figure who cannot be tolerated in a democracy—that is, the heedless, greedy person who dehumanizes and degrades others, who makes them of no account by denying their inherent dignity and worth, who is ignorant of oneness.[109]

Whitman does not deny that there are enemies in a democracy. He does not ask us to love our enemies. Instead, he challenges us to recognize that those who hate are still divine. Furthermore, he challenges us to welcome those haters to the table, for everyone is included in the all.[110] At a time when many people have given up on rhetoric and the hope that it might be possible to persuade our adversaries to see things as we do, Whitman's call for inclusive communication is revolutionary. It might also sound hopelessly naive, less like a philosophical doctrine and more like a recipe for abuse. Why give voice to the hateful, to the heedless? Whitman argues that they must be included in the democratic conversation, I believe, because he recognizes that to muzzle or exclude such voices is counterproductive. Banning the hateful perpetuates a sense of victimhood, creating fertile ground for what I call *the politics of resentment.*[111] Resentment is a powerful but ultimately toxic democratic emotion. Often it begins in a legitimate sense of grievance, but resentment is easily manipulated by demagogues who shift targets, gaining power over their audiences by telling us who to blame. When the goal becomes the punishment and humiliation of wrongdoers rather than addressing the genuine—generally systemic and structural—causes of suffering, then democracy runs off track as hatred takes hold. Were Whitman to ban haters from the table, this would serve only to reinforce their sense of grievance.

Let the heedless speak! Though this is Whitman's counsel, he does not validate their hatred. He allows them to speak so that they can reveal their *avidya* and heedlessness to all who have eyes to see and ears to hear. *Democratic speech is a revelation.* What it reveals becomes grounds for civic judgment. And what are we collectively judging? From the perspective of the ethics of oneness, what are the new stasis points of democratic controversy? The question is not who is rational and who is not. The question is not who is civil and who is not. Instead, reading democracy alongside Whitman, the question is who is mindful and who is not. The question is who recognizes oneness and who does not. The question, in short, is who recognizes and enacts the human dignity due to divine beings and who does not. To mark people as heedless is a profound, powerful, and poignant gesture of dissent. Indeed, Whitman models one way to enact dissent's disruptive gesture, especially in a time when the value of human life is frighteningly low.

Unfortunately, it seems that the rhetoric of hatred has been normalized as legitimate political speech today. Whitman's poetry takes away any and all possible warrant for the hateful tyrannizing of our fellow human beings. By allowing the hateful and the tyrannical to speak while condemning their hatred as heedlessness, Whitman's poetry redraws democracy's battle lines. It is never easy, in democratic politics, to identify one's enemies. For Whitman, the enemy is clear: it is the one who lacks faith, who denies the interconnectedness of all beings, who is heedless of the divinity of other humans. It is the scorner who divides the all in order to exclude and humiliate. It is the tyrant who degrades other beings in order to dominate and destroy them. Though

Whitman repeatedly calls for contentment, and though he models a grateful appreciation of the miracle of life in his poetry, he does not demand accommodation to injustice. He is not a poet of acquiescence.

Whitman rejects no one prima facie; he welcomes all. However, in Whitman's poetry people can reject themselves with their words and actions. To permit all creates the rhetorical warrant to forbid tyrants and scorners. This is not a liar's paradox to be exploited by the practitioners of hatred—much as free speech laws are exploited today—but instead a basic ethical challenge of democracy. If we are truly devoted to oneness, then it becomes easy to recognize tyrants as tyrants when they out themselves by speaking heedlessly in the language of domination and disrespect. It is then up to us as the demos to determine how best to deal with them. Again, democracy is a *dharmakshetre*.

Beyond Indifferentialism and Acquiescence

In the closing chapter of *Pragmatism* (1907), William James offers a more upbeat and sympathetic reading of Whitman's poetry than he did five years earlier in *The Varieties of Religious Experience*. James observes that while "serious" philosophers shun religion—perhaps they really do believe that it is the opiate of the masses—for the pragmatist, religion is of signal importance, not as a reflection of some otherworldly truth, but instead as a map to life that has profound consequences on the conduct of individuals in the world of people and things. To pretend that religion doesn't matter is to ignore a big part of the human experience. James pledges to treat religious claims as hypotheses and to judge all religion by a pragmatic test, to ask "if consequences useful to life flow from it." As a test case, James chooses Whitman's poem "To You," an intimate poem in which Whitman's narrator practices communication as yoga by repeatedly addressing an anonymous friend or lover as an incarnation of the divine.[112]

Ever fond of binaries, James contends that there are two ways to read this poem. "One is the monistic way, the mystical way of pure cosmic emotion," which entails reading the poem as a statement of ontological truth: the universe is one, all people are interconnected and divine, so let us be grateful for existence and fret not about the world. "Whatever may happen to you, whatever you may appear to be, inwardly you are safe. Look back, *lie* back, on your true principle of being!" "This is the famous way of quietism, of indifferentialism . . . a spiritual opium." For James, philosophies of oneness necessarily result in quietism. If the world is truly one and all is God, then there is nothing that can be—that need be—done. (Though he sets his sights on Whitman with these words, perhaps it would be more appropriate to mention

Emerson's celebration of acquiescence.) The second way to interpret the poem is "the pluralistic way," which James associates with a pragmatic philosophy of becoming rather than being. In this interpretation, Whitman does not celebrate the reality of divinity but instead addresses his friend or lover with such beautiful words in order to inspire them to be better than they presently are. "Forget the low in yourself, then, think only of the high. Identify your life therewith, then, through angers, losses, ignorance, ennui, whatever you thus make yourself, whatever you thus most deeply are, picks its way." The first interpretation emphasizes "the static One"; the second presents "possibles in the plural, genuine possibles, and it has all the restlessness of that conception."[113]

I hope that *The Ethics of Oneness* has demonstrated, conclusively and emphatically, that this is a false binary. Oneness need not be static. Indeed, in Whitman's poetry, oneness is active—it is an active justification for democracy, and also an active call for a better, more respectful, more just democracy. Oneness lends democracy divine sanction, and, according to Whitman, it is up to us to elaborate this oneness in the world by seizing on the many possibles that life consistently presents to us. Whitman's oneness is not restless in the sense of lacking foundations; its restlessness is found in a giddy excitement at the possibility of a better world that recognizes divinity and embraces vulnerability. This is a calm and centered excitement, sure, but that is no less worthy than the anxious, striving, discontented excitement our culture tends to laud.

The oneness that Whitman celebrates—that I celebrate, too—does not lord over us, requiring mystical magisterial translators who gain tremendous power through their exclusive access to the truth.[114] This oneness is not something we've somehow become separated from and must be reconnected to. As Vedanta and many other spiritual traditions teach, oneness has been there all along; it's just that we've chosen to commit ourselves to different ideals, including separation, competition, hierarchy, enemyship, exclusion, and domination.[115] The ethics of oneness of *Leaves of Grass* is a project of making what is true, real. We cannot sit back and wait for the world to fix itself with confident indifference. We must actively commit ourselves to making oneness a reality through our everyday democratic obligations. And we can only do this by starting locally, with how we address everyone we meet—strangers and friends and foes—and how we address ourselves, too.

Conclusion

One.
Such a simple word and yet so
hard to pronounce.
What's the deal?
The trouble is not our mouths.
The trouble is our minds and their investments.

Sometimes
when the words won't come
the problem is the words.
Sometimes
when the words won't come
the problem lies deeper.

Devoted to "duelity"
habituated to seeing
Division. Borders. Walls. Lines. Stops.
We miss continuity and
the field where life grows like leaves of grass.

The truth is,
life is a practice.
The truth is,
we get good at what we practice.
The truth is
a practice,
too.

What did that kind Chennai bookseller mean when she handed me a copy of Ralph Waldo Emerson's *Essays: First Series* and commented that it was the best book on yoga "for me"? I don't think she was being condescending. I don't think she was implying that as a white Westerner I couldn't understand—or wouldn't appreciate—the good stuff, the real, genuine texts of yogic wisdom. I also don't think that she somehow peered deeply into my soul and knew exactly which book would satisfy the desperate longings of my heart. My first job during high school was working in a bookstore. One of the marks of a good bookseller is the ability, carefully honed over thousands of interactions, to recommend the right book to the right person at the right moment (it's a skill that continues to come in handy, I must say, as a professor). When the merchant recommended Emerson to me, I think it likely she believed that, as an American, I might find Emerson accessible and useful in my yogic journey because Emerson *spoke my language*. She was right.

The more I reflect on that exchange, the more playful and even rebellious it seems to me. With her recommendation, she took a small stand against orthodoxy. It is a common belief, in both India and the United States, that yoga must be practiced within particular religious traditions or philosophical lineages in order to be legitimate. This perspective has become even more prevalent in India today with the ascendency of a militantly intolerant Hindu fundamentalism that seeks to color all yoga saffron (in no small part by re-branding the Bhagavad Gita as a Hindu nationalist text).[1] It is also a common belief in the United States, where tracing the roots of the tree of yoga back to a particular Indian guru or lineage acts as a badge of honor and a marker of legitimacy. I studied yoga philosophy for several weeks at the world-famous Krishnamacharya Yoga Mandiram, which is why I was in Chennai; and after completing a course there, an American yoga teacher back home remarked to me that now I was a legitimate yogi, for I had a respectable lineage.

The argument can be made that Tirumalai Krishnamacharya (1888–1989) was indeed the most influential yoga teacher of the twentieth century—*Yoga Journal* calls him "the father of modern yoga," for during his years teaching yoga at the Mysore Palace in the 1930s and '40s he instructed three of the figures who would come to dominate American yoga: B. K. S. Iyengar, founder of Iyengar yoga; Pattabhi Jois, founder of Ashtanga yoga; and Indra Devi, author of *Forever Young, Forever Healthy* (1953) and one of the first yoga teachers to cement the connection between yoga and health, beauty, and longevity in public opinion.[2] When the Chennai bookseller handed me a copy of Emerson's essays, I believe she was implying that lineage—at least, in the way it is commonly understood—is not as important as many make it out to be. It is possible to find yogic wisdom in unexpected places, for countless others have also been on this path, and their sagacity is worth heeding even when it comes from outside the canon (whatever that is). Though I am not for certain, I think she also might have wanted to broach an important question for me and other spiritual pilgrims: Is it really necessary to travel all the way to India, or to wrestle with Sanskrit, to understand yoga?

Like many contemporary yogis, I struggle with how best to respond to the destructive legacy of European colonialism in India and the complex issues surrounding cultural appropriation. There are few easy answers here, and little moral certainty, either. It's easy to posture and pose, more difficult to consider and contemplate. Yoga's future is something that no one person can decide alone. It is something that yogis need to determine together, through cross-cultural conversations that will demand much of us—including that we get better at sitting with the various prejudices we carry around with us like historical baggage. We must become more skilled at turning *toward*, rather than *away from*, the difficult topics that, if we had our druthers, we would avoid.[3] To me, reckoning with prejudice is a core practice of *svadhyaya*, self-study; it is also a clarion call for communication and conversation with others. Yogis should really add dialogue and deliberation to their daily meditation practices, for talking is as much an opportunity for yoga as *virabhradrasana* (warrior pose). I think it inescapable: conversation is as much a part of an ethical life as the other *yamas* and *niyamas*, including *ahimsa* (nonviolence) and *satya* (truthfulness).

The tree of yoga first took root in India. Does this mean that one can only learn yoga there? Or if one was born there? Many people have told me exactly this. But here I recall the praise that Indian intellectuals lavished on Emerson for his efforts at articulating an American Vedanta. They did not dismiss Emerson because he did not study with a master guru in an ashram for years, which was then, and remains today, an unrealistic option for most people anyway. I have been privileged to travel to India multiple times, but this is not a privilege that most Americans can afford, in time or money. However, I do not believe anyone is condemned to a watered-down, second-class yoga. Yogic wisdom can be found everywhere.

I have no doubt that my grasp of yoga has been infinitely enriched by studying in India and by my halting efforts to decipher a new language, and it would be awfully arrogant of me to suggest that Westerners can ignore yoga's long history in India and the world. We cannot. In fact, I would argue that we have an ethical obligation to understand, comprehend, and discuss this history. In the end, however, I can understand yoga only through the lens of my own experience as shaped by the time, and place, in which I live, which has its own history, language, culture, and traditions. Writing this book, I've come to recognize that these traditions—American to the core but also cross-cultural and international—have value, too. We must begin the procession from where we find ourselves now, and while this journey may and perhaps should take us to new lands, we need not feel shame at being who or where we are right now.

In her book *Biography of a Yogi: Paramahansa Yogananda and the Origins of Modern Yoga* (2017), the yoga studies scholar Anya Foxen contests Elizabeth De Michelis's influential argument that modern yoga is "the graft of a Western branch onto the Indian tree of yoga."[4] Foxen writes, "I'm inclined to modify the metaphor. Modern yoga is less a graft and more an inosculation—the place where two trees, each with their own ancient root system, have entwined so intimately that they have become one."[5] When it comes to yoga, we're dealing not with a tree or trees but a forest. Foxen's project, to recover the Western traditions (like "harmonialism") that influenced the formation of modern "yoga" practice (she often wonders if we can even call it that), is sure to be controversial.[6] In *The Ethics of Oneness*, I have pursued a related recovery project but from a different angle. Studying Emerson and Whitman on the Bhagavad Gita is like studying a transcendentalist graft onto an ancient tree, and as the new branch grows, it drops its own seeds that sprout and become new trees (transcendentalism, Emersonianism, religious liberalism, Whitmanism, New Thought, mind cure, positive thinking) in a new land with very different soil and weather. As far as I can tell, communication as yoga is an American invention—inspired by the Gita, certainly, but unlike the practices of the divine song or anything I experienced while studying in India. Like Foxen, I want to resist attempts to say that American practices of yoga are nothing more than bad copies of true and proper Indian practices, for as scholars have shown, Indian yoga itself has undergone almost constant change since the time of the Bhagavad Gita. It's not that there is no there there, it's that the there that is there is constantly changing. When it comes to contemporary yoga, we're dealing with something new built out of something old—and that is exciting, especially when we revisit the old to better understand how it informs the new.

As I turned to leave the magical Chennai bookshop, the bookseller gave me a beautiful gift: a 1960s paperback reprint of Franklin Edgerton's 1944 translation of the Bhagavad Gita, originally published in the Harvard Oriental Series. While I was putting the finishing touches on *The Ethics of Oneness*, I cracked open this volume one more time—and, amazingly, I discovered the same rebelliousness therein that I spied in the bookseller who offered it to me. Edgerton was an American linguist who served as the Salisbury Professor of Sanskrit and Comparative Philology at Yale University from 1926 until his retirement in 1953. His translation of the Gita is said to be "extremely literal,"[7] and it was widely used by American students for decades. However, Edgerton made at least one rhetorically daring choice that departed from conventional wisdom—he employed the Emersonian language of the "over-soul." Repeatedly, Edgerton translates *adhyatma*—the Sanskrit word that represents a person's inner soul as a manifestation of cosmic divinity—as "over-soul," and so, for instance, in chapter 3 Krishna advises Arjuna to proceed "with mind on the over-soul."[8] To focus on the oversoul, here, is to practice one-pointed focus on the divinity of all people and to remember this divinity when interacting with everyone. Sanskrit scholars have critiqued this unique and unabashedly Emersonian translation of the Gita for introducing an American philosophical concept into an Indian text.[9] That's fair. But I'd like to think that, in his translation, Edgerton—whose knowledge of Sanskrit was unmatched in the United States and Europe—was deliberately gesturing to a rich tradition of American yoga in which the Gita meets transcendentalism in order to encourage American readers of the Gita to learn more about their own nation's history with the text.

The yoga of Emersonianism and Whitmanism reached the apex of its influence during the late nineteenth and early twentieth centuries. These traditions inspired the New Thought movement, whose positive-thinking dogma has become a form of American common sense. In this way the wisdom of Emerson and Whitman lives on, though in ways that the authors would likely not recognize.[10] When I began studying yoga philosophy and meditating as a teenager, part of yoga's appeal was its apparent timelessness. Yoga is just so ancient! Reading widely in the scholarly literature, I now know that while yoga is indeed ancient, it is not timeless. The study and practice of yoga has undergone profound shifts throughout the centuries. There is no yoga—there are only yogas in the plural.

The story of twentieth- and twenty-first-century yoga is a remarkable tale of *parinama*, change, for yoga has transformed from a countercultural practice—several Americans claiming to teach yoga in the early 1900s were jailed, immigrants (including yoga gurus) from India were denied citizenship in 1906 and banned from immigrating entirely from 1917 to 1965, and anti-yoga hysteria graced the headlines of major American newspapers ("Latest Black Magic Revelations about Nefarious American Love Cults," promised one expose of a yoga "cult" in William Randolph Hearst's *New York Journal*)—to one of the twenty-first century's most profitable consumer industries.[11] Contemporary yoga, like so many forms of spirituality, has been captured and corrupted by the rhetoric of a neoliberal, fundamentalist capitalism that encourages us to measure everything in terms of its profitability and to always focus on our "brand." The religious studies scholar and courageous cultural critic Andrea R. Jain has narrated the story of yoga's transformation brilliantly in her books *Selling Yoga: From Counterculture to Pop Culture* (2015), *Peace Love Yoga: The Politics of Global Spirituality* (2020), and a number of associated articles.[12] I hope that my book has added at least one chapter to the history of contemporary yoga as narrated by Jain, Foxen, and others, including the *New York Times* columnist Michelle Goldberg, author of a scintillating biography of Indra Devi titled *The Goddess Pose: The Audacious Life of Indra Devi, the Woman Who Helped Bring Yoga to the West* (2015).[13] The story of American yoga is one of triumph—yoga has become a dominant force in American culture—and also one of loss, as older yogic traditions including the ethics of oneness have been forgotten. This is unfortunate, because the ethics of oneness is a potential antidote to a greedy, profit-obsessed culture of isolated and lonely individualism, and also to the many forms of yoga Americans practice today that reinforce the fracturing of the world.

It is sad that many later writers who embraced certain aspects of Emersonianism and Whitmanism—including Ralph Waldo Trine, whose *In Tune with the Infinite* (1897) was a sensation, selling over 1.5 million copies in the United States; Richard Bucke, Whitman's biographer and the popular author of *Cosmic Consciousness* (1901); and Swami Vivekananda, the founder of "modern yoga" whose vision of yoga was shaped by his reading of the transcendentalists in India[14]—presented oneness through an individualistic lens. Swami Vivekananda was clear that it was possible to practice karma yoga in the world, but he also called Whitman "the Sannyasin of America," a sannyasin being a monk who renounces the world.[15] Vivekananda elevated individual *strength* to a core yogic virtue, and strength, he taught spiritually hungry Americans, could be found by practicing team sports and the type of individual meditations recommended by the mind-cure movement. In the years since, American yoga has become emphatically individualistic. To commune with the oversoul, the New Thought writers suggested that people must make themselves solitary and alone, withdrawing to quiet places of contemplation, sequestered from the busy world around them. Bucke characterized the precise moment when various great "men" throughout history (his sages were exclusively male) awoke to cosmic consciousness and were touched by "the Brahmic Splendor" (most were between thirty-four and thirty-six years old)—and it is striking that almost all these great men were alone when they achieved enlightenment.[16]

These writers capture one side of the mystic experience in the Bhagavad Gita—as we saw in chapter 4, Krishna does grant Arjuna a temporary "divine eye" so that he can experience the true nature of *brahman*. This vision changes Arjuna; afterward, he knows the truth, *tat tvam asi*, and though he remains afraid, he is determined to fight. However, these writers uniformly missed something important about Emersonianism and Whitmanism—namely, that both writers envisioned enlightenment as a social and a relational process involving communication as yoga. For them, enlightenment can and must be found through social interaction. Both Emerson and Whitman are true to the Gita on this point. Indeed, Arjuna is prepared for his mystic vision by the dialogue he has with Krishna on the battlefield. Arjuna has a personal realization, but his awakening to the all is not solitary. Krishna's rhetoric readies him for his enlightenment. It is through our interactions with others that we come to know the truth of oneness.

Though the Gita continues to be widely studied today, the "textbook" that many contemporary yogis use to understand the philosophy and practice of yoga is the Yoga Sutra, composed and compiled by Patanjali.[17] Patanjali taught an austere, monastic yoga aimed at "stilling the fluctuations of the mind."[18] The Yoga Sutra of Patanjali attained notoriety in India and then, for nearly seven hundred years, was completely forgotten. In the late 1880s, the Theosophical Society latched onto the Yoga Sutra, interpreting the text in a way that reinforced their esoteric teachings but with little understanding of its history or meaning.[19] Swami Vivekananda then almost single-handedly recovered the Yoga Sutra from obscurity by appending a loose translation to his influential book *Raja Yoga* (1896). Vivekananda promised that the practice of yoga in the Patanjali tradition would bring "the liberation of the soul through perfection."[20] Decades later in Mysore and Chennai, Krishnamacharya presented the Yoga Sutra as a manual for healthy living, as did his many disciples who found fame in the United States.[21] During my time at the Krishnamacharya Yoga Mandiram in Chennai we studied, memorized, and learned to chant Patanjali's sutras in the proper Vedic style (even though the language of the Yoga Sutra is closer to the hybrid Sanskrit of the early Mahayana Buddhist scriptures than the Sanskrit of the Vedas) because, our teachers told us, these timeless verses have a magical power that connects contemporary yogis back to the primordial Vedic sages who first saw the truth of oneness and then lit the fires of human wisdom with their words.[22] Contemporary yoga is a study of transformation, but in the midst of this change, one thing has remained relatively constant: for the past century, Americans have sought health and heavenly perfection though the esoteric wisdom of Patanjali. It is no understatement to say that Patanjali has been canonized in contemporary American yoga.[23]

Like any classical wisdom text, the Yoga Sutra of Patanjali can be read in many ways. There are only four verbs in the entire book; the threadbare sutras leave plenty of room for interpretation and improvisation. Every time I teach this text, however, my students and I invariably arrive at a troubling conclusion: that Patanjali professes a philosophy bordering on nihilism. Life is suffering, and to overcome suffering, we must reject almost everything that makes life worth living. Swami Vivekananda interprets the dualistic Patanjali through the lens of Advaita Vedanta, putting a monistic spin on a text that is fundamentally dualistic. However, the practice of yoga in the Yoga Sutra of Patanjali is less about unification—as Advaitins insist—and more about detachment of the soul (the *purusha*) from the material world (the *prakriti*). Patanjali claims that the goal of yoga is *kaivalya*, "aloneness" or "isolation" from existence and escape from the bonds of mortal life. "When the soul realizes that it depends on nothing in the universe, from gods to the lowest atom, that is called Kaivalya (isolation) and perfection," Vivekananda summarized.[24] Consequently, the famed German Indologist Georg Feuerstein (1947–2012) insists that if we take Patanjali seriously, "we turn our back on all things of the world, on life itself."[25] Patanjali's yoga "is entirely a process of negation of everything that is ordinarily considered as typically human."[26] Michelle Goldberg comes to a similar conclusion: "The point of Patanjali's philosophy is to reject and transcend this world, not to function more easily within it. His yoga is a tool over self-obliteration rather than self-actualization."[27] Patanjali talks with enticing language about the superpowers (*siddhi*) that yogis develop in their practice, but in the end his yoga is not superhuman, it is antihuman.

Swami Vivekananda claimed to hold the Yoga Sutra in such high regard because this text offers a detailed, step-by-step guide to the practice of meditation. However, I find it ironic that Patanjali's Yoga Sutra is so popular today, for even though many yogis turn to this text to provide the philosophical foundation for the yoga they practice, it is largely out of step with the spirit of contemporary yoga. Contemporary yogis crave affirmation. For us, yoga is less about figuring out how to get out of life and instead about determining how to get the most out of life. Yoga is about enriching existence, not rejecting it. And yet we rely on a philosophical foundation that reinforces—and in fact champions the pursuit of—the very same isolation and atomization that is a chief source of suffering in the contemporary world.

As yoga has exploded in popularity, Americans have lost touch with their own yogic history, including the tradition that teaches an ethics of oneness.[28] I believe this to be a profound loss, for today we desperately need a conversation about oneness—an awakening to what unites us as embodied human beings seeking sure footing in a world on fire. We require practices that promote healthy forms of oneness that prepare us to meet the challenges of a shared democratic life of mutual vulnerability, in all its beauty, in all its ugliness, and ultimately in all its perplexity. I hope *The Ethics of Oneness* helps people find their balance—and find hope—in an uncertain, unstable world shaken to its very foundations by oneness panic. This is not just an academic book to me. It's a book about life, a book born from life, a book that breathes.

After writing this book, I was inspired to change how I teach yoga philosophy, both at the university and at the yoga studio I co-own in downtown State College, Pennsylvania, with my brilliant wife Anna Sunderland Engels and three other dear friends and devoted yogis (Mark Agrusti, Ariel Xu, and Kristen Boccumini). Our studio is called Yoga Lab; our slogan is "A Space for Self-Discovery." And there, for the past several years on Thursday evenings, I have regularly taught a *vinyasa* class called Philosophy in Practice.[29] Americans have long understood yoga to be a practice of self-discovery: that much remains consistent across the decades. But what does it mean to discover oneself? Before writing *The Ethics of Oneness*, I tended to think about self-discovery, or *svadhyaya*, through the Yoga Sutra of Patanjali, for that is what I learned while training to be a yoga teacher in India and the United States.[30] In this tradition, yoga means *the stilling of the fluctuations of the mind*, and it involves denying unhealthy connections to the world, to others, and even to one's body. Basically, Patanjali's yoga prepares us to become the atomized, isolated, lonely individuals that late fundamentalist capitalism preys upon. Now, having learned more about the history of yoga in my country and having investigated how my cultural ancestors wrestled with the challenges of living a unitive life, I am determined to teach and practice a very different kind of yoga. This yoga is *an awakening to oneness*, a practice of one-pointed focus on the all that underlines diversity and unites us in a common project—namely, life.

As this book was going to press, people around the world were being asked to "shelter in place" and practice "social distancing" to mitigate the spread of a deadly pandemic. Most spiritual traditions contend that oneness is beyond argument, but I can think of no more persuasive case for acknowledging oneness than a global pandemic. With our heroic effort, this pandemic will pass and we will pick up the pieces. I hope that this crisis proves the ontological truth of oneness and impresses it so deeply on our collective memory that we won't ever forget it. If we remember, then the next time humanity confronts a collective challenge like this, perhaps we will avoid the oneness panic that has shocked American society to its very core. Oneness is beautiful, but it can also be terrible; Krishna proves this when he reveals his divine form to Arjuna. We are never in control as much as we'd like, which is why Emerson calls on us to get better at letting go and to practice acquiescing to the oversoul. And yet we are not powerless—this is Whitman's point. It is possible, within certain limits, for people to manage their shared vulnerability, but only together, democratically. It is possible to build a world true to the ontological reality of oneness that also nurtures the best of the human spirit. Just as we are learning new habits for personal hygiene and social interaction, we can also learn new democratic habits like addressing each other as divine and sanctifying the body as we seek shared solutions to common problems. We erect borders; disease and rising seas knock them down. Perhaps we need less division and more collaboration? If the pandemic has proven anything, it is that we desperately need the ethics of oneness.

As the pandemic spread, it forced us into isolation, especially those of us with underlying health conditions (I have had bad asthma since I was a child). Though I firmly believe that the world will never be the same, at some point restrictions will be lifted and we will be able to see our friends, our families, our communities again. We will delight in hugs and handshakes. We will celebrate life and mourn those who were lost. We will walk in parks and on busy city streets. We will return to the now-shuttered yoga studios, coffeehouses, and record stores, if they survive. We will go to movies, plays, and concerts. We might even smile when strangers invade our personal space (though we might be too shell-shocked for this—who knows). I am hopeful that we will soon again celebrate togetherness, but we shouldn't forget that American culture is deeply individualistic. Loneliness is part of our existential condition. It can be hard to connect with others and with the world, when most of us have been trained in the arts of separation since childhood. Our culture thrives on anxiety, and anxiety tends to atomize. Our culture builds walls, and so do we. The oneness panic we have experienced has the potential to intensify our anxiety, our atomization, our desire to build walls for years to come. Even in the face of a shared, global problem, the rhetoric from many American leaders has placed the responsibility, and the blame, for illness on individuals. We are told that our problems are solely our responsibility, and warned not to count on public help. And so we sit at home and watch films and shows that celebrate "heroes" who face their problems alone—rugged heroes, superheroes, vigilantes. In the postpandemic period, we will need a yoga that challenges such individualistic distortions. We must remember that yoga means connection. We should demand a yoga that takes the ethics of oneness seriously so that the connections we build are healthy, nourishing, and sustainable.

After one of the very first presentations I made of the research that would become *The Ethics of Oneness*, a senior colleague posed a question that has stuck with me to the end. He asked, Why do we need another book about the history of yoga? That history has already been told, he quipped, and he pointed to Goldberg's *The Goddess Pose* as evidence. You're not going to add anything to what she says, he insisted, and so you had better work on a different project. I love Goldberg's book. In fact, I adore several of the insightful histories of yoga that have recently been published, and I would be proud if *The Ethics of Oneness* sits next to them on bookshelves physical and digital. But to say that the story of yoga has been told—or to say that any story has ever been told so well that it can't be told anew, with fresh eyes—is not just flatly wrong, it is extremely arrogant. The story is never finished, because we are never finished. The reality is that most contemporary authors pay scant attention to Emersonianism and Whitmanism and the ethics of oneness. Goldberg mentions neither philosopher-poet in her book. I point this out not to fault her—neither Emerson nor Whitman seems to have influenced that great twentieth-century publicist of yoga, Indra Devi, in the slightest. I point this out to acknowledge that there are many traditions of American yoga, and not all have equal claim on the present. Some have been forgotten. Some have been watered down so much that they have lost their bite. Hence, the importance of *old beginnings*, of returning to older traditions—like the ethics of oneness—to discover what they can teach us about life in the present. When it comes to oneness, I believe we have much to learn from the past, especially right now.

When Emerson says that the oversoul is the "Supreme Critic" on all matters, I take him to mean that oneness is an ontological reality—we are one, like blades of grass on a field—and also an ethical aspiration. Certainly, it is not the case that we should petition the oversoul or the all for judgment and then sit around in meditation waiting for a response. We would be waiting for a long time. Instead, we must actively devote ourselves to oneness in our interpersonal relationships so that oneness becomes real in the social, political, and democratic world. We must, in short, practice communication as yoga. And what does this practically entail? To practice communication as yoga involves:

- Acknowledging the divine in all things.
- Avoiding talk of divinity that makes it appear as though the divine stands apart from us, in judgment, or as though nature itself is not divine.
- Approaching other people as avatars of divine oneness, for everyone, whether they realize it or not, is an incarnation of the divine all.
- Asking, Is this how I would address God?—for that is what we are doing every time we talk to another person, we are conversing with a divine body incarnated on earth and not an object to be used for our selfish purposes.
- Picturing the body as sacred and every individual life as a miracle.
- Treating others with dignity, respect, and reverence, even when we disagree—and make no mistake, we will disagree, for oneness does not mean sameness. While we are ontologically one, our experiences of that oneness are diverse, conditioned as we are by our life stories and experiences and expectations and maps and languages. A oneness that refuses to respect difference is unethical.
- Listening for oneness as it illuminates another's words and letting this oneness be the common ground on which relationships and communities and governments and nations are built.

- Reimagining those with whom we disagree—even those who are hateful—as heedless of oneness rather than inherently evil. Doing this will give us a map for redrawing the lines of what is tolerable and what is intolerable in our world.
- Becoming critical genius hunters and treating the words of gurus and prophets and saviors and populists with extreme caution. We must never forget that there are many who will attempt to promote a false oneness for their own selfish greedy ends.
- Rejecting the all-too-common practices of enemyship and the politics of resentment, which rely on emotions (anger, fear, hatred) that nurture division and fracture the world into "us" and "them."
- Watching out for those moments when oneness begets twoness, when an "us" creates a "them," when openness becomes exclusivity; and resisting such duality.
- Learning to recognize the signs of oneness panic, and coming to grips with it.
- Transcending our dualistic rhetorical habits and consciously committing ourselves to using language that highlights interconnectedness and the fundamental solidarity of being.
- Honoring the ontological truth that life is a shared procession of mutual vulnerability. Though our culture teaches us that we must go it alone, in fact we walk a common path.

I understand communication to be a practice of unconscious devotion. Every time we open our mouths and speak as we have been taught to speak, we are actively devoting ourselves to the cultural ideas that have led us collectively to this moment in time. We use god terms of separation and exclusion and isolation and every-man-for-himself, then wonder why our world is so fractured! To be human is to live a life in communication, and so, at a very minimum, social change demands a change in how we talk. For transcendentalists like myself, a new and more democratic world becomes possible only once we make such rhetorical commitment to practicing communication as yoga, as difficult as this will be.

Many of my students come to yoga because they want to make the world a better place. It's easy to dismiss such motivation as naive, but I find that charges of naivety often silence the eager in service of the status quo. In my experience, my students' desire is urgent, genuine, and true. One definition of yoga is union: yoga brings us into greater harmony with what we might call, following Whitman, the cosmic pulse. A strong and steady pulse for change beats just below the surface of this country, of this world. The voices of hatred and greed are louder, as they echo through loaded chambers; but from time to time we hear this pulse. Rarely do we know what to do when we do. To practice yoga is to take a courageous stand against the conventional belief that people must be wolves to each other. Yoga is at its most powerful when it is at its most democratic. Yoga is at its most democratic when it awakens people to oneness—to the reality that as human beings we are divinely equalized with each other and interconnected with the world we inhabit, to the fact that while no one else can gain enlightenment for us, nevertheless we are on this journey together.

In turn, the meaning of democracy changes when it becomes a kind of yoga, a yoga of devotion to the oneness that underlines life's magnificent variety. If the Bhagavad Gita is right, such devotion is the path to enlightenment. Perhaps so, perhaps not—I'm not sure. After writing this book, I am convinced that Emerson and Whitman are right and that devotion to oneness can be a first step toward remaking the world as a more just, equal, and democratic place. In the traditions of Emersonism and Whitmanism, oneness is an invitation to see the world differently, from a higher plane, with a more expansive, cosmic viewpoint. For some reason that none of us can explain (though there is no shortage of explanations), each of us has been incarnated on earth in this time and this place and this body. Living life means setting out on a journey that our culture tells us is solitary but that, in fact, is shared. In spite of what our culture, and our capitalism, might say, *we are all in this together*—not as comrades fighting a common enemy, but as brothers and sisters living a common life and who will meet a common destiny. What might it mean, then, dear readers, if we heed this invitation to the all? What might it mean if we devote ourselves to oneness rather than twoness, to cooperation rather than competition, to interconnectedness rather than exclusivity, to reverence rather than derision, to gratitude rather than grasping, to love rather than hate? Those who want things to remain the same surely will laugh at these questions, but the truth is that we don't know the answers, because we have never really tried.

Proudly accepting my place in the philosophical lineage of American transcendentalism, I understand oneness as an ontological truth and an ethical challenge to live a different kind of life than the one my culture has said will bring me happiness. A genuine commitment to oneness is not easy, especially in a world so deeply committed to division. Oneness requires the courage to challenge convention. If we can gin up this courage together, then our collective commitment has the power to reinvent our dying democracy and reinvigorate our lives as citizens of the world. As the Gita teaches, that to which we devote ourselves has a way of becoming real for us. This is why oneness is the greatest secret, the password primeval, of democracy. "Yo yat shraddhah sa eva sah."

Acknowledgments

This book is dedicated to Anna, my best friend, my wife, my life partner, my other half, my everything, my brilliant beautiful generous kindhearted witty world-traveling photo-snapping companion. I dedicate this book to you because you are the sun. I love you.

My dearest friends are like a good cup of coffee (and those who know me best know what a good cup of coffee means to me)—sending much love and all my gratitude to Mark & Ariel, Jess & Joe, Sarah & Tahru, Shaner, Boone, Kirt, Kristen & Theo, Josh, Derek, Ira, Nathan, Scott, Patrick, and Greg. Thanks also to Lara Heimann, my yoga teacher and friend. Love to my mentors, Andrew & Kay Davis, Greg Shepherd, and David Zarefsky. My family means home—thanks to Mom & Dad, Jim & Marylou, Nate & Karen, and Kate & Sam for everything. Yoga Lab is my home away from home, my retreat, my *sangha*. Thanks to all the teachers and students there, whose collective cheer, conviviality, and goodwill make it a wonderful community.

During the summer of 2018, I was privileged to participate in a seminar at Yale University sponsored by the National Endowment for the Humanities called "The Bhagavad Gita: Ancient Text, Modern Readers." I'd like to thank Richard Davis, the brilliant director of the seminar, for facilitating such a great experience. Richard has become a friend and mentor, and his generosity in sharing his knowledge of the Gita has made this a much better book. Thanks to Richard and to the other seminarians, who taught me so much.

Over the past few years I've made several visits to the Vedanta Society of New York and one memorable visit to the Vedanta Society of Northern California. Thank you to Swami Sarvaprinayanda in Manhattan and Swami Tattwamayananda in San Francisco for the thoughtful conversations about life and the Gita (and also for permitting me access to the society's archives for research). Thank you, too, to the librarians and staff at the Penn State University Libraries in University Park, the New York Public Libraries in Manhattan and Brooklyn, the Houghton Library at Harvard, the Beinecke Rare Book and Manuscript Library at Yale, the Library of Congress, and the British Library in London for their assistance as I researched this book.

In 2018 I traveled to India twice to tour Belur Math in Kolkata, which is the international headquarters of the Vedanta Society and the Ramakrishna Mission, and to visit the Shri Krishna Museum and see the sites in Kurukshetra, where the Gita is set. Thanks to everyone who made those trips possible and pleasant.

I'm blessed with amazing colleagues who make it a joy to walk into Sparks; thanks to all of you for all that you do. I'd especially like to thank my department, my college, and the Rock Ethics Institute at Penn State for supporting my research, both domestic and international. And speaking of international travel, gratitude to my buddy and fellow philosopher-rhetorician Scott Stroud, who is one of the few kindred scholars in my field to also take a deep interest in Indian philosophy. I've had many enjoyable conversations with Scott about the delights and travails of conducting research in India, and I always learn something new from him.

My book benefited tremendously from the late-stage prose wizardry of Johanna Rosenbohm, who is the copy editor that all authors dream of. A big thank you, too, to my bud Patrick McCartney, who read through the manuscript in its entirety and provided me with many helpful suggestions (and a graduate seminar's worth of readings!).

The longtime philosophy and rhetoric editor at the University of Chicago Press, Doug Mitchell, passed away while I was completing this book. Doug was a true champion of rhetorical scholarship, and so this is a big loss for the field of rhetorical studies; but more than that, Doug was a good guy, and so it is a much bigger loss for those close to him. I send my condolences to his family and friends, and hope that they take some comfort in the fact that his name and good work will live on in the scholarship that he championed, including this book. The editor who stepped into Doug's shoes, Kyle Wagner, has proven to be the perfect editor: brilliant, patient, funny, and very insightful. It has been a delight to work with Kyle, and I look forward to our future conversations and collaborations (and perhaps, if we're smart, a bucket of tater tots).

Lastly, thanks to all my students. You give me hope for the future.

Notes

Works by Ralph Waldo Emerson and Walt Whitman are frequently cited below. Publication details are given here for the shortened cites in the notes.

Emerson

Collected Poems and Translations, Library of America ed. Edited by Harold Bloom and Paul Kane. New York: Literary Classics of the United States, 1994.

"Brahma"

The Collected Works of Ralph Waldo Emerson, vol. 7. Edited by Ronald A. Bosco and Douglas Emory Wilson. Cambridge, MA: Harvard University Press, 2007.

Society and Solitude (1870): "Works and Days"

Emerson: Essays & Lectures, Library of America ed. Edited by Joel Porte. New York: Literary Classics of the United States, 1983.

The Conduct of Life (1860): "Fate," "Power," "Illusions," "Worship"

Essays: First Series (1841): "Circles," "Compensation," "Friendship," "Intellect," "The Over-Soul," "Politics," "Self-Reliance," "Spiritual Laws"

Essays: Second Series (1844): "Character," "Experience," "Gifts," "New England Reformers," "Nominalist and Realist," "The Poet"

Nature (1836)

Representative Men (1850): "Goethe; Or, The Writer," "Montaigne; Or, The Skeptic," "Plato; Or, The Philosopher"

Single essays: "An Address to the Senior Class in Divinity College, Cambridge, July 15, 1838" ["Divinity School Address"], "The Method of Nature: An Address to the Society of the Adelphi, in Waterville College, Maine, August 11, 1841," "The Transcendentalist: A Lecture Read in the Masonic Temple, Boston, January 1842"

The Journals and Miscellaneous Notebooks of Ralph Waldo Emerson. 16 vols. Edited by William H. Gilman et al. Cambridge, MA: Harvard University Press, 1960–82.

The Letters of Ralph Waldo Emerson. 6 vols. Edited by Ralph L. Rusk. New York: Columbia University Press, 1939.

Notebook Orientalist. In *The Topical Notebooks of Ralph Waldo Emerson*, vol. 2. Edited by Ronald A. Bosco. Columbia: University of Missouri Press, 1993.

Whitman

Complete Poetry and Collected Prose, Library of America ed. Edited by Justin Kaplan. New York: Literary Classics of the United States, 1982.

Democratic Vistas (1871)

Leaves of Grass, 1st ed. (1855)

Leaves of Grass, final "deathbed" ed. (1891–92)

Specimen Days (1882): "Carlyle from American Points of View"

Single poems: "A Backward Glance o'er Travel'd Roads," "The Base of All Metaphysics," "By Blue Ontario's Shore," "By That Long Scan of Waves," "Eidolons," "In Cabin'd Ships at Sea," "I Sing the Body Electric," "Laws for Creations," "Of the Terrible Doubt of Appearances," "Out of the Rolling Ocean the Crowd," "Passage to India," "Salut au Monde!," "Song of Myself," "A Song for Occupations," "A Song of the Rolling Earth," "Song of the Exposition," "Song of the Open Road," "Starting from Paumanok," "The Sleepers," "Thoughts," "To You," "When Lilacs Last in the Dooryard Bloom'd"

Introduction

1. See Nathan Crick, *The Keys of Power: The Rhetoric and Politics of Transcendentalism* (Columbia: University of South Carolina Press, 2017); Roger Thompson, *Emerson and the History of Rhetoric* (Carbondale: Southern Illinois University Press, 2017); and Sean Ross Meehan, *A Liberal Education in Late Emerson: Readings in the Rhetoric of Mind* (Rochester, NY: Camden House, 2019).

2. See William James, *The Varieties of Religious Experience*, Library of America ed. (1902; New York: Literary Classics of the United States, 2000), 38; Cornel West, *The American Evasion of Philosophy: A Genealogy of Pragmatism* (Madison: University of Wisconsin Press, 1989); and Stanley Cavell, "The Philosopher in American Life," in *Emerson's Transcendental Etudes* (Stanford, CA: Stanford University Press, 2003), 33–58.

3. There have been a number of fine scholarly works describing the influence of Eastern thought on the transcendentalists. See Frederic Ives Carpenter, *Emerson and Asia* (1930; New York: Haskell House, 1968); Arthur Christy, *The Orient in American Transcendentalism: A Study of Emerson, Thoreau, and Alcott* (1932; New York: Octagon Books, 1978); Dale Riepe, *The Philosophy of India and Its Impact on American Thought* (Springfield, IL: Charles C. Thomas, 1970); J. P. Rayapati, *Early American Interest in Vedanta: Pre-Emersonian Interest in Vedic Literature and Vedantic Philosophy* (New York: Asia Publishing House, 1973); Carl T. Jackson, *The Oriental Religions and American Thought: Nineteenth-Century Explorations* (Westport, CT: Greenwood Press, 1981); R. K. Gupta, *The Great Encounter: A Study of Indo-American Literary and Cultural Relations* (Riverdale, MD: Riverdale, 1987); Arthur Versluis, *American Transcendentalism and Asian Religions* (New York: Oxford University Press, 1993); Catherine L. Albanese, *A Republic of Mind and Spirit: A Cultural History of American Metaphysical Religion* (New Haven, CT: Yale University Press, 2007), 330–93; Robert C. Gordon, *Emerson and the Light of India: An Intellectual History* (New Delhi, India: National Book Trust, 2007); and Michael J. Altman, *Heathen, Hindoo, Hindu: American Representations of India, 1721–1893* (New York: Oxford University

Press, 2017). Interestingly, and strikingly, the influence of Indian thought on the transcendentalists is absent from the major histories of American philosophy, including West's *The American Evasion of Philosophy*; Louis Menand's *The Metaphysical Club: A Story of Ideas in America* (New York: Farrar, Straus and Giroux, 2001); Bruce Kuklick's *A History of Philosophy in America* (Oxford: Oxford University Press, 2002); and, though more journalistic than scholarly, Carlin Romano's *America the Philosophical* (2012; New York: Vintage, 2013).

4. Emerson, *Journals and Miscellaneous Notebooks*, 10:360.

5. Emerson, 10:360.

6. Emerson, 9:467.

7. Emerson, "The Over-Soul.," 385. On Emerson's water metaphors, see Branka Arsic, *On Leaving: A Reading in Emerson* (Cambridge, MA: Harvard University Press, 2010).

8. Bhagavad Gita, 11.1, 18.68.

9. Bhagavad Gita, 6.31.

10. Here I would point to two scholarly studies that link Emerson closely with liberalism: Christopher Newfield, *The Emerson Effect: Individualism and Submission in America* (Chicago: University of Chicago Press, 1996); and George Katab, *Emerson and Self-Reliance* (1995; Lanham, MD: Rowman & Littlefield, 2002). These scholars find ample evidence of the liberal Emerson in his writings. It is striking, however, how many Emersons we can find if we look.

11. Emerson, "Self-Reliance," 272.

12. Emerson, "Gifts," 536.

13. Patrick J. Deneen, *Why Liberalism Failed* (New Haven, CT: Yale University Press, 2018), 4–5. The founders of the United States replaced civic republicanism with a philosophical liberalism that was concerned primarily with advancing individual freedom and with managing the inevitable battles between individuals pursuing their happiness. See Gordon S. Wood, *The Creation of the American Republic, 1776–1787* (1969; Chapel Hill: University of North Carolina Press, 1998), 471–518; and Jeremy Engels, "The Trouble with 'Public Bodies': On the Anti-Democratic Rhetoric of *The Federalist*," *Rhetoric & Public Affairs* 18, no. 3 (2015): 505–38.

14. On the arrival of the Indian philosophical and religious texts in Europe, see Raymond Schwab, *The Oriental Renaissance: Europe's Rediscovery of India and the East, 1680–1880*, trans. Gene Patterson-Black and Victor Reinking (1950; New York: Columbia University Press, 1984); in the United States, see Rayapati, *Early American Interest in Vedanta*; and Altman, *Heathen, Hindoo, Hindu*. Texts like the Gita were immediately put into dialogue with mystical texts from many other traditions, including Platonism and Neoplatonism, Sufism, Quakerism, Romanticism, and Christian mysticism.

15. Emerson, "Divinity School Address," 79.

16. Scholars call this urge to render the value of all things in dollar terms of the market *neoliberalism*. See Ned O'Gorman, *The Iconoclastic Imagination: Image, Catastrophe, and Economy in America from the Kennedy Assassination to September 11* (Chicago: University of Chicago Press, 2015); and Wendy Brown, *Undoing the Demos: Neoliberalism's Stealth Revolution* (New York: Zone Books, 2015). In her brilliant book *Genealogies of Citizenship: Markets, Statelessness, and the Right to Have Rights* (Cambridge: Cambridge University Press, 2008), Margaret R. Somers uses the term *fundamentalist capitalism* rather than *neoliberalism*. Perhaps *systemic greed* would also be a useful and more accessible synonym.

17. Jeremy David Engels, *The Art of Gratitude* (Albany: State University of New York Press, 2018).

18. According to Emerson, Americans were much too hung up on the miracles performed by saints like Jesus, when they should recognize, as Jesus did, that the real miracle is life itself:

"He spoke of miracles; for he felt that man's life was a miracle, and all that man doth, and he knew that this daily miracle shines, as the character ascends. But the word Miracle, as pronounced by Christian churches, gives a false impression; it is Monster." Emerson, "Divinity School Address," 80.

19. The essence of the perennial philosophy, according to Aldous Huxley, is the Upanishadic dictum *tat tvam asi*, "you are that"—you are divine, all is one. Oneness is the essence of things, and, Huxley observes, in many of the world's languages, "The root meaning 'two' should connote badness. . . . Obscurely and unconsciously wise, our language confirms the findings of the mystics and proclaims the essential badness of division—a word, incidentally, in which our old enemy 'two' makes another decisive appearance." Aldous Huxley, *The Perennial Philosophy* (New York: Harper & Brothers, 1945), 11. Stephen Prothero offers an invective against the perennial philosophy in *God Is Not One: The Eight Rival Religions That Run the World* (New York: HarperOne, 2010), contending that this philosophy papers over the significant divisions between the world's religions in its attempt to find unity between them. This is a valid critique, but it seems to break down whenever Prothero discusses the mystical traditions within the world's religions, which share more than divides them. Here I would also point to Karen Armstrong's *A History of God: The 4,000-Year Quest of Judaism, Christianity and Islam* (New York: Gramercy Books, 1993), for Armstrong's chapter "The God of the Mystics" (209–56) is particularly helpful on Christian mysticism and the mystical strains of Judaism and Islam. Armstrong alludes to the similarities of the mystical traditions between the world's religions here and elsewhere in her book.

20. Henry Wood, *Ideal Suggestion through Mental Photography: A Restorative System for Home and Private Use, Preceded by a Study of the Laws of Mental Healing* (Boston: Lee and Shepard, 1893), 71.

21. See Jeremy Engels, *Enemyship: Democracy and Counter-Revolution in the Early Republic* (East Lansing: Michigan State University Press, 2010), 67–111; and Jeremy Engels, *The Politics of Resentment: A Genealogy* (University Park: Pennsylvania State University Press, 2015), 50–69.

22. Emerson, "Character," 501.

23. Engels, *Enemyship*, 207–22.

24. Whitman, *Democratic Vistas*, 960.

25. See Engels, *Enemyship*.

26. Philosophical maps orient us ontologically. Here I follow Scott Stroud, who suggests that communication scholars should focus their attention on how rhetoric persuades through "ontological orientation." See Scott R. Stroud, "Ontological Orientation and the Practice of Rhetoric: A Perspective from the *Bhagavad Gita*," *Southern Communication Journal* 70, no. 2 (2005): 146–60. I also think of William Ernest Hocking, who mused, "*There is no such thing as a pure adventure:* for when you have cancelled path, peak, sky, star, all distinguishable points in space, the adventure itself is abolished." William Ernest Hocking, *The Meaning of God in Human Experience: A Philosophic Study of Religion* (New Haven, CT: Yale University Press,1912), xii.

27. Emerson, "New England Reformers," in *Essays: Second Series* (1844), 607.

28. William James, *Pragmatism* (1907; Buffalo, NY: Prometheus Books, 1991), 23.

29. Emerson, "Spiritual Laws," 316.

30. Richard H. Davis, *The Bhagavad Gita: A Biography* (Princeton, NJ: Princeton University Press, 2015), 22.

31. James, *Pragmatism*, 58.

32. I should be more specific: the question of this book is not if oneness is true. This is a question of profound interest to me that I hope to take up in later work, though it will require a different approach than I adopt here.

33. Here I allude to Thomas Farrell's definition of *rhetoric* as "the art, the fine and useful art, of making things matter." See Thomas B. Farrell, "Sizing Things Up: Colloquial Reflection as Practical Wisdom," *Argumentation* 12, no. 1 (1998): 1.

34. Here I allude to Debra Hawhee's definition of *rhetoric* in "Looking into Aristotle's Eyes: Toward a Theory of Rhetorical Vision," *Advances in the History of Rhetoric* 14, no. 2 (2011): 139–65. The practice of rhetoric involves a kind of psychological "transport" that the ancient Greeks called *phantasia*; Michele Kennerly contends that "rhetoric's work often consists of giving presence to the *unseeable*—something not yet or never capable of being seen—or to the *unseen*—something visible but ignored." Michele Kennerly, "Getting Carried Away: How Rhetorical Transport Gets Judgment Going," *Rhetoric Society Quarterly* 40, no. 3 (2010): 269.

35. There is a very succinct and helpful summary of the plot of the Mahabharata in Gurcharan Das, *The Difficulty of Being Good: On the Subtle Art of Dharma* (2009; New Delhi: Penguin, 2012), xvi–xxx. I also found the summary in Devdutt Pattanaik's *Jaya: An Illustrated Retelling of the Mahabharata* (Haryana: Penguin Books India, 2010), to be enjoyable and illuminating. For the still-unmatched study of the Gita's place in the Mahabharata, see J. A. B. Van Buitenen, *The Bhagavadgītā in the Mahabharata* (Chicago: University of Chicago Press, 1981).

36. Davis, *The Bhagavad Gita: A Biography*, 6.

37. The Bhagavad Gita was the product of a bitter war over patronage. According to a number of scholars, it is fundamentally a counterrevolutionary treatise. As Buddhists and Jains gained in popularity—and won the sponsorship of kings and other wealthy benefactors—Brahmins struck back, marking their rivals as enemies of the state in the Puranas (the Kalki Purana in particular calls for the killing of all *mlecchas*, heretics, including Buddhists and Jains) and the Gita. In later chapters of the Bhagavad Gita, Krishna extols the wisdom of Brahmins (see 18.41–44) and attacks their rivals, including Buddhists, Jains, Lokayayikas, and Charvakas (see 16.23–24). See Wendy Doniger, *Against Dharma: Dissent in the Ancient Indian Sciences of Sex and Politics* (New Haven, CT: Yale University Press, 2018), 132–41; Johannes Bronkhorst, *How the Brahmins Won: From Alexander to the Guptas* (Leiden: Brill, 2016), 249; and Geoffrey Samuel, *The Origins of Yoga and Tantra: Indic Religions to the Thirteenth Century* (Cambridge: Cambridge University Press, 2008).

38. Bhagavad Gita, 7.7. This mirrors Krishna's later description of the nature of God in 9.15–19, where he describes himself as a "scaffold" (*bharta*) and "home" (*nivasa*).

39. Jarrod L. Whitaker, *Strong Arms and Drinking Strength: Masculinity, Violence, and the Body in Ancient India* (Oxford: Oxford University Press, 2011).

40. Bhimrao Ambedkar, "Philosophic Defence of Counter-Revolution: Krishna and His Gita," in *Writings and Speeches*, vol. 3, ed. Vasant Moon and Hari Narake (1987; New Delhi: Ambedkar Foundation, 2014), 364. According to Stefanie Syman in *The Subtle Body: The Story of Yoga in America* (New York: Farrar, Straus and Giroux, 2010): "Krishna's message is this: Know me. With this knowledge, you can murder without sinning" (21).

41. On the Romantics' reading of the Gita, see Bradley L. Herling, *The German Gita: Hermeneutics and Discipline in the German Reception of Indian Thought, 1778–1831* (New York: Routledge, 2006).

42. Mahatma Gandhi, *The Bhagavad Gita according to Gandhi*, ed. John Strohmeier (Berkeley, CA: North Atlantic Books, 2009), xvii. Two additional examples, from many: Eknath

Easwaran downplays the Bhagavad Gita's situatedness in the Mahabharata, and, following Gandhi, contends that it forwards the strongest defense of nonviolence possible. "Just base your life on the Gita sincerely and systematically and see if you find killing or even hurting others compatible with its teachings" (it is not, both contend, hence marking the Gita as a masterpiece of *ahimsa*, "nonviolence"). Easwaran frames the Gita "as metaphor for the perennial war between the forces of light and the forces of darkness in every human heart. Arjuna and Krishna are then no longer merely characters in a literary masterpiece. Arjuna becomes Everyman, asking the Lord himself, Sri Krishna, the perennial questions about life and death—not as a philosopher, but as the quintessential man of action. Thus read, the Gita is not an external dialogue but an internal one: between the ordinary human personality, full of questions about the meaning of life, and our deepest Self, which is divine." Eknath Easwaran, trans., *The Bhagavad Gita* (1985; Tomales, CA: Nilgiri Press, 2007), 19, 20, 21. Sri Swami Satchidananda argues that "the entire dialogue between Krishna and Arjuna, and the war itself can be seen as allegory. The historic Kurukshetra battlefield is symbolic of the human frame. Life centered in the body is a kind of warfare. . . . So this Kurukshetra battle didn't happen just once some thousands of years ago. It's constantly happening. It's within each of us. If the good tendencies will allow their conscience to guide them, they can have the grace and friendship of the Lord, and they can win the battle of life." Sri Swami Satchidananda, *The Living Gita: The Complete Bhagavad Gita, A Commentary for Modern Readers* (1988; Yogaville, VA: Integral Yoga Publications, 2012), xv.

43. Bhagavad Gita, 1.1.

44. On the question of dharma, I found the following work especially helpful: Alf Hiltebeitel, *Dharma: Its Early History in Law, Religion, and Narrative* (Oxford: Oxford University Press, 2011); for a discussion of dharma in the Bhagavad Gita, see 517–624.

45. We are deluded, Krishna teaches, "by" or "because of duality delusion" (*dvandvamohena*). Bhagavad Gita, 7.27.

46. Whitaker, *Strong Arms and Drinking Strength*, 8–9.

47. Bhagavad Gita, 7.17.

48. Barbara Stoler Miller, trans., *The Bhagavad-Gita: Krishna's Counsel in Time of War* (New York: Bantam, 1986), 33 (6.29).

49. Bhagavad Gita, 6.29.

50. Bhagavad Gita, 6.31, 6.28.

51. Bhagavad Gita, 13.30.

52. On Advaita Vedanta, see Eliot Deutsch, *Advaita Vedanta: A Philosophical Reconstruction* (Honolulu: University of Hawaii Press, 1969); and David Loy, *Nonduality: A Study in Comparative Philosophy* (Amherst, NY: Humanity Books, 1988). This was the interpretation preferred by the late nineteenth-century Indian reform movements including the Brahmo Samaj and reformers including Swami Vivekananda, who read both the Gita and the dualistic Yoga Sutra through the lens of Advaita.

53. K. N. Upadhyaya, "The Impact of Buddhism on Early Buddhism on Hindu Thought (with Special Reference to the Bhagavadgita)," *Philosophy East and West* 18, no. 3 (1968): 163–73; and Doniger, *Against Dharma*, 140–42.

54. See, for instance, chapter 13 of the Bhagavad Gita, "The Field and the Knower of the Field."

55. Mark Singleton, *Yoga Body: The Origins of Modern Posture Practice* (New York: Oxford University Press, 2010).

56. Chapter 6 of the Bhagavad Gita is where Krishna offers his most concrete and practical advice on how to meditate. He uses a number of verbs for *controlling* and *focusing* in this book,

with the result that his vision of meditation and yoga that sounds remarkably like Patanjali's definition of yoga as *citta vrtti nirodha*, the stilling of the fluctuations of the mind.

57. Bhagavad Gita, 6.19.

58. See, for instance, Philip Goldberg, *American Veda: From Emerson and the Beatles to Yoga and Meditation—How Indian Spirituality Changed the West* (New York: Three Rivers Press, 2010), 26, which suggests that Whitman is a "direct heir" to Emerson's reading of Advaita.

59. And, indeed, Whitman represents a dissenting voice to the hegemony that Advaita Vedanta exercised over nineteenth-century visions of yoga, a hegemony that in many ways continues up to the present via the long shadow that Swami Vivekananda has cast over "modern yoga." On Vivekananda's influence, see Elizabeth De Michelis, *A History of Modern Yoga* (2004; London: Continuum, 2008); for a powerful dissenting view, see Andrea R. Jain, "No, I Don't Owe My Yoga Mat to Vivekananda," *Religion Dispatches*, October 5, 2011, http://religiondispatches.org/no-i-dont-owe-my-yoga-mat-to-vivekananda/.

60. Whitman, "Song of Myself," 246.

61. Whitman, "Of the Terrible Doubt of Appearances," 275.

62. Emerson, "Divinity School Address," 83.

63. This is the motto of the Vedanta Society that Swami Vivekananda established in the United States in 1894, taken from Rig Veda 1.164.46.

64. James, *The Varieties of Religious Experience*, 36. James believed that Americans had so deeply imbibed "Emersonian optimism" that it had become part of their civic temperament (38).

65. Emerson, "Spiritual Laws," 318.

66. Emerson, "Fate," 944.

67. John Dewey, *The Public and Its Problems* (1927; Athens, OH: Swallow Press, 1954), 184.

68. Whitman, *Democratic Vistas*, 989.

69. Whitman, 965.

70. Whitman, 989.

71. Political philosopher Danielle S. Allen explores the stakes of the metaphors we use to represent the *demos*—arguing emphatically for a metaphor of "wholeness" over the more common metaphor of "oneness"—in *Talking to Strangers: Anxieties of Citizenship since* Brown v. Board of Education (Chicago: University of Chicago Press, 2004), 13–20. I believe her critique to be valid for political visions of oneness in the Hobbesian tradition, *e pluribus unum* oneness, oneness based on enemyship, which is intended to erase difference and negate the sacrifices that minorities are asked to make in the name of democracy. Whitman's ethics of oneness escapes many of these critiques while offering a rich vision of democratic communication that does not suffer from a tendency toward transactionality.

72. Emerson, "The Poet," 457.

73. On Theosophy, see Albanese, *Republic of Mind and Spirit*, 271–83, 330–93, and 448–71. It is true that the Theosophical Society also enumerated a philosophy of oneness. In the first of three volumes on the Bhagavad Gita published by an author calling themselves "The Dreamer," the author forwards an allegorical interpretation of the Gita invested in helping "in the realization of the Oneness of Life, which is at the basis of a true Brotherhood of Humanity." See the Dreamer, *Studies in the Bhagavad Gita: The Yoga of Discrimination* (London: Theosophical Publishing Society, 1902), 6. Interestingly enough, the Dreamer talks warmly of oneness but then reads the Gita through the lens of dualistic Sankhya philosophy. Though the Theosophical Society, especially under Annie Besant, made important contributions to the history of European and American yoga, it was generally not interested in democracy and was in fact antidemocratic, so

I do not consider it at length in this book. To me, the best Theosophical treatment of the Gita is Annie Besant, *Hints on the Study of the Bhagavad Gita* (Benares, India: Theosophical Publishing Society, 1908).

74. On spiritual bypassing, see John Welwood, *Toward a Psychology of Awakening: Buddhism, Psychotherapy, and the Path of Personal and Spiritual Transformation* (Boston: Shambhala Press, 2000), 11–21.

Chapter One

1. Goldberg, *American Veda*, 26–46; Syman, *The Subtle Body*, 11–25.

2. Singleton, *Yoga Body*.

3. Emerson included the word *yoga* in his list of Sanskrit vocabulary. See Emerson, *Notebook Orientalist*, 135, 138.

4. Henry David Thoreau to Harrison G. O. Blake, November 20, 1849, in Henry David Thoreau, *Letters to a Spiritual Seeker*, ed. Bradley P. Dean (New York: W. W. Norton, 2004), 50.

5. Bhagavad Gita, 6.29–32.

6. On the colonial encounter between Europe and India, see Schwab, *The Oriental Renaissance*; J. J. Clarke, *Oriental Enlightenment: The Encounter between Asian and Western Thought* (London: Routledge, 1997); and Peter van der Veer, *Imperial Encounters: Religion and Modernity in India and Britain* (Princeton, NJ: Princeton University Press, 2001). Specifically between the United States and India, see Rayapati, *Early American Interest in Vedanta*; and Altman, *Heathen, Hindoo, Hindu*.

7. See Thomas R. Trautmann, *Aryans and British India* (Berkeley: University of California Press, 1997).

8. It should be noted that in general the Brahmin priests did not share these texts with lower-class Indians, either, who had to rely on learned priests for access because they did not read Sanskrit.

9. On the travels of the Gita to Europe and the United States, see Davis, *The Bhagavad Gita: A Biography*, 72–114.

10. Quoted in Vans Kennedy, *Researches into the Nature and Affinity of Ancient and Hindu Mythology* (London: Longman, 1831), v. Here, it would be more accurate to say that the Bhagavad Gita represents the late eighteenth- and early nineteenth-century Brahminical opinion of Calcutta elites when they were asked by the British what the equivalent of their "Bible" was. See Davis, *The Bhagavad Gita: A Biography*, 72–114.

11. David White observes that " 'yoga' has a wider range of meanings than nearly any other word in the entire Sanskrit lexicon." David Gordon White, introduction to *Yoga in Practice*, ed. David Gordon White (Princeton, NJ: Princeton University Press, 2012), 2. For a helpful history of yoga's varied traditions in India, see David Gordon White, *Sinister Yogis* (Chicago: University of Chicago Press, 2009).

12. Charles Wilkins, *Bhăgvăt-Gēētā, or Dialogues of Krēēshnă and Ărjŏŏn; in Eighteen Lectures; with Notes, Translated from the Original, in the Sănskrēēt, or Ancient Language of the Brāhmăns* (London: C. Nourse, 1785), 140.

13. A. W. Schlegel, *Bhagavad-Gita, id est THESPESION MELOS sive Almi Chrishnae et Arjunae Colloquium de rebus divinis, bharateae episodium. Textum recensuit, Adnotationes criticas et interpretationem Latinam adiecit* (Bonn: Eduard Weber, 1823). On Schlegel's translation of the Gita, see Herling, *The German Gita*, 157–201, and specifically 191–95 for Schlegel's translation of the word *yoga*.

14. Schlegel quoted in Helmut Gipper, "On the Translation of the Bhagavadgita," in *Studies in Western Linguistics*, ed. Theodora Bynon and Frank Robert Palmer (Cambridge: Cambridge University Press, 1986), 119.

15. See Dorothy M. Figueira, *The Exotic: A Decadent Quest* (Albany: State University of New York Press, 1994), 49–89.

16. On Hegel's reading of the Gita, see Figueira, *The Exotic*, 72–80; and Herling, *The German Gita*, 220–53. Hegel and later Victor Cousin were the sources of what Figueira (74, 83–84) calls "the moral dilemma of fatalism" common to nineteenth-century Orientalist readings of India and the yoga-is-quietism trope.

17. Victor Cousin, *Cours de L'Histoire de la Philosophie: Histoire de la Philosophie due XVIII Siecle* (Paris: Pichon et Didier, 1829), 213.

18. Cousin, *Cours de L'Histoire de la Philosophie*, 213.

19. Cousin, 174.

20. Cousin, 217.

21. Victor Cousin, *Cours de Philosophie: Introduction a L'histoire de la Philosophie* (Paris: Pichon et Didier, 1828), lecture 3, 14–15.

22. Cousin, *Cours de Philosophie*, lecture 3, 15.

23. Cousin, lecture 3, 15.

24. Cousin, *Cours de L'Histoire de la Philosophie*, 229.

25. Cousin, *Cours de Philosophie*, lecture 3, 16.

26. Amit Majmudar, trans., *Godsong: A Verse Translation of the Bhagavad-Gita, with Commentary* (New York: Knopf, 2018), 21 (2.58).

27. Schlegel, *Bhagavad-Gita*, 138.

28. Cousin, *Cours de L'Histoire de la Philosophie*, 229: "Il se recueille en soi, 'comme une tortue qui se retire en ellememe.'"

29. On Romanticism and the importance of inward experience as a means by which cosmic order could be discovered within, see Charles Taylor, *Sources of the Self: The Making of Modern Identity* (Cambridge, MA: Harvard University Press, 1989), 368–90, 456–93; Charles Taylor, *A Secular Age* (Cambridge, MA: Harvard University Press, 2007), 299–376; and Frederick C. Beiser, *The Romantic Imperative: The Concept of Early German Romanticism* (Cambridge, MA: Harvard University Press, 2003).

30. Cousin, *Cours de L'Histoire de la Philosophie*, 225: "En ce monde, le veritable devot dedaigne toute action." Cousin here quotes Schlegel's translation from *Bhagavad-Gita*, 137 ("mente devotus in hoc aevo utraque dimittit, bene et male facta"). Steven Adisasmito-Smith also presents the problems with the translation of this passage in "Transcendental Brahmin: Emerson's 'Hindu' Sentiments," in *Emerson for the Twenty-First Century*, ed. Barry Tharaud (Newark: University of Delaware Press, 2010), 139.

31. Bhagavad Gita, 3.20. For an argument that *lokasamgraha* is the neglected ethical heart of the Bhagavad Gita, see Satya P. Agarwal, *The Social Role of the Gita: How and Why* (New Delhi: Motilal Banarsidass Publishers, 1993).

32. Schlegel, *Bhagavad-Gita*, 137.

33. See White, *Sinister Yogis*.

34. Hannah Adams, *A Dictionary of All Religions and Religious Denominations, Jewish, Heathen, Mahometan, Christian, Ancient and Modern* (1817; Atlanta: Scholars Press, 1992), 322. On Adams, see Altman, *Heathen, Hindoo, Hindu*, 11–28.

35. On Roy, see Altman, 38–45; on human sacrifice in colonial India, see Crispin Bates, "Human Sacrifice in Colonial Central India: Myth, Agency, and Representation," in Crispin Bates, *Beyond Representation: Colonial and Postcolonial Constructions of Indian Identity* (New Delhi: Oxford University Press, 2006), 19–54. Unbelievably, human sacrifice continues to persist in certain Hindu communities today. See Puja Changoiwala, "India's Killer 'Godmen' and their Sacrificial Children," *This Week in Asia*, April 14, 2018, https://www.scmp.com/week-asia/society/article/2141250/indias-killer-godmen-and-their-sacrificial-children.

36. "Theology of the Hindoos, as Taught by Ram Mohun Roy," *North American Review* 6 (March 1818): 386, 389.

37. Altman, *Heathen, Hindoo, Hindu*, 46.

38. Emerson, *Journals and Miscellaneous Notebooks*, 1:50. The answer, he concluded, had to do with climate: "It is because a flaming sky boils their blood & blackens their skin & maddens their nature enervating the mind while it renders it fiercer & more brutal" (1:50).

39. Versluis, *American Transcendentalism and Asian Religions*, 50.

40. Bryan W. Van Norden, *Taking Back Philosophy: A Multicultural Manifesto* (New York: Columbia University Press, 2017), 27. As Edward Said writes, for the Orientalist, especially the reader of the Arab world, "the Oriental is irrational, depraved (fallen), childlike, 'different'; thus the European is rational, virtuous, mature, 'normal.'" Edward W. Said, *Orientalism* (1978; New York: Vintage, 1994), 40.

41. Norden, *Taking Back Philosophy*, 27.

42. Lawrence Buell, *Emerson* (2003; Cambridge, MA: Harvard University Press, 2004), 154. Here, Buell is describing Emerson's attraction to Persian poetry, but the same can be said for his attraction to Indian philosophy.

43. Emerson, "Divinity School Address," 78–79.

44. Lawrence Buell labels the move made by Mozoomdar, Vivekandanda, and other Indian intellectuals "the Indianization of Emerson." Buell, *Emerson*, 192.

45. Protap Chunder Mozoomdar, "Emerson as Seen from India," in *The Genius and Character of Emerson: Lectures at the Concord School of Philosophy*, ed. F. B. Sanborn (Boston: James R. Osgood, 1885), 371.

46. Mozoomdar, "Emerson as Seen from India," 367.

47. For a helpful study of Vivekananda's rhetoric, see Scott R. Stroud, "Hinduism for the West: Swami Vivekananda's Pluralism at the World's Parliament of Religions," in *Thinking Together: Lecturing, Learning, & Difference in the Long Nineteenth Century* (University Park: Pennsylvania State University Press, 2018), 169–86.

48. David Kopf, *The Brahmo Samaj and the Shaping of the Modern Indian Mind* (Princeton, NJ: Princeton University Press, 1979), 16.

49. Swami Vivekananda, *The Complete Works of Swami Vivekananda*, 9 vols. (Calcutta: Advaita Ashram, 1978), 4:95.

50. Emerson, *Journals and Miscellaneous Notebooks*, 10:360.

51. Robert D. Richardson Jr., *Emerson: The Mind on Fire* (Berkeley: University of California Press, 1995), 114.

52. Walter Harding, *Emerson's Library* (Charlottesville: University Press of Virginia, 1967), 70–71.

53. Versluis, *American Transcendentalism and Asian Religions*, 246.

54. Ralph Waldo Emerson to Max Muller, August 4, 1873, in *The Letters of Ralph Waldo Emerson*, ed. Ralph L. Rusk, 6 vols. (New York: Columbia University Press, 1939), 6:246. Muller

dedicated his *Introduction to the Science of Religion* (1873), the foundational work of comparative religion, to Emerson.

55. Emerson, "Plato; Or, The Philosopher," 640–41.

56. Cousin, *Cours de L'Histoire de la Philosophie*, 230.

57. Crick, *The Keys of Power*, 9.

58. Crick, 9.

59. Emerson, "New England Reformers," 601; italics added.

60. Shanta Acharya, *The Influence of Indian Thought on Ralph Waldo Emerson* (Lewistown, UK: Edwin Mellen Press, 2001), 122.

61. Buell, *Emerson*, 165.

62. Emerson, "The Over-Soul," 398.

63. Emerson, *Nature*, 7.

64. See Alan D. Hodder, *Emerson's Rhetoric of Revelation: "Nature," the Reader, and the Apocalypse Within* (University Park: Pennsylvania State University Press, 1989).

65. Mark A. Noll, *America's God: From Jonathan Edwards to Abraham Lincoln* (Oxford: Oxford University Press, 2002), 309.

66. Emerson, "Divinity School Address," 82–83.

67. Emerson, 82–83.

68. Emerson, 89.

69. John 1:3: "πάντα δι' αὐτοῦ ἐγένετο, καὶ χωρὶς αὐτοῦ ἐγένετο οὐδὲ ἕν ὃ γέγονεν": "All things were made by/through him; and without him was not any thing made that was made" (my translation).

70. Rayapati, *Early American Interest in Vedanta*, 77–78.

71. Arsic, *On Leaving*, 165.

72. Richard Poirier, *Poetry and Pragmatism* (Cambridge, MA: Harvard University Press, 1992), 30.

73. Emerson, "Self-Reliance," 268, 269, 272, 277.

74. Emerson, "Compensation," 292.

75. Emerson, "The Over-Soul," 385, 386, 389, 390, 392, 393, 396, 397, 398, 399.

76. Emerson, *Journals and Miscellaneous Notebooks*, 7:167.

77. Emerson, "The Over-Soul," 385–36.

78. Emerson, 386–87.

79. Richardson, *Emerson: The Mind on Fire*, 114.

80. There is evidence to suggest that as a student at Harvard in 1821, Emerson initially encountered the Bhagavad Gita in the appendix to Robert Southey's epic poem *The Curse of Kehama* (1810)—though he continued to attest to the influence of Cousin on his interpretation of the Gita. See Kenneth W. Cameron, "Young Emerson's Orientalism at Harvard," in *"Indian Superstition," by Ralph Waldo Emerson, Edited with a Dissertation on Emerson's Orientalism at Harvard* (Hanover, NH: Friends of the Dartmouth Library, 1954), 13–48; and Adisasmito-Smith, "Transcendental Brahmin," 135–36. For an argument that Roy's work exercised a profound influence on Emerson, see Alan Hodder, "Emerson, Rammohan Roy, and the Unitarians," *Studies in the American Renaissance* (1988): 133–48. Emerson also likely encountered the Gita through his reading in late 1830 of Joseph de Gerando's three-volume *Histoire comparée des systèmes de philosophie*. See Richardson, *Emerson: The Mind on Fire*, 102–5, 115. I initially thought that Emerson might have encountered the philosophy of the Gita through a reading of Abraham-Hyacinthe Anquetil-Duperron's two-volume Latin translation of the Persian translation of the Upanishads,

L'Oupnek'hat (vol. 1, 1801, vol. 2, 1802), but Emerson read Anquetil-Duperron's works on Zoroastrianism, not Hinduism. See Richardson, *Emerson: The Mind on Fire*, 121–22, 603n8. Emerson did quote a passage from *L'Oupnek'hat* in his journals. See Christy, *The Orient in American Transcendentalism*, 284. However, as J. P. Rao Rayapati points out, this quotation is secondhand, for Anquetil-Duperron's words were originally quoted in Gerando's *Histoire comparée des systèmes*, and this quotation is embedded in the notes Emerson was taking on that book. Rayapati concludes, "Emerson probably never saw Duperron's *L'Oupnek'hat*, much less read it." Rayapati, *Early American Interest in Vedanta*, 99.

81. Rammohan Roy, *Translation of the Several Principle Books, Passages, and Texts of the Vedas, and of Some Controversial Works of Brahmunical Theology* (1832), in *Two Brahman Sources of Emerson and Thoreau*, ed. William Bysshe Stein (Gainesville, FL: Scholars' Facsimiles and Reprints, 1967): "universal soul" (85), "soul of the universe" (75, 111), "all-pervading soul" (112).

82. Abbe J. A. Dubois, *Description of the Character, Manners, and Customs of the People of India; And of their Institutions, Religious and Civil* (London: Longman, Hurst, Rees, Orme, and Brown, 1817), 180. This work was reprinted in Philadelphia in 1818 by M. Carey & Son; see Rayapati, *Early American Interest in Vedanta*, 67.

83. William Ward, *A View of the History, Literature, and Mythology of the Hindoos: Including a Minute Description of Their Manners and Customs, and Translations from Their Principle Works* (1822), in Stein, *Two Brahman Sources of Emerson and Thoreau*, 115, 181.

84. Henry Thomas Colebrooke, "Essay on the Philosophy of the Hindus, Part II," *Transactions of the Royal Asiatic Society of Great Britain and Ireland* 1, no. 1 (1824): 94, 97. Moreover, Colebrooke observed, in Indian philosophy the word for individual soul, *atman*, is often translated as "universal soul" and "individual souls, emanating from the supreme one, are likened to innumerable sparks issuing from a blazing fire." Henry Thomas Colebrooke, "Essay on the Philosophy of the Hindus, Part V," *Transactions of the Royal Asiatic Society of Great Britain and Ireland* 2, no. 1 (1829): 13, 35. Colebrooke's essays were one of the chief sources for Cousin's understanding of yoga.

85. Cousin, *Cours de L'Histoire de la Philosophie*, 199.

86. Stein, *Two Brahman Sources of Emerson and Thoreau*, x–xi.

87. John S. Harrison, *The Teachers of Emerson* (New York: Sturgis & Waldon, 1910), 277.

88. Swami Paramananda, *Emerson and Vedanta* (Boston: Vedanta Centre, 1918), 65.

89. Versluis, *American Transcendentalism and Asian Religions*, 66.

90. In Sanskrit, both *adhi* and *para* serve the same semantic function as a prefix meaning "above" and "over."

91. Emerson, "The Over-Soul," 398.

92. For Emerson, each individual is "a finite human being made of infinite—divine, impersonal—substance," and "a voluntary power or the 'me' that emerges within impersonal forces—sensations, affections, perceptions—with which the 'me' has to establish relations." Arsic, *On Leaving*, 96.

93. Emerson's "me" is relational, through and through. See Sharon Cameron, "The Way of Life by Abandonment: Emerson's Impersonal," *Critical Inquiry* 25, no 1 (1998), 3.

94. On the troubles with "ragged individualism" (a phrase he adopts from John Dewey's *Individualism Old and New*, though his brilliant analysis extends far beyond Dewey's in its contemporary relevance), see Nathan Crick, *Dewey for a New Age of Fascism: Teaching Democratic Habits* (University Park: Pennsylvania State University Press, 2019), 11–27.

95. "In this country, the emphasis of conversation, and of public opinion, commends the practical man." Emerson, "Goethe; Or, The Writer," 748.

96. Emerson, "The Over-Soul," 385.

97. See paragraphs 76–77 of Kant's *Third Critique.*

98. Schlegel quoted in Schwab, *The Oriental Renaissance*, 13.

99. Emerson, "The Over-Soul," 387.

100. Bhagavad Gita, 9.1.

101. See Knut A. Jacobsen, *Yoga in Modern Hinduism: Hariharananda Aranya and Samkhyayoga* (New York: Routledge, 2018).

102. Swami Vivekananda, *Karma Yoga* (1896), in *Complete Works*, 1:42.

103. Vivekananda, *Karma Yoga*, 1:40.

104. "To eat meat is surely barbarous, and vegetable food is surely purer—who can deny that? For him surely is a strict vegetarian diet whose one end is to lead solely a spiritual life. But he who has to steer the boat of his life with strenuous labor through the constant life-and-death struggles and the competition of the world must of necessity take meat. So long as there will be in human society such a thing as the triumph of the strong over the weak, animal food is required, or some other suitable substitute for it has to be discovered; otherwise the weak will naturally be crushed under the feet of the strong." Vivekananda, "The East and the West," in *The Complete Works of Swami Vivekananda*, 5:485. On Vivekananda's call for a "muscular" yoga, see Singleton, *Yoga Body*, 100–101.

105. Whitaker, *Strong Arms and Drinking Strength*, 8–9.

106. Emerson, "Plato; Or, The Philosopher," 637.

107. Emerson, 638.

108. Emerson, 639.

109. The Rig Veda ties "yoga" to war, as does the Bhagavad Gita (in the form of Krishna's war rhetoric, and his denunciation of heretics who do not recognize his divinity or the authority of the Vedas and the Vedas' interpreters, the Brahmins). Many of the Puranas (including Emerson's beloved Vishnu Purana) invoked yoga in order to extend Brahminical rule over hated rivals like the Buddhists. Yoga has never been one thing, nor has it ever been pure. The same is true of India itself. See Burton Stein, *A History of India*, 2nd ed. (Malden, MA: John Wiley & Sons, 2010), 93–94.

110. Emerson, 637.

111. Altman, *Heathen, Hindoo, Hindu*, 78.

112. Emerson, "The Over-Soul," 386.

113. Emerson, 386.

114. Davis, *The Bhagavad Gita: A Biography*, 20.

115. Emerson, "The Over-Soul," 398.

116. Friedhelm Hardy makes the useful distinction between "intellectual bhakti" and "emotional bhakti" in *Viraha Bhakti: The Early History of Krishna Devotion in South India* (Delhi: Oxford University Press, 1983). On the development of Vaishnavism and the emotional bhakti traditions in South India, see June McDaniel, *The Madness of the Saints: Ecstatic Religion in Bengal* (Chicago: University of Chicago Press, 1989).

117. Majmudar, *Godsong*, 94 (12.1). "The Over-Soul" marks an important transition in Emerson's engagement with Indian philosophy. Steven Adisasmito-Smith argues that the Laws of Manu's doctrine of karma and its suggestion that divine law is manifested within each individual's

heart influenced Emerson's earliest thoughts on Indian philosophy. These themes are central to "The Over-Soul," though, proving that he is more than a simple conduit; Emerson gives them his own spin. "Emerson differs from Manu in that the supreme spirit within is not only a spectator or witness. God acts through the individual's hands." In speaking about God as incarnation, or *avatar*, Emerson is closer to the salvational theism of Vaishnavite Hinduism (which he encountered in the Bhagavad Gita and the Vishnu Purana) than Brahminical puritanism of the Laws of Manu. Adisasmito-Smith, "Transcendental Brahmin," 148.

118. Cousin paraphrased Schlegel's translation of the opening of chapter 12 (*Bhagavad-Gita*, 170) in *Cours de L'Histoire de la Philosophie*, 236.

119. See Loy, *Nonduality*.

120. Deutsch, *Advaita Vedanta*, 9. Deutsch argues that "Brahman" in the Bhagavad Gita "is used in several senses. In some passages it is used as a substitute for the term *prakriti* ('unconscious nature') and in others as a synonym for the term *Veda*. The general Upanishadic metaphysical meaning of Brahman, though, is retained and unless otherwise noted, it has this signification." See Eliot Deutsch, trans., *The Bhagavad Gita* (Lanham, MD: University Press of America, 1968), 12.

121. Swami Nikhilananda, *Brihadaranyaka Upanishad*, in *The Upanishads, A New Translation*, 4 vols. (New York: Ramakrishna-Vedanta Center, 1956), 3:172 (2.3.6).

122. Deutsch, *Advaita Vedanta*, 11, 62.

123. At times, however, Advaitins break this rule; for the types of arguments they tend to make for the necessary existence of *brahman*, see Deutsch, *Advaita Vedanta*, 27–45.

124. For the Sanskrit text of the Gita, I use Winthrop Sargeant, trans., *The Bhagavad Gita*, 25th Anniversary ed., ed. Christopher Key Chapple (Albany: State University of New York Press, 2009), 351 (8.3), 369 (8.21).

125. Majmudar, *Godsong*, 65 (8.13).

126. Wendy Doniger, *On Hinduism* (Oxford: Oxford University Press, 2014), 14–15.

127. Doniger, *On Hinduism*, 152.

128. Emerson, "Worship," 1057. About Emerson, Stanley Cavell writes: "The universe is what constantly and obediently answers to our conceptions. It is what can be all the ways we know it to be, which is to say, all the ways we can be." *The Senses of Walden*, expanded ed. (Chicago: University of Chicago Press, 1992), 128.

129. Henry David Thoreau, *A Week on the Concord and Merrimack Rivers*, ed. Robert F. Sayre, Library of America ed. (New York: Literary Classics of the United States, 1985), 54.

130. James, *Pragmatism*, 31.

131. Emerson, "An Address to the Senior Class in Divinity College," 81.

132. Indeed, Swami Abhedananda—who frequently cited Emerson in his books and lectures—explains that "the universal substance" "is the 'Over-Soul' of Emerson; while in Vedanta it is called 'Brahman,' the absolute substance of the universe, the infinite and eternal source of matter and mind, of object and substance. This substance is not many but one." Swami Abhedananda, *Vedanta Philosophy: Self-Knowledge (Atma-Jnana)* (New York: Vedanta Society, 1905), 23, 24.

133. James, *The Varieties of Religious Experience*, 36.

134. "Revelation is the disclosure of the soul." Emerson, "The Over-Soul," 393.

135. Emerson, "Fate," 955.

136. Bronkhorst, *How the Brahmins Won*, 249–54.

137. See Stephen Knapp, "Kalki: The Next Avatar of God and the End of Kali-yuga," accessed March 2020, https://www.stephen-knapp.com/kalki_the_next_avatar_of_God.htm.

138. Emerson, "The Method of Nature," 116–17.

139. Emerson, "The Divinity School Address," 90; "The Transcendentalist," 196.

140. Emerson, "The Over-Soul," 392.

141. In the American context, that is. There is evidence that such rhetoric historically had more power in India. See Stephen E. Lindquist, "Literary Lives and a Literal Death: Yajnavalkya, Sakalya, and an Upanisadic Death Sentence," *Journal of the American Academy of Religion* 79, no. 1 (2011): 33–57.

142. Emerson, "The Over-Soul," 390, 391.

143. Emerson, 386.

144. Emerson, 390.

145. On nineteenth-century American mysticism, see Albanese, *A Republic of Mind and Spirit*. And, indeed, as Albanese argues emphatically, a central concept in American metaphysical religion is dualism—the dualism between higher and lower worlds typical of Western occult traditions. She reads Emerson's *Nature* as a definitive statement of metaphysical religion (160–69). I would argue that later works, including "The Over-Soul," challenge this framework by presenting oneness as an alternative to dualism, which is just another social convention that frustrates self-reliance.

146. John Durham Peters, *Speaking into the Air: A History of the Idea of Communication* (Chicago: University of Chicago Press, 1999), 88; on nineteenth-century spiritualism, see 89–108. On Locke's vision of the self, see Taylor, *Sources of the Self*, 159–76; for a helpful discussion of the influence of Locke's psychologism on rhetorical theory during the eighteenth and nineteenth centuries, see Thomas M. Conley, *Rhetoric in the European Tradition* (1990; Chicago: University of Chicago Press, 1994), 188–228.

147. Emerson, "The Over-Soul," 391.

148. Bhagavad Gita, 17.3.

149. Emerson, "Spiritual Laws," 311.

150. Emerson, "The Over-Soul," 385. On Emerson's water metaphors, see Arsic, *On Leaving*.

151. Emerson, 385.

152. Emerson, "The Over-Soul," 392.

153. Emerson, 398. This theme of an expanding heart is also present in Roy's *Translation of the Several Principal Books, Passages, and Texts of the Veds*, 58: "I am, however, not without a sanguine hope that, through Divine Providence and human exertions, they will sooner or later avail themselves of that true system of religion which leads its observers to a knowledge and love of God, and to a friendly inclination towards their fellow-creatures, impressing their hearts at the same time with humility and charity, accompanied by independence of mind and true sincerity."

154. In *American Transcendentalism: A History* (New York: Hill and Wang, 2007), Philip Gura makes this split between self-culture and the community reformers central to his history of transcendentalism.

155. Emerson, "New England Reformers," 596.

156. Robert N. Hudspeth, ed., *The Letters of Margaret Fuller*, 6 vols. (Ithaca, NY: Cornell University Press, 1983–1984), 2:108.

157. See C. B. Macpherson, *The Political Theory of Possessive Individualism: Hobbes to Locke* (Oxford: Clarendon Press, 1962).

158. Emerson, "The Over-Soul," 386.

159. Emerson, 398.

160. Emerson, 385.

Chapter Two

1. On the various editions of *Leaves of Grass*, see Library of Congress, "Revising Himself: Walt Whitman and *Leaves of Grass*," exhibition, http://www.loc.gov/exhibits/whitman/leavesofgrass.html#0010.

2. Emerson said this to his friend Frank Sanborn after first reading Whitman's *Leaves of Grass*, as recounted in Frank E. Sanborn, "Reminiscent of Whitman," *Conservator*, May 1897, 38. Note that Romain Rolland views Whitman (along with Emerson and Thoreau) as paving the way for the yogis to come to the United States. See Romain Rolland, *Prophets of the New India*, trans. E. F. Malcolm-Smith (London: Cassell, 1930), 267–85.

3. Om Prakash Sharma, "Walt Whitman and the Doctrine of Karman," *Philosophy East and West* 20, no. 2 (1970): 170.

4. For two of the strongest cases for the influence of the Gita and Vedanta on Whitman, see V. K. Chari, *Whitman in the Light of Vedantic Mysticism* (Lincoln: University of Nebraska Press, 1964); and T. R. Rajasekharaiah, *The Roots of Whitman's Grass* (Rutherford, NJ: Fairleigh Dickinson University Press, 1970).

5. V. K. Chari, "Whitman in India," in *Walt Whitman and the World*, ed. Gay Wilson Allen and Ed Folsom (Iowa City: University of Iowa Press, 1995), 398.

6. Whitman, "A Backward Glance o'er Travel'd Roads," 664–65. To be fair, Whitman mentions a number of sources for *Leaves of Grass* here, reflecting its true eclecticism.

7. Whitman, "Passage to India," 531, 539.

8. He does demonstrate his familiarity with the Mahabharata and likely the Bhagavad Gita in *Democratic Vistas*. "The literature, songs, esthetics, &c., of a country are of importance principally for the women and men of that country, and enforce them in a thousand effective ways," he writes, describing "Yudishtura, Rama, Arjuna" as among many male models of ethical conduct: "These, I say, are models, combined, adjusted to other standards than America's, but of priceless value to her and hers" (959). According to William James, "In mystic states we both become one with the Absolute and we become aware of our oneness. This is the everlasting and triumphant mystical tradition, hardly altered by differences of clime or creed. In Hinduism, in Neoplatonism, in Sufism, in Christian mysticism, in Whitmanism, we find the same recurring note." James, *The Varieties of Religious Experience*, 378.

9. Whitman, "Starting from Paumanok," 180. On Whitman inventing a new religion, see David Kuebrich, *Minor Prophecy: Walt Whitman's New American Religion* (Bloomington: Indiana University Press, 1989).

10. James, *The Varieties of Religious Experience*, 378.

11. Richard Maurice Bucke, *Cosmic Consciousness: A Study in the Evolution of the Human Mind* (1901; Philadelphia: Innes & Sons, 1905), 2.

12. Whitman, "Song of Myself," 192.

13. For Whitman's uses of *rapport*, see "In Cabin'd Ships at Sea," 166; "Salut au Monde!," 296; and "By Blue Ontario's Shore," 470.

14. Whitman, *Democratic Vistas*, 943.

15. Beiser, *The Romantic Imperative*, 60; Emerson, "Fate," 955; Whitman, "Carlyle from American Points of View," 894. Whitman notes its rarity in *Democratic Vistas*, 943.

16. Whitman, *Democratic Vistas*, 988.

17. Whitman, "Song of Myself," 203.

18. In specialist works, this *dvandva* compound would be indicated by a diacritical mark: *bhedābheda* (in Devanagari: भेदाभेद).

19. On Bhedabheda Vedanta, see Richard King, *Indian Philosophy: An Introduction to Hindu and Buddhist Thought* (Washington, DC: Georgetown University Press, 1998), 221–22; and Roy W. Perfect, *An Introduction to Indian Philosophy* (Cambridge: Cambridge University Press, 2016), 135, 166.

20. Bhagavad Gita, 15.7.

21. In *The Hindu Gita*, Arvind Sharma describes the interpretation of Bhaskara, an early commentator who identified as a proponent of Bhedabheda—and who thus acts as an important counterpoint to the Advaitic interpretation of Shankara that became dominant in the nineteenth- and early twentieth-century United States (Shankara's interpretation acts as the monist equivalent to the late Emerson in the schema I've developed in this book). See Arvind Sharma, *The Hindu Gita: Ancient and Classical Interpretations of the Bhagavadgita* (La Salle, IL: Open Court, 1986), 16–41.

22. Whitman, "Starting from Paumanok," 179.

23. See Stroud, "Ontological Orientation and the Practice of Rhetoric."

24. According to the philosopher Charles Taylor, "We cannot do without some orientation to the good. . . . We each essentially are (i.e., define ourselves at least inter alia by) where we stand on this." Taylor, *Sources of the Self*, 33.

25. On the good as based on ontology, see Remi Brague, *The Wisdom of the World: The Human Experience of the Universe in Western Thought*, trans. Teresa Lavender Fagan (1999; Chicago: University of Chicago Press, 2003). Charles Taylor traces the changing conceptions of the sources of the good during the nineteenth century in *A Secular Age*, 299–321.

26. Whitman, preface to *Leaves of Grass*, 1st ed., 18.

27. Whitman, *Democratic Vistas*, 985.

28. Whitman, 989.

29. Kenneth Burke, *The Rhetoric of Religion: Studies in Logology* (1961; Berkeley: University of California Press, 1970), 25–27; Richard Weaver, *The Ethics of Rhetoric* (1955; Davis, CA: Hermagoras Press, 1985), 212. As Burke notes (91, 180), god terms, which organize our vision of the good, are central to governance.

30. Burke, *Rhetoric of Religion*, 25, 26.

31. Weaver, *The Ethics of Rhetoric*, 214.

32. Weaver, 15, 18.

33. Whitman, "A Song for Occupations," 360, 362.

34. Whitman, "Song of Myself," 246.

35. Bhagavad Gita, 17.3.

36. See Deutsch, *Advaita Vedanta*.

37. Abhedananda, *Vedanta Philosophy: Self-Knowledge*, 23–24. On Swami Abhedananda and the Vedanta Society of New York, see Carl T. Jackson, *Vedanta for the West: The Ramakrishna Movement in the United States* (Bloomington: Indiana University Press, 1994), 50–57.

38. West, *The American Evasion of Philosophy*.

39. Whitman, "Out of the Rolling Ocean the Crowd," 263. He specifically describes the earth in terms of *rondure* in "Song of the Exposition," 348; and "A Passage to India," 533.

40. Whitman, "Starting from Paumanok," 183.

41. Whitman, "Laws for Creations," 511.

42. "My three-score years of life summ'd up, and more, and past,
By any grand ideal tried, intentionless, the whole a nothing,
And haply yet some drop within God's scheme's ensemble—some way, or part of wave,
Like one of yours, ye multitudinous ocean"

Whitman, "By That Long Scan of Waves," 620. Whitman notes that in moments of rapport, we become aware of our "manifold and oceanic qualities." *Democratic Vistas*, 943.

43. Whitman, "Starting from Paumanok," 181.

44. Whitman, *Leaves of Grass*, 1st ed., 50.

45. Brague, *The Wisdom of the World*, 19.

46. Brague, 19.

47. Brague, 33.

48. Alexander von Humboldt, *Kosmos: A General Survey of the Physical Phenomena of the Universe*, vol. 1 (London: Hippolyte Bailliere, 1845), 5, 6.

49. See Griffith Dudding, "The Function of Whitman's Imagery in 'Song of Myself,' 1855," *Walt Whitman Review* 13 (1967), 3–11; and David S. Reynolds, *Walt Whitman's America: A Cultural Biography* (New York: Vintage, 1995).

50. Roger Asselineau, "Foreign Language Borrowings," in *The Routledge Encyclopedia of Walt Whitman*, ed. J. R. LeMaster and Donald D. Kummings (New York: Routledge, 1998), 227.

51. Weaver, *The Ethics of Rhetoric*, 23.

52. As Anna Julia Cooper astutely observed in 1892, the year of Whitman's death: "It is these magic words, 'I *believe*.' That is power." Anna Julia Cooper, *A Voice from the South* (1892), in *The Voice of Anna Julia Cooper*, ed. Charles Lemert and Esme Bhan (Lanham, MD: Rowman & Littlefield, 1998), 195. A few years later, William James observed—sounding very much like Walt Whitman—that "there are, then, cases" in which "faith in a fact can help create the fact." William James, "The Will to Believe," in *The Will to Believe and Other Essays in Popular Philosophy* (1897; New York: Dover, 1956), 25.

53. Joshua Gunn and Dana L. Cloud, "Agentic Orientation as Magical Voluntarism," *Communication Theory* 20, no. 1 (2010): 50–78.

54. For a summary statement of New Thought by one of its most prominent participants, see Henry Wood, *The New Thought Simplified: How to Gain Harmony and Health* (Boston: Lee and Shepard, 1903).

55. Whitman, "Song of the Open Road," 299.

56. Whitman, "Song of Myself," 194.

57. Whitman, "Salut au Monde!," 296.

58. Whitman, 296.

59. Emerson, "The Over-Soul," 391–92.

60. Emerson, 386.

61. Emerson, 390. On the paradoxes and challenges of Emerson's vision of "the impersonal," see Cameron, "The Way of Life by Abandonment."

62. Margaret Fuller, *Woman in the Nineteenth Century* (1845), in *The Portable Margaret Fuller*, ed. Mary Kelley (New York: Penguin, 1994), 241; italics added.

63. On Fuller and Emerson, see Christina Zwarg, *Feminist Conversations: Fuller, Emerson, and the Play of Reading* (Ithaca, NY: Cornell University Press, 1995).

64. Emerson, "The Over-Soul," 398.

65. Emerson, "Friendship," 350.

66. Emerson, 354.

67. Whitman, "Starting from Paumanok," 183. According to Helena Born, writing in the early twentieth century in a judgment that continues to hold up today, "Whitman's hopes for humanity embrace the female equally with the male." Helena Born, *Whitman's Ideal Democracy and Other Writings* (Boston: Everett Press, 1902), 9.

68. Whitman, *Democratic Vistas*, 955. On Whitman's connection to the women's rights movement of the 1850s, see Sherry Ceniza, *Walt Whitman and Nineteenth-Century Women Reformers* (Tuscaloosa: University of Alabama Press, 1998).

69. On the oppressive norms of Victorian sexuality, see Michel Foucault, *The History of Sexuality: An Introduction, Volume 1*, trans. Robert Hurley (1976; New York: Vintage Books, 1990).

70. Whitman, *Democratic Vistas*, 955.

71. Lottie L. Guttry, "Walt Whitman and the Woman Reader," *Walt Whitman Review* 22, no. 1 (1976): 104.

72. Whitman, "A Song for Occupations," 356.

73. Whitman, *Democratic Vistas*, 978, 988.

74. Whitman, "The Base of All Metaphysics," 275.

75. Charles E. Morris III, "Pink Herring and the Fourth Persona: J. Edgar Hoover's Sex Crime Panic," *Quarterly Journal of Speech* 88, no. 2 (2002): 228–44.

76. See Gary Schmidgall, *Walt Whitman: A Gay Life* (New York: E. P. Dutton, 1997); and John Marsh, *In Walt We Trust: How a Queer Socialist Poet Can Save America from Itself* (New York: Monthly Review Press, 2015).

77. Michael Robertson, *Worshipping Walt: The Whitman Disciples* (Princeton, NJ: Princeton University Press, 2008), 144. Significantly, though often they did meet in person, the relationships between these admirers and Whitman were generally carried on through romantic letters. On the queering of romantic letters, see Pamela VanHaitsma, *Queering Romantic Engagement in the Postal Age: A Rhetorical Education* (Columbia: University of South Carolina Press, 2019).

78. Whitman, "Song of Myself," 244–45.

79. Peters, *Speaking into the Air*.

80. Peters, 166, 167.

81. Peters, 167.

82. Peters, 167.

83. Peters, 167.

84. Whitman imagines a truly universal community unbounded by any borders, and while this vision is beautiful, philosophers argue that it is difficult to sustain any such rhetoric of universality, which is perpetually breaking down into more restrictive rhetorics that claim *we* are divine but *they* are not. When such supercharged rhetorics have been yoked to claims about family or blood, it has led to the worst types of violence in human history. So we must be on guard. Here, I have learned much from the ongoing debate in French philosophy between Jean-Luc Nancy and Jacques Derrida about the viability of community as a democratic ethic. For a starting place, see Jean-Luc Nancy, *The Inoperative Community*, ed. Peter Conner, trans. Peter Connor, Lisa Garbus, Michael Hollander, and Simona Sawhney (Minneapolis: University of Minnesota Press, 1991); and Jacques Derrida, *The Politics of Friendship*, trans. George Collins (London: Verso, 2006).

85. There are a number of democratic theorists who assume as an a priori that any practice of social inclusion or community building will inherently be exclusionary. There is of course ample historical evidence for this, but what concerns me here is when theorists start from this premise rather than subjecting it to the same criticism that they give to other theories. For example, Chantal Mouffe argues in *The Democratic Paradox* (London: Verso, 2000, 12–13, 21) that there is always a "constitutive outside" in democratic politics that is rooted in the nature of the social and in the essence of language itself. "Antagonism, then, can never be eliminated and it constitutes an ever-present possibility in politics. A key task of democratic politics is therefore

to create the conditions that would make it less likely for such a possibility to emerge" (13). Democracy entails antagonism and exclusion by its very nature for Mouffe, and for many critical and rhetorical scholars influenced by her work (and by the work of those she cites). What would it mean to take the "constitutive outside" not as an inevitability but instead as a potential to be negotiated?

86. Whitman, *Leaves of Grass*, 1st ed., 31, 79, 87.

87. Danielle S. Allen explores the stakes of the metaphors we use to represent the demos in *Talking to Strangers*, 13–20.

88. Whitman, "The Sleepers," 549.

89. Whitman, "By Blue Ontario's Shore," 480.

90. Whitman, *Leaves of Grass*, 1st ed., 44.

91. James, *The Varieties of Religious Experience*, 83.

92. I describe the history of the debt of gratitude in Engels, *The Art of Gratitude.*

93. Robert A. Emmons, *Thanks! How Practicing Gratitude Can Make You Happier* (Boston: Houghton Mifflin, 2007), 29.

94. Robert A. Emmons and Michael E. McCullough, eds., *The Psychology of Gratitude* (Oxford: Oxford University Press, 2004), viii.

95. See Engels, *The Art of Gratitude.*

96. See Engels. The emotions most closely associated with mystical traditions, and how these emotions are handled rhetorically, is also the topic of research I would like to undertake in the coming years.

97. Carole Satyamurti, *Mahabharata: A Modern Retelling* (New York: W. W. Norton, 2015), 90.

98. Satyamurti, *Mahabharata*, 232. Later, the narrator notes of Duryodhana:

> He had used wealth to ingratiate himself
> with the citizens, and to win support
> from neighboring kings, securing promises
> that they would fight for him when the time came.
> He was resolved: no argument on earth
> would make him yield his cousin's former kingdom (275).

99. Emerson, "Gifts," 536. "The expectation of gratitude is mean, and is continually punished by the total insensibility of the obliged person. . . . It is a very onerous business, this of being served, and the debtor naturally wishes to give you a slap," Emerson concluded (537).

100. Swami Vivekananda, *Raja Yoga*, in *Complete Works*, 1:190.

101. Bhagavad Gita, 16.1.

102. Bhagavad Gita, 16.15.

103. "Spiritual wealth is considered to be for freedom, the wealth of an *asura*, for bondage." Swami Dayananda Saraswati, *Bhagavad Gita: Home Study Course*, 9 vols. (Chennai, India: Arsha Vidya Research and Publication Trust, 2011), 8:180 (16.5).

104. Debra Hawhee, "Rhetoric's Sensorium," *Quarterly Journal of Speech* 101, no. 1 (2015): 2–17.

105. See Lisa Feldman Barrett, *How Emotions Are Made: The Secret Life of the Brain* (New York: Houghton Mifflin Harcourt, 2017).

106. Whitman, "A Song of the Rolling Earth," 362.

107. Whitman, *Leaves of Grass*, 1st ed., 110.

108. Whitman, "Song of Myself," 207.

109. Whitman, 188.

110. Macpherson, *The Political Theory of Possessive Individualism.*

111. Whitman, "Song of Myself," 209.

112. Thomas A. Tweed, *The American Encounter with Buddhism, 1844–1912: Victorian Culture and the Limits of Dissent* (Chapel Hill: University of North Carolina Press, 1992), 29.

113. This is the essence of Stephen Prothero's critique of the perennial philosophy in *God Is Not One.*

114. See Jon Kabat-Zinn, *Meditation Is Not What You Think: Mindfulness and Why It Is So Important* (New York: Hachette, 2018); and Thich Nhat Hanh, *The Miracle of Mindfulness* (New York: Beacon Press, 1999).

115. Whitman, "Song of Myself," 218.

116. Thich Nhat Hanh, *The Heart of Understanding: Commentaries on the Prajnaparamita Heart Sutra*, ed. Peter Levitt (Berkeley, CA: Parallax Press, 1988), 3–4.

117. Whitman, *Leaves of Grass*, 1st ed., 93. The 1891–92 edition makes slight amendments to this passage ("A Song for Occupations," 358).

118. Whitman, "Song of the Open Road," 307.

119. Whitman, 302.

120. Whitman, *Leaves of Grass*, 1st ed., 78.

121. To be thrown into the world is to learn to measure our words, our thoughts, and even our self-worth against *doxa*, which is made rhetorically productive, in part, through god terms. Foucault calls this process "veridiction." See Michel Foucault, *The Birth of Biopolitics: Lectures at the Collège de France 1978–1979*, ed. Michel Senellart, trans. by Graham Burchell (2004; New York: Picador, 2008), 27–50; and Michel Foucault, *Subjectivity and Truth: Lectures at the Collège de France, 1980–1981*, ed. Frederic Gros, trans. Graham Burchell (2014; London: Palgrave, 2017), 11–13, 221, 237–39.

122. For a helpful study of Kant's philosophy and his rhetoric of morality, see Scott R. Stroud, *Kant and the Promise of Rhetoric* (University Park: Pennsylvania State University Press, 2014).

123. Pierre Hadot, *Philosophy as a Way of Life: Spiritual Exercises from Socrates to Foucault*, ed. Arnold I. Davidson, trans. Michael Chase (Malden, MA: Blackwell, 1995), 81–109.

124. Soteriology is often bound up with metaphysical concerns about the true nature of being and goodness, especially in Indian philosophy. As Mircea Eliade observes, "In India metaphysical knowledge always has a soteriological purpose." Mircea Eliade, *Yoga: Immortality and Freedom*, trans. Willard R. Trask (1954; Princeton, NJ: Princeton University Press, 2009), 13.

125. Whitman, *Leaves of Grass*, 1st ed., 9. Whitman repeats this passage, with slight variation, in his later poem "By Blue Ontario's Shore," 475.

Chapter Three

1. See John Michael Corrigan, *American Metempsychosis: Emerson, Whitman, and the New Poetry* (New York: Fordham University Press, 2012).

2. Gordon, *Emerson and the Light of India*, 88–89.

3. Emerson, *Journals and Miscellaneous Notebooks*, 14:275. Elsewhere, Emerson wrote: "Every history in the world is my history. . . . I can as readily find myself . . . in the Vedas as in the New Testament" (7:389).

4. Emerson, 9:467.

5. Versluis, *American Transcendentalism and Asian Religions*, 74–76.

6. On the *philosophia perennis*, see Huxley, *The Perennial Philosophy*.

7. Emerson, "Plato; Or, The Philosopher," 638. According to Robert Gordon, for Emerson, "the philosophical arguments which lie at the heart of 'Plato' were derived entirely from Indian philosophy." Gordon, *Emerson and the Light of India*, 131.

8. Emerson, "Plato; Or, The Philosopher," 640–41. It is worth noting here that Emerson linked Jesus's wisdom to the East: "Europe has always owed to oriental genius, its divine impulses. What these holy bards said, all sane men found agreeable and true. And the unique impression of Jesus upon mankind, whose name is not so much written as ploughed into the history of this world, is proof of the subtle virtue of this infusion." Emerson, "Divinity School Address," 78–79.

9. Richardson, *Emerson: The Mind on Fire*, 355, 357–58.

10. Garry Wills, *Lincoln at Gettysburg: The Words That Remade America* (New York: Simon & Schuster, 1992), 64.

11. Emerson, 473.

12. Richardson, *Emerson: The Mind on Fire*, 359.

13. Emerson, "Experience," 472.

14. Emerson, 473.

15. Emerson, 473.

16. Emerson, "Nominalist and Realist," 577.

17. Emerson, "Plato; Or, The Philosopher," 638; and note that Emerson in his journals attributes this passage to the Vishnu Purana (*Journals and Miscellaneous Notebooks*, 9:320). Later, in his essay "Illusions," he offers a similar quote: "The Hindoos, in their sacred writings, express the liveliest feeling, both the essential identity, and of that illusion which they conceive variety to be. 'The notions, '*I am*,' and '*This is mine*,' which influence mankind, are but delusions of the mother of the world. Dispel, O Lord of all creatures! the conceit of knowledge which proceeds from ignorance'" (1123).

18. Acharya, *The Influence of Indian Thought on Emerson*, 120; Zwarg, *Feminist Conversations*.

19. Emerson, "Experience," 473.

20. Emerson, "Illusions," 1118.

21. Fuller, *Woman in the Nineteenth Century*, 242.

22. Fuller, 243.

23. Fuller, 244.

24. Fuller, Arthur Versluis notes, "devoted almost no time to Asian religions" and "demonstrated very little interest in the East." Versluis, *American Transcendentalism and Asian Religions*, 11, 3.

25. On the macho world of the Mahabharata, see Whitaker, *Strong Arms and Drinking Strength*.

26. There are moments in the Mahabharata where this ideal is resisted, especially in the figure of Draupadi. See Wendy Doniger, *The Hindus: An Alternative History* (New York: Penguin, 2009), 199–303.

27. Bhagavad Gita, 3.20. For an argument that *lokasamgraha* is the neglected heart of the Bhagavad Gita, see Agarwal, *The Social Role of the Gita*.

28. Bhagavad Gita, 16.19–20.

29. And indeed, feminist writers correctly point out the relational nature of agency. See Karlyn Kohrs Campbell, "Agency: Promiscuous and Protean," *Communication and Critical/Cultural Studies* 1, no. 2 (2005): 1–19.

30. Emerson, "New England Reformers," 599.

31. Emerson, 599.

32. The poem that precedes Emerson's essay "Friendship" begins: "A ruddy drop of manly blood . . ." In this essay, he speaks of "friends" with masculine pronouns; women are instead spoken of as "lovers." Perhaps for Emerson only men are capable of the "roughest courage" that friendship demands, though surely women are also capable of the "tenderness" that true friendship rests on. Either way, friendship seems to be the realm of men: "Can another be so blessed, and we so pure, that we can offer him tenderness? When a man becomes dear to me, I have touched the goal of fortune." Emerson, "Friendship," 343, 346, 348.

33. Emerson quoted in Cavell, *Emerson's Transcendental Etudes*, 131.

34. K. R. Chandrasekharan reads "Brahma" in light of the Advaita of the Bhagavad Gita. See K. R. Chandrasekharan, "Emerson's Brahma: An Indian Interpretation," *New England Quarterly* 33, no. 1 (1960): 506–12.

35. Carpenter, *Emerson and Asia*, 110–11.

36. Emerson, "Brahma," 159.

37. Christy, *The Orient in American Transcendentalism*, 164.

38. "Emerson Travestie," *New York Times*, November 12, 1857.

39. "Emerson Travestie."

40. "Editor's Easy Talk," *Graham's American Monthly Magazine of Literature, Art, and Fashion*, 52, no. 3 (March 1858): 273.

41. Deutsch, *Advaita Vedanta*, 32.

42. Deutsch, 32.

43. Deutsch, 32.

44. Majmudar, *Godsong*, 15 (2.16).

45. Majmudar, 31 (3.35).

46. "There is no getting around it: the extent of Krsna's 'rational assessment of the situation,' at least as far as ethics is concerned, is that Arjuna is a ksatriya and so must—and will—fight." Simon Pearse Brodbeck, "Calling Krsna's Bluff: Non-attached Action in the Bhagavadgita," *Journal of Indian Philosophy* 32, no. 1 (2004): 98.

47. Here, Krishna speaks to a cultural conflict at the time in India between two competing models of the dharma of a king, the warrior king and the renunciant king. See Samuel, *The Origins of Yoga and Tantra*, and Hiltebeitel, *Dharma*.

48. Majmudar, *Godsong*, 15–16 (2.19–21).

49. Henry David Thoreau, *Walden: A Fully Annotated Edition*, ed. Jeffrey S. Cramer (New Haven, CT: Yale University Press, 2004), 287.

50. Thoreau, *Walden*, 288.

51. See Richard H. Davis, "Henry David Thoreau, Yogi," *Common Knowledge* 24, no. 1 (2018): 56–89.

52. Thoreau, *A Week on the Concord and Merrimack Rivers*, 115, 111.

53. Thoreau, 113–14.

54. Thoreau, 114.

55. Thoreau observed that "there is such a thing as caste, even in the West; but it is comparatively faint; it is conservatism here. It says, forsake not your calling, outrage no institution, use no violence, rend no bonds; the State is thy parent. Its virtue or manhood is wholly filial." He then invokes the familiar Orientalist trope of an essential clash between "the Oriental and the Occidental," offering the totalistic view of India as a land of pure contemplation and fatalism. Thoreau, *A Week on the Concord and Merrimack Rivers*, 114. In the Bhagavad Gita, Krishna portrays himself as the creator of the four *varnas*, or classes; he has little to nothing to say about *jati*,

or caste. These categories of course share several characteristics, including endogamy and hierarchy; but Krishna's emphasis, especially in describing *svadharma*, is on *varna*, not *jati* (though the Gita would certainly come to be associated with *jati* in later Indian thought). This distinction was largely lost on American readers, who adopted the view, from European authorities like Cousin and Hegel, that the Gita was a text of caste.

56. In his notes on Wilkins's *Bhăgvăt-Gēētā*, Emerson copied out the following passage: "The man who believeth that it is the soul which killeth & he who thinketh that the soul may be destroyed, are both alike deceived; for it neither killeth, nor is it killed. It is not a thing which a man may say, it hath been, it is about to be, or is to be hereafter; for it is a thing without birth; it is ancient constant & eternal, & is not to be destroyed in this its mortal frame." This is Emerson's gloss of the Bhagavad Gita 2.11–30 in Emerson, *Notebook Orientalist*, 131. Emerson copied a similar passage into his notebooks from Wilson's translation of *The Vishnu Purana*, which he borrowed from James Elliot Cabot in 1845: "What living creature slays or is slain? What living creature preserves or is preserved? Each is his own destroyer or preserver, as he follows evil or good." Emerson, *Journals and Miscellaneous Notebooks*, 9:319.

57. Perry Miller, *Errand into the Wilderness* (1956; Cambridge, MA: Harvard University Press, 1984), 187. On Orientalism in today's academy, see Norden, *Taking Back Philosophy*.

58. Richardson, *Emerson: The Mind on Fire*, 527.

59. Richardson, 527, 528. As Richardson points out, "Whitman wrote one piece in 1880 in which he denied ever being seriously influenced by Emerson. In the conversations from which Horace Traubel constructed his splendid memoir *With Walt Whitman in Camden*, we get another story. Emerson is a constant, almost obsessive presence in this record; there are over three hundred references to Emerson, many of them extended discussions, over a period of two and half years" (529).

60. Emerson, "The Poet," 457.

61. Emerson, 459.

62. See Peter Simonson, "A Rhetoric for Polytheistic Democracy: Walt Whitman's 'Poem of Many in One,'" *Philosophy and Rhetoric* 36, no. 3 (2003): 353–75.

63. Whitman, "By Blue Ontario's Shore," 475.

64. Whitman, 470.

65. Whitman, "Song of Myself," 207.

66. On Whitman's use of a "pulse" metaphor for the divine in his poetry, see Kuebrich, *Minor Prophecy*, 20–21.

67. See A. A. Long, *Greek Models of Mind and Self* (Cambridge, MA: Harvard University Press, 2015), esp. chap. 3.

68. As Larry Siedentop argues, "in its basic assumptions, liberal thought is the offspring of Christianity. It emerged as the moral intuitions generated by Christianity were turned against the authoritarian model of the Church." Larry Siedentop, *Inventing the Individual: The Origins of Western Liberalism* (Cambridge, MA: Harvard University Press, 2014), 332.

69. See Engels, "The Trouble with 'Public Bodies.'"

70. "All goes to show that the soul in man is not an organ, but animates and exercises all the organs; is not a function, like the power of memory, of calculation, of comparison, but uses these as hands and feet; is not a faculty, but a light; is not the intellect or the will, but the master of the intellect and the will; is the background of our being, in which they lie." Emerson, "The Over-Soul," 386–87.

71. Whitman, "I Sing the Body Electric," 250.

72. Whitman, 254.

73. Mircea Eliade, *The Sacred and the Profane: The Nature of Religion*, trans. Willard R. Trask (1957; Orlando, FL: Harvest, 1987), 11, 12.

74. In the Christian tradition, *hierophany* maintains an ambience of separation and secrecy. Indeed, in his *American Dictionary of the English Language* (1828), s.v. "sacred," Noah Webster observes that the sacred "is removed or separated from that which is common, vulgar, polluted, or open, public." He makes plain the connection between *sacredness* and *secrecy*, both words (he surmises) derived from the Latin *sacer*. Webster also observes that someone or something that "is accursed is separated from society or the privileges of citizens, rejected, banished." These cultural dynamics will be familiar to students of the philosopher Giorgio Agamben and his concept of *homo sacer*.

75. Taylor, *A Secular Age*, 300.

76. Taylor develops this thesis in *A Secular Age*; see also Marcel Gauchet, *Le désechantement du monde* (Paris: Gallimard, 1985).

77. He could not be the one true son of God, because, according to Emerson in the "Divinity School Address," everyone is an incarnation of God—a fact that Jesus himself recognized. "Thus is he, I think, the only soul in history who has appreciated the worth of a man" (80).

78. Susan Jacoby, *Freethinkers: A History of American Secularism* (New York: Metropolitan/Owl, 2004), 149–85.

79. Eliade, *The Sacred and the Profane*, 203.

80. See James Turner, *Without God, without Creed: The Origins of Unbelief in America* (Baltimore: Johns Hopkins University Press, 1985); and Jacoby, *Freethinkers*.

81. This nonreligious person has a strong ethics, but it is not rooted in *hierophany*, as there is nothing beyond what we immediately see to manifest itself as sacred. For one productive discussion of the ethics of Eliade's "modern nonreligious man," see Charles Taylor, *The Ethics of Authenticity* (1991; Cambridge, MA: Harvard University Press, 2018).

82. Robertson, *Worshipping Walt*, 4.

83. Whitman, *Democratic Vistas*, 949. In his poem "Starting from Paumanok," 180, Whitman observes similarly:

> I say that the real and permanent grandeur of these States must be their religion,
> Otherwise there is no real and permanent grandeur;
> (Nor character nor life worthy the name without religion,
> Nor land nor man or woman without religion.)

84. Whitman, "I Sing the Body Electric," 254–55.

85. Corrigan, *American Metempsychosis*, 1–2.

86. Whitman, "I Sing the Body Electric," 255.

87. See Gerald Horne, *The Apocalypse of Settler Colonialism: The Roots of Slavery, White Supremacy, and Capitalism in Seventeenth-Century North America and the Caribbean* (New York: Monthly Review Press, 2018): and Cheryl I. Harris, "Whiteness as Property," *Harvard Law Review* 106 (1993): 1709–91. The Thirteenth Amendment banned slavery "except as punishment for a crime whereof the party shall have been duly convicted," allowing slavery to continue in the prison system in a nation that disproportionately jails racial minorities. See Whitney Benns, "American Slavery, Reinvented," *Atlantic*, September 21, 2015, https://www.theatlantic.com/business/archive/2015/09/prison-labor-in-america/406177/; and Stephen John Hartnett, ed., *Challenging the Prison-Industrial Complex: Activism, Arts, and Educational Alternatives* (Urbana: University of Illinois Press, 2010).

88. See Ibram X. Kendi, *Stamped from the Beginning: The Definitive History of Racist Ideas in America* (New York: Nation Books, 2016); David Roediger, *Working toward Whiteness: How America's Immigrants Became White: The Strange Journey from Ellis Island to the Suburbs* (2005; New York: Basic Books, 2018); and Shannon Sullivan, *White Privilege* (New York: Polity, 2019).

89. "After the first blush of sin comes its indifference," Thoreau writes—and it is that indifference, that acquiescence, that disinterest, that is as good as assent to slavery and war. "The broadest and most prevalent error requires the most disinterested virtue to sustain it." Henry David Thoreau, "Civil Disobedience," in *Collected Essays and Poems*, Library of America ed., ed. Elizabeth Hall Witherell (New York: Literary Classics of the United States, 2001), 210.

90. Jack Turner, *Awakening to Race: Individualism and Social Consciousness in America* (Chicago: University of Chicago Press, 2012), 21.

91. Danielle Allen, *Our Declaration: A Reading of the Declaration of Independence in Defense of Equality* (New York: Norton, 2014), 22.

92. See Martin Klammer, *Whitman, Slavery, and the Emergence of "Leaves of Grass"* (University Park: Pennsylvania State University Press, 1995).

93. Whitman, "Song of Myself," 197.

94. See Saidiya Hartman, *Scenes of Subjection: Terror, Slavery, and Self-Making in Nineteenth-Century America* (New York: Oxford University Press, 1997).

95. Whitman, "I Sing the Body Electric," 255–56.

96. Whitman, 256–57.

97. Edward Carpenter, *Towards Democracy* (London: T. Fisher Unwin, 1892), 29.

98. Whitman, "Song of Myself," 188.

99. Whitman, 225.

100. See White, *Sinister Yogis*.

101. Whitman, "Song of Myself," 225.

102. See Kenneth Burke, "The Rhetoric of Hitler's 'Battle,'" in *The Philosophy of Literary Form* (Baton Rouge: Louisiana State University Press, 1941), 191–220; Robert L. Ivie, "Images of Savagery in American Justifications for War," *Communication Monographs* 47 (1980), 279–94; and Engels, *Enemyship*.

103. Majmudar, *Godsong*, 16 (2.26–27). On "anticipatory grief," see Elizabeth Kubler-Ross and David Kessler, *On Grief and Grieving: Finding the Meaning of Grief Through the Five Stages of Loss* (New York: Scribner, 2005).

104. Majmudar, *Godsong*, 19 (2.48).

105. Yoga Sutra of Patanjali, 2.48.

106. Satyamurti, *Mahabharata*, 635.

107. Chitra Banerjee Divakaruni, *The Palace of Illusions* (2008; New York: Anchor, 2009).

108. Whitman, "When Lilacs Last in the Dooryard Bloom'd," 459.

109. James, *The Varieties of Religious Experience*, 83.

110. Whitman, "When Lilacs Last in the Dooryard Bloom'd," 459.

Chapter Four

1. See Daniel Kahneman, *Thinking, Fast and Slow* (New York: Farrar, Straus and Giroux, 2011), 50–58. In education, psychologists call the self-fulfilling effects of expectations the Pygmalion effect (for positive expectations) and the golem effect (for negative expectations).

2. Majmudar, *Godsong*, 120 (17.3). Swami Chinmayananda explains *shraddha* as "supreme faith" rather than "blind belief": "Shraddha is 'my belief in something I do not know, so that I may come to know what I believe in.'" Swami Chinmayananda, *The Holy Geeta* (Mumbai: Central Chinmaya Mission Trust, 2013), 837 (commentary on 12.2). At the Krishnamacharya Yoga Mandiram in 2013 and 2014, the teachers repeatedly testified to the importance of *sraddha*; we students were told that it is the essence of the Upanishads, the Bhagavad Gita, and the Yoga Sutra—the essence, in fact, of yoga.

3. J. Cockburn Thompson, trans., *The Bhagavad-Gita; Or, A Discourse between Krishna and Arjuna on Divine Matters* (Hertford: Stephen Austin, 1855), 110 (17.3).

4. Thompson, *Bhagavad-Gita*, 110–11. Not all Rakshasas are evil in the Mahabharata.

5. Bhagavad Gita 4.40.

6. William James, "The Sentiment of Rationality," in *The Will to Believe and Other Essays in Popular Philosophy* (1897; New York: Dover, 1956), 97.

7. See Loy, *Nonduality*; and Deutsch, *Advaita Vedanta*.

8. Majmudar, *Godsong*, 84 (11.1).

9. This is not the first time that Krishna reveals his divine form in the Mahabharata. Devdutt Pattanaik points out that "long before the war, when negotiations for peace had broken down, Krishna had revealed his cosmic form (virat-swarup)—the same form he shows Arjuna during the course of his discourse—to both Dhritarashtra and Duryodhana, perhaps to impress upon the father and son that his words needed to be taken seriously. But Dhritarashtra, granted momentary sight, had simply declared his helplessness before such awesomeness and shrunk back into blindness, while Duryodhana had seen it as a magician's trick. Both father and son refused to see what was shown. They clung to the view that they were the victims. Thus, showing does not guarantee seeing. Telling does not guarantee hearing. Gyana is not vi-gyana." Devdutt Pattanaik, *My Gita* (New Delhi: Rupa, 2015), 39.

10. Majmudar, *Godsong*, 85 (11.8).

11. Majmudar, 84 (11.7).

12. The other memorable example that jumps to mind is chapter 35 of Herman Melville's *Moby Dick*, "The Mast-Head," in which the narrator ascends to the crow's nest and sees below him the interconnectedness of all creation as an emanation of God. Notably, this vision ends with a warning: "Over Descartian vortices you hover. And perhaps, at mid-day, in the fairest weather, with one half-throttled shriek you drop through that transparent air into the summer sea, no more to rise for ever. Heed it well, ye Pantheists!"

13. Emerson, "The Poet," 457.

14. On polyphony, see Mikhail Bakhtin, *Problems of Dostoevsky's Poetics*, ed. and trans. Caryl Emerson (1984; Minneapolis: University of Minnesota Press, 2003), 21–22.

15. I say at least three, because the vision is being told in the future by Vaishampayana to King Janamejaya. Another interesting feature of the divine vision is that there are substantial meter changes in the divine vision. Most of the Gita is composed in the *anusthubh* meter, but parts of the divine vision are presented in a much older meter more common to the Vedas, the *tristubh*. Some scholars raise the possibility that the *tristubh* sections are older, and perhaps closer to the original. I am not a Sanskrit scholar, so I cannot evaluate these claims. But they are interesting. See Dennis Hudson, "Arjuna's Sin: Thoughts on the Bhagavad-Gita in its Epic Context," *Journal of Vaisnava Studies* 4, no. 3 (1996): 65–84.

16. Majmudar, *Godsong*, 85 (11.13).

17. Majmudar, 87 (11.23–25).

18. Majmudar, 87 (11.27).

19. Majmudar, 88 (11.31).

20. Majmudar, 88 (11.32–34).

21. James A. Hijiya, "The *Gita* of J. Robert Oppenheimer," *Proceedings of the American Philosophical Society* 144, no. 2 (2000): 125.

22. Swami Tyagishananda, who observes that "the special teachings of the Gita are to be found in every part of the M.bh.," provides a long and detailed list of how the Gita's teachings inform key aspects of the Mahabharata. See Swami Tyagishananda, *Srimad Bhagavad Gita: Insights and Significance* (Kolkata: Ramakrishna Mission, 2019), 3. For a helpful grounding of the doctrines of the Bhagavad Gita in the narrative of the Mahabharata, see Van Buitenen, *The Bhagavad Gita in the Mahabharata*; and Angelika Malinar, *The Bhagavadgita: Doctrines and Contexts* (Cambridge: Cambridge University Press, 2007).

23. On the complex and contested meaning of *samadhi*, see Stuart Ray Sarbacker, *Samadhi: The Numinous and Cessative in Indo-Tibetan Yoga* (Albany: State University of New York Press, 2005).

24. Satyamurti, *Mahabharata*, 421. This is Sanjaya's comment to King Dhritarashtra immediately following the Bhagavad Gita.

25. Duryodhana is not included here, because his beef was primarily with Arjuna's older brother Bhima. Again, however, there is a common theme of trickery to his death, as he is killed by a blow that is quite literally below the belt. For a description of the philosophy of warfare in the Mahabharata, see Kaushik Roy, *Hinduism and the Ethics of Warfare in South Asia: From Antiquity to the Present* (Cambridge: Cambridge University Press, 2012), 13–39.

26. Satyamurti, *Mahabharata*, 499.

27. Satyamurti, 524.

28. Satyamurti, 545.

29. Up to this point, Yudhishthira's chariot had glided above the earth, a symbol that he was above many of the worst human foibles; from this point forward his wheels touch the ground.

30. Satyamurti, *Mahabharata*, 548.

31. On Karna's status anxiety and his tragic flaws, see Das, *The Difficulty of Being Good*, 151–82.

32. According to David Dean Shulman, "There is, perhaps, no more popular hero in India's classical literature than Karna, the 'hidden' eldest brother to the five Pandava heroes of the Mahabharata." David Dean Shulman, *The King and the Clown in South Indian Poetry and Myth* (Princeton, NJ: Princeton University Press, 1985), 380.

33. Satyamurti, *Mahabharata*, 539.

34. Satyamurti, 539.

35. Satyamurti, 583.

36. Majmudar, *Godsong*, 90 (11.49).

37. Bhagavad Gita, 16.1

38. Saraswati, *Bhagavad Gita: Home Study Course*, 7:37.

39. Saraswati, 7:41

40. Saraswati, 7:49.

41. Martha Nussbaum, "The Costs of Tragedy: Some Moral Limits of Cost-Benefit Analysis," *Journal of Legal Studies* 29, no. 2 (2000): 1006–8. Nussbaum eloquently explores the power of asking tragic questions in *The Fragility of Goodness: Luck and Ethics in Greek Tragedy and Philosophy* (1986; Cambridge: Cambridge University Press, 2001), 23–84.

42. This tension plays out repeatedly in the figure of Yudhishthira, who is bound by cultural norms to be a warrior king but who clearly prefers the peaceful, ascetic life of a renunciant. Bhishma's teachings to Yudhishthira after the war about what it means to be a king can be seen as a Brahminical education in warrior kingship. See Alf Hitlebeitel, *Rethinking the Mahabharata: A Reader's Guide to the Education of the Dharma King* (Chicago: University of Chicago Press, 2001).

43. To be fair, it is often Arjuna who makes the most persuasive case for war during these conversations, making his sudden thoughtfulness at the beginning of the Gita somewhat out of character.

44. Nussbaum, "The Costs of Tragedy," 1007.

45. For a discussion of conflicts over Indian visions of dharma, see Doniger, *Against Dharma.*

46. Whitman, "Salut au Monde!," 287.

47. Whitman, 287.

48. See Elizabeth Belfiore, "A Theory of Imitation in Plato's Republic," *Transactions of the American Philological Association* 114 (1984): 121–46. Plato assigns eidolons and other mental images to the lowest rung in the divided hierarchy of being at *Republic* 509d.

49. Ingrid E. Holmberg, "Euripides' Helen: Most Noble and Most Chaste," *American Journal of Philology* 116, no. 1 (1995): 19–42.

50. Whitman, "Eidolons," 168.

51. Whitman, 170.

52. Whitman, 169–70.

53. Whitman, "Of the Terrible Doubt of Appearances," 275.

54. Whitman, "Salut au Monde!," 287

55. Whitman, 288.

56. Whitman, 288–89.

57. Whitman, 291, 293, 294.

58. Whitman, 296.

59. Whitman, 294.

60. Whitman, 296.

61. Whitman, 292.

62. See Marsh, *In Walt We Trust.*

63. At times, Krishna suggests that the war will serve a larger purpose in cosmic history—time is cyclical, and the war at Kurukshetra is a necessary "sacrifice," a "cosmic dissolution," that will create the conditions for the birth of a new world. See the translator's introduction to W. J. Johnson, trans., *The Sauptikaparvan of the Mahabharata: The Massacre at Night* (Oxford: Oxford University Press, 1998), ix–xli.

64. "Salut au Monde!" was originally published in 1856 and revised in 1881.

65. Kenneth Burke, "Definition of Man," in *Language as Symbolic Action: Essays on Life, Literature, and Method* (Berkeley: University of California Press, 1966), 13.

66. Burke, *The Rhetoric of Religion*, 314–15.

67. Burke, "Definition of Man," 9–10.

68. See Kenneth Burke, *The War of Words*, ed. Anthony Burke, Kyle Jensen, and Jack Selzer (Berkeley: University of California Press, 2018).

69. Emerson, "The Transcendentalist," 205; Emerson, "Fate," 966.

70. Emerson, "Compensation," 290.

71. Emerson, "The Over-Soul," 385–86.

72. Whitman, "Starting from Paumanok," 183.

73. Whitman, "By Blue Ontario's Shore," 480.

74. Emerson, "Self-Reliance," 270.

75. Emerson, 270.

76. Emerson, 270.

77. Emerson, "New England Reformers," 598.

Chapter Five

1. Newfield, *The Emerson Effect.*

2. Emerson, "The Poet," 457. The genius, Emerson concludes, is able to put words to realities that are beyond words and reconnect parts to the whole, helping others see the oneness of the world. The genius "re-attaches things to nature and the Whole" with his words (455).

3. Emerson, "New England Reformers," 608. Here Emerson echoes one way to understand the central teaching of the Bhagavad Gita, which is, according to Swami Tyagishananda, "nothing else than the spiritualizing of life on the basis of the spiritual realizations of realized persons like Sri Krishna." Tyagishananda, *Srimad Bhagavad Gita*, 15.

4. Emerson, 606.

5. Emerson, "The Over-Soul," 386.

6. Emerson, 396.

7. Bhagavad Gita, 18.61.

8. In his journal for 1845, Emerson copied the following passage from Wilson's translation of the *Vishnu Purana*: "the goddess Yoganidra, the great illusory energy of Vishnu, by whom, as utter ignorance, the whole world is beguiled" (*Journals and Miscellaneous Notebooks*, 9:322). This passage is later reprinted, slightly paraphrased, in Emerson's essay "Montaigne," 705.

9. Emerson, "Illusions," 1117.

10. Emerson, "The Divinity School Address," 84.

11. See Albanese, *A Republic of Mind and Spirit*, 160–69.

12. See Catherine L. Albanese, *Nature Religion in America: From the Algonkian Indians to the New Age* (Chicago: University of Chicago Press, 1990).

13. Emerson, "New England Reformers," 608; Emerson, "Montaigne," 705.

14. Emerson, *Journals and Miscellaneous Notebooks*, 15:106.

15. Emerson, "Fate," 952: "In the Hindoo fables, Vishnu follows Maya through all her ascending changes, from insect and crawfish up to elephant; whatever form she took, he took the male form of that kind, until she became at least woman and goddess, and he a man and a god. The limitations refine as the soul purifies." This essay presents a further refinement of the basic point that Emerson made twenty years earlier in his essay "Circles."

16. Emerson, "Works and Days," 7:87.

17. As David Loy writes about nondual philosophical systems, including especially Advaita: "Unlike Western philosophy, which prefers to reflect on the dualistic experience accessible to all, these systems make far-reaching epistemological and ontological claims on the basis of counterintuitive experience accessible to very few—if we accept their accounts, only to those who are willing to follow the necessarily rigorous path, who are very few. It is not that these claims are not empirical, but if they are true, they are grounded on evidence not readily available." Loy, *Nonduality*, 4. Remember that in chapter 11 of the Gita, Krishna reminds Arjuna how rare his

cosmic vision of the divine is. Again, a marker of Advaita Vedanta is the argument that enlightenment is rare; other philosophical systems are more democratic.

18. Patrick Olivelle, trans., *The Katha Upanishad*, in *The Upanishads* (1996; New York: Oxford University Press, 2008), 240 (3.14).

19. Majmudar, *Godsong*, 91 (11.52).

20. Emerson, *Journals and Miscellaneous Notebooks*, 9:307.

21. Emerson, 9:307.

22. Emerson, "The Over-Soul," 390.

23. Emerson, "New England Reformers," 601.

24. Gordon, *Emerson and the Light of India*, 136.

25. Emerson, "New England Reformers," 607, 606.

26. See Emerson's essay "Power," which to a certain extent counterbalances "Fate" in *The Conduct of Life*.

27. Emerson, "Fate," 945. Here he mentions the Lisbon earthquake and "race living at the expense of race"—that is, slavery—as examples of injustice on both a cosmic and a human scale.

28. Emerson, "Fate," 954, 944.

29. Famously, Emerson observed that "a foolish consistency is the hobgoblin of little minds," and so I think we are meant to read this consistency as an expression of deep wisdom. Emerson, "Self-Reliance," 265.

30. Emerson, "Self-Reliance," 264.

31. Benjamin Franklin, *Poor Richard Improved* (1757), in *Benjamin Franklin: Writings*, Library of America ed., ed. J. A. Leo Lemay (New York: Literary Classics of the United States, 1987), 1293.

32. Emerson, "Self-Reliance," 263.

33. Emerson, "Spiritual Laws," 310.

34. Emerson, "Self-Reliance," 260.

35. Majmudar, *Godsong*, 31 (3.35).

36. Majmudar, 19 (2.48).

37. Emerson, "Compensation," 297.

38. Emerson, 294, 297.

39. Other peoples' esteem is the foundation of morality, when internalized as the "impartial spectator," as Adam Smith describes it in *The Theory of Moral Sentiments*, ed. D. D. Raphael and A. L. Macfie (1759; Indianapolis: Liberty Fund, 1976).

40. Emerson, "Compensation," 289.

41. Emerson, 288.

42. Emerson, 292.

43. Emerson, 290.

44. Emerson, 291.

45. Alexis de Tocqueville remarked, "I think there is no country in the civilized world where they are less occupied with philosophy than the United States," so focused are they on the demands of "practical life." Alexis de Tocqueville, *Democracy in America*, trans. Harvey C. Mansfield and Delba Winthrop (1835; Chicago: University of Chicago Press, 2000), 403, 404. On the history of American pragmatism, see also West, *The American Evasion of Philosophy*; and John Kaag, *American Philosophy: A Love Story* (New York: FSG, 2017).

46. James, *Pragmatism*, 96.

47. James, 27.

48. Majmudar, *Godsong*, 19 (2.47).

49. Emerson, "Self-Reliance," 261.

50. Emerson, "Spiritual Laws," 317.

51. Emerson, 321.

52. Emerson, "Self-Reliance," 275. "In morals," Emerson writes elsewhere, "the capital virtue" is "self-trust." Emerson, "Experience," 490.

53. Emerson, "Spiritual Laws," 312.

54. Emerson, "The Over-Soul," 392–93.

55. Emerson, 387.

56. Engels, *The Art of Gratitude*, 104.

57. Benjamin Anastas, "The Foul Reign of Emerson's 'Self-Reliance,'" *New York Times Magazine*, December 2, 2011, http://www.nytimes.com/2011/12/04/magazine/riff-ralph-waldo-emerson.html. For further critiques of Emerson's politics as a defense of capitalism, liberalism, and conformity, see Gura, *American Transcendentalism: A History*, and Newfield, *The Emerson Effect*.

58. Emerson, "Gifts," 536.

59. Emerson, "Experience," 483.

60. The norms of self-culture were explored in William Ellery Channing, *Self-Culture* (Boston: James Munroe & Company, 1843).

61. Eliade, *Yoga: Immortality and Freedom*, 235.

62. There is a subtle lexical change here, with the *d* at the end of *ad* assimilating to *c* to match the initial consonant sound of the verb: *ad* + *quiescere* thus becomes *acquiescere*.

63. Lewis and Short's *Latin Dictionary* defines the meaning of *acquiescere* as "to become physically quiet, to come to physical repose." This sense of a process of coming to rest, of finding calm and mental peace, is crucial for understanding the etymology of *acquiescence*. Here, I nod to the crucial connection between *acquiescere* and its synonym *requiescere*, to quiet down.

64. Henk Van Den Belt, *The Authority of Scripture in Reformed Theology: Truth and Trust* (Leiden, The Netherlands: Koninklijke Brill NV, 2008), 100–102.

65. Majmudar, *Godsong*, 136 (18.65–66).

66. Davis, *The Bhagavad Gita: A Biography*, 32.

67. Emerson, "Compensation," 289–90.

68. Emerson, "Fate," 952.

69. Emerson, "Spiritual Laws," 320.

70. Emerson, "Fate," 967–68.

71. Emerson, "The Over-Soul," 387.

72. As Jack Turner argues, "To Emerson, Thoreau, Douglass, Ellison, and Baldwin, personal responsibility entailed at minimum (1) a refusal to be complicit in injustice, (2) a commitment to examine oneself for complicity, and (3) a willingness to overcome whatever complicity one finds. Their sense of what counted as complicity was expansive: one is complicit in injustice insofar as one authorizes it politically or enables it socially or economically." Turner, *Awakening to Race*, 2.

73. Emerson, "Spiritual Laws," 320.

74. See Gary Lindberg, *The Confidence Man in American Literature* (Oxford: Oxford University Press, 1982). Interestingly enough, Frank Baum attended the talks at the World's Parliament of Religions in 1893, and was also a member of the Theosophical Society. The parallels between Dorothy's journey and the devotee is not hard to trace. Philip Goldberg writes, "I leave it to others to find mystical themes in the journey of Dorothy and her companions, although it

is hard to resist noting the pure Vedanta of waking up to find that you've come home—and that you never left." Goldberg, *American Veda*, 52.

75. Emerson, "Politics," 563.

76. Jeremy Engels, "Demophilia: A Discursive Counter to Demophobia in the Early Republic," *Quarterly Journal of Speech* 97, no. 2 (2011): 131–54. For a concurrent example of demophilia to Emerson's *Essays: First Series*, see George Sidney Camp, *Democracy* (New York: Harper and Brothers, 1841).

77. Emerson, "Nominalist and Realist," 583.

78. Emerson, "Fate," 960.

79. Emerson, "The Over-Soul," 398.

80. Edward Tyrrel Channing, *Lectures Read to the Seniors in Harvard College*, ed. Dorothy I. Anderson and Waldo W. Braden (1856; Carbondale: Southern Illinois University Press, 1968), 17.

81. Channing, *Lectures Read to the Seniors*, 16.

82. Emerson, "Spiritual Laws," 316.

83. Emerson, 310.

84. Emerson, "New England Reformers," 602–3.

85. Emerson, "The Over-Soul," 386.

86. Emerson, "New England Reformers," 601.

87. Emerson, 608.

88. Emerson, "The Over-Soul," 395.

89. Emerson, "New England Reformers," 606.

90. See Jeremy Engels and William Saas, "On Acquiescence and Ends-Less War: An Inquiry Into the New War Rhetoric," *Quarterly Journal of Speech* 99, no. 2 (2013): 225–32.

91. Emerson, "New England Reformers," 601. Emerson explains his reference: "You remember the story of the poor woman who importuned King Philip of Macedon to grant her justice, which Philip refused: the woman exclaimed, 'I appeal': the king, astonished, asked to whom she appealed: the woman replied, 'From Philip drunk to Philip sober.' The text will suit me very well" (601).

92. Emerson, "The Over-Soul," 397.

93. Emerson, "New England Reformers," 605.

94. Emerson, "The Over-Soul," 398.

95. Emerson, 398.

96. Emerson, 397.

97. Emerson 397. Also: "Great is the soul, and plain. It is no flatterer, it is no follower; it never appeals from itself. It believes in itself" (399).

98. Emerson, 398.

99. Emerson, 397.

100. Emerson, 397.

101. For two particularly powerful and heart-wrenching recent exposés, see Benjamin Lorr, *Hell-Bent: Obsession, Pain, and the Search for Something Like Transcendence In Competitive Yoga* (New York: St. Martin's Griffin, 2012); and Matthew Remski, *Practice and All Is Coming: Abuse, Cult Dynamics, and Healing in Yoga and Beyond* (Rangiora, New Zealand: Embodied Wisdom Publishing, 2019).

102. See Sarah Herrington, "Yoga Teachers Need a Code of Ethics," *New York Times*, June 7, 2017, https://www.nytimes.com/2017/06/07/opinion/yoga-code-of-ethics-bikram-choudhury.html.

103. Here I follow Michel Foucault, who cautions critics against fetishizing "the author." For Foucault, focusing on "the author" is a way of coping with the dangerousness of discourse: with the twin facts that authors are nodes through which discourse is articulated, meaning that discourse transcends the author; and that discourse represents infinite and multiple possibilities for interpretation and action. Demonizing an author for dangerous speech is a feeble attempt to contain that speech. Removing a speaker from conversation does not kill discourse—though it can intimidate speakers into silence, which is one of the ways that political regimes hoping to avoid outward violence against citizens have ruled throughout history. Michel Foucault, "What Is an Author?," in *The Foucault Reader*, ed. Paul Rabinow (New York: Pantheon Books, 1984), 101–20.

Chapter Six

1. Whitman, *Democratic Vistas*, 960.

2. Whitman, "Carlyle from American Points of View," 894; Whitman, *Democratic Vistas*, 989; italics added.

3. Whitman, "Carlyle from American Points of View," 894.

4. Whitman, 894.

5. Whitman, "Song of Myself," 246.

6. Whitman, *Democratic Vistas*, 985.

7. This theme goes back at least to Plato and Socrates. For the best contemporary discussion, see Allen, *Our Declaration*, 21–22, especially given that Allen contests what philosopher Chantal Mouffe (following Norberto Bobbio) calls the "democratic paradox"—the conflict between equality and liberty. Allen makes a convincing argument that liberty and equality are not in conflict but that, in fact, liberty is enriched by, and only possible on the foundation of, equality.

8. Whitman, *Democratic Vistas*, 989.

9. Taylor, *A Secular Age*, 300. For a brilliant critique of liberalism's vision of a prepolitical, presocial self that can be isolated from the world, see Elisabeth R. Anker, *Orgies of Feeling: Melodrama and the Politics of Freedom* (Durham, NC: Duke University Press, 2014). This is also a core goal of my book *The Art of Gratitude*, to critique, and offer an alternative to, liberalism's econo-centric definition of the individual.

10. Whitman, *Democratic Vistas*, 989.

11. Whitman, "Song of Myself," 210.

12. Whitman, "Song of the Open Road," 301.

13. For an argument that James viewed Whitman as his philosophical foil and adversary, especially in *The Varieties of Religious Experience* (1902), see John Tessitore, "The 'Sky-Blue' Variety: William James, Walt Whitman, and the Limits of Healthy-Mindedness," *Nineteenth-Century Literature* 62, no. 4 (2008): 493–526.

14. See William James, *A Pluralistic Universe* (New York: Longmans, Green, 1909).

15. James, *The Varieties of Religious Experience*, 77.

16. James, 131.

17. "The solid meaning of life is always the same eternal thing—the marriage, namely, of some unhabitual ideal, however special, with some fidelity, courage, and endurance; with some man's or woman's pains.—And whatever or wherever life may be, there will always be the chance for that marriage to take place." William James, "What Makes a Life Significant," in *Writings*

1878–1899, Library of America ed., ed. Gerald E. Myers (New York: Literary Classics of the United States, 1992), 878.

18. James, 864.

19. James, 878.

20. James, *The Varieties of Religious Experience*, 103.

21. James, 152.

22. James, 152.

23. James, 82.

24. James, 83.

25. James, 84.

26. James, 378, 83.

27. Bucke, *Cosmic Consciousness*, 2.

28. James, *The Varieties of Religious Experience*, 359–61.

29. On Emerson, see Bucke, *Cosmic Consciousness*, 240–41. Bucke did not believe that Emerson ever advanced much past this essay, and that his experiences of cosmic consciousness were not nearly as frequent, or as profound, as Whitman's.

30. James, *The Varieties of Religious Experience*, 182–83, quoted in Bucke, *Cosmic Consciousness*, 82–83. Know that this was false, that Whitman was often roiled by foul moods—he was, after all, human.

31. Bucke, 183, 186.

32. Bucke, 189.

33. James, *The Varieties of Religious Experience*, 361.

34. James, 132.

35. James, 91.

36. Annie Payson Call, *Power through Repose* (1891; Boston: Roberts Brothers, 1893), 13.

37. Call, *Power through Repose*, 131.

38. Hopkins quoted in Horowitz, *One Simple Idea*, 55.

39. Ralph Waldo Trine, *In Tune with the Infinite: Or Fullness of Peace, Power, and Plenty* (New York: Thomas V. Crowell, 1897), 42.

40. Horowitz, *One Simple Idea*, 68.

41. James suggested that the mind-cure movement was responsible for introducing Americans to meditation, and historian Leigh Eric Schmidt concurs: "He was right about that: meditation came to more and more Americans not through a retrieval of venerable Christian practices, but through the rise of 'New Thought,' as the optimistic gospel of mental healing and positive thinking was then dubbed." Leigh Eric Schmidt, *Restless Souls: The Making of American Spirituality from Emerson to Oprah* (San Francisco: HarperCollins, 2005), 17.

42. Wood, *The New Thought Simplified*, 10.

43. Wood, 35.

44. Horatio W. Dresser, *The Power of Silence: An Interpretation of Life in its Relation to Health and Happiness* (Boston: Geo. H. Ellis, 1895), 10.

45. Dresser, *The Power of Silence*, 11.

46. Wood, *Ideal Suggestion through Mental Photography*, 110, 108–9.

47. Wood, 119, 125, 121, 133; Trine, *In Tune with the Infinite*, 58, 92.

48. The relationship between Indian thought generally, and the Bhagavad Gita specifically, and New Thought is a worthy subject for future research. For hints, see Charles S. Braden, *Spirits*

in Rebellion: The Rise and Development of New Thought (1963; Dallas: Southern Methodist University Press, 1987), 270; and Horowitz, *One Simple Idea*, 94.

49. Horatio W. Dresser, *A History of the New Thought Movement* (New York: Thomas Y. Crowell, 1919), 3. The importance of Emerson to New Thought is also emphasized in Braden, *Spirits in Rebellion*, 35, 37; and Schmidt, *Restless Souls*, 148.

50. Wood, *New Thought Simplified*, 98–99, 99, 100.

51. Dresser, *The Power of Silence*, 12.

52. Wood, *New Thought Simplified*, 102, 102–3.

53. Wood, *Ideal Suggestion through Mental Photography*, 71; italics added.

54. Horowitz, *One Simple Idea*, 7.

55. Horowitz, 67–111. On the prosperity gospel, see Kate Bowler, *Blessed: A History of the American Prosperity Gospel* (New York: Oxford University Press, 2013); and Costi W. Hinn, *God, Greed, and the (Prosperity) Gospel: How Truth Overwhelms a Life Built On Lies* (Grand Rapids, Michigan: Zondervan, 2019).

56. Wood, *New Thought Simplified*, 101.

57. Wood, 100–101.

58. Wood, 103.

59. Wood, *Ideal Suggestion through Mental Photography*, 58. He continued: "We must 'think no evil,' dwell only in the good, and build nothing else into the walls of our soul-temple" (89).

60. Wood, 144.

61. Wood, 93.

62. See Philip Deslippe, "The Swami Circuit: Mapping the Terrain of Early American Yoga," *Journal of Yoga Studies* 1 (2018): 5–44.

63. According to Elizabeth De Michelis, Vivekananda's philosophy was "strongly influenced by the New Thought style of Metaphysical teachings that pervaded the American cultic milieu to which he had acculturated." De Michelis, *A History of Modern Yoga*, 168–69; see esp. 91–126. "Making his way in the metaphysical culture of the United States, which lionized him after 1893, Vivekananda quickly learned the American metaphysical dialect, and he creolized his presentation of already combination Indian-Western spirituality to please American ears and tastes," writes Albanese in *A Republic of Mind and Spirit*, 355.

64. According to Mark Singleton, Yogi Ramacharaka and several other popular early twentieth-century yoga writers "belong more properly to the distinct 'New Thought' subgenre of modern yoga." Singleton, *Yoga Body*, 130. See also Braden, *Spirits in Rebellion*, 288; and Albanese, *A Republic of Mind and Spirit*, 358–59.

65. Albanese, *A Republic of Mind and Spirit*, 362–63; Robert Love, *The Great Oom: The Improbable Birth of Yoga in America* (New York: Viking, 2010).

66. These frames are not mutually exclusive. Antifoundationalists value dissent, and most dissent-oriented scholars in rhetoric reject ultimate foundations. Nor are these frames exhaustive, for there are of course myriad ways to study democracy; see David Held, *Models of Democracy*, 3rd ed. (Stanford, CA: Stanford University Press, 2006).

67. For examples of the Deweyan antifoundationalist frame in rhetorical and communication studies, see Gregory J. Shepherd, "Community as the Interpersonal Accomplishment of Communication," in *Communication and Community*, ed. Gregory J. Shepherd and Eric W. Rothenbuhler (Mahwah, NJ: LEA, 2001), 25–35; Robert Asen, "A Discourse Theory of Citizenship," *Quarterly Journal of Speech* 90, no. 2 (2004): 189–211; William M. Keith, *Democracy as Discussion: Civic Education and the American Forum Movement* (Lanham, MD: Lexington Books,

2007); Robert Danisch, *Pragmatism, Democracy, and the Necessity of Rhetoric* (Columbia: University of South Carolina Press, 2007); Nathan Crick, *Democracy and Rhetoric: John Dewey on the Arts of Becoming* (Columbia: University of South Carolina Press, 2010); Scott R. Stroud, *John Dewey and the Artful Life: Pragmatism, Aesthetics, and Morality* (University Park: Pennsylvania State University Press, 2011); and Brian Jackson and Gregory Clark, eds., *Trained Capacities: John Dewey, Rhetoric, and Democratic Practice* (Columbia: University of South Carolina Press, 2014).

68. Louis Menand, *The Metaphysical Club: A Story of Ideas in America* (New York: Farrar, Straus and Giroux, 2001), x.

69. Charles Sanders Peirce's "The Fixation of Belief," *Popular Science Monthly*, November 1877, 1–15. Though Dewey has become famous for his antifoundationalism—which is expounded memorably in part 1 of Richard Rorty's *Contingency, Irony, and Solidarity* (Cambridge: Cambridge University Press, 1989) and in a number of Rorty's interviews collected in *Take Care of Freedom and Truth Will Take Care of Itself* (Stanford, CA: Stanford University Press, 2005)—it is, of course, Peirce who first articulates the antifoundationalist ethos.

70. For two particularly poignant and convincing arguments for Dewey's continued importance to the study of democracy, see Eddie S. Glaude Jr., *In a Shade of Blue: Pragmatism and the Politics of Black America* (Chicago: University of Chicago Press, 2007); and Crick, *Dewey for a New Age of Fascism*.

71. John Dewey, *Experience and Nature* (1925), in *John Dewey: The Later Works, 1925–1953*, ed. Jo Ann Boydston (Carbondale: Southern Illinois University Press, 1988), 1:132. Like Emerson, Dewey saw communication as a practice of transcendence. Here I think of Gregory J. Shepherd's definition of "communication as transcendence." "Communication is *the simultaneous experience of self and other*. That's what I mean by *transcendence*," he writes in "Communication as Transcendence," in *Communication as . . . Perspectives on Theory*, ed. Gregory J. Shepherd, Jeffrey St. John, and Ted Striphas (Thousand Oaks, CA: Sage, 2006), 22.

72. Crick, *Democracy and Rhetoric*; Stroud, *John Dewey and the Artful Life*.

73. John Dewey, "Creative Democracy: The Task before Us" (1939), in John Dewey, *The Later Works, 1925–1953*, ed. Jo Anne Boydston (1988; Carbondale: University of Southern Illinois University Press, 1991), 14:227.

74. I track this definition of democracy in essay 1 of Engels, *The Politics of Resentment*.

75. Robert L. Ivie, "Enabling Democratic Dissent," *Quarterly Journal of Speech* 101, no. 1 (2015): 49.

76. For a discussion of the role of resentment in democracy, see Engels, *The Politics of Resentment*. My doctoral adviser makes a very helpful argument about the importance of joy rather than anger or resentment to dissent and the battle for social justice. See Stephen J. Hartnett, "Communication, Social Justice, and Joyful Commitment," *Western Journal of Communication* 74 (2010), 68–93. For a vision of democracy based in gratitude rather than resentment, see Engels, *The Art of Gratitude*.

77. Dewey, *The Public and Its Problems*, 184.

78. William James reported that "many persons to-day regard Walt Whitman as the restorer of the eternal natural religion." James, *The Varieties of Religious Experience*, 83.

79. Rorty, *Contingency, Irony, and Solidarity*.

80. Macpherson, *The Political Theory of Possessive Individualism*; R. W. B. Lewis, *The American Adam: Innocence, Tragedy, and Tradition in the Nineteenth Century* (Chicago: University of Chicago Press, 1955).

81. Whitman, "Song of Myself," 188.

82. "Democracy is not an alternative to other principles of associated life. It is the idea of community life itself." Dewey, *The Public and Its Problems*, 148. The fact that democracy draws people together into associations, or "public bodies," is what has long frightened demophobes, including the founders of the United States. See Engels, "The Trouble with 'Public Bodies.'"

83. See Allen, *Talking to Strangers.*

84. Richard Rorty, "Religion as Conversation-Stopper," *Common Knowledge* 3, no 1 (1994): 1–6.

85. Robert Asen, "Neoliberalism, the Public Sphere, and a Public Good," *Quarterly Journal of Speech* 103, no. 4 (2017): 335–36.

86. Swami Prabhavananda, *The Sermon on the Mount According to Vedanta* (1963; Hollywood: Vedanta Society, 1992), 22.

87. Whitman, "Song of Myself," 211. For one of the clearest and most provocative accounts of Whitman's vision of democracy as an art of mobilizing for a common good, see Marsh, *In Walt We Trust*, esp. 179–224.

88. Carpenter, *Towards Democracy*, 42, 9.

89. Whitman, "Song of Myself," 203.

90. Whitman, *Democratic Vistas*, 989.

91. Bootstrapping became so common that John Dewey—who viewed it as "futile" and fundamentally bad advice—devoted much of his work in the late 1920s and '30s, including *The Public and Its Problems* (1927), *Individualism Old and New* (1930), and *Liberalism and Social Action* (1935), to arguing against the normative force of "old liberalism" (i.e., the new bootstrapping). For Dewey's critique of bootstrapping, see John Dewey, *How We Think* (1910), in *The Middle Works*, ed. Jo Ann Boydston (Carbondale: Southern Illinois University Press, 1978), 6:190.

92. See Campbell, "Agency: Promiscuous and Protean."

93. See Engels, "The Trouble with 'Public Bodies.'"

94. According Danielle Allen, rhetoric is "the art of trust production." *Talking to Strangers*, 141.

95. Kenneth Burke, *Attitudes toward History* (1937; Berkeley: University of California Press, 1984), 41.

96. For a brilliant and eye-opening conversation about the "rhetoric of evil," see the special issue of *Rhetoric & Public Affairs* 6, no. 3 (2003). For a critique of the rhetoric of evil written from the perspective of Deweyan antifoundationalism, see Richard J. Bernstein, *The Abuse of Evil: The Corruption of Politics and Religion since 9/11* (Cambridge, UK: Polity Press, 2005).

97. In Sanskrit, *lokatantra* means a "people system" and hence something close to democracy.

98. I make this argument in *The Art of Gratitude*. According to Robert Ivie, "The rhetorical invention of dissent's affirming gesture is crucial to the enactment of its disruptive gesture." Ivie, "Enabling Democratic Dissent," 54, 56.

99. For a description of the sacrificial dynamics of violence that illustrates why I find the democratic invitation to violence so alarming, see René Girard, *Violence and the Sacred*, trans. Patrick Gregory (1972; Baltimore: Johns Hopkins University Press, 1979).

100. Whitman, "Starting from Paumanok," 180.

101. Whitman, "Thoughts," 600; *Specimen Days*, 897; *Democratic Vistas*, 937, 939, 962. Emerson uses this word, too, in a similar sense of a lack of faith in education that can train the soul to reconnect with the oversoul, a lack that is filled by selfishness and showmanship. Its opposite?—"infinite hope." See Emerson, "New England Reformers," 600, 601.

102. Whitman, "By Blue Ontario's Shore," 478; *Democratic Vistas*, 937, 939, 953, 962.

103. Whitman, "By Blue Ontario's Shore," 475.

104. Building on Whitman's rhetoric of infidelity, Edward Carpenter draws out the importance of cultivating faithfulness for democracy's future: "Democracy just begins to open her eyes and peep! and the rabble of unfaithful bishops, priests, generals, landlords, capitalist, lawyers, kings, queens, patronisers and polite idlers goes scuttling down into general oblivion. Faithfulness emerges, self-reliance, self-help, passionate comradeship. Freedom emerges, the love of the land . . ." Carpenter, *Towards Democracy*, 62.

105. Whitman, "Starting from Paumanok," 180.

106. Norman Fischer, *Opening to You: Zen-Inspired Translations of the Psalms* (New York: Penguin Compass, 2002), 3.

107. Simonson, "A Rhetoric for Polytheistic Democracy," 353–75.

108. Whitman, "Song of the Open Road," 296; Whitman, *Democratic Vistas*, 949.

109. Whitman, "By Blue Ontario's Shore": "the tyrant," 479; "the menacing one" and "the scorner," 473.

110. Whitman, "Song of Myself," 205.

111. See Engels, *The Politics of Resentment*. What I call the politics of resentment is premised on an understanding of what rhetorical scholars call the victimage ritual as being central to American politics. See Jeremy Engels, "The Politics of Resentment and the Tyranny of the Minority: Rethinking Victimage for Resentful Times," *Rhetoric Society Quarterly* 40, no. 4 (2010): 303–25.

112. See Whitman, "To You," 375–77; James, *Pragmatism*, 119–21.

113. James, *Pragmatism*, 121.

114. I am thinking of the Theosophical Society here, founded in 1875 by Henry Steel Olcott and Helena Petrovna Blavatsky. Blavatsky claimed that there were "Masters" who were in contact with the spiritual realm and could manipulate the material world, and claimed in her first book, *Isis Unveiled* (1877), to take direct dictation from these Masters. Her assumption was that "Spiritualism, in the hands of an adept, becomes Magic, for he is learned in the art of blending together the laws of the Universe, without breaking any of them and thereby violating Nature." See Albanese, *A Republic of Mind and Spirit*, 274–75, 279.

115. For a discussion of the overlap between Buddhist conceptions of emptiness and yogic philosophies of oneness, see Robert Wright, *Why Buddhism Is True: The Science and Philosophy of Meditation and Enlightenment* (New York: Simon & Schuster, 2017), 193–214. For an overview of Chinese philosophies and spiritual practices of oneness, see Philip J. Ivanhoe, *Oneness: East Asian Conceptions of Virtue, Happiness, and How We Are All Connected* (Oxford: Oxford University Press, 2017).

Conclusion

1. For a helpful discussion of the relationship between Hindu fundamentalist nationalism, yoga, and neoliberalism in India, see Patrick McCartney, "Politics Beyond the Yoga Mat: Yoga Fundamentalism and the 'Vedic Way of Life,'" *Global Ethnographic* 4 (2017): 1–18; and Robert F. Worth, "The Billionaire Yogi behind Modi's Rise," *New York Times*, July 26, 2018, https://www.nytimes.com/2018/07/26/magazine/the-billionaire-yogi-behind-modis-rise.html. On how Hindu nationalists enlisted the Gita in their cause, see Akshaya Mukul, *Gita Press and the Making of Hindu India* (New Delhi: Harper Collins, 2015).

2. A. G. Mohan with Ganesh Mohan, "Memories of a Master," *Yoga Journal*, April 5, 2017, https://www.yogajournal.com/yoga-101/memories-of-a-master. For a history of Krishnamacharya's teaching at Mysore, see N. E. Sjoman, *The Yoga Tradition of the Mysore Palace* (1996; New Delhi: Abhinav Publications, 1999). For a forceful critique of the Krishnamacharya mystique, see David Gordon White, *The Yoga Sutra of Patanjali: A Biography* (Princeton, NJ: Princeton University Press, 2014), 197–224.

3. For a model of the type of awareness we need to cultivate and also the types of deliberations we need to have, see Rhonda V. Magee's truly inspirational *The Inner Work of Racial Justice: Healing Ourselves and Our Communities through Mindfulness* (New York: Tarcher Perigee, 2019).

4. De Michelis, *A History of Modern Yoga*, 2. De Michelis adopts this arboreal metaphor from Iyengar's *Tree of Yoga*, hence enacting, in her rhetorical choices, the very philosophical position she wishes to defend.

5. Anya Foxen, *Biography of a Yogi: Paramahansa Yogananda and the Origins of Modern Yoga* (Oxford: Oxford University Press, 2017), xii.

6. Late in the process of writing this book, I was fortunate to get a sneak peak of an early copy of Professor Foxen's new book while it was still in copyediting, and I am curious, and excited, to see how it challenges our conversations about contemporary postural yoga. See Anya Foxen, *Inhaling Spirit: Harmonialism, Orientalism, and the Western Roots of Modern Yoga* (Oxford: Oxford University Press, 2020).

7. M. B. Emeneau, "Franklin Edgerton," *Language* 40, no. 2 (1964): 111.

8. Franklin Edgerton, trans., *The Bhagavad Gita* (1944; New York: Harper Torchbooks, 1964), 21 (3.30). Majmudar renders *adhyatman* here as "metaself" (*Godsong*, 31), and Sargeant translates it as "supreme Spirit" (*The Bhagavad Gita*, 187). Edgerton also translates *adhyatman* as "over-soul" at 7.29 (41), 8.1 (42), 13.11 (66), and 15.5 (73).

9. See R. C. Zaehner, trans., *The Bhagavad-Gita, with a Commentary Based on the Original Sources* (London: Oxford University Press, 1966), 173, which critiques Edgerton's translation of 3.30: "E's 'over-soul' (which he had presumably borrowed from Emerson) introduces a wholly new concept and is quite unjustified."

10. See Horowitz, *One Simple Idea*; and Schmidt, *Restless Souls*.

11. See Robert Love, "Fear of Yoga," *Columbia Journalism Review*, November/December 2006, https://archives.cjr.org/essay/fear_of_yoga.php; and Deslippe, "The Swami Circuit."

12. See Andrea R. Jain, *Selling Yoga: From Counterculture to Pop Culture* (New York: Oxford University Press, 2015); Jain, *Peace Love Yoga: The Politics of Global Spirituality* (New York: Oxford University Press, 2020); and, for example, Jain, "No, I Don't Owe My Yoga Mat to Vivekananda."

13. See Michelle Goldberg, *The Goddess Pose: The Audacious Life of Indra Devi, the Woman Who Helped Bring Yoga to the West* (New York: Knopf, 2015).

14. On Trine: Schmidt, *Restless Souls*, 153; on Bucke: De Michelis, *A History of Modern Yoga*; on Vivekananda, Kopf, *The Brahmo Samaj and the Shaping of the Modern Indian Mind*.

15. Chari, "Whitman in India," 307.

16. Bucke, *Cosmic Consciousness*, 8, 68.

17. De Michelis, *A History of Modern Yoga*, 178. For a helpful discussion of the history of the Yoga Sutra, see White, *The Yoga Sutra of Patanjali: A Biography*.

18. "Yogash citta vrtti nirodhah." Yoga Sutra of Patanjali, 1.2.

19. See, for instance, William Q. Judge, *The Yoga Aphorisms of Patanjali* (New York: Path, 1889), a Theosophical interpretation of the text and one of the first English translations. Albanese

notes in *A Republic of Mind and Spirit*, 353: "After Vivekananda's pathbreaking work, though, Theosophists learned more clearly that the 'aphorisms' of Patanjali they so admired were, in fact, an exposition of raja yoga, containing techniques for stilling the fluctuations of the mind and promoting mental concentration in order to attain Samadhi, participation in the bliss of the divine consciousness. What they did not realize in this new learning was that they were being encouraged to read the dualistic Patanjali work in ways that were monistic. They were learning, in effect, no longer the isolation of the soul from matter and desire but the presence of a divine source of bliss within an embodied individual consciousness."

20. Vivekananda, *Raja Yoga*, 122.

21. To study yoga philosophy at the Krishnamacharya Yoga Mandiram in Chennai means studying the Yoga Sutra—and also learning to properly chant the sutras. The oral recitation of the sutras acted, we were told, as a link to the past, connecting us to Krishnamacharya and his teachers, just as it connected Krishnamacharya back to Patanjali himself.

22. White, *The Yoga Sutra of Patanjali: A Biography*, 10.

23. Both the Bhagavad Gita and Patanjali's Yoga Sutra are listed as part of the "Yoga Humanities" requirements for Yoga Alliance's Common Core Curriculum for yoga teachers (https://www.yogaalliance.org/New_RYS_Standards/Common_Core_Curriculum_for_RYS_200); Patanjali's ashtanga yoga and, in particular, his *yamas* and *niyamas* are central to Yoga Alliance's Code of Conduct and Scope of Practice for yoga teachers.

24. Vivekananda, *Raja Yoga*, 288 (commentary on sutra 3.56). Commenting on sutra 3.51, where Patanjali introduces the idea of *kaivalya*, Swami Vivekananda explains: "He attains aloneness, independence and becomes free. When one gives up even the ideas of omnipotence and omniscience, there comes entire rejection of enjoyment, of the temptations from celestial beings" (286).

25. Georg Feuerstein, *The Yoga-Sutra of Patanjali: A New Translation and Commentary* (1979; Rochester, VT: Inner Traditions International, 1989), 10. Though we tended to work directly from the Sanskrit when memorizing, chanting, and interpreting the sutras, my teachers at the Krishnamacharia Yoga Mandiram approved of this translation. I should note that there are many contemporary scholars who contest the nihilistic interpretation of Patanjali's Yoga Sutra, reading it in a way that is more affirmative of life than Feuerstein (or I) do. The most compelling case for a worldly Patanjali is Michael Stone, *Yoga for a World Out of Balance: Teachings on Ethical and Social Action* (Boulder, CO: Shambhala Press, 2009). See also Ian Whicher, *The Integrity of the Yoga Darśana: A Reconsideration of Classical Yoga* (Albany, NY: State University of New York Press, 1998); Christopher Key Chapple, *Yoga and the Luminous: Patanjali's Spiritual Path to Freedom* (Albany: State University of New York Press, 2008); Edwin F. Bryant, *The Yoga Sutras of Patanjali: A New Edition, Translation, and Commentary* (New York: North Point Press, 2009); and Stephen Cope, *Yoga and the Quest for the True Self* (New York: Bantam, 2000).

26. Feuerstein, *The Yoga-Sutra of Patanjali*, 11.

27. Goldberg, *The Goddess Pose*, 98–99.

28. Today, according to the communication scholar Kristen Blinne, we are witnessing the *yogification* of the public sphere. Kristen C. Blinne, *Defining Pop Culture Yoga: A Communication Remix* (Lanham, MD: Lexington Books, 2020).

29. See more about Yoga Lab in State College, Pennsylvania, at http://www.statecollegeyogalab.com.

30. Hence the central role that Patanjali plays in my book *The Art of Gratitude*. I would absolutely write the last part of that book differently after completing *The Ethics of Oneness*.

Index